CHILD, FAMILY, AND STATE

NOMOS

XLIV

NOMOS

Harvard University Press

I	*Authority* 1958, reissued in 1982 by Greenwood Press

The Liberal Arts Press

II	*Community* 1959
III	*Responsibility* 1960

Atherton Press

IV	*Liberty* 1962
V	*The Public Interest* 1962
VI	*Justice* 1963, reissued in 1974
VII	*Rational Decision* 1964
VIII	*Revolution* 1966
IX	*Equality* 1967
X	*Representation* 1968
XI	*Voluntary Associations* 1969
XII	*Political and Legal Obligation* 1970
XIII	*Privacy* 1971

Aldine-Atherton Press

XIV	*Coercion* 1972

Lieber-Atherton Press

XV	*The Limits of Law* 1974
XVI	*Participation in Politics* 1975

New York University Press

XVII	*Human Nature in Politics* 1977
XVIII	*Due Process* 1977
XIX	*Anarchism* 1978
XX	*Constitutionalism* 1979
XXI	*Compromise in Ethics, Law, and Politics* 1979
XXII	*Property* 1980
XXIII	*Human Rights* 1981
XIV	*Ethics, Economics, and the Law* 1982
XXV	*Liberal Democracy* 1983
XXVI	*Marxism* 1983

XXVII *Criminal Justice* 1985
XXVIII *Justification* 1985
XXIX *Authority Revisited* 1987
XXX *Religion, Morality, and the Law* 1988
XXXI *Markets and Justice* 1989
XXXII *Majorities and Minorities* 1990
XXXIII *Compensatory Justice* 1991
XXXIV *Virtue* 1992
XXXV *Democratic Community* 1993
XXXVI *The Rule of Law* 1994
XXXVII *Theory and Practice* 1995
XXXVIII *Political Order* 1996
XXXIX *Ethnicity and Group Rights* 1997
XL *Integrity and Conscience* 1998
XLI *Global Justice* 1999
XLII *Designing Democratic Institutions* 2000
XLIII *Moral and Political Education* 2001
XLIV *Child, Family, and State* 2002
XLV *Secession and Self-Determination* (in preparation)
XLVI *Political Exclusion and Domination* (in preparation)

NOMOS XLIV
Yearbook of the American Society for Political and Legal Philosophy

CHILD, FAMILY, AND STATE

Edited by

Stephen Macedo, *Princeton University*
and
Iris Marion Young, *University of Chicago*

NEW YORK UNIVERSITY PRESS • *New York and London*

NEW YORK UNIVERSITY PRESS
New York and London

Library of Congress Cataloging-in-Publication Data
Child, family, and state / edited by Stephen Macedo and
Iris Marion Young.
p. cm. — (Nomos ; 44)
"Emerged from a group of papers and commentaries presented at the annual meeting of the American Society for Political and Legal Philosophy in September of 1999, held in conjunction with the annual meeting of the American Political Science Association in Atlanta, Georgia"—Pref.
Includes bibliographical references and index.
ISBN 0-8147-5682-4 (cloth : alk. paper)
1. Children's rights—United States—Congresses. 2. Children—Legal status, laws, etc.—United States—Congresses. 3. Parent and child (Law)—United States—Congresses. 4. Adoption—United States—Congresses. 5. Child welfare—United States—Congresses. 6. Education—Parent participation—United States—Congresses. 7. Children of Gay parents—United States—Congresses.
I. Macedo, Stephen, 1957– II. Young, Iris Marion, 1949–
III. American Society for Political and Legal Philosophy. Meeting (1999 : Atlanta, Ga.) IV. American Political Science Association Meeting (1999 : Atlanta, Ga.) V. Series.
HQ792.U5 C4195 2002
305.23'0973—dc21 2002010992

New York University Press books are printed on acid-free paper, and their binding materials are chosen for strength and durability.

Manufactured in the United States of America
10 9 8 7 6 5 4 3 2 1

This volume of *Nomos* is dedicated, with gratitude, to Alan Ritter, Visiting Professor of Political Philosophy at the University of Connecticut Law School, formerly of the University of Virginia and Indiana University. Professor Ritter has been both a participant in and a benefactor of the activities of the American Society for Political and Legal Philosophy for many years.

Professor Ritter's many writings on anarchism, freedom, Rousseau, and Proudhon include *Anarchism: A Theoretical Analysis* (Cambridge, 1980), *The Political Thought of Pierre-Joseph Proudhon* (Princeton, 1969), and "The Anarchist Justification of Authority" in *Nomos XIX: Anarchism.* His longstanding and generous support for the Association is deeply appreciated.

CONTENTS

Preface xi

Contributors xiii

Introduction 1
STEPHEN MACEDO AND IRIS MARION YOUNG

PART I: ADOPTION, RACE, AND PUBLIC POLICY

1. Toward New Understandings of Adoption: Individuals and Relationships in Transracial and Open Adoption 15
MARY LYNDON SHANLEY

2. Placing the Adoptive Self 58
CAROL SANGER

3. The Child Welfare System's Racial Harm 98
DOROTHY E. ROBERTS

4. Is Complaint a Moral Argument? 134
LAWRENCE M. MEAD

5. Comments on Dorothy Roberts's "The Child Welfare System's Racial Harm" 148
EVA FEDER KITTAY

6. Legal Fictions and Family Romances: Contesting Paradigms of Child Placement 170
MORRIS B. KAPLAN

PART II: EDUCATION AND PARENTAL AUTHORITY

7. Parents, Government, and Children: Authority over Education in the Liberal Democratic State 211
William A. Galston

8. Taking Children's Interests Seriously 234
Martha L. A. Fineman

9. The Proper Scope of Parental Authority: Why We Don't Owe Children an "Open Future" 243
Shelley Burtt

PART III: SAME-SEX FAMILIES

10. Children's Rights in Gay and Lesbian Families: A Child-Centered Perspective 273
Barbara Bennett Woodhouse

11. Relationship Rights for a Queer Society: Why Gay Activism Needs to Move Away from the Right to Marry 306
Valerie Lehr

PART IV: BIRTHRIGHT CITIZENSHIP

12. Children of a Lesser State: Sustaining Global Inequality through Citizenship Laws 345
Ayelet Shachar

13. Moral Equality and Birthright Citizenship 398
Michael Blake

Index 411

PREFACE

This volume of *NOMOS*—the forty-fourth in the series—emerged from a group of papers and commentaries presented at the annual meeting of the American Society for Political and Legal Philosophy in September 1999, held in conjunction with the annual meeting of the American Political Science Association in Atlanta, Georgia. Since that meeting, the original authors have revised their work significantly, with careful attention to the ideas that developed out of the conference. Meanwhile, additional authors have added further essays and new commentaries to round out the present volume. All of these authors have worked painstakingly to contribute first-rate work related to a series of contemporary family issues that have been unavoidable in courtrooms but that remain underdeveloped in the realms of political and legal philosophy. They deserve our heartfelt thanks for their noteworthy efforts.

Thanks are also due to an outstanding production team at New York University Press, especially to Stephen Magro and Despina Gimbel.

Finally, thanks to Managing Editor John Holzwarth, who has contributed in important ways to every aspect of this project, from the organization of the meetings to the preparation of the final manuscript. His care and good sense have been essential.

CONTRIBUTORS

MICHAEL BLAKE
Kennedy School of Government, Harvard University

SHELLEY BURTT
Political Science, Yale University (through 1998)

MARTHA L. A. FINEMAN
Law, Cornell University

WILLIAM A. GALSTON
Institute for Philosophy and Public Policy, University of Maryland

MORRIS B. KAPLAN
Philosophy, Purchase College, State University of New York

EVA FEDER KITTAY
Philosophy, Stony Brook University, State University of New York

VALERIE LEHR
Government and Gender Studies, St. Lawrence University

STEPHEN MACEDO
Politics and University Center for Human Values,
Princeton University

LAWRENCE M. MEAD
Politics, New York University

DOROTHY E. ROBERTS
Law, Northwestern University

CAROL SANGER
Law, Columbia University

AYELET SHACHAR
Law, University of Toronto

MARY LYNDON SHANLEY
Political Science, Vassar College

BARBARA BENNETT WOODHOUSE
Law, University of Florida

IRIS MARION YOUNG
Political Science, University of Chicago

INTRODUCTION

STEPHEN MACEDO AND
IRIS MARION YOUNG

Some of the most difficult and divisive moral and legal issues facing contemporary societies concern the regulation of parenting, child rearing, and family relations. Parenting is a profound personal responsibility: parents generally claim and exercise a great deal of authority and control over their children. This concentration of sustained responsibility for the well-being of fragile and dependent others helps make parenting the most serious, difficult, and rewarding project that most adults will undertake in their lives. Raising children is, for most adults, a central, if not *the* central, project in their lives: a source of profound satisfaction or disappointment.

The family has sometimes been viewed as a prepolitical institution: a set of relations that precede political authority. Certainly families at their best are forms of community whose bonds and purposes transcend those of politics, and much parental power is exercised in the privacy of the home. Nevertheless, the state has always taken a great interest in family relations. Children are future citizens and independent beings with interests of their own. Authority over child rearing and education has long been divided between parents and political institutions (and sometimes religious authorities). There are certain things parents may not do to their children, and there are some forms of care and education that parents *must* provide to children, according to even the most liberal and democratic societies. It has been increasingly recognized that children are not the property of their parents, though some believe that the law still allows parents in effect to tyrannize their children.

Among the basic conflicts involving children, families, and the state are, therefore, those concerning the degree of control that parents should be allowed to exercise over their children, the range of responsibility properly claimable by public institutions, and the conditions under which public institutions may not only regulate the upbringing and education of children but even remove children from the care of their parents. Besides regulating the relations between parents and children, the law plays an important role in deciding who can be a parent and under what conditions.

This volume turns to questions such as these in an era in which the conditions of parenting and our thinking about the acceptable forms of parenting and the best interests of children are changing in remarkable ways. While the ideal of the two-parent family continues to exert a powerful pull on the imaginations of many, the realities of parenting and child rearing are no longer expected to mirror the old norms. Divorce rates escalated sharply in the decades following World War II. The number of children being born out of wedlock has risen sharply, as has the number of children being raised by a single parent. The "nuclear family" is far more fluid and complex than it was once thought to be.

Societies have dealt with these changes in different ways. If the 1960s and 1970s witnessed the culmination of a social revolution in family life, the politics of subsequent decades have often been defined by reaction. Segments of the U.S. population have seemed in the grip of a moral panic over declining parental responsibility and inadequate care of children. Some bemoan the "decline" of older family patterns and blame an increasingly permissive culture and flawed social welfare policies. Others embrace the new variety of family forms and argue that public education and welfare policy should do far more to help single parents and poorer parents raise and educate their children.

An important theme running through many debates over public policy concerning family and parenting might be called the "normalization question." In what ways should the law seek to reflect and facilitate or oppose and resist parenting and child-rearing practices that depart from the ideals of old? What should the stance of the law be toward single-parent families, unwed motherhood, lesbian motherhood, or the adoption of children by gay and lesbian parents? For all its tolerance, contemporary American society still makes many assumptions about what families with children ought to look like. While policy has become more flexible in some areas, the law still often operates on the assumption that children should have two parents, of different sexes, that it is best that these be biological parents, and, if not, that the adopting parents should be as much as possible like biological parents, which is to say, young, married, straight, and of the same race. Public policy, including laws governing adoption and child custody, often reflect and enforce these assumptions.

The essays that follow do not constitute an exhaustive inquiry into the philosophical, political, and legal dilemmas surrounding children, families, and the state. They do, however, join in serious debate over some of the most difficult and divisive questions concerning the future of child rearing and parental authority. These essays share the recognition that the law can do much to shape and structure parent-child relations: all of our authors embrace the idea that patterns of family life and parenting are in important part the product of moral, political, and legal choices. Our essayists also share the conviction that fundamental questions of justice are often at stake in these choices and the conflicts that swirl around them. Our authors disagree deeply but respectfully about many basic questions.

The essays that follow fall into four parts: "Adoption, Race, and Public Policy," "Education and Parental Authority," "Same-Sex Families," and "Birthright Citizenship."

How should the state limit and structure the law of adoption? To what extent should the fact of adoption be shrouded in secrecy? Should the rules governing adoption seek to break and conceal all links between a child and his or her biological mother and father in order to facilitate the creation of exclusive parent-child bonds in the new adoptive family? Should the law, as Mary Shanley asks in her essay, seek to create "as if" biological families on the basis of adoption? Or is the norm of "closed" adoption based on outmoded and invidious assumptions about the shame of illegitimacy? Ought public authorities try to match adoptive children and parents on the basis of race? How much weight, if any, should adoption policies give to the maintenance of same-race families? And with respect to all of these questions, who should decide? The biological mother? Public agencies? The adopted child?

Questions surrounding the law of adoption make it plain that the law is not a passive spectator or a neutral facilitator with respect to children and parenting. Nowhere is the law's power more evident, however, than with respect to parents who find their rights as parents challenged by child welfare agencies. The awesome power of the state intervenes most drastically in the most intimate and intense of personal relations when parents, especially mothers, are deemed unworthy to continue to act as parents. Given America's history of slavery and racism, it is sobering to consider the disproportionate tendency for child welfare agencies to intervene in black families and other minority families, and indeed to remove black children from their homes. Is this disproportion, as Dorothy Roberts asks, a manifestation of the continued effects of past and present racism?

Perhaps no aspect of the proliferation of family forms is more controversial than parenting and adoption by gay and lesbian couples. Should adoption by gay men and lesbians be facilitated or resisted by public policy? What policy best serves the best interests of children? On the other hand, does the extension to gays and lesbians of the right to participate equally in marriage and parenting in effect extend the power of what has long been an oppressive institution, especially for women?

Control over the upbringing of children is an enduring source of conflict among adults. Many feel passionately that the education of children should be guided by parents. Others concede that the public properly has a substantial interest in the education of children, both because those children are future citizens and because they are independent beings with their own interests and needs. The previous volume in this series focuses on educational conflicts (*NOMOS XLIII: Moral and Political Education*).[1] Nevertheless, three essays here also consider the contest over who shall control children's education. Should children be regarded as self-developing individuals independent of their parents, or should society respect parents' preferences about their children's upbringing?

Our authors also debate the neglected question of whether it is an injustice to base the granting of citizenship on birthright (defined in terms of blood or soil). Does the seeming "naturalness" of birthright citizenship obscure the unfairness of a system that arbitrarily denies membership in wealthy and privileged societies to children who happen to be born to the "wrong" parents?

Mary Shanley opens Part I with an essay that discusses two very different debates concerning the ethics and policy of adoption: debates about whether adoptions should be "closed" or "open" and debates about whether transracial adoption is acceptable. According to Shanley, in these debates and others about child welfare, law and policy usually vacillate between two assumptions: either the child is a rights-bearing individual whose individual interests must trump other concerns, or children are embedded in relations with family, community, and culture that have significant claims on forming a child's upbringing. Shanley aims to craft a framework of principles that accommodates both these moral imperatives. A key move in developing that framework consists in rejecting two assumptions that continue to lie as background to adoption practice in the United States: first, that the goal of adoption placement should be to try to replicate a biological family, and second, that biological mothers who offer their children for adoption have "abandoned" them, rendering them parentless. Shanley argues that the birth mother's position and voice are central for mediating issues of the child's best interest and the child's embeddedness in racial, ethnic, or religious communities. While the birth mother's wishes need not be decisive, her connection to the child gives her a prima facie claim to decide whether the child should have access to knowledge about the birth parents or continued connection with them. Inasmuch as the birth mother or birth parents are embedded in relationships of community solidarity that are meaningful to them, moreover, they have a prima facie claim to decide on the child's behalf whether such connections should form a significant place in the child's life.

While Carol Sanger agrees with most of Shanley's substantive conclusions, she rejects Shanley's underlying appeal to the value of embeddedness in community. Sanger appeals, rather, to the principle of autonomy to argue that birth mothers should have significant voice in decisions about the placement of their children and the amount of knowledge those children should have about their mothers. Embeddedness in communities and relationships, Sanger argues, is a poor guide for policy: it offers no means for deciding which sorts of connections should have significance for a child's life. Furthermore, we cannot be confident, says Sanger, that birth mothers will reliably mediate between the child and the community connections in which he or she is embedded. Sanger concludes that birth mothers should indeed have a significant role in setting the terms of adoption and the child's placement, but solely on individualist grounds of decisional autonomy. Law and policy ought to recognize maternal prerogatives as part of the authority of being a parent.

Dorothy Roberts interrogates the causes and consequences of racial disparities in every aspect of the child welfare systems of the United States. She argues that there are reasons to think that these disparities are due at least in part to cultural bias in the welfare system, a bias manifested in a disproportionate tendency to remove children from black families. Roberts admits that evidence of racial bias in the foster care system is contested and difficult to gather. Far clearer, however, is the connection between foster care and poverty, and in the United States both the legacy of past racism and continuing racial discrimination create disproportionate poverty among African Americans. Roberts argues that whether or not racism is a major cause of the disproportionate interaction of blacks with child protection systems, this circumstance has harmful consequences, both for individual blacks and for blacks as a group. The foster care system disrupts already fragile families and helps reinforce the stigmatization of blacks, especially black mothers. Drawing on her earlier work on the history of the influence of ideologies of black motherhood on law and social policy in the United States, Roberts argues that racial disparities in foster care should be placed within the wider narrative of the denigration of black mothers and elevation of white families.

Lawrence Mead, in response, contends that Roberts's argument takes the form of a private complaint rather than a political appeal. For citizens to engage one another in political argument, Mead claims, they must agree on the facts about their social problems. Their political debate then turns on what values and priorities they decide embody the general interest. Disagreement about the causes of racial disparities in foster care, along with disagreement about the causes of most other complex social conditions, is endemic and unresolvable, and for this reason public policy cannot address them. It is indisputable that black families are disproportionately involved with the welfare system, Mead allows, but it is not at all clear why. Roberts asserts that part of the explanation is racism, but Mead charges that Roberts has not demonstrated that those who designed and administer the child welfare system are racists: she has not shown that the disproportionate impact of the child welfare system on blacks is explained by particular racist actions. Even if we did agree on the facts sufficiently to demonstrate that such disparities signal unfairness, however, an argument for public action to remedy the inequalities must show that such action would serve the general interest and not just the interests of blacks. Roberts does not appeal to such a general interest, according to Mead, and thus ignores the imperatives of proper political argument. Roberts, charges Mead, would revive the failed, excessively permissive, social policies of the 1960s and 1970s.

Eva Feder Kittay generally agrees with Roberts's position that services for children should not be so disruptive and punitive toward troubled families and instead ought to provide families with greater support. To the analysis of the reasons for alleged current inequities in U.S. foster care systems, Kittay adds sexism to racism. The problems of the foster care system should be understood in the context of widespread assumptions about dependency that tend both to minimize the extent to which people are dependent on one another and to hold individual families—

which in practice usually means women—responsible for the care of those who are inevitably dependent, such as infants and frail old people. Kittay argues that social policy ought to make dependency a more central concern: society should assume greater responsibility for the material support of both dependents and their caretakers, and we should value and support particular relationships of caring. Greater social support for care would help address the underlying conditions that now lead to the crises that bring children to the attention of child protection agents. Public policy would then have a less punitive and more supportive set of protocols to help parents with their children. On this model, everyone's family caretaking would receive greater social support, not just that of poor or black people. To the extent that African American families must contend with unique conditions of stigma and stereotype, however, Kittay suggests that some social policies should be specifically targeted at black families.

Morris Kaplan closes Part I with further reflections on the essays by Shanley and Roberts. Contemporary controversies surrounding adoption make clear, Kaplan argues, the extent to which family relations are socially constructed rather than natural: legal kinship can be made and unmade by law. This frank recognition that family relations are socially constructed represents a sharp break with, and real advance on, the political tradition. Public policy should facilitate the development of new and complex forms of family relations. Kaplan draws on work in developmental psychology to argue that young children need to bond early and consistently with at least one adult: maintaining biological connectedness is not important, but sustaining a stable pattern of caregiving and love is crucial. History rather than genetics should be at the center of determinations of child custody and adoption. Kaplan further emphasizes the arbitrariness of the obstacles that continue to impede adoptions by same-sex individuals or couples. He also joins Roberts in decrying the impact of social welfare policy on black families. The speedy placement of every parentless child ought to be regarded as an emergency, and more support should be given to poorer families in order to support successful parenting.

In Part II, William Galston takes up the vexing question of state authority over the education of children. He asserts that three values come into play in weighing the appropriate scope of state regulation of education against the right of parental discretion about the content and setting of their children's education. First, the education of children must promote their normal development, prepare them for becoming contributing members of society, and equip them to make independent judgments. Second, the liberal democratic state must act to promote the effective functioning of its core institutions. Third, education policy must recognize the special relationship between parents and children and the parents' expressive interest in teaching children about the values and ways of life to which they are committed. For Galston, these values are equally important and may conflict. Although key Supreme Court decisions give considerable weight to parental authority over educational decisions (within the limits of child welfare and civic competence), Galston finds that recent moral and legal discussions of education neglect parents' relational and expressive interests in the education of their children. Parents ought to have the liberty to school their children in those beliefs and practices that give meaning to their lives. States thus should allow substantial scope for school diversity and parental choice in education. Galston suggests that such diversity and choice are best guaranteed by permitting a wide scope for parental choice among educational options, so long as these choices are consistent with "the maintenance of civic unity and stability."

Martha Fineman denies that parents should be regarded, to the extent that Galston would have it, as the custodians of their children's educational interests. She points out that families often pressure children to conform to familial and community norms in ways that damage children's individuality. Fineman also questions Galston's assumption that public education tends toward uniformity and private education toward diversity. In the United States, local control over public education results in considerable diversity among public schools, both within and across districts. And while private schools can in principle be very diverse, the actual variety of private school types remains within a narrow range in the United States today. Many private schools are more homogeneous than their public school counterparts, moreover, and parents often choose them for that reason. Fineman suggests that a liberal democracy concerned to foster individuality and diversity among its citizens should make public education mandatory and universal. To the extent that parents have legitimate expressive interests to promote through their children's education, these can be met through institutions that supplement public schools.

Shelley Burtt argues against the view that good parents must struggle to limit the influence that they exert over their children's choices and values. Parental authority should not be conceived of as limited to preparing children to be autonomous choosers: parents are not duty bound to avoid shaping the substantive convictions of their children. Burtt emphasizes what she calls the "comprehensive neediness" of children: their need for intense and pervasive forms of care and attention from particular adults if they are to grow and mature. Children's progress toward adulthood involves far more than the development of rationality or critical reflection: they must develop a host of skills, capacities, and emotional resources to thrive as adults. Since parents have such extensive responsibilities, they should be allowed to try to raise their children to respect their particular values. Parents should, moreover, be able to choose among a broad array of educational options for their children.

In Part III, Barbara Bennett Woodhouse explores the rights of children in gay and lesbian families from a child-centered perspective, a viewpoint that keeps the best interests of the child at center stage. Woodhouse deplores what she describes as the traditional tendency to focus on the competing rights of adults in child custody disputes. Legal decisions involving custody, adoption, marriage, and assisted conception by same-sex couples will have important implications for the well-being of children in these families. Woodhouse examines a variety of scenarios representing actual legal disputes over the parenting rights of same-sex partners. She argues that when legal disputes such as these are analyzed on the basis of the best interests of children, it becomes clear that it is unconstitutional to single out children for less favorable treatment because of the sexual orientation of their parents. Children who are cared for by persons in same-sex relationships have the same needs to maintain close ties to particular adults as do children in heterosexual households. The children's developmental needs speak strongly in favor of ending the arbitrary inequalities imposed upon same-sex couples.

Valerie Lehr's chapter voices disappointment that gays and lesbians are not forming coalitions with other social groups to press a progressive agenda for greater democracy and equality. The quest for gay marriage, she argues, often ignores the radical implications of gay and lesbian families and so is a distraction from the true goals of a more progressive politics. Rather than seeking equal access to traditional forms of marriage and family, gays and lesbians should embrace a "queer politics" that would "make history" by challenging these and other traditional social forms. The campaign for nondiscriminatory access to marriage—typically conducted by white, middle-class gay men—ignores the oppressive dimensions of traditional family life, including its perpetuation of gender inequality. Proponents of "gay marriage" could even strengthen the forces of inequality and oppression. Lehr ends by sketching an agenda for "queer democracy" that would radically challenge traditional ways of conceiving and constructing family and parenting.

In Part IV, Ayelet Shachar calls into question the two principal grounds on the basis of which political societies automatically attribute citizenship to children: birth to certain parents (*jus sanguinis*) or birth within a certain territory (*jus soli*). Birthright citizenship in either form, argues Shachar, is both unjust and mystifying: it operates to grant some children unfair access to wealth and opportunity, while insulating these distributive effects from normative assessment because of the apparent naturalness of citizenship based on birthright. Shachar argues that the distribution of citizenship—the processes by which we assign citizenship to children—ought to be subject to principles of distributive justice. In our world, citizenship is, in effect, a valuable form of property, and the laws by which we decide who qualifies for citizenship sustain massive global inequalities. The unfairness of the current rules for access to citizenship is covered over by the false naturalness of birthright citizenship.

Michael Blake responds by acknowledging the injustice of current inequalities of access to wealth and power. He further allows that our current rules for allocating citizenship—whether based on parentage or soil—are arbitrary rather than "natural."

He denies, however, that the arbitrariness of the rules for allocating citizenship is the crux of the injustice. Membership in states, like membership in families, is indeed distributed in somewhat arbitrary ways, and these ways lead to unequal access to wealth and power. The crux of the problem is not the membership criteria themselves, however, but some of (not all of) the inequalities that flow from the distribution of citizenship. The real problem, according to Blake, is that gross forms of poverty and degradation are allowed to persist in the poorest nations. These can and should be addressed, and doing so does not require scrapping the current rules allocating membership in political societies based on birthright.

These essays will not settle, but hopefully they will help illuminate, the moral questions that lie before policy makers and citizens contemplating the future of children and families.

NOTES

1. Stephen Macedo and Yael Tamir, eds., *NOMOS XLIII: Moral and Political Education* (New York: NYU Press, 2002).

PART I

ADOPTION, RACE, AND PUBLIC POLICY

1

TOWARD NEW UNDERSTANDINGS OF ADOPTION: INDIVIDUALS AND RELATIONSHIPS IN TRANSRACIAL AND OPEN ADOPTION

MARY LYNDON SHANLEY

Adoption, the conscious severing of the legal ties between biologically related persons and the creation of legal ties between biologically unrelated persons, is a social practice and legal procedure that makes us consider the nature of the ties that are important to children's identity, to family life, and to larger social groups. Although adoption is generally favorably regarded in the United States, people disagree strongly over whether children should be placed across ethnic or racial lines, and whether adoption records should be open and parties to adoption should be able to know one another's identities or even meet. These controversies about transracial and open adoption raise issues that go beyond adoption itself. They illuminate a central dilemma in liberal political theory: Should the infant available for adoption be understood as an individual who needs to be placed quickly so that a parent-child relationship can be formed or as someone with ties to persons outside the adoptive family—genetic kin or a racial group—that deserve social and legal recognition?[1] Should a Catholic child be placed only with Catholic parents and a Muslim child only with Muslim parents? Should a black child be placed only with black parents and a Filipino child only with Filipino parents? Should adoptees have access to their original birth certificates, and should birth parents be able to know who adopted their child? I suggest that taking the child's status as *both* a rights-bearing individual and a relational being into account would allow us to reframe the controversies concerning secrecy versus nonsecrecy and race neutrality versus race matching in ways that would be beneficial to all parties to adoption.

People usually think of family ties as created "by nature": the dominant cultural image of family in the United States consists of a heterosexual couple and their offspring (even though such households are not in the majority). Except for the choice of whom to marry, people do not usually choose their relatives, whether parents, children, siblings, aunts, uncles, nieces, nephews, grandparents, or grandchildren. Adoption complicates this picture by suggesting both that family ties can be severed and that the parent-child bond as well as the marital bond can be assumed voluntarily. Adoption concerns both ending an existing set of relationships or potential relationships and establishing new ones. In addition to these biological ties, adoption may remove a child from parents of one religious, ethnic, or racial group and place him or her in a family with different identities and social ties.

The tension between framing adoption policy to reflect the child's status either as a freestanding individual or as a person to whom these biological and social relationships are of continuing significance infuses the debates about both secrecy and transracial placement in adoption. Proponents of secrecy in adoption tend to regard the infant as an "unencumbered individual" whose primary need is the establishment of strong parent-child bonds. They worry that unsealed records and open adoption suggest that the biological tie is in some way defining of who a person is and may impede the forging of strong relationships in the adoptive family.[2] People who advocate doing away with secrecy argue that knowledge of the genetic link between biological parents and child is part of the identity of both the biological parents and the child, and must not be permanently inaccessible to either.[3] Advocates of race-blind placement, for their part, argue that an infant awaiting adoption should be treated as an unencumbered individual who should be placed without regard to race so that neither child nor adoptive parents will experience discrimination. They contend that children's primary interests are in rapid, permanent placement regardless of race and that even when race matching causes no delay it is a capitulation to a kind of biologism that flies in the face of equal treatment for every individual.[4] Opponents of transracial placement insist that being a member of a racial minority gives the child an interest in being raised by others of that minority and gives the group an interest in raising the child.[5]

Although these issues of adoption policy involve assertions about the rights of birth parents, adoptive parents, minority groups, and children alike, it is the child who should be at the center of discussion.[6] The purpose of adoption is to provide care to children. Children have not only physical needs for food, shelter, and clothing, but also psychological needs for love and permanence. Emotional security is perhaps the most important component of successful identity formation. This need argues for timely and permanent placement with parents who not only regard themselves as entitled to act as the child's parents, but are supported by law and social practice in their caregiving efforts. In addition, children benefit from information about their origins, and the formation of their religious, racial, cultural, and ethnic identities may be facilitated by knowledge of their birth parents. Although arguments for the preservation of these ties are often made in the name either of birth parents' right to knowledge of their child or of a group's right to keep the child as a member of that community, the more important claim is that of the child. It is the child's multiple needs for security and identity that should engage those trying to deal with the tension between regarding the child as an unencumbered individual or as an embedded self with ties to individuals and groups that require legal recognition.

Giving priority to children and their needs does not in itself, however, provide unambiguous answers to the questions of whether adoption records should be open or closed or whether placement should be made across racial lines. Transracial adoption pits values of equality against community, interracial community against multiculturalism, and individuality against racial-ethnic community.[7] Disputes about secrecy pit values of privacy against those of knowledge and freedom of information. All of these values are fundamental to pluralist democracy in the United States. The complex moral and policy issues involved in open and transracial adoption are, in Janet Farrell Smith's words, "not resolvable without remainder." That is, in situations involving "a complex set of conflicting practical demands, each tied to a set of apparently morally reasonable supports, taking up one of these positions will not nullify moral demands of the alternatives not taken."[8] But in the real world where all of us must act, we cannot avoid judgments and policy choices that will favor one side or the other. For example, the law will either prohibit or allow disclosure of identifying information about the parties to an adoption; and the law will either prohibit or allow placement of children across racial lines.

While the existence of such intractable issues may force recognition of a moral remainder, it may also suggest the desirability of reconfiguring the discourse and policies surrounding adoption to minimize the conflict between values. Two shifts have emerged in the discourse and practice concerning adoption that point to the possibility of reframing the way we talk about adoption to reflect the child's status as *both* a rights-bearing individual and a relational being with links to biological relatives and social groups. One is the shift away from trying to make the adoptive family an "as if" family, one in which the children from all appearances might have been born to the parents, to recognizing the adoptive family as different from the biological family and valid on its own terms. Replacing the "as if" model of the adoptive family with that of a more complex family structure might increase respect for a variety of family forms, including blended families, single-parent families, and gay and lesbian families. The other shift in the discourse on adoption is away from regarding the child available for adoption as a "parentless" child, often as one "abandoned" by the original parents, to recognizing the significance of the original parents in adopted children's construction of identity. This change might increase respect for birth parents, particularly birth mothers, who release a child for adoption.

I begin the exploration of these issues in Section I by giving a brief overview of the history of adoption policy and law. I show the ways in which traditional practice tended both to construct the adoptive family as an imitation of the biological family and to treat the child awaiting adoption as a "parentless" individual. In Section II, I discuss the ways in which the effort to create "as if" adoptive families shaped policies regarding both secrecy and same-race placements and how those policies might be changed. In Section III, I examine how policies concerning secrecy and transracial placement reflected the notion that the child available for adoption was now "parentless," and I suggest ways those policies might be changed. In Section IV, I use the discussions of the "as if" adoptive family and the "parentless" child to develop policy positions concerning nonsecrecy and race-neutral placement. I suggest that nonsecrecy—achieved through adoption registries, unsealed records, or full or partial "open adoption"—should be the rule rather than the exception in adoption. Although some regard public recognition of both sets of parents as a capitulation to biologism, I believe that it need not blur the distinction between biological and social parenthood or undermine the custodial authority of the adoptive parents. I also suggest that since the birth parents are the concrete link between child and racial group, the birth parents' understanding of their racial identity and its meaning to them are relevant to the question of whether a specific child should be placed across racial lines. Attention to the wishes of birth parents, often in fact only the birth mother, is a way to counteract the disparagement of women (particularly women of color) who place their children for adoption. Policies and practices surrounding adoption cannot eliminate, although they can reduce, the tension between regarding the child as an autonomous individual and as a person shaped by personal and social relationships. While that tension is particularly striking in adoption and other areas of family law, it is an ineradicable part of all law that strives to foster freedom and individualism as well as commitment and communal ties.

I. Traditional Policy and Practice Surrounding Adoption

In the United States until the mid-nineteenth century the biological tie was a necessary, if not a sufficient, condition for gaining legal recognition as a child's parent. But while adoption statutes in the nineteenth century and new reproductive technologies in our own day have made the disaggregation of genetic and social parenthood seem like a relatively recent development, legal convention, and not biology alone, has always determined who would enjoy status as a legal parent. As Thomas Hobbes pointed out, while maternity could be observed at the time of parturition, knowledge of paternity depended on the not always reliable word of the mother.[9] Bastardy laws proclaimed that biological fathers would be recognized as legal fathers only if they were married to the mother of their child. Not all women who gave birth were regarded as legal mothers of their offspring: slave mothers (along with slave fathers) did not have parental rights.

The creation of legal adoption in the mid-nineteenth century was a radical innovation because it dissolved the "natural" (blood) ties that bound families together and replaced them with "artificial" (legal) ties of kinship.[10] Although members of a child's extended family sometimes adopted the child, the paradigmatic model of formal adoption was "stranger adoption." In the American understanding of kinship, according to anthropologist David Schneider, "family" is constituted by biological parents and their child, and

> [t]he relationship which is "real" or "true" or "blood" or "by birth" can never be severed, whatever its legal position. Legal rights may be lost, but the blood relationship cannot be lost. It is culturally defined as being an objective fact of nature, of fundamental significance and capable of having profound effects, and its nature cannot be terminated or changed.[11]

Statutes allowing legal adoption disrupted this traditional understanding of the indestructible and involuntary nature of family bonds by severing the legal tie between original parents and offspring and then by creating a new legal tie by convention and choice.[12]

But although adoptive families were created "artificially" by a legal procedure, from the mid-nineteenth to the mid-twentieth century most adoptive families were constructed in such a way as to give the *appearance* that they had resulted from sexual relations between the parents. Parents were of the age to have borne the child and were of the same race and often the same religion as the child's biological parents. The dissolution of the child's legal ties to its original parents made possible the "construct[ion of] the adoptive family as an 'as-if' biological family, reflecting the deeply embedded notion in the ideology of American kinship that the only 'real' relation is a blood relation and, by extension, the only experience of authentic identity is bestowed by blood ties."[13] In line with this cultural belief, adoption laws were designed to make adoptive families imitate nature.

Adoption statutes rested upon an individualistic and voluntaristic understanding of family ties that permitted the legal bond between biological parents and offspring to be severed and another legal bond between adoptive parents and child to be formed through the consent of both sets of parents. The creation of an "as-if" adoptive family thus incorporated a model of the individual and social ties consonant with the assumptions of liberal individualism and liberal political theory. Infant adoption, in particular, seemed to rest on the notion that at least for a brief period after birth, the child could be regarded as an individual who could be moved from one family to another and could be expected to take on an identity shaped by the roles, status, and obligations that membership in the new family entailed. Adoption discourse focused on the right of the child to a permanent home and the obligation of the state to protect the child by placing him or her with adults who were financially and emotionally capable of providing care. The intermediary role performed by the adoption agency that accepted the child from the birth parents and then placed the child with adoptive parents reflected the fact that for a moment the child was a ward of the state not bound to any other specific persons, an individual awaiting the creation of lasting family ties by an adoption decree.

At the same time that adoption law drew upon notions of individuality and voluntarism that allowed for the construction of nonbiological families, it assumed that the family of which the child would become a member would have a particular configuration. There would be two (and only two) parents, of different sexes, and of the same race as the child. The sealing of adoption records reflected the legal assumption that parenthood was an exclusive status that could belong to only two persons at a time with respect to any particular child. Underlying same-race placement of children with adoptive parents was the social fact that interracial marriage had been the exception rather than the rule in the United States (only in 1967 did the Supreme Court hold that state prohibitions on interracial marriage violated the Constitution). Adoptive families reflected the assumption that constructed families should imitate what was seen as a norm given by nature.

Society also dealt with unmarried motherhood differently depending on the race of the mother. Before World War II, adoption was not common among whites in the United States.[14] During the first two decades of the twentieth century, a woman who bore a child outside marriage was considered a "fallen woman" and morally deficient. A child born out of wedlock was labeled "illegitimate," a "child of sin," and was considered likely to grow up to be a delinquent. Society expected the mother to raise the child herself as punishment for her transgression and as a "lesson" to other women tempted to engage in illicit (i.e., unmarried) sex, and the mother and child were stigmatized. In the 1930s, the social condemnation of extramarital pregnancy continued, but the advice on what to do changed. An unmarried white woman was now counseled to hide her pregnancy, give the child up for adoption, and never see the child again in order to "get on with her life" (hopefully marrying and bearing "legitimate" children).

Blacks' experience of adoption was different from whites'. Both during and after slavery, black children who were orphaned or separated from their parents were often taken in by other families. There was a long history of informal adoption in black communities.[15] By contrast, formal relinquishment of children for adoption because of unwed pregnancy was rare. Because of the rape and sexual exploitation of black women by their white masters during slavery, black communities have tended not to stigmatize black children born out of wedlock.[16] Many black infants, therefore, were placed with and raised by members of a woman's extended family, often without formal legal adoption. Raising such a child was regarded not only as caring for an individual child, but as contributing to the well-being of the black community. Black women who bore children out of wedlock were labeled by white society as loose or without morals, but they were not provided the services of maternity homes and adoption agencies to help them in their pregnancies and with the placement of their children. In addition, many black families could not meet some of the criteria agencies used to select adoptive homes (e.g., family income or number of bedrooms in the house).

After World War II, the stigma and embarrassment about sexual or reproductive inadequacy still haunted infertile couples, and the stigma attached to out-of-wedlock pregnancy for the white mother became more complex. Although moral condemnation of out-of-wedlock pregnancy continued, some social workers (influenced by psychoanalytic theory and by the scarcity of newborn white infants to adopt) began to shift their view of the unwed mother from someone morally deficient and incorrigible to someone caught in the throes of a psychological conflict that had led her (unconsciously) to seek to bear a child.[17] By and large, the stigma that had been attached to white children born out of wedlock disappeared, and they began to be regarded as innocent and desirable. This acceptance did not extend to the black mother or infant.

> Public and private agencies and government policies viewed both black and white women as breeders, but with a major and consequential distinction. The former were viewed as socially unproductive breeders, constrainable only by punitive, legal sanctions. . . . White unwed mothers in contrast were viewed as socially productive breeders whose babies, unfortunately conceived out of wedlock, could offer infertile couples their only chance to construct proper families.[18]

Thus race significantly influenced the status of birth mothers and the value attached to their mothering capabilities.

These factors contributed to a shift in adoption practices meant to facilitate the adoption of white infants. During the 1940s many jurisdictions began to seal adoption records, making it impossible for anyone to examine the records to discover the identity of the biological parents of an adopted child.[19] E. Wayne Carp has argued that what he calls the shift from confidentiality (records closed to all but "the parties of interest": i.e., birth parents, adoptive parents, and child) to secrecy (records inaccessible to everyone except by a court order) arose from a complex set of factors, including social workers' desire "to defend the adoptive parents, protect the privacy of unwed mothers, increase their own influence and power, and bolster social work professionalism."[20] Adoptive parents tried to avoid the stigma of infertility and the fear that the birth parents might reappear by pushing for secrecy. Unwed mothers sought secrecy in order to be spared the social condemnation that accompanied nonmarital pregnancy. Seeking to avoid investigation of their life circumstances and the six-month delay in placement that were often standard in state agencies, unwed mothers turned to private, unlicensed adoption agencies that would guarantee their privacy. As a result, state agencies shifted their procedures and urged legislatures to mandate the sealing of adoption records.

The invisibility of the child's biological parents through sealed records made possible the construction of the adoptive family as an "as-if" biological family. "The adoptive parents were supposed to be people who, by physical appearance and age, could have conceived the infant."[21] A variety of practices developed that made possible the construction of the "as if" family. Unwed white pregnant women would often leave their home communities, telling friends and neighbors that they were traveling or visiting relatives, and reside in homes for unwed mothers. Upon the birth of the child, the birth mother signed a document in which she irrevocably severed her rights and responsibilities to the child. The adoption agency took custody of the child and matched the characteristics of adoptive and original parents. Statutes and court decisions "used tests of adoptive parental fitness and strict eligibility standards to make the artificial family approximate the legal ideal of a proper natural one in age, race, affection, and legal authority."[22] When the adoption became final, usually after a probationary period of six months to a year, the court sealed the original birth certificate and adoption records and entered into the public record a new birth certificate, which contained only the names of the adoptive parents. The sealed records could be opened only by court order after a showing of "good cause." (In some states, a petitioner could establish good cause by demonstrating medical necessity; in others, a strongly felt psychological need to establish a personal identity came to constitute cause.) In addition to these practices, the general exclusion of single persons and of gay and lesbian couples from the pool of adoptive parents maintained the custom of making the adoptive family resemble a biological family.

These practices in both U.S. and international adoptions have become known as the "clean break" approach to adoption, in which the integration of a child into an adoptive family "is premised on the complete severance of ties with the biological family."[23] In an intercountry adoption, the clean break model also involves the child's assumption of a new "national identity—as 'Swedish' or 'American' rather than 'South Korean,' 'Colombian,' or 'Chinese.'"[24] Paradoxically, as Barbara Yngvesson notes, the clean break model, which incorporates an individualistic model of the child who can be moved from one family to another across all kinds of cultural and geopolitical lines in order to be placed in a family environment, also suggests that the ties between child and birth parent are so strong that unless the child is rendered "parentless" (e.g., by being declared legally "abandoned"), new ties cannot be created.[25]

Many factors, both sociological and ideological, have in recent years challenged the model of the adoptive family as a mirror or imitation of the biological family and of the infant voluntarily relinquished for adoption as a "parentless" child. The relatively low number of white babies available for adoption, due in part to contraceptive use and abortion and in part to the decreasing stigma associated with unwed motherhood, has made the efforts of many people to locate healthy infants more visible through ads or notices seeking women waiting to place a child for adoption. Single persons and gay and lesbian couples have found ways to adopt children. Some people have adopted across racial lines, making the constructed nature of at least some adoptive families readily visible. Some people have entered into open adoptions, in which members of both the family of origin and the adoptive family are known to everyone involved.

The emergence of families through nonsecret and transracial adoptions has thrown into question the traditional assumption that the goal of voluntary infant adoption is to create an "as if" family through the incorporation of a "parentless" child. Adoption is creating a variety of new forms of families. In the case of nonsecrecy or open adoption, the birth parents' and the child's rights to know one another's identities are at issue; in transracial adoption, both the child's right to a particular cultural identity and the group's right to raise "its own" are at issue. I bring the policy debates over secrecy versus nonsecrecy and same-race versus transracial adoption together here because both raise the question of whether or to what extent the law should treat an infant available for adoption as an autonomous individual in need of a family or as an individual in part defined by relationships to persons or groups beyond the adoptive family.

II. The "As If" Adoptive Family

A. Nonsecrecy and Open Adoption

Both open adoption and transracial adoption challenge the notion that adoptive families should mirror the nuclear family composed of a heterosexual couple and their biological offspring. David Schneider has pointed out how strongly the possibility of having biological offspring a couple could raise together influenced the American understandings both of "family" and of legitimate sexual relations:

> Sexual intercourse between persons who are not married is fornication and improper; between persons who are married but not to each other is adultery and is wrong; between blood relatives is incest and is prohibited; between persons of the same sex is homosexuality and is wrong; with animals is sodomy and is prohibited; with one's self is masturbation and wrong; and with parts of the body other than the genitalia themselves is wrong. All of these are defined as "unnatural sex acts" and are morally, and in some cases, legally, wrong in American culture.[26]

Schneider might have noted that intercourse across racial lines was also prohibited by both cultural and legal rules, on the grounds that it was "unnatural" and an offense to both custom and morality. Interracial marriage was a crime in some states until the Supreme Court struck down antimiscegenation statutes in *Loving v. Virginia* in 1967.[27] As late as 1984, Florida argued before the Supreme Court that a divorced white woman should be denied custody of her white child because the mother's new marriage to a black man would create social difficulties for the child as she grew up. The Court rebuffed Florida's reasoning, saying that "[t]he question . . . is whether the reality of private biases and the possible injury they might inflict are permissible considerations for removal of an infant child from the custody of its natural mother. . . . The Constitution cannot control such prejudices [as exist against interracial marriage], but neither can it tolerate them."[28] Even as the Court rejected any legal validity to the notion that families had to be racially homogeneous, it acknowledged the power of such an idea in Americans' imagination and social practice.

The primacy of blood ties in many Americans' understanding of family deeply affected the practice of secrecy in adoption. Initially, adoption records were kept confidential in order to protect the privacy of all parties, particularly the birth mother, from outsiders; confidentiality was not meant to block the exchange of nonidentifying information among parties to the adoption. Carol Sanger has pointed out the stigma attached to *all* birth mothers, married and unmarried alike, who decided not to raise their children or who were forced by circumstance or social pressure not to do so.[29] The shame attached to unmarried women bearing children did tremendous harm to individual women and children and played a large role in the subordination of women as a group. Women were often "ruined" by an act from which men might walk away unscathed. Fear of such dire social consequences increased the pressure on women to marry and surrounded premarital sexual activity with fear and anxiety. The practice of hiding one's pregnancy and childbirth in order to resume a "normal" life was the best many women could do in the face of these social pressures, but the toll such secrecy exacted was tremendous.

The practice of open adoption developed in response to the realization of white birth mothers that "the agencies needed them, rather than birth mothers needing the agencies," and it has received considerable support from the adoptees' rights movement. The adoptees' rights movement is made up of adult adoptees and others who contend that to be denied access to knowledge of one's genetic history may impede the development of a person's identity and sense of self-worth. In a typical formulation, Vermont

State Senator Richard Sears (Democrat—Bennington), who was adopted as a child, argued in favor of a proposed statute to open Vermont's adoption records, saying that adoptees "are the only people in the nation who are denied the basic right of knowing who they are."[30] Most people take knowledge of their genetic origins for granted; members of the adoptees' rights movement contend that access to such information is a basic civil and human right.

Notwithstanding the development of the practice of open adoption and pressure from various quarters to abandon sealed records, not everyone agrees that *all* adult adoptees should have access to their adoption records. In their eyes, the right of the birth parents to anonymity is very strong and may override the adoptee's right to know the identity of his or her birth parents, particularly if the birth records were sealed at the time of the adoption. State laws vary quite a bit in their provisions for disclosure and secrecy.[31] Some advocates of secrecy worry that if birth parents cannot be guaranteed confidentiality, some birth mothers will choose to terminate the pregnancy or retain custody. Even some birth parents who might go through with adoption will face the dilemma of acknowledging the pregnancy and adoption to a future spouse and children or will live in dread of being contacted by the grown child later in life.

It seems to me, however, that except in cases in which knowledge that she had once borne and relinquished a child would put a woman in grave danger, the adult adoptee's right to know his or her specific history overrides an adult's right to privacy (particularly eighteen years after the birth). The original parents are under no obligation to meet their offspring, much less develop a social relationship (although they may do so if they all agree); indeed, original parents may get legal protection from unwanted overtures that are harassing or threatening.[32] The adoptee does not have a right to an actual social relationship with the original parents; the child's right to be cared for and to be parented has been met by the adoptive parents. But adult adoptees should not be deprived of the information they need to construct a coherent story of origin, an explanation of how they came into the world.

We humans think of ourselves as temporal beings, as coming out of a past and being formed by what has gone before us, and of having a connection with the future. We are shaped by and shape the world in many ways, including physical procreation, works of craftsmanship and art, friendships, and material or spiritual legacies. Our sense of history and continuity, extending back into the past and forward into the future, is part of what gives a sense of meaning to our existence and our works. It is this experience of ourselves as beings in time that underpins a person's right to specific knowledge of his or her origins.

Although some people contend that nonsecrecy and open adoption idealize the blood tie by continuing the contact between birth parents and child, I think these practices would undercut the blood-based understanding of family bonds by giving custodial authority to adoptive parents *even though* the identity of the birth parents was known. Whereas secrecy suggests that only if the original family is rendered invisible and inaccessible can new family ties be forged, nonsecrecy and open adoption suggest that a child can have multiple sources of family identity and multiple mothers. The identity of the child is constructed neither exclusively by the original family nor exclusively by the adoptive family, but by the child's knowledge of or contact with both of these families.

But as Barbara Yngvesson has shown, for a child to occupy space between two families, a radical transformation in the understanding of "family" must take place. This is because the traditional understanding of the family "as constituted by shared biological heritage, by the 'mystical commonality' of mother and child, and as whole rather than split (it excludes difference, it is complete in itself)—is fundamental to the tension surrounding the place, and lack of place, of the birth mother in the adoptive family."[33] The practice of secrecy, Yngvesson notes, reflects the belief that the adoptive family can mirror the unity and inevitability of the biological family only if the birth mother is rendered invisible. "Only by outlawing her (splitting her off) through various forms of legal and social closure—sealed records, rewritten birth certificates, the silences that meet revelations that one is a birth mother or that one is a child with 'two mothers'—can the adoptive family *become* a family, 'as if' it were biological, and the adoptive mother become 'real.'"[34] For the adoptive mother to become "real," the birth mother has to become a nonmother; and for the birth mother to "get on with her life," she has to leave her pregnancy and child behind her as if they never existed.

Nonsecrecy, whether achieved by unsealed records or open adoption, simultaneously recognizes children as distinct individuals *and* as beings for whom the relationships that led to their births may be significant. The adopted child has two sets of parents; the birth parents do not need to be obscured for the other parents (or parent) to assume their role in the child's life. In making the identities of birth parents either known or ascertainable at a later date, nonsecrecy in adoption has marked a departure from the traditional practice of creating an "as if" family. Yet while nonsecrecy and open adoption recognize the child both as an individual and as a being-in-relationship with the family of origin, discussions of nonsecrecy have rarely addressed the issue of the child's relationships to a distinct *group* of origin. That question, however, has sparked a heated controversy about transracial adoption, a practice that also challenges the "as if" adoptive family.

B. Transracial Adoption

The public debate over whether children, particularly black and Native American children, should be adopted by people of other races has brought a whole raft of distinct considerations to the question of whether the "as if" adoptive family should be the norm. To what extent should the freedom to adopt or to be adopted be constrained by the requirement that the race of the child and that of the adoptive parents match? Underlying that question are assumptions about individualism and group identity. Should children available for adoption be treated as individuals and placed as quickly as possible with a suitable family regardless of race, or should children be treated as members of a racial group and matched with parents of that race? And who should have a say concerning whether race should play any part in placing a child: the birth parents, the adoptive parents, the adoption agency, the child's racial community of origin, and, in the case of Native American children, the tribe?

The controversy over transracial adoption has its roots in both sociological and ideological legacies of the civil rights movement.

Although both advocates and opponents of transracial adoption oppose the legacy of racial discrimination and seek greater social opportunity and justice for people of color, they differ markedly in their judgments about what strategies are likely to create a society free from the scourge of racism. Over the past three decades the debate has gone through a number of phases, which together illuminate these strategies.

Before the 1960s, there were very few transracial adoptions. Racial prejudice and segregation meant that interracial families were stigmatized, even though many American families were of mixed white, black, Native American, or Hispanic ancestry. The "normal" family, whether biological or adoptive, was racially homogeneous in appearance. The civil rights movement of the 1950s and 1960s, however, led some whites to adopt black children as a way of manifesting their belief that love could occur across racial lines and as a way of providing for children likely to grow up in poverty. In the early 1970s the Child Welfare League, which had long opposed adoption across racial lines, reversed its previous position and endorsed transracial adoption. By 1972, approximately twenty thousand black children had been adopted by white parents, and the number of Native American children adopted by white parents had also risen significantly.[35]

Adoption of black and Native American children by whites did not sit well with all advocates of civil rights, however. In 1972, the National Association of Black Social Workers (NABSW) went on record opposing transracial adoption. They contended that transracial adoption was a form of cultural genocide and that black children could develop neither "Black pride and a Black identity" nor the practical "survival skills" necessary to live in a society infused with racism unless they were raised in black families.[36] In 1985 William Merritt reiterated the NABSW position: "We view the placement of Black children in white homes as a hostile act against our community. It is a blatant form of race and cultural genocide."[37] In the face of this opposition, adoption of black children by whites fell off immediately and continued to decline.

Similarly, in the 1970s, many Native Americans began to see transracial adoption as a threat to the preservation and cultural integrity of Indian tribes. In states with large Indian populations, studies suggested that perhaps as many as 25 to 35 percent of all

Indian children were removed from their homes by the state and placed in adoptive homes, foster homes, and institutions like the boarding homes run by the Bureau of Indian Affairs; the vast majority of such placements were in non-Indian homes.[38] Indian rights advocates urged Congress to adopt the Indian Child Welfare Act of 1978 (ICWA), which declared it to be "the policy of this Nation to protect the best interests of Indian children and to promote the stability and security of Indian tribes and families by the establishment of minimum Federal standards for the removal of Indian children from their families."[39] The ICWA stipulated that when an adoption concerned the child of a member of a recognized Indian tribe, the tribe should have jurisdiction over the adoption, or, if the matter remained in the hands of the state courts, the court should try to place the child first with a member of the child's extended family, then with a member of the tribe, then with another Indian family, and only as a last resort with non-Indians.

This approach of accepting transracial placement only when placement with parents of the same race proved impossible appealed to James Bowen, who in a law review article in 1987 suggested that Congress pass an Afro-American Child Welfare Act modeled on the ICWA.[40] Bowen's proposed act would have established an Afro-American Child Welfare Commission to review all cases in which the removal of black children from their biological parents was contemplated and would have required such measures as mandatory appointment of counsel and state payment of attorney's fees if the parents were indigent. Bowen proposed giving subsidies to adults who had informally adopted children (usually members of the extended family) and establishing "a procedure to flush out potential non-related same-race adoptive parents in case no relative comes forward."[41] Bowen's suggestions for recruiting minority adoptive parents and scrutinizing the criteria used in decisions to remove children from their homes were picked up by many workers in the field. His proposal that transracial adoption be prohibited unless no adoptive parents of the same race could be found for a child was not acted upon, however, and Congress has since forbidden the use of race in the adoption of non-Indian children.

Federal law thus currently treats the part race may play in the placement of Native American and black children very differently. While the ICWA required that tribal membership be taken into account in placing Indian children, Congress required adoption agencies to ignore race in foster and adoptive placement of non-Indian children. Indeed, Congress has strengthened that prohibition in recent years. In 1994, Congress passed the Multiethnic Placement Act (MEPA), which stipulated that while adoption agencies receiving federal funds might take the "racial background of the child and the capacity of the . . . adoptive parents to meet the needs of a child of this background" into account as one of a number of factors in making an adoptive placement, these considerations could not preclude or even greatly delay permanent placement of a child.[42] Despite this tone of compromise, MEPA offended some activists on both sides of the transracial adoption controversy. Because it did not *require* an effort at same-race placement, MEPA failed to satisfy proponents of race matching; because it did not *prohibit* race matching altogether, it failed to satisfy proponents of race-blind placement. Those opposed to race matching got their wish when in 1996 Congress incorporated the Adoption Anti-Discrimination Bill into the Small Business Job Protection Act. Known as the Interethnic Placement Act (IEPA), that law stipulated that federal funds would be denied to any state or private agency that used race as a criterion for the placement of a child.[43] The IEPA explicitly exempted proceedings involving Indian children covered by the ICWA.[44]

In prohibiting the use of race as a factor in adoption of non-Indian children, Congress was responding to the kinds of arguments put forward in Elizabeth Bartholet's 1991 article "Where Do Black Children Belong?"[45] That article, which took issue with the practice of making transracial placements only after attempts at in-race placement had failed, set the terms in which transracial adoption would be debated throughout the 1990s. The article began with an account of Bartholet's experience as she began her quest, as a single, divorced white woman, to adopt a child: "When I first walked into the world of adoption, I was stunned at the dominant role race played. . . . It was central to many people's thinking about parenting. And it was a central organizing principle for the agencies which had been delegated authority to construct adoptive families."[46] Bartholet, who had worked in the civil rights movement of the 1960s, was disturbed by the role race played in both the attitudes of potential adoptive parents and the policies of adoption agencies. "The large majority of the people actively looking to adopt in this country are white and for the most part they want white children, at least initially."[47] The shortage of healthy children to adopt is in reality a shortage of white children and of infants—there are many older children of color available for adoption. "The familiar refrain that there are no children available for adoption is a reflection of the racial policies of many adoption agencies and the racial preferences of many adoptive parents."[48] There are many older children available in foster care: "The proportion of [children of color] in foster care is three times greater than in the nation's population. . . . More than half of the children waiting for adoption nationally are children of color, and this population is rapidly increasing in most states."[49]

Bartholet argued that adoption agencies should change their policies not only to allow white parents to adopt black children, but also to encourage such adoptions through counseling potential adoptive parents. Many people who might not initially think of adopting a child of a different race or an older child might be receptive to the idea if asked to consider doing so. She argued that the preference for same-race placement violates the principle of antidiscrimination, harms children waiting to be adopted by delaying their placement (and thereby sometimes preventing it altogether because older children are harder to place), and harms prospective adoptive parents by depriving them of the chance to nurture and love a child.

Although Bartholet was mainly concerned with the adoption of older children in foster care, many of whom had become available for adoption when the state terminated the parental rights of their parents, she and other opponents of race matching did not limit their opposition to such cases. Even when efforts at race matching would not delay the placement (e.g., of an infant voluntarily relinquished at birth), she thought that a preference for racial homogeneity in the family was offensive; arguments that families should be racially homogeneous reflected an "inappropriate separatist agenda."[50] Randall Kennedy struck a similar note, contending that "[r]acial matching is a disastrous social policy both in how it affects children and in what it signals about our current attitudes regarding racial distinctions."[51] In his eyes, "Racial matching reinforces racialism. . . . It buttresses the notion that people of different racial backgrounds are different in some moral, unbridgeable, permanent sense."[52] Most important, racial matching in adoption or marriage "belies the belief that love and understanding are boundless and instead instructs us that our affections are and should be bounded by the color line regardless of our efforts."[53] Hawley Fogg-Davis concurred: a race-neutral adoption system would "send a powerful message to all Americans that racial ascription should not be a barrier to the intimate association of family life."[54] Public policy allowing agencies to restrict placement across racial lines would reflect misguided biologism and would fail to affirm the human capacity to love beyond racial boundaries. Lifting those restrictions would deal a blow to the model of the "as if" adoptive family.

Opponents of race matching put forward various proposals to guarantee race neutrality in adoption practices. Bartholet and Kennedy lobbied during the debates on both the MEPA and IEPA to prohibit any effort at race matching when there were qualified adoptive parents of any race who wanted to adopt the child. Guaranteeing adoption choice was in their eyes the way to make sure that the child's equal protection right to expeditious permanent placement was not violated. Richard Banks and Hawley Fogg-Davis went even further, arguing not only that adoption agencies should be prohibited from race matching but that prospective adoptive parents should not be permitted to signify what race child they want or what race(s) they wish to exclude from consideration. Banks proposed that agencies that receive any government funding should not be allowed to classify or list children by race, a practice he called "facilitative accommodation."[55] Once agencies ceased to maintain lists of children "sorted" by race, prospective adoptive parents would have to consider each child as an individual. In addition, eliminating the adopter's choice would compel prospective parents to envision themselves as members of a multiracial family.

Fogg-Davis similarly supported a prohibition on listing children by race. For one thing, she considered it inappropriate for an adoption agency to decide to which racial group any particular child belongs. Although people in the United States are perceived through racial categories, individuals should not passively accept third-party racial identification, but rather "challenge existing racial meanings by creating flexible racial self-understandings in a lifelong process of self-reflection and -revision."[56] Particularly for a mixed-race or a transracially adopted child, racial identity is not a "given" but is arrived at by what Fogg-Davis termed "racial navigation." Racial identity is influenced but not determined either by one's biological parents or by the groups to which one's parents belong; it is always in part to be negotiated or navigated by the individual herself or himself.[57] In both Banks's and Fogg-Davis's view, "Adoption is about matching a parent to a child, not a parent to a race."[58]

In these debates, individual rights are pitted against group rights; a self with a fluid and "negotiable" racial identity is contrasted to a self with a fixed and inherited racial identity; ideals of integration and the "melting pot" are set against ideals of ethnic nationalism and cultural difference. Advocates of transracial adoption frame the issue as one of antidiscrimination, focusing on the rights of the waiting child (or parents) to equal protection. In Randall Kennedy's terms, "There was a time when forward-looking people would have thought it praiseworthy for prospective adoptive parents to have said to a state welfare agency, 'we are willing to raise a parentless child regardless of the child's race.'" Race matching, even the version authorized by the MEPA, by contrast, "denigrates such people, portraying them as a mere fallback for parentless children of a different race than they."[59] It is telling that Kennedy spoke of "parentless" children, drawing attention to the need of the child already in state custody to find a permanent adoptive home. The need to place parentless children directs the attention of those thinking about adoption policy forward from the present into the future, not back into the past: "forward-looking people" would applaud transracial placement.

Underlying the dispute over race matching are different views about whether the child available for adoption should be viewed as an individual or as a person with links to his or her racial group of origin. As Twila Perry noted, proponents of transracial adoption tended to adhere to a highly individualistic model of liberal theory, while proponents of race matching, like herself, tended to be more communitarian and group oriented in outlook.[60] The insistence on seeing black children awaiting adoption strictly as individuals disconnected from blacks as a group is, as critics of race-blind placement contended, double-edged. While the assignment of rights by race can constitute invidious and unconstitutional discrimination, people in the contemporary United States neither perceive nor treat one another as raceless. Throughout their lives black children's position in and experience of society will be linked to the position of blacks in general. Critics of race-neutral adoption policy correctly pointed out that federal law dictating that black children must be placed without regard to race in the case of adoption may perpetuate notions about the inadequacy of black families and black parenting that will be harmful to these children and other blacks.

A policy of nondiscrimination may also divert attention from the social problems, including racism, that lead so many minority children to be in the adoption and foster care system. When proponents of race-neutral placement insist that what parentless black children need is "not 'white,' 'black,' 'yellow,' 'brown,' or 'red' parents but loving parents,"[61] they focus on the individual child rather than the systemic social forces that put their birth parents under such strain that they relinquish the child for adoption. The disproportionate number of black children awaiting adoption is

> an indicator of a web of racial disadvantage in American society: the fact that blacks are more likely to be poor than whites, that poor blacks are more likely than poor whites to have their parental rights terminated by a court, that white women who give birth to biracial babies may be motivated by racist social pressure to surrender their children for adoption.[62]

Transracial adoption may gradually diminish social attitudes that insist upon racial uniformity in intimate and family relationships. But transracial adoption does not attack the "web of racial injustice that makes so many black children available for adoption in the first place."[63]

Transracial adoption thus poses a dilemma for advocates of racial equality and nonsubordination. Multiracial families give testimony to the ability of people to love and take responsibility for one another across racial lines. At the same time, when white parents adopt children of color, they may reinforce white privilege and a sense of entitlement to whatever they desire and may contribute to the denigration of blacks and Native Americans as parents. While this dilemma cannot be entirely done away with in contemporary society, certain changes in the discourse and practice of adoption might undercut some of the dynamics of white privilege. As both transracial adoption and nonsecrecy have begun to weaken the hold of the "as if" adoptive family (and hence of the racially homogeneous family) on our social imagination, so they might also undermine the notion that the child available for adoption is a "parentless" child. These changes are linked; the virtual disappearance of the family of origin in the construction of the "as if" adoptive family suggested that the child available for adoption was an unencumbered individual, a person without ties to parents, simply awaiting placement with new parents to begin a new life. Under the traditional model of adoption, the child was treated as figuratively "abandoned" and so without roots. It is possible, however, to change both practice and discourse so that they do not suggest that adoption entails a clean break from the original family following their abandonment of the child, but instead suggest that many parents relinquish their children because they cannot give them the care they need. This change would counteract the disparagement of people, primarily women, who place their children for adoption and in particular would give dignity and voice to women of color.

III. The "Parentless" Child

While there have always been a significant number of adoptions, formal or informal, in which children were placed with family members or friends who maintained ties with the original parents, the traditional model for legal adoption was "stranger adoption." Under this model, social practice and law made a clean break between the family of origin and the child and then placed the now "parentless" child in an adoptive family. In domestic adoptions, the clean break was facilitated by sealing adoption records. In international adoptions, U.S. law required that for a foreign-born child with two surviving parents to qualify for "orphan" status, which is necessary for adoption in the United States, the child had to be legally "abandoned" by both parents. These measures were designed to prevent kidnapping and involuntary relinquishment, but they also constructed the child as "a kind of open cultural space (little, cute, girl) which simply needed to be filled with love."[64] In both domestic and international adoptions, the child was often represented as a foundling, a generic child without traceable roots in a specific past, even though in most voluntary adoptions the birth parents planned the relinquishment of the child, whether to an agency, doctor, or lawyer.

The legal and cultural construction of the child available for adoption as a "parentless" child affected the way people viewed not only the child, but also the adoptive parents and the original parents. The adoptive parents were often portrayed as rescuers, and the original parents were imagined as people who had "abandoned" their child. By and large, society did not judge those who relinquished a child for adoption kindly or compassionately. Except in the most extraordinary circumstances, like the air raids during World War II that led parents in London to send their children to live in the countryside, separating from one's child, particularly if one was a woman, was "marked as evidence of self-interest and assumed antithetical to the welfare of children."[65] The widely accepted procedure of confidentiality and issuance of a new birth certificate "lock[ed] into place the notion that relinquishing one's child need[ed] to be hidden" and "sustain[ed] the view that the separation itself was inherently bad."[66]

The understanding of the adoptable child as parentless and the practices that contributed to it started to change, however, when some states began mandating unsealed records and permitting open adoption. These changes, as Carol Sanger noted, occurred partly in response to birth mothers' realization that they controlled "a desirable commodity in short supply" and so could "think through the terms under which they might be willing to part with it."[67] This exercise of agency or decision-making authority by the birth mother or birth parents altered the depiction of the child available for adoption as "parentless" or "abandoned." In open adoption the birth mother changed from supplicant to partner in making a decision about the placement of her child; the terms of adoption, once thought to be absolute, became negotiable to some extent; and the original parents remained a presence in the life of their child.

With open adoption, even though a definitive transfer of custody took place, the child and the birth parents did not disappear entirely from each other's lives. As Barbara Yngvesson and Maureen Mahoney persuasively contend, the child could be understood as an individual who, though separated from his or her family of origin and joined permanently to another family, was also partially constituted by his or her origins, which did not need to be concealed for the new bonds to be deep and truly familial. The original parents (often only the birth mother) were understood as individuals for whom the fact of having begotten the child could not be obliterated.[68]

In an essay recounting her experience as a birth mother when a college student, Maureen Sweeney stated that she now wished to "develop adoption into an empowering option for pregnant women who feel that they cannot raise the child they are carrying."[69] Sweeney was not arguing for open adoption per se, but for the development of a "new paradigm" of adoption based on the experiences and observations of many people that adoption is not a temporally singular "event," not something that people experience and then "get over," but rather an ongoing reality in the lives of birth parents, adoptive parents, and adoptee. Sweeney's analysis paid particular attention to the ways society could view birth mothers as taking steps to provide care for their children, both by relinquishing parental rights and by their willingness to be known by and accessible to their offspring. Relinquishing a child for adoption, in such a view, would be seen not as an act of abandonment (although this is not to deny that some parents do abandon their children) but as a responsible act for the good of the child, arising from "an ethic of care for and responsibility to all those whose lives are indelibly changed by the adoption experience."[70] The birth mother would be seen as taking steps to make sure others would take care of the child in the future.

The consideration of the birth parents' concern for the child is largely absent from arguments on *both* sides in the transracial adoption debate. Given the terms in which that argument has been framed, this is understandable. Those who have asserted that adoption agencies should not be able to place children according to race do not want to allow birth parents to insist on same-race placement. Those who have favored race matching do not want to allow anyone, even birth parents, to select adoptive parents of a different race. Given the focus on the racial composition of the adoptive family, the disputants rarely have asked whether the birth parents—in particular the birth mother—should have a say in where their child is to be placed.

On the few occasions when someone has raised the question of whether birth parents should have a say in the placement of their child, the answer has almost universally been that they (or she) should not. For example, Donna J. Goldsmith argued against giving the gestational mother any opportunity to influence the placement of her offspring under the ICWA: "The concept that a mother has the right to remove her child from its extended family and community, thereby depriving the child of its heritage . . . is foreign to American Indian cultures."[71] Evelyn Blanchard gave similar testimony before Congress in 1988:

> Indian people have two relationship systems. They have a biological relational system, and they have a clan or band relational system. It is the convergence, if you will, of these two systems in tribal society that creates the fabric of tribal life. And each of us as an Indian person has a very specific place in the fabric. Those responsibilities are our rights, individual rights. And even our mother has no right to deny us those rights.[72]

There is, of course, no legally recognized body like a tribe that might be given authority to place children of other ethnic groups. When James Bowen faced the question of how the group of origin could have weight in the placement of black children, he proposed that the law give "any blood relative" of a child awaiting adoption the right to petition the court regarding custody of the child and to order the court to give preference to the wishes of the extended family.[73]

Twila Perry did pay attention to the birth mother, arguing that race-blind placement could reinforce the subordination of racial minorities, particularly minority women. Responding directly to Bartholet's "Where Do Black Children Belong?" in an article she published at about the time Congress adopted MEPA, Perry explained that, contrary to Bartholet (and hence contrary to MEPA's opposition to race matching), she preferred placing black children with black adoptive parents when possible. Her preference did not stem from consideration about the survival of the group, since black survival is not really threatened by transracial adoption; the psychological well-being of children adopted by parents of another race, since many of these children seem to be very well adjusted as children and as adults; or the transmission of cultural values, since the acquisition of a culture is distinct from being of a particular race. Rather, Perry objected that the *discourse* about transracial adoption did nothing to challenge, and even reinforced, notions of white superiority and black inferiority. Discourse about the benefits to a black child of being adopted by whites suggested that white women were superior mothers. To say, "We will place this child without regard to color," simply because there was a white adult or family who wanted the child, seemed to give whites the power to decide whether and when to "disconnect" the child from the black community.[74] Indeed, in practice, "transracial adoption" has referred only to the adoption of black children by white families, not to a true color-blind system in which all children are assigned to prospective adoptive parents without regard to race.[75] Perry did not propose such a color-blind system; instead, she advocated attempting to match parents and child by race first, then turning to transracial placement if necessary.

Lying behind Perry's opposition to color-blind adoption was the realization that all too often society portrays black women as "inadequate to the task of mothering Black children, while white women are seen as competent to raise children of any race."[76] Viewing transracial adoption as a way to help black children can mask the ways in which the rhetoric, and possibly the practice, can perpetuate the notion that black women's bodies, and their offspring, can be appropriated or put to use by others. Similarly, Dorothy Roberts demonstrated that the denigration of black motherhood has a long history, stretching from slavery, to the exclusion of most black women from "mothers' pensions" in the 1920s and 1930s, to criticism of black matriarchy in the Moynihan Report, to excoriation of the "welfare queen" in the 1990s. Roberts warned that the abandonment of race matching in adoption could contribute not only to the desirable goal of defying racist assumptions that would limit love by race but also to the continuation of "a system designed to provide childless white couples with babies and with the type of babies they prefer."[77] While transracial adoption can and does help specific black children and defies segregationist practices, "[i]t does nothing to diminish the devaluation of Black childbearing."[78] Required race matching acknowledges black families' child-rearing abilities but undercuts efforts to form families across racial lines.

I am uneasy with arguments both for and against race matching that do not make the birth parents' wishes concerning the race of the adoptive parents part of the placement decision. Arguments for race matching run up against the fact that in other contexts, liberal theory and law abjure the notion of assigning identity or rights by blood. Painful as it may be for others, when someone changes nationality, converts to a new religion, or forges a racial identity different from that of his or her relatives, a liberal society allows such self-definition. Indeed, I find it important to the legitimacy of the ICWA that the parents' tribal membership, not simply their race, creates the grounds for transferring jurisdiction to tribal courts. As long as people can exit from the tribe, the parents' tribal membership is in some ways a stand-in for the parents' understanding of their own identities. Until children grow up to decide such matters for themselves, their parents' declarations of self-understanding and intent may properly be taken as a proxy for their own. Parents have this authority not because they "own" their children, but because someone must speak for the child, and liberty is best protected if parents, not the state or other individuals or groups, assume this responsibility. If parents are tribal members, it is proper that the tribal courts have jurisdiction in matters concerning the custody of their children.

What about situations in which adoption cases involving Native American children are heard by state courts? I am not convinced that these courts should be bound to place the child with Native American adoptive parents regardless of the declared wishes of the birth parents. The child available for adoption cannot be dealt with simply as an individual so "embedded" in a racial group that the group can claim the child regardless of the parents' (often the birth mother's) wishes; I am loath to take away agency and voice from a woman in difficult circumstances, and I would side with her even in the face of tribal opposition.[79]

At the same time, however, I find suggestions that birth parents should not be able to request same-race placements disturbing. Parents with vibrant ties to a group may express their hope that their children be placed where they will have the opportunity to forge similar ties. Richard Banks argued that because white privilege confers so much power, he found parental choice by minority-race parents more acceptable than the exercise of such choice by white parents.[80] Giving choice to black birth parents would undermine racism regardless of whether they sought same-race or different-race placement; black birth parents' choice of same-race placement would empower blacks as a group, while their choice of transracial placement would create multiracial families. White birth parents' choice of same-race placement, however, would replicate racial hierarchy, and whites would be unlikely to choose to place their children with parents of a racial minority group. These considerations are strong arguments for a racially differentiated policy. But the equal protection clause of the Constitution prohibits laws that on their face treat individuals of different races differently. Giving the state the power to exclude expressions of parental choice by white but not by black birth parents raises difficult equal protection issues and would in practice do so little to dismantle existing racial hierarchies that I reject it.

I propose reframing the issue of where to place the Native American or African American child from one that pits equal individual rights (of the adoptive parents or the child) against group rights (of the child's racial or ethnic group) to one that reinserts the birth parents, particularly the birth mother, into the discussion. The relative invisibility of the birth parents—usually a single mother—in the debates about transracial adoption reveals the way in which gender and race combine to marginalize birth mothers who are members of a racial minority or mothers of biracial children. One would think that the birth parents, as the concrete link between the child and the racial group claiming an interest in or jurisdiction over the child's placement, would be the appropriate persons to present their understanding of their own and the child's racial identity, but neither ICWA nor MEPA gives birth parents much voice. Unfortunately, the dismissal of the birth mother's views and wishes in the context of adoption reinforces presumptions about the irrelevance or the irresponsibility of women who relinquish their children for adoption.

Listening to birth mothers cannot, of course, unravel the web of social and economic injustice—including poverty, lack of access to birth control, and stigmatization of unwed motherhood—that leads women both in the United States and abroad to relinquish their children for adoption. But attending to and recording a birth mother's views at least makes it harder to regard her simply as the supplier of a resource (babies) for others (adoptive parents). The child available for adoption cannot be dealt with simply as an unencumbered individual without ties to specific others, but must be seen as someone with a specific story of origin. Again, this recognition that a child available for adoption needs to be viewed both as an individual and as a person constituted by various relationships offers an alternative to the norm of the "as if" adoptive family and the image of the "parentless" child. Adoption discourse and practice that recognize the possibility of a variety of family forms, and the multiple relationships that shape adoptee, birth parents, and adoptive parents alike, will make life better not only for families touched by adoption but also for other families that do not conform to the traditional model of the two-parent heterosexual family in which the social and biological parents are one and the same.

IV. Reflections on Policy

The dilemma over whether the infant available for adoption should be regarded as an autonomous self or as a person with significant ties to others is illuminated in practical and concrete terms by the debates over nonsecrecy and transracial adoption.

Both nonsecret and transracial adoption challenge the construction of the "as if" adoptive family and raise questions about whether the child available for adoption should be regarded as having been "abandoned" by birth parents or a group of origin. Taken together, nonsecret and transracial adoption suggest that it may be useful to recognize in discourse and public policy that not every child has two, or only two, "parents," even though custodial authority properly rests with the social parents who are the child's daily caregivers.

Advocates of nonsecrecy challenge the biologism of the "as if" family by opposing the sealing of birth records that makes the identity of the original parents impossible or difficult to ascertain. They suggest that a family does not have to have impermeable borders that shut out all adults except the legal parents in order to be "real," stable, and enduring.[81] In some independent open adoptions, however, both birth and adoptive parents who choose "people who are 'like' themselves or an idealized image of who they might be . . . 'match' themselves to one another and perpetuate the notion that a real family is one that mimics biologically-based 'likeness.'"[82] Thus although open adoption may encourage nonessentialist thinking that does not equate motherhood with a biological relationship and in this way may contribute to a pluralization of family forms, it may also encourage people to try to form a family with people like themselves and in that way to mirror the biologic family.

Most advocates of transracial adoption, for their part, in focusing on the child awaiting adoption and his or her right to be placed in a permanent family, draw attention away from the birth parents. The birth parents have relinquished their parental rights, severing the child's ties to a specific family and history. The adoptable child is generalized, a being innocent and deserving of love; the child is like all other children, and his or her race is irrelevant. For opponents of transracial adoption, however, the child's ties to the group of origin, and hence his or her race, are relevant. For these advocates of same-race placement, focusing on the group draws attention away from the birth parent(s).

Brought into dialogue with one another, these discussions of nonsecret and transracial adoption highlight the ways that gender, race, and class are implicated in adoption policy. All adoptions challenge the gender norm that has defined the capacity to bear a child as a woman's preeminent characteristic. Adoption says that a woman may decide not to raise a child she has borne and that a woman who has not borne a child may decide to be a mother. In severing the connection between childbearing and child rearing, adoption suggests both that a woman does not require a birth father to become a mother and that men as well as women can engage in the "hands-on" work of parenting.[83]

Finding ways to acknowledge adoption as a cooperative endeavor may be particularly difficult when the adoptive parents occupy a quite different position in the social, racial, and economic hierarchies of their society (including global society in the case of intercountry adoption) than the birth mothers (or parents) do. As Yngvesson's reflections on the experience of adoptive families in both the United States and Sweden suggest, in nonsecret adoption, when parents are aware that their child may someday meet his or her birth parent(s), they must do more than accept the "motherless" child, the abandoned innocent. They must receive the child in his or her specificity and acknowledge his or her social history. They must not only love their child but also make room in their lives for those things that "belong to" their child, although the extent of such sharing will vary greatly.[84] To engage in nonsecret or open adoption should involve not only love for and acceptance of the child, but acknowledgment of and respect for the original parent(s).

If public policy encouraged soliciting birth parents' wishes with respect to specifying either the race of their child or the role (if any) that race should play in the child's placement, some of the objections to transracial adoption voiced by Twila Perry, Ruth-Arlene Howe, Dorothy Roberts, and others would be mitigated. Were the birth parent(s) to have a say in the placement of the child, to exchange letters and photographs with the adoptive parents during the child's minority, and to know that the adoptee might contact them when he or she reached age eighteen, transracial placements would be less likely to suggest that (white) adoptive parents can appropriate the children of (black) women when it suits their purposes.

As adoption practice moves toward greater "openness" and the exchange of specific information about the adopted child, general awareness of kinds of coercive contexts in which a woman may "choose" to relinquish her child for adoption will probably increase. One kind of coercion stems from social customs and mores that make bearing a child out of wedlock a cause of stigma and "social death" for a woman. Another stems from economic conditions that put some people in circumstances where they cannot provide a child with food, clothing, and shelter (much less adequate education). There can be no greater indictment of structurally produced economic inequalities than that they cause some people to have to give up their children.

Transforming the model of the "as if" adoptive family created by the incorporation of the "parentless" child entails seismic shifts in the ways we view both women and children. The birth mother remains knowable; the child is treated both as an individual and as someone with ties to people outside the adoptive family. Regarding the child under these two aspects emphasizes the fact that the child is no one's possession, and that parenthood is better understood as stewardship than as proprietorship.[85] "There is a deep and profound sense that we do not own our children. All children can escape the confines of what we would make of them."[86] That parenthood is not a proprietary relationship is true of all families but is easier to see when two sets of parents must cooperate (even if only in the moments of relinquishing and assuming custody) to provide for a child's needs.

Adoption practice should reflect the idea that the responsibility for children's well-being is not a matter to be left to private arrangements, but a public responsibility. The laws governing adoption are important not only to those personally touched by them, but to the larger society as well. Those laws express what society understands families and family obligations to be. One symbolic benefit of agency adoptions over independent adoptions is that oversight by the agency suggests that providing physical and psychological nurturance to children is a social and public responsibility, not simply a matter to be arranged between individuals. The agency represents the public's commitment to assume responsibility for the well-being of the child, even though another family may almost immediately take custody of the child. The proper form of family is not given in nature but is constructed through social practice, reflective discussion, and legal regulation. Public discussion of policies regulating adoption should remind us of society's responsibility to ensure that all children are provided with care.

Robert Gordon has suggested that the power exerted by a legal regime "consists less in the force that it can bring to bear against violators of its rules than in its capacity to persuade people" of the fitness and desirability of "the world described in its images and categories."[87] My aim in this essay has been to suggest the appropriateness of a legal regime in which adoptive families would be seen as a distinct and valuable kind of family, not as an imitation of the biologic family, and in a world in which the decision to place a child for adoption would be regarded as an effort to secure care for the child, not as an act of abandonment. In such a world, the relinquishment of a child for adoption by one set of parents and the assumption of parental rights by another would be seen as interrelated efforts to secure care for the child. There would still be conflicts that could not be settled without moral remainder. Policy, practice, and discourse, however, would be shaped both to place a child securely and permanently in an adoptive family and to recognize the relevance of acknowledging (and in some cases maintaining) relationships between a child and birth parents or racial groups. The shift away from the model of the "as if" adoptive family formed by incorporation of the "abandoned" child would carry with it difficulties and stresses, but it would more accurately reflect what happens in adoption and would do greater justice to all those involved in the adoption process.

NOTES

I wish to thank Diane Churchill, Ann Congleton, Madelyn Freundlich, Hawley Fogg-Davis, Mona Harrington, Alice Hearst, Joan Hollinger, Morris Kaplan, Steve Macedo, Susan Okin, Dorothy Roberts, Carol Sanger, and Patricia Wallace for their comments on an earlier version of this essay.

1. Readers familiar with debates in political theory will recognize that this examination of adoption engages aspects of the dispute between liberals and communitarians, particularly the contrast Michael Sandel draws between the "unencumbered individual" and the "embedded

self." See Sandel, *Liberalism and the Limits of Justice* (New York: Cambridge University Press, 1982), and *Democracy's Discontent* (Cambridge, Mass.: Harvard University Press, 1996).

2. A. D. Kraft et al., "Some Theoretical Considerations on Confidential Adoptions. Part III: The Adopted Child," *Child and Adolescent Social Work Journal* 2 (Fall 1985): 139–53. Jerome Smith reviews some of the literature that expresses reservations about open adoption in *The Realities of Adoption* (Lanham, Md.: Madison Books, 1997), 40–44.

3. A. Baran and R. Pannor, "Open Adoption," in *The Psychology of Adoption*, ed. D. M. Brodzinsky and M. Schechter (New York: Oxford University Press, 1990); Jeanne Lindsey, *Open Adoption: A Caring Option* (Buena Vista, Calif.: Morning Glory Press, 1987); Katherine Bartlett, "Rethinking Parenthood as an Exclusive Status: The Need for Legal Alternatives When the Premise of the Nuclear Family Has Failed," *Virginia Law Review* 70, no. 5 (1984): 879–963; Barbara Yngvesson, "Negotiating Motherhood: Identity and Difference in 'Open' Adoptions," *Law and Society Review* 31, no. 1 (1997): 31–80.

4. Elizabeth Bartholet, "Where Do Black Children Belong? The Politics of Race Matching in Adoption," *University of Pennsylvania Law Review* 139 (1991): 1163–1256; Randall Kennedy, "Orphans of Separatism: The Painful Politics of Transracial Adoption," *American Prospect* 17 (Spring 1994): 38–45; Richard Banks, "The Color of Desire: Fulfilling Adoptive Parents' Racial Preferences through Discriminatory State Action," *Yale Law Journal* 107 (1998): 875–964; Hawley Fogg-Davis, "Choosing Children: A Proposal for Race-Neutral Adoption Policy," unpublished paper, University of Wisconsin, Madison, 1999.

5. Twila L. Perry, "The Transracial Adoption Controversy: An Analysis of Discourse and Subordination," *New York University Review of Law and Social Change* 21 (1993–94): 33–108; Ruth-Arlene Howe, "A Review of *Family Bonds*," *Golden Gate University Law Review* 24 (1994): 299–305; James S. Bowen, "Cultural Convergences and Divergences: The Nexus between Putative Afro-American Family Values and the Best Interest of the Child," *Journal of Family Law* 26, no. 3 (1987–88): 487–544.

6. Barbara Woodhouse has developed a child-centered analysis in many of her writings on family law; see "Hatching the Egg: A Child-Centered Perspective on Parents' Rights," *Cardozo Law Review* 14 (1993): 1747–1806, and "'Out of Children's Needs, Children's Rights': The Child's Voice in Defining the Family," *Brigham Young University Journal of Public Law* 8 (1994): 321–41.

7. Janet Farrell Smith, "Analyzing Ethical Conflict in the Transracial Adoption Debate: Three Conflicts Involving Community," *Hypatia* 11, no. 2 (Spring 1996): 2.

8. Ibid.

9. Thomas Hobbes, *De Cive,* chap. 9, para 3, in *Man and Citizen,* ed. Bernard Gert (New York: Doubleday Anchor, 1972), 213.

10. Michael Grossberg, *Governing the Hearth: Law and the Family in Nineteenth-Century America* (Chapel Hill: University of North Carolina Press, 1985), 268–84. On the history of adoption law in the United States, see Jamil S. Zainaldin, "The Emergence of a Modern American Family Law: Child Custody, Adoption, and the Courts, 1796–1851," *Northwestern University Law Review* 73 (1979): 1038–89; and Stephen B. Presser, "The Historic Background of the American Law of Adoption," *Journal of Family Law* 11 (1971): 443–516.

11. David M. Schneider, *American Kinship: A Cultural Account* (Chicago: University of Chicago Press, 1968), 24.

12. We tend to think of the parent-child bond as more fundamental than the marriage bond. Marriage partners are chosen from among many possible mates, and marriage bonds can be legally severed by divorce. By contrast, each child conceived and born is experienced as unique and "given," not individually chosen, and often not intentionally conceived. Although children are expected in our culture to separate from their parents and leave home, and although parents and children can become seriously estranged, we tend to think of the parent-child bond as "forever."

13. Barbara Yngvesson and Maureen Mahoney, "'As One Should, Ought and Wants to Be': Belonging and Authenticity in Identity Narratives," *Theory, Culture and Society* 17, no. 6 (2000): 85. On the ways in which U.S. culture emphasizes blood ties, see Dorothy Roberts, "The Genetic Tie," *University of Chicago Law Review* 62 (1995): 207–73; and Schneider, *American Kinship.*

14. Rickie Solinger, *Wake up Little Susie: Single Pregnancy and Race before Roe v. Wade* (New York: Routledge, 1992).

15. Andrew Billingsley, *Climbing Jacob's Ladder: The Enduring Legacy of African-American Families* (New York: Simon and Schuster, 1992); Patricia Hill Collins, *Black Feminist Thought* (Boston: Unwin Hyman, 1990); Jaqueline Jones, *Labor of Love, Labor of Sorrow* (New York: Vintage, 1986); Herbert Guttman, *The Black Family in Slavery and Freedom 1750–1925* (New York: Pantheon, 1976); Carol Stack, *All Our Kin* (New York: Harper and Row, 1974).

16. Joyce Ladner observed that most blacks considered a child born out of wedlock to have a right to live in the community without stigmatization. Joyce Ladner, *Tomorrow's Tomorrow: The Black Woman* (Garden City, N.Y.: Doubleday, 1972), cited in Twila Perry, "Transracial and International Adoption: Mothers, Hierarchy, Race,

and Feminist Legal Theory," *Yale Journal of Law and Feminism* 10 (1998): 112.

17. On the causes of the change in attitudes toward unwed (white) mothers, see E. Wayne Carp, *Family Matters: Secrecy and Disclosure in the History of Adoption* (Cambridge, Mass.: Harvard University Press, 1998), and Solinger, *Wake up Little Susie.*

18. Solinger, *Wake up Little Susie,* 24.

19. See Joan Heifetz Hollinger, "Aftermath of Adoption: Legal and Social Consequences," in *Adoption Law and Practice,* vol. 2, ed. Joan Heifetz Hollinger (New York: Matthew Bender, 1998; Supp. 2000), chap. 3.

20. Carp, *Family Matters,* 102, 109–12, and see generally chap. 4, 102–37. Carp viewed the unwed mothers' demand for privacy as the prime reason for the increasing tendency to shroud adoption in secrecy and to use state law to seal adoption records, but it seems more likely that it was pressure from adoptive parents—the ones paying the agencies—that led to greater secrecy.

21. S. Katz, quoted in Ruth-Arlene Howe, "Adoption Practice, Issues, and Laws 1958–1983," *Family Law Quarterly* 17 (1983): 178. In 1977, in *Drummond v. Fulton County Department of Family and Children's Services* [563 F.2d 1200 (5th Cir. 1977) (en banc)], the Fifth Circuit Court of Appeals found that white foster parents of a mixed-race child had not been deprived of their rights under the equal protection clause of the Fourteenth Amendment when the state decided to remove the child for permanent placement in another home. The Court held that while automatic and conclusory use of race is prohibited, race may be used as one of the factors in placing a child for adoption. The adoption agency, the court held, did not violate the Constitution when it tried to "duplicate the biological, natural environment of the child as part of the agency mission." Drummond, 563 F.2d at 1205–6, quoted in Bowen, "Cultural Convergences and Divergences," 515. This use of race would now be prohibited by the Interethnic Placement Act; see below, Section III.

22. Grossberg, *Governing the Hearth,* 275.

23. Barbara Yngvesson, "Un Niño de Cualquier Color: Race and Nation in Intercountry Adoption," in *Globalizing Institutions: Case Studies in Regulation and Innovation,* ed. Jane Jenson and Boaventura de Sousa Santos (Aldershot, England: Ashgate, 2000), 171.

24. Ibid. On the notion of a "clean break" in intercountry adoption, see William Duncan, "Regulating Intercountry Adoption: An International Perspective," in *Frontiers of Family Law,* ed. Andrew Bainham and David S. Pearl (New York: John Wiley, 1993). The Hague Convention on Protection of Children and Co-operation in Respect of Intercountry

Adoption both speaks of a child's right to the preservation of its identity (Article 30) and favors adoptions that sever the tie between adoptee and birth parents (Articles 26 and 27).

25. The ties to the past, however, visibly follow intercountry adoptees: "their names, skin color, facial configuration and manner tie them to a past that will always haunt the present, connecting adoptive parent to child, [receiving country] to its immigrant adoptees, and adoptees to the country of birth that made them 'adoptable.'" Yngvesson, "Un Niño de Cualquier Color," 171.

26. Schneider, *American Kinship*, 38.

27. *Loving v. Virginia*, 388 U.S. 1 (1967).

28. *Palmore v. Sidoti*, 466 U.S. 429 (1984).

29. Carol Sanger, "Separating from Children," *Columbia Law Review* 96, no. 2 (1996): 375–517.

30. Quoted in Yngvesson and Mahoney, "'As One Should,'" 91. The bill passed by the Vermont legislature in May 1996 provided for unsealing adoption records on a case-by-case basis, a more limited measure than Sears and others had sought.

31. States have taken various approaches to the question of making identifying and nonidentifying information available to adult adoptees. Most permit the release of nonidentifying background information about birth parents if the adoptee requests it. Several have a "mutual consent registry" whereby both birth parent(s) and adoptee must consent to the release of identifying information. Some have "search and consent" procedures, whereby if an adult adoptee requests his or her birth record, the state must search for the birth parents and request their consent to release the record. If the birth parents cannot be found, or withhold their consent, the adoptee can petition the court to release the record on a showing of good cause. See Peter Swisher, Anthony Miller, and Jana Singer, *Family Law: Cases, Materials, and Problems* (New York: Matthew Bender, 1995), 750–2. My thanks to Milton C. Regan, Jr., for this reference.

Naomi Cahn and Jana Singer, "Adoption, Identity, and the Constitution: The Case for Opening Closed Records," *University of Pennsylvania Journal of Constitutional Law* 1 (December 1999): 150–94, make a strong case for not opening all adoption records retroactively but requiring the state to conduct a confidential search for the birth parents and to request their consent to the release of identifying information.

32. A Tennessee statute reflects the kind of approach I am advocating. It states that an adult adoptee over the age of twenty-one may obtain identifying information about his or her birth parent(s) upon request. Birth parents, however, may register to prevent contact by the adoptee,

and an adoptee who despite this contacts the birth parent(s) may be subject to legal liability. The statute was upheld against a constitutional challenge in *Doe v. Sundquist,* 106 F.3d 702 (6th Cir.), cert. denied, 118 S. Ct. 51 (1997). My thanks to Milton C. Regan, Jr., for this information.

33. Yngvesson, "Negotiating Motherhood," 71.

34. Ibid.

35. Smith, "Analyzing Ethical Conflict," 1–13, 5.

36. National Association of Black Social Workers, "Position Paper," April 1972, quoted in Elizabeth Bartholet, *Family Bonds: Adoption and the Politics of Parenting* (Boston: Houghton Mifflin, 1993), 94.

James Bowen described survival skills as "abilities to ignore racial insults, to decipher the appropriateness of fighting back or submission, to emphasize black strength, beauty and worth as a countermeasure to the denigration of Blacks in America." Bowen, "Cultural Convergences and Divergences," 510. Eloquent testimony to the difficulties white parents face in transmitting survival skills to black children came from white as well as black parents. For example, J. Douglas Bates writes of the errors and oversights he and his wife committed in raising their two black daughters in *Gift Children: A Story of Race, Family, and Adoption in a Divided America* (New York: Ticknor and Fields, 1993).

37. Testimony before the Senate Committee on Labor and Human Resources, 99th Cong., 1st Sess., June 25, 1985, quoted in Perry, "The Transracial Adoption Controversy," 47.

38. Halting (or at least slowing) this placement of Indian children away from reservations and Indian homes was meant to serve the interests of both the children and the tribes. Witness after witness at congressional hearings on the ICWA testified that Indian children placed away from Indian families were frequently placed in a series of foster homes or institutions and did not find permanent homes. Moreover, those children raised without any knowledge of or exposure to Native American culture seemed to fare less well psychologically than those who were raised with an appreciation of Native American culture. Senate Select Committee on Indian Affairs, *Indian Child Welfare Act: Hearings on S. 1214 before the Senate Select Comm. on Indian Affairs,* 95th Cong., 1st Sess., 1977, 46–47, quoted in Alice Hearst, "The Indian Child Welfare Act," unpublished paper, Smith College, Northampton, Mass., 1996, 17–18.

39. 25 U.S.C.A. § 1902. For testimony before Congress see Senate Select Committee on Indian Affairs, *Indian Child Welfare Act*; and Senate Committee on Interior and Insular Affairs, Subcommittee on Indian Affairs, *Indian Child Welfare Program: Hearings before the Subcomm. on Indian Affairs of the Senate Comm. on Interior and Insular Affairs,* 93rd Cong., 2d Sess., 1974.

40. James S. Bowen, "Cultural Convergences and Divergences," 487–544, esp. 522–32.

41. Ibid., 523, 531.

42. 42 U.S.C.A. § 5115a (West 1995).

43. 42 U.S.C.A. § 1996b (1) sec. 1808.

44. Martha Minow explains the difference as stemming from Congress's perception that the "extraordinarily frequent wrenching of Indian children from Indian parents, and the cultural insensitivity of child welfare agencies removing those children," made Indian children a special case. The differences also stem from the residence of many Indians on reservations, the distinct constitutional status of Indian tribes, and the existence of tribal courts that may make decisions regarding the custody of Indian children. Martha Minow, *Not Only for Myself: Identity, Politics and the Law* (New York: New Press, 1997), 75.

45. Bartholet, "Where Do Black Children Belong?" 1163.

46. Ibid., 1164–65.

47. Ibid., 1166.

48. Ibid.

49. Judith K. McKenzie, "Adoption of Children with Special Needs," *Future of Children* 3 (1993), 62, 68–69.

50. Bartholet, "Where Do Black Children Belong?" 1248.

51. Kennedy, "Orphans of Separatism," 39.

52. Ibid., 40.

53. Ibid.; see also Kennedy, "How Are We Doing with *Loving*? Race, Law and Intermarriage," *Boston University Law Review* 77 (October 1997): 815–22.

54. Fogg-Davis, "Choosing Children," 4–5.

55. Banks, "The Color of Desire," 943 (ref. omitted).

56. Hawley Fogg-Davis, *The Ethics of Transracial Adoption: Public Policy and Parental Choice* (Ithaca, N.Y.: Cornell University Press, 2001), 2.

57. The contrast between this view of racial navigation and racial self-definition and the view of racial identity and group membership underlying the ICWA is striking. Under the ICWA, if one of a child's parents is a tribal member, and the child fits the criteria for membership in that tribe, the tribe has jurisdiction in all custody matters concerning the child, or any state court must try to place the child with a tribal member or another Indian family. In the case of Indian children, racial identity is relevant to adoptive placement, and that racial identity is transmitted by blood or tribal membership.

58. Banks, "The Color of Desire," 909.

59. Kennedy, "Orphans of Separatism," 40.

60. Perry, "The Transracial Adoption Controversy," 65–67, 77–78.

61. Kennedy, "Orphans of Separatism," 41.
62. Fogg-Davis, "Choosing Children," 4.
63. Ibid.
64. Yngvesson, "Un Niño de Cualquier Color," 173.
65. Sanger, "Separating from Children," 377.
66. Ibid., 445.
67. Ibid., 490.
68. Yngvesson, "Negotiating Motherhood"; Yngvesson and Mahoney, "'As One Should.'" Adam Pertman, *Adoption Nation: How the Adoption Revolution Is Transforming America* (New York: Basic Books, 2000), advocates open adoption, drawing on social science data; interviews with birth parents, adoptive parents, and adoptees; and his own experience as an adoptive parent.
69. Maureen A. Sweeney, "Between Sorrow and Happy Endings: A New Paradigm of Adoption," *Yale Journal of Law and Feminism* 2, no. 2 (1990): 335.
70. Ibid.
71. Donna J. Goldsmith, "Individual vs. Collective Rights: The Indian Child Welfare Act," *Harvard Women's Law Journal* 13 (1990): 8.
72. Senate Select Committee on Indian Affairs, *To Amend the Indian Child Welfare Act: Hearings on S. 1976 before the Senate Select Comm. on Indian Affairs,* 100th Cong., 2d Sess., 48, 1988, 97–98 (Statement of Evelyn Blanchard).
73. "If the Afro-American child's extended family shall establish a different order of preference [than that drawn up by the court] by resolution, the agency or court effecting the placement shall follow such order. . . . Where appropriate, the preference of the Afro-American child or parent shall be considered." Bowen, "Cultural Convergences and Divergences," 539.
74. Perry "The Transracial Adoption Controversy," 81.
75. Ibid., 106.
76. Perry, "Transracial and International Adoption," 121.
77. Dorothy Roberts, *Killing the Black Body: Race, Reproduction, and the Meaning of Liberty* (New York: Pantheon, 1997), 276.
78. Ibid.
79. I do not think that obliteration of the voice of the mother is necessary to defend tribes from unjustifiable incursions by state courts. It is important to liberal society that people be able to change affiliations, such as religious affiliation. Although he may not share these particular views, my thinking about respecting both liberal principles and cultural pluralism is indebted to Will Kymlicka, *Liberalism, Community and Culture* (New York: Oxford University Press, 1989), esp. 162–82.

80. Banks, "The Color of Desire," 943–44.

81. This attitude of advocates of open adoption is akin to that of advocates of "limited parent status" for genetic parents (an argument developed with respect to known sperm donors of children born to lesbian couples). See Brad Sears, "Winning Arguments/Losing Themselves: The (Dys)functional Approach in *Thomas S. v. Robin Y*," *Harvard Civil Rights-Civil Liberties Law Review* 29 (1994): 559–80; Fred Bernstein, "This Child Does Have Two Mothers . . . and a Sperm Donor with Visitation," *New York University Review of Law and Social Change* 22 (1996): 1–58; Kate Harrison, "Fresh or Frozen: Lesbian Mothers, Sperm Donors, and Limited Fathers," in *Mothers in Law: Feminist Theory and the Legal Regulation of Motherhood*, ed. Martha Albertson Fineman and Isabel Karpin (New York: Columbia University Press, 1995). On extending some rights (but not custodial rights) to adults other than the parents involved in raising a child, see Bartlett, "Rethinking Parenthood."

82. Yngvesson and Mahoney, "'As One Should,'" 86.

83. On the importance of caregiving work to families and to the larger society, see Mona Harrington, *Care and Equality* (New York: Knopf, 1999); Eva Feder Kittay, *Love's Labor* (New York: Routledge, 1999); and Susan Moller Okin, *Justice, Gender, and the Family* (New York: Basic Books, 1989).

84. Yngvesson, "Negotiating Motherhood"; Yngvesson, "Un Niño de Cualquier Color"; Yngvesson and Mahoney, "'As One Should.'"

85. For an analysis of proprietary understandings of parenthood, see Janet Farrell Smith, "Parenting and Property," in *Mothering: Essays in Feminist Theory*, ed. Joyce Trebilcot (Totowa, N.J.: Rowman and Allenheld, 1983).

86. Drucilla Cornell, "Reimagining Adoption and Family Law," in *Mother Troubles*, ed. Julia Hanigsberg and Sara Ruddick (Boston: Beacon, 1999), 224.

87. Robert Gordon, "Critical Legal Histories," *Stanford Law Review* 36 (1984): 109.

2

PLACING THE ADOPTIVE SELF

CAROL SANGER

I. Introduction

In "Toward New Understandings of Adoption" (Chapter 1 of this book), Mary Shanley drops adoption into the cauldron of liberal political philosophy and asks us to consider whether, for purposes of permanent placement, children are better viewed as unencumbered individuals or as embedded selves with "ties to persons outside the adoptive family—genetic kin or a racial group."[1] The characterization of adoptable children as either unencumbered or embedded selves matters tremendously in terms of how adoption is understood and how policies are set: who gets adopted, by whom, how quickly, and under what terms. For the last thirty years or so, the issue has played itself out (though not always using the exact vocabulary of political philosophy) in two much disputed areas of adoption: transracial adoption (the placement of children across color lines) and open adoption (where both birth parents and adoptive parents possess some degree of identifying information about each other from the start). The basic argument is this. If children are essentially unencumbered, then it makes sense on developmental grounds to place them quickly with the first qualified family who wants them so that they can get on with whatever shape their newly situated little lives may take. That is, if the defining aspects of the self are made rather than derived, what matters for a child's well-being is familial permanence, not "continuity." Under this view, no regulatory deference is owed (at least under the auspices of embeddedness) to the characteristics, traditions, or preferences of the child's original parents or community. Indeed, the child is no longer "their" child but rather a freestanding someone who, once adopted, can proceed with family life and the business of becoming encumbered anew. The policy implications of this autonomous measure of the self for transracial and open adoption seem clear. Rather than waiting for an adoptive placement that honors the constitutive significance of race, children may be placed across racial lines. In the United States this has most often meant the placement of darker children with whiter families. With regard to open adoption, the unencumbered child may be placed without the identification or participation of birth parents beyond their initial consent, as has long been the standard practice in traditional "clean break" adoptions.

In contrast, if children (even newborns) are linked significantly to their families of origin in ways that necessarily affect who they are and who they will go on to be, then racial or cultural or other significant sources of identity should count heavily in the selection of adoptive parents even at the cost to the child of delaying permanent placement. The constitutive links may be to individuals—typically the birth parent(s)—or to groups such as a racial or ethnic community. Depending on how we size up the importance of the links, the individual or the group may even be granted participatory rights in the placement decision. The rules governing the placement of Indian children on reservations provide an illustration. The federal Indian Child Welfare Act gives jurisdiction in custody matters to tribal courts and creates a legal presumption that the best interests of Indian children are served by placement with tribal members.[2] Deference to *individual* ties is found in the increasing number of states that permit the birth parent(s) to articulate preferences regarding the social, cultural, and demographic traits of the adoptive parents, including their amenability to ongoing birth parent contact with the child.[3]

Shanley explains all this as part of her project to reconcile these competing visions of the self as they play out not just in the liberal-communitarian debate but in the very real context of adoption placement policies. She wants to consider "whether or to what extent the law should treat an infant available for adoption as an autonomous individual in need of a family or as an individual in part defined by relationships to persons or groups beyond the adoptive family." To that end, Shanley sets up three guiding principles. The first is simply that "the *child* should be at the center of the discussion"; after all, as Shanley reminds us, the very "purpose of adoption is to provide care to children."[4] This mirrors the familiar "best interests of the child" standard invariably announced (at least in law) whenever children are involved. The second principle repudiates the "biologism" of traditional adoption: that is, the established practice of treating adoptive families as if they were *identical* to biological ones—long the fiction that was encouraged by such social work policies as placing red-headed children with red-headed parents and by such legal requirements as replacing the child's original birth certificate with a postadoption certificate identifying the adoptive mother as the birth mother.[5] The third principle is the reconceptualization of adoptable children from "parentless" and "abandoned" to children necessarily tied to their families—and particularly their mothers—of origin.[6]

By sticking to these principles, Shanley is able to synthesize competing theories of the self and devise a regulatory scheme that "minimize[s] the conflict between values." She sensibly insists that children have needs for both security (the codeword for the demands of autonomous infants) *and* identity (the codeword for the demands of the embedded ones). Respecting security means that adoptable children require prompt placement with an eye to the adoptive family's availability rather than its similarities to the child's original parents or community. This is just as those on the "unencumbered" side of the debate would have it. Indeed, as things stand with regard to federal legislation, and excepting Indian children, they *do* have it: the 1996 Multiethnic Placement Act withholds federal funds from any adoption agency that uses race as a placement criterion.[7] But along with security, children's concurrent (*eventual* may be more accurate) need for identity means that adoptable children are also entitled to information about their birth family or group. The child "cannot be dealt with simply as an unencumbered individual without ties to specific others, but must be seen as someone with a specific story of origin." Under Shanley's plan, that story of origin is acknowledged and effected by giving birth mothers—and not the child's collective race or group—some voice in expressing their understanding of their child's race and their preference (if any) for the kind of family in which the child will be placed. Moreover, a policy that honors ancestral ties must run in both directions. Thus Shanley favors nonsecrecy with regard to adoption records and supports legislation authorizing adult adoptees to find out who their biological parents are—not the right to a "social relationship" but at least the right "to know [their] specific history."

In this essay I want to focus on the special relationship Shanley establishes among placement decisions, embeddedness, and birth mothers. I shall later argue that the law should respect a different special relationship—one that also links mothers to placement decisions but that drops embeddedness from the equation. But Shanley's argument and the general case for birth mothers first. Their importance—even centrality—emerges from Shanley's formal project of "minimiz[ing] the conflict in values" between embeddedness and autonomy.[8] To be sure, she is very fair in considering the interests of *all* the players in the adoption triad—children should always come first, adoptive parents should be permitted to assert their racial preferences. But birth mothers are given a special place at the table, and for good reasons. For the last half century, birth mothers were denied much of a place at all. Their function in adoption was twofold: consent and disappear. This directive was not always unwelcome; part of the impetus for the confidentiality of adoption records in the 1950s came from birth mothers who feared (quite rightly) the stigma of unwed motherhood.[9] Since then, the legal and social consequences of illegitimacy for the much smaller number of post-*Roe* women who continue unplanned pregnancies have improved for both mother and child. But the increased acceptability (indeed praiseworthiness) of maternal decisions to *keep* a nonmarital child (to use the new vocabulary) is unmatched when it comes to mothers' decisions to *relinquish* the same child for adoption. Indeed, many young unmarried pregnant women now consider placing a child for adoption more stigmatizing than keeping it.[10] Thus until recently certain traditional adoption practices held steady. Birth mothers (if no longer *unwed* mothers) remained invisible and uninvolved. As birth mother Jan Waldron has observed, "[T]here are millions of birthmothers in this country, yet most people will tell you they've never met *one*."[11]

Shanley aims to improve this situation. In keeping with her third guiding principle (rejecting the adoptee-as-abandoned-by-uncaring-mother fantasy), birth mothers are now to be recognized for the work they do. Special consideration is given throughout to how one or another placement policy would improve their status and treatment.[12] Rather than being erased from the birth process (literally, when one thinks about the substitute birth certificate), birth mothers are to be meaningfully considered and included. Thus Shanley notes that open adoptions not only satisfy an adopted child's need for identity but also benefit birth mothers. Because adoptive parents know that their child may one day meet its birth mother, they will be more likely to demonstrate "not only love for and acceptance of the child, but acknowledgment of and respect for the original parents." Again, "recognizing the significance of the original parents in adopted children's construction of identity . . . might increase respect for birth parents, particularly birth mothers." Such recognition is especially necessary to offset the "structurally produced economic inequalities . . . that . . . cause some people to have to give up their children." The people Shanley has insistently in mind here are minority birth mothers. Noting "the disproportionate number of black children awaiting adoption," Shanley explains that attending to a birth mother's placement preferences "at least makes it harder to regard her simply as the supplier of a resource (babies) for others (adoptive parents)"; further, it would "counteract the disparagement of people, primarily women, who place their children for adoption and in particular would give dignity and voice to women of color."[13]

But the real power (and likely source of increased respect) that Shanley confers upon birth mothers is the link she establishes between birth mothers and embeddedness. To the extent that embeddedness is to be honored in placement decisions, Shanley gives the claim to birth mothers. The communitarian conception of the embedded self might seem to favor ascriptive characteristics associated with group identity, rather than mothers' preferences. But Shanley goes with the latter. Limiting her immediate argument to race, she urges that birth mothers be solicited with respect to specifying "the race of their child" and "the role (if any) that race should play in the child's placement." Her reasons make sense. Faulting the failure of federal adoption legislation to include the preferences of birth mothers, Shanley argues, "One would think that the birth parents, as the concrete link between the child and the racial group claiming an interest in or jurisdiction over the child's placement, would be the appropriate persons to present their understanding of their own and the child's racial identity" and concludes that "until children grow up to decide such matters for themselves, their parents' declarations of self-understanding and intent may properly be taken as a proxy for their own." I would modify this analysis slightly. While parental decisions are proxylike, the theory behind them is less one of substituted judgment than of superior judgment. The Supreme Court expressed it thus in *Parham v. J.R.*: "The law's concept of family rests on a presumption that parents possess what children lack in maturity, experience, and capacity for judgment required for making life's difficult decisions. More important, historically it has recognized that the natural bonds of affection lead parents to act in the best interests of their children."[14] There may be reasons in certain cases to subject the Court's observation about assumed bonds of affection to sharper scrutiny. *Parham* itself, where frustrated parents and guardians were institutionalizing mentally ill children is such an example. Yet the legal and intuitive starting point is clear: parents' decisions about their children's well-being are understood to be well-intended and presumptively right. Thus *whatever* parents decide on behalf of their children is in the child's best interests, whether or not it is proxy for what we imagine either the child or even some more knowing entity, such as an adoption agency, would decide.

There will certainly be unhappiness with Shanley's policy conclusions by many in the adoption debates. Those who side with the long influential 1972 position statement of the National Association of Black Social Workers will dislike her dismissal of group interests or claims (other than as reflected in the birth mother's preferences); Elizabeth Bartholet and Richard Banks will be dissatisfied with her refusal to dismiss race-based preferences of either birth mothers or adoptive couples.[15] Adoptive parents may balk at the endorsement of adoptee access to identifying information, and birth mothers may wonder whether Shanley's suggestion that they be "listened to" means that their opinions are to be heeded as well as heard.

But Shanley has prepared her readers for these various disappointments early on by introducing an idea from moral philosophy: the concept of moral remainder. This is the notion that the resolution of complex problems may not be as tidy and complete as our moral (or arithmetical) instincts might desire. In situations involving "a complex set of conflicting practical demands, each tied to a set of apparently morally reasonable supports, taking up one of these positions will not nullify moral demands of the alternatives not taken."[16] Thus even when the problem has been solved—that is, a workable policy has been set—there may simply be something left over and unresolved. In adoption, the remainder is some unsatisfied aspect of a morally reasonable claim asserted by one or more of the participants. At the same time, amidst all this justifiable dissatisfaction, children will have been placed in what we expect are permanent homes with parents who want them. The normative importance of the sheer fact of placement is a point worth emphasizing, for adoption is not simply an interesting problem upon which to test philosophical theories of the self. It is a practice (bordering on an industry) carried out by layers of participants applying shifting rules in multiple jurisdictions. The needs and desires of those involved—mothers, fathers, grandparents, and siblings from both the birth and adoptive families, not to mention lawyers, judges, social workers, and adoptees themselves—are concrete, often heartfelt, and likely to conflict. It is unlikely, then, that the theoretical basis of each player's interests will be wholly satisfied, and some will necessarily bear the weight of the unsatisfied remainder.

II. Three Arguments

I agree with Shanley's conclusions that birth mothers should, if they desire, have considerable say about where their children are placed. I disagree, however, about tying the position to the notion of embeddedness, and for several reasons. The first concerns the difficulties inherent in defining this much contested term so that its implementation in the real world of placement decisions will be clear, fair, and manageable. Thus while Shanley limits her argument (more or less) to ties created by race and ethnicity, we might ask if other claims to community or heritage also fall under the penumbra of embeddedness. Should a birth parent's religion, nationality, hair color, or union background matter in deciding where a child is placed? My second concern involves the problem of defection. If mothers are designated as spokeswomen for their babies' constitutive ties, what are we to do about birth mothers uninterested in maintaining them, mothers who decide they would rather start their child off in an entirely new direction? Should the law act on maternal preferences only if the decision honors an appropriate link (i.e., a link acceptable to the proponents of embeddedness), or may birth mothers decline the invitation as well?[17]

There is, however, a third reason to defer to birth mother preferences that is unconnected to the role of embeddedness in the construction of identity. I endorse giving birth mothers power over their child's destiny (or at least over the child's adoption placement) on the grounds that the right to choose substitute caretakers for one's child—even permanent ones—falls within the scope of authority all parents have, without special reference to adoption or to whether the birth mother votes communitarian or liberal. I argue that the decisional autonomy inherent in maternal status prevails over claims the child or group may have for communal affiliation (recognizing that in practice the preferences of mother, group, and child may coincide).

These points—the contours of embeddedness, the ungovernable nature of birth mothers' placement decisions, and an alternative basis for maternal involvement—are developed in the following three sections. First, however, I want to be clear about the facts on which this discussion proceeds. Adoption covers a huge sweep of circumstances: there are stepparent adoption, special needs adoption, fost-adopt programs, kinship adoption, and so on. Yet all of these proceed under one of two initiating events. Either the birth parents have consented to the adoption, or their rights have been terminated involuntarily by the state. In the latter cases, where children have been removed from their families rather than relinquished by them, the children are often older, may well know their birth parents, and are more likely to have spent time in foster care. Certainly, considerations of embeddedness look quite different in such cases. The child may have its feet squarely in *two* families, a choice made not by policy but by circumstance. Claims regarding ties to families, customs, and communities of origin seem immediately more persuasive in cases where a child knows or may be returned to his or her family.

Shanley focuses our attention not on the predicament of older children in foster care but on "voluntary infant adoption" cases where the mother has decided from the very start to give up her baby for reasons satisfactory to her. Recognizing that such decisions are often made under constraints of time and circumstance, the law now attempts to safeguard their integrity through such mechanisms as (short) revocation periods, preconsent counseling, the removal of financial incentives, and permitting consent only after childbirth. Once such criteria have been met, the law credits the mother's decision as voluntary.[18] These are the cases Shanley posits here. While numerically a far smaller group than children in foster care, voluntarily relinquished infants test us more sharply on the potential limits of embeddedness and on the justifications for the birth mother's authority over the infant's postadoption self. Voluntarily relinquished infants also distance us from the difficult question of whether the state should concentrate on reunifying rather than terminating parents from their children in foster care, and the significance of embeddedness for that debate. Finally, because voluntarily relinquished infants are particularly marketable, they (or those concerned with the terms of their placements) drive agency practices and legal reform with special interest and vigor.

III. The Contours of Embeddedness

To the extent that children are, in Shanley's phrase, relational beings with ties to persons or groups outside the adoptive family, exactly which ties are deserving of respect for purposes of a placement regime? I have already noted that Shanley focuses on race, as debated in the adoption of black children by white families, and on ethnicity, as incorporated in the Indian Child Welfare Act. That focus has much appeal. In a society like ours, where racial distinctions are crucial to how life is experienced from cradle to grave, race is worth fighting about—or at least getting as right as we can—in the cradle context of adoption. This is especially so in light of racial practices in adoption over the last fifty years, where the pattern of traffic has gone entirely in one direction. The adoption by white parents of Indian and black children, and more recently of Chinese girls, has led to claims of ethnic plundering from members of at least the first two birth communities. Shanley urges maternal participation in placement decisions as a way to acknowledge, not sever, children's racial or ethnic ties and to remedy the "reinforce[ment of] white privilege" produced under the earlier regimes. But are there *other* ties similarly crucial to the construction of the (infant) self that justify extending placement suffrage to additional categories of birth mothers? Should, for example, a pious birth mother be entitled to a say with regard to her child's religious upbringing? Can a union mom insist on prolabor adoptive parents? Locating the borders of embeddedness is central to deciding with whom a child will be placed (and for what reasons) and who gets to make the decision (and why they do).

I want to suggest that at least in the context of adoption, embeddedness should be understood to mark a very small circumference. That is, if we take the notion of embeddedness to be based on a thesis about the way that a community constitutes the individual self, only a very few characteristics will make it onto the embeddedness shortlist. In thinking about what properly counts as such a marker, I want to distinguish embeddedness not from rival theories of autonomy but from characteristics or aspects of the self that are biological, genetic, or innate.[19] Shanley sometimes blurs the two, as when she contrasts the "freestanding individual" with "a person to whom these biological and social relationships are of continuing significance" or when she aligns advocates who "argue that knowledge of the genetic link between biological parents and child is part of the identity of both the biological parents and the child" on the side of embeddedness. But if embeddedness is to serve as the justification for maternal participation in placement decisions, it is important to identify its limits. This is especially so in an age when mothers discharged from maternity wards are given not only instructions on bathing the newborn but (soon enough) detailed maps to their child's entire genetic structure—and therein potential claims to and by all sorts of genetically based communities.[20]

Let us then be clear: embeddedness refers to the effects of a social process, not a natural process (though of course it may be a social process that chooses to make something social of a natural process or an innate characteristic). The circumstances of a child's birth *may* support a claim of embeddedness (i.e., that links to the birth family or community are constitutively important), but, as we shall see, only when the community (either the birth community or the adoptive community) attaches great importance to the circumstances of the child's birth. Thus the background of the birth parent may be significant for a child adopted out of that background, but only if the adopted child has subsequent dealings with the interested birth community or if the adoptive community itself regards the child's birth circumstances as significant. An example of the first might be the adoption of a black child into a white family in a racially diverse and divided society. An example of the second would be the efforts of white adoptive parents of Chinese girls to honor their daughters' origins (Chinese names, Chinese language training, and so on).[21] To be sure, the distinction between communitarian-based markers and innate ones is sometimes blurry; certain ties between child and group would seem to be both social (tribal membership) and biological (tribal membership because one's mother is a member of the tribe). Such confusion is understandable, especially when the characteristic in question seems apparent: we think we know it when we see it.[22] But as the following cases illustrate, race (or color) is not always a reliable marker for potential claims of embeddedness. It is unexpectedly malleable, and racial assessments are not always correct.

The malleability of racial categories is revealed in a telling episode from the early twentieth century. In 1904, the New York Sisters of Charity sent a group of Irish orphans out west for placement with hardworking Catholic families in a remote Arizona mining town.[23] When the train arrived at its destination, the children were distributed by the priest to the eager prospective parents, all screened and approved by the local priest. Thus Anna Doherty was handed to Abigail and Andres De Villescas; Henry Potts went to Josefa and Rafael Holguin, Edward Gibson to Trancita and Francisco Alvidrez, and so on. Within the day, the white people of the town, having grasped that *Mexicans* were adopting the orphans, formed a posse and seized the children back by force. The aftermath—legal, social, and economic—was long and hard-fought, and the children were never returned to the Mexican families. And how had this violent "misunderstanding" come about? Historian Linda Gordon explains the effect of the trip west:

> Seven days on a train had left [the children] restless and cranky, but the nuns dressing them in their finest communicated to them the solemnity of the occasion waiting. Their long train ride had transported them from orphanhood to son and daughter. . . . [The children] did not grasp that this trip was to offer them not only parents but also upward mobility. Even less did they know that mobility took the form of a racial transformation unique to the American Southwest, that the same train ride had transformed them from Irish to white.[24]

The transformation (or improvement or confusion) of racial categories continues to the present. In recognition of the inadequacy of such gross classifications as "black" or "white," the 2000 census permitted respondents for the first time to check off multiple categories of race.[25] This reform resulted in part from lobbying by the parents of mixed-race children who argued that they could not accurately describe their children's racial composition under the existing "one or the other" system. The recognition of multiply raced people further complicates implementing embeddedness. The concept does not tell adoption agencies how to resolve conflict or competition among different communities of origin—when, for example, a child is Indian *and* black *and* Catholic *and* Brazilian.

The instability of categories—their amenability to expansion and redefinition—raises doubts about embeddedness as a basis for bestowing very much in the way of decision-making authority. Similar concerns also arise outside of race. What should be made, for example, of a Catholic birth mother faithful to the tradition of the Latin mass who places her child for adoption with a Catholic family just when Vatican II and the vernacular guitar folk mass make an appearance? Has her preference been met—is the adoptive family what the mother understood "Catholic" to mean? Or would some nice Unitarians have done as well? Putting aside the fluidity of categories whether the changes come from within (internal reform) or without (social reclassification), should religion be considered an embedded characteristic in the first place? In New York, for example, at least for children adopted out of foster care, religion is treated as presumptively embedded: "[W]henever a child is placed in the home or custody of any person other than its adopted parents, such placement must, when practicable, be with a person of the same religious faith or persuasion as that of the child."[26] And how is the newborn's religion determined? Unless the parents have expressly stated otherwise, "it shall be presumed that the parent wishes the child to be reared in the religion of the parent."[27]

Even if we assume that racial or religious categories are fixed, our confidence about them is still challenged by a practical problem: the inability even of experts and intimates to know what they see. The problem arose in a tragic "switched-at-birth" adoption case from Georgia.[28] In 1983, two white mothers each gave birth to a baby boy on the same day at the same hospital. Jody Pope, married to a white man, gave birth to Melvin. Tina Williams, unmarried and planning to relinquish her child for adoption, gave birth to Cameron, whose father was black. Both mothers had seen their babies in the hospital several times, and each certified upon discharge that she had examined and was taking home her own child. In fact, through astonishing negligence, the two babies had been switched in the hospital sometime between birth and checkout. Pope therefore took home biracial Cameron, and white Melvin was placed with a foster mother pending his adoption by a mixed-race couple (white mother, black father) who had especially wanted a biracial child. The foster mother, aware of Melvin's pending placement, expressed concern to the adoption social worker that the infant looked so relentlessly white. An adoption consultant was brought in to help "resolve ambiguities" as to Melvin's racial make-up, and advised that "biracial children sometimes appear to be white in early infancy but experience skin darkening over time." Melvin was then adopted by the mixed-race couple. When the children were four, the switch was discovered, and predictable negligence suits and custody battles followed.[29]

The case indicates both the importance attributed to color and its precariousness as a marker for race. Imagine a roomful of infant orphans who have kicked off their identification tags. How would social workers begin to sort them for purposes of successful adoption placement? The answer of the influential Child Welfare League of America is that "at the present time, children placed with adoptive families with similar distinctive characteristics, e.g., color, can become more easily integrated into the average family and community." Thus, as researchers note, "the conventions perpetuated by agencies, not the legal system, guarantee that created families will be homogeneous in looks and specifically, as the CWLA advises, in *color.*"[30]

Switched-at-birth cases—real or imagined—are useful in thinking through the nature of embeddedness claims for adoption.[31] In a sense, traditional adoption has endorsed a switched-at-birth model: the adopted child is treated as if he or she were the adoptive parents' biological child from the moment of birth. And how do parents, community, and the switchees themselves respond upon learning they are not who they thought they were (or that the people they thought were their birth parents are not)? Let us imagine that Al Gore and George W. Bush were switched at birth and that each was then raised by the other's parents. Years later the mistake is uncovered. Gore, now the Republican candidate for president, learns that in fact he is from a long line of Democrats. Bush, the Democratic candidate, receives mirror-image facts.[32] To test whether this unintended swap matters, we might ask whether each man will now feel he has been "living a lie." Or will the revelation of political ancestry seem to each more like an interesting but vaguely remote historical fact? The second question directs us toward a more autonomous view of the self. What each man *chooses* to make of the information determines its importance, not the mere fact of it.

Would this be different if the essential switch were not one of political party but one of religion or class—say a baby placed by his Jewish parents with Christian parents in 1940 Germany? Or the child of a disappeared Argentinean trade unionist placed with parents from the military elite? Or an American Indian child removed from the reservation and placed with white Protestant parents, a practice ended only by the Indian Child Welfare Act in 1978? These are but a few examples from among the many the last century richly offered up. Of course, in each of these cases, coercion, not choice, provoked the placement. The claims of parents (and perhaps of the parents' group) for recognition and continuity may seem stronger where the very point of the placement was to obliterate the characteristic that linked parent to child.

IV. Birth Mother Preferences

Shanley argues that birth mothers should participate in placement decisions because "as the concrete link between the child and the racial group claiming an interest in or jurisdiction over the child's placement, [they] would be the appropriate persons to present their understanding of their own and the child's racial identity." Indeed, when there is no apparent or participating father, the birth mother may be the only one who even knows what the universe of potential ties is. Moreover, having likely been part of the relevant community, she can most vividly understand the importance of continued association, whether in the form of immediate placement or subsequent disclosure of information.

Yet designating birth mothers as the spokeswomen for embeddedness does not guarantee that birth mothers will choose to honor the child's relational ties. The birth mother may have her own view of how a child of hers might flourish, a view that envisions a way of life quite different from that in which she was raised. From an embeddedness point of view, this looks like maternal contrariness or ingratitude. What explains this form of defection, and what should the law make of it? The Supreme Court has concluded that at least with regard to Indian children, a mother may not so choose. In the 1989 Supreme Court case of *Mississippi Band of Choctaw Indians v. Holyfield*, an unmarried Indian couple wanted the Holyfields, a white family, to adopt their newborn twins.[33] (Years earlier, Mr. Holyfield had been the birth mother's pastor.) In an attempt to defeat the tribe's jurisdiction over the matter, the birth mother "went to some efforts to see that [the babies] were born outside the confines of the Choctaw Indian Reservation." The Supreme Court held that her efforts failed: no matter where the babies were born, their domicile—the key to tribal jurisdiction under the Indian Child Welfare Act—followed that of their mother and *she* was still domiciled on the reservation.

There is much of legal interest in the case—federal legislation elevating group rights over those of individual parents or over the interests of the child, for example.[34] But the facts alone are of interest to us here. The birth parents deliberately chose for their children lives different from their own. Reasons for doing so may differ. Birth parents may have a special fondness for particular prospective parents, as was likely part of the explanation in *Holyfield.* They may want a better material life for their children than they experienced or believe likely in the birth community. Parents may also affirmatively seek to distance the child from the very characteristic that is the source of their authority under an embeddedness delegation. Thus while in New York religious matching is the default rule, parents may choose differently. The statute makes clear that "religious wishes of a parent shall include wishes that the child be placed in the same religion as the parent or in a different religion from the parent or with indifference to religion or with religion a subordinate consideration."[35] In this regard, recall George Eliot's description of the long awaited reunion between Daniel Deronda and his mother. At their meeting, Deronda learns not only that his mother (and therefore he) is Jewish but that this was exactly why she gave him up: "And the bondage I hated for myself I wanted to keep you from. What better could the most loving mother have done? I relieved you from the bondage of having been born a Jew."[36] Whether children accept, applaud, or reject such decisions, and at what stages in their lives, we cannot reliably know. But suppressing communities of origin is not limited to birth mothers. Parents in general reinvent their family histories and lose religious or racial identification as they like.[37] Thus in nonadoptive contexts, parents may indeed "defect." Since we do not impose restrictions on apostasy or "passing" generally, it is not clear why we should burden such a decision in the context of adoption.

Some breakaway preferences spike maternal concerns about a child's future well-being with a kind of petulance. A short story by Canadian author Elyse Gasco describes a Catholic home for unwed mothers from the point of view of the unhappy, waddling residents: "And one day, when a nun was slightly short with her, unusually sour, her habit freshly ironed and stiff, [my roommate] said: 'I'm telling you. Give it to the Jews. They know how to laugh at themselves. They're even iffy on this hell thing.'"[38] And what I have called petulance is sometimes described by experts as a predictable stage in adolescent development.[39] The musings of columnist Dan Savage capture both perspectives. Having satisfied all the adoption agency's requirements, Savage anxiously waited to be chosen by some birth mother somewhere. But why, he wondered, would any young woman pick him and his male partner from among the agency's catalogue of attractive married heterosexual couples applying for the same position? Savage found comfort in the idea that there *was* a birth mother who would choose them: the hypothetical "Susan." Susan is sixteen and the daughter of strict fundamentalist Christians who are upset about her promiscuity, her punk boyfriend, and her pregnancy. They are, however, happy that she is "choosing life" over abortion, even if she insists on relinquishing their grandchild for adoption. Susan comes to the adoption agency, reads the resumes, and finds her revenge: she chooses the gay couple.[40]

While Savage's actual anxieties were eventually relieved (he was chosen), his daydream was recently acted out in a Tennessee Chancery Court, where the grandparents of a baby placed by its fifteen-year-old mother with a lesbian sought to set the adoption aside in favor of themselves. The grandparents argued that the "non-traditional structure" of the adoptive mother's home was not in the child's best interests.[41] The trial rejected their claim, relying on the near-glowing home study provided to the court. The appellate court affirmed that an adoptive parent's lifestyle *is* a factor but "does not control the outcome of custody or adoption decisions, particularly absent evidence of its effects on the child." The facts (and ultimate success) of the Tennessee case notwithstanding, it may well be that few birth mothers will choose gay parents for their children. Certainly gay couples are regularly informed that their chances for adoption will improve if they will accept a "special-needs" child—one who is older than two, of color, handicapped, or already in foster care. There is also a reported case of a birth mother who surrendered her child to an agency in a traditional closed adoption, later discovered the child was adopted by a same-sex couple, and sought (unsuccessfully) to rescind the adoption.[42]

I present these examples not to suggest that birth mothers are particularly idiosyncratic or prejudiced but simply to point out that, like other parents, they too have preferences about how they would like their children raised. Their preferences are not always predictable or admirable or comfortable. But in this regard, their decisions are not so unlike the evaluations unmarried adults make in deciding whether a potential partner will be the kind of person they could imagine raising their child. In choosing a future mate/co-parent, singles are free to choose a partner from the same community or from a different one. Racial or ethnic similarity is not required; that was resolved in *Loving v. Virginia* in 1967.[43] So too, one could argue, with adoptive parents. A birth mother may insist on continuity, or she may not. If she is permitted to participate, there is no way to ensure that she will honor rather than disrupt relational ties between her child and any community of origin.

V. Alternative Bases of Maternal Authority

To review, using embeddedness as the basis for a birth mother's placement authority is problematic on several counts. Putting aside the deep question of how policy makers (or psychologists or political theorists) can be sure what constitutes the self, serious practical problems remain regarding the definition, scope, and enforceability of embeddedness in a placement regime. But while honoring birth mothers' preferences may disappoint those who would see them as an exercise of communitarian values, the practice is now actively supported for at least two other reasons.[44] The first urges placement authority as a reward or inducement for birth mothers not to abort. The second is market driven: giving birth mothers placement authority, if that is what birth mothers want, ought to increase the number of desirable infants released onto the adoption market. I put forth a third reason, which, in contrast to the first two, plays no role at present in the politics of placement. It is that choosing adoptive parents for one's child is within the scope of custodial authority vested in all parents and is justified on that basis alone. I find only this third rationale appealing, even as it includes the first two, for reasons I shall set forth below. I begin, however, with an overview of the roles of morals and markets.

Morality first. Since the legalization of abortion in 1973, the commitment of many antiabortion advocates has broadened to include what might be seen as companion issues. An example from the 1980s was the heated dispute over the federal "Baby Doe" regulations, which reclassified parental decisions to withhold care from severely disabled newborns from the acceptable realm of parental authority to that of child abuse and discrimination. In piecing together why withholding care from newborns (in contrast, say, to withholding it from the elderly) became such a focus of public concern, Robert Mnookin explained that "[n]otwithstanding their defeat in Roe v. Wade, many right-to-lifers wish to carry on the political battle over abortion. . . . [T]he issue of the proper treatment of handicapped newborns serves important political ends by connecting abortion rights to children's rights."[45] Adoption works in much the same way but with broader appeal, as would-be adoptive parents may also benefit. The starting point for adoption activists motivated by pro-life beliefs is simply that adoption is "the *best* solution for an unwed mother: Adoption clearly rises above abortion as a beneficial alternative for both mother and child, and arguably is superior in most instances to other life-affirming alternatives such as single parenting."[46] William Pierce, president of the National Council for Adoption, an umbrella organization now supporting agencies that oppose open records, contends that adoption is simply "not on the public agenda."[47] Much blame for this is laid at the door of abortion providers, who, it is argued, do not even "raise the issue of adoption with pregnant clients."[48] Others blame the federal government for the adoption movement's purported inability to "fight on level ground": "[S]ome women have always had abortions or single-parented, but the number has swelled to its present extent only when the federal government overrode state and local preferences and enshrined the worst choice as a fundamental legal right, and the mediocre choice as a fundamental economic right."[49] How, then, from this perspective, can adoption be put back onto the public agenda of policy makers and the private agenda of birth mothers?

The marrying of proadoption and antiabortion advocacy has crept into public policy in a variety of enterprising ways. There are the "Adoption, Not Abortion" bumper stickers.[50] Sticking to the vehicular, there are also proadoption license plates. Drivers in Florida may now select "Choose Life" from among the forty specialized license plates ("Save the Manatee"; "Remember the Challenger Astronauts") offered by the Department of Motor Vehicles. Proceeds from the sales of "Choose Life" plates go to adoption agencies. When questioned why the license plates do not say "Choose Adoption," Tom Gallagher, the Florida Education Commissioner explained that "'Choose Life' basically is talking about adoption. And that's pretty much what it says."[51]

Beyond these rhetorically significant moves, prolife adoption advocates have had a serious impact on adoption agency practices. This is seen in the significant policy change of the many affiliates of Catholic Charities. Once faithful practitioners and proponents of traditional closed adoption, many Catholic adoption agencies now offer and promote open adoption, at least with regard to consensual contact or communication between birth mothers and adoptive parents.[52] A typical Catholic Charities adoption Web page now urges comparison shopping along the following lines:

> *Compare! All adoption agencies are not the same.*
> *Birthmothers*
> *You have all the choices!*
> *No obligation.*
> * You can choose either to have an open or closed adoption
> * You can choose to select & meet the family
> * Option to receive photos of & letters from your child as they grow
> * Direct placement—Never any foster care
> * Available day, night, weekend, & holidays—whenever you need us
> * Click here for more information[53]

The pitch here is directed wholly to the imagined preferences of the relevant consumer, the birth mother.

The second basis of support for birth mother participation in placement decisions is more directly concerned with the laws of supply and demand. The goal here is less to prevent abortion than to increase the supply of desirable candidates in the adoption pool. And here the issue of voluntary infant relinquishment becomes pertinent. There are adoptable American children in foster care, but they are generally older and wiser in ways that make them less marketable to the traditional clients of adoption agencies and lawyers.

As the National Committee for Adoption explained in 1989, "More than a million couples are chasing the 30,000 white infants available in this country each year."[54] To get those babies, agencies have sought to make adoption more attractive to birth mothers who, as the overwhelming majority of them already do, will otherwise choose either single parenthood or abortion. In the most comprehensive study of the shift in agency practices from closed to open adoption, the causal factors listed most often by agency staff were "client demand, changes in agency values, and competition from independent adoptions and other private agencies [already] offering openness in adoption placements."[55] Curiously, only five of the sixty-three agencies canvassed in 1993 listed "It's a right or entitlement" as a reason to offer open adoption, though whether the right referred to is that of the child or of the birth mother is not clear. In any event, by the 1990s, birth mothers had indisputably become the primary clients of agencies, and what they seem to want is some form of open adoption.[56]

And exactly why is open adoption desired by birth mothers? I put the case very simply. Open adoption recognizes birth mothers as *mothers* rather than as transient, anonymous participants in the adoption process. Traditional adoption, through requiring the strict confidentiality of records and complete termination of the parent-child relationship, sought to deny the fact. Consider the language of unconditional surrender required of parents whose children are adopted out of foster care in New York: "[T]he parent [acknowledges she is] giving up all rights to have custody with, visit with, speak with, write to, or learn about the child, forever."[57] One young birth mother described the experience of the termination hearing:

> It was a paper already written out, just saying that once I signed those papers that I'd given up all right and say in the baby's life, legally. I just, that was it. And to someone to kind of just put a very large period at the end of a sentence like that was like, whoa, it, it hit hard. But, it's written blunt like that so you know. They can't make it cushy and comfortable in that respect 'cause you have to realize what is going on, and boy, did it! And it was pretty much went through in a matter of minutes, and that was it.[58]

In our society, however, motherhood is not usually experienced in a matter of minutes. It is generally understood as a more enduring undertaking. Of course, therein lies the policy conundrum of adoption. Is someone who voluntarily gives up a child to be counted as a mother for any purposes? Motherhood is a complicated status in our society, one that is revered and rewarded, but also one that is regulated, in part to make sure that mothers live up to the kind of behavior deserving of reverence. Distancing oneself from motherhood, whether by not having children at all or—perhaps worse—by giving away the children one has, is therefore a suspect act fraught with personal and social significance. Thus maternal decisions to separate from children under circumstances far less momentous than adoption—something as ordinary as going to work in the morning—are taken seriously, both by mothers themselves and by those who judge them. Such decisions are heavily influenced by dominant cultural views about the importance of children to women's identity and reputation.[59] Birth mothers, like everyone else, are keenly aware of this. In a study comparing two groups of birth mothers, "placers" and "keepers," more than half of the "keeper" group explained that "they could not emotionally handle the thought of placing their child for adoption," and many "placers" feared "peer reaction which views their behavior as selfish, unloving, and even incomprehensible."[60] The consequence of all this for adoption is that mothers who might in fact want to give a child up sometimes decide not to.

But if we accept that birth mothers are, at least for some finite period, full-scale mothers, it cannot surprise us that some may miss or mourn or wonder about a child relinquished for adoption. As one birth mother put it, "[I]f I'm going to give this baby up, I don't need to know an exact location, but, did they take this baby off, like and they're working him on a farm, or is he in the city?"[61] Another birth mother wrote to the lawyer arranging the adoption of her son: "Dear Mr. Kaplan, It would ease my heart to know that Finn is healthy and happy. Is there any way? Many thanks, Diana." Until the 1980s, the legal answer to these questions was a flat "no."[62] Around that time, however, encouraged by the success of adult adoptees in obtaining records and occasional (consensual) reunions, birth mothers began to "come out," to organize, and to move subtly from therapy to lobbying.[63] Through such organizations as Concerned United Birth Parents, they have pressed for greater (that is to say, any) openness in adoptions from the very start of the adoption process, rather than twenty-one years later and then only at the adoptee's initiative. To be sure, not all birth mothers want a continued connection or some vestige of authority over their child, but many do. The form, degree, and desire for openness differ. Some mothers want simply to name the child and ask the adoptive parents to honor that significant selection. Others seek the promise of information, such as a yearly letter or photo, or the adoptive parents' agreement to give the child a memento or letter from its mother when it is older. Still others want to select the adoptive parents and sometimes to negotiate some form of ongoing contact. All of these arrangements are included within the parameters of what is now called open adoption, and almost all agencies now offer it to their clients.

Whether or not these various agreements brokered ("mediated" in agency speak) by agencies will be upheld by courts is another matter. Courts initially asked to enforce such agreements, most often by birth mothers whose visitation had been cut off, commonly refused to do so on grounds of public policy.[64] Open adoption agreements were understood to violate the letter and spirit of existing laws severing all ties between birth mother and child for the purpose of establishing the child securely in its new family. Slowly, however, courts began to detect and to articulate a public policy that *favored* enforcement. Thus the Maryland Court of Appeals noted that such agreements might well "foster [adoption] in those cases where the natural parent and adoptive parent are known to each other and the natural parent is reluctant to yield all contact with his or her child."[65] Open adoption was seen not simply as benefiting a particular child but as central to sustaining adoption as a social institution.[66] About twenty-five states have now authorized "post-adoption agreement contact statutorily."[67] Most provide that enforcement is contingent on the court's determination that the agreed-on contact is in the best interests of the child.

But in addition to (perhaps) offering an alternative to abortion and (perhaps) increasing the number of infants in the adoption pool, there is a third and independent reason to honor birth mother participation in the placement process. The case is straightforward: making decisions about the care and custody of one's child falls within a well-established bundle of parental rights. These include the right—and the obligation—to provide care for one's children, whether personally or by arranging for a surrogate caretaker. We see this in a variety of circumstances outside the context of adoption as parents regularly determine where and with whom and for how long their children will live. Thus parents may send children to summer camp or to boarding school or to live with Aunt Louise. And even when the child's new placement is not with kindly Aunt Louise but in a mental institution—a decision not always taken with the child's interests exclusively in mind—the Supreme Court has made clear that "our precedents permit the parents to retain a substantial, if not the dominant, role in the decision."[68] Divorcing parents too are entitled to decide between themselves which one will have custody of the kids, and under such agreements, one parent may significantly decrease or even cease contact with the children. Nonetheless, such decisions are rubber-stamped by courts as a matter of course.[69] And in cases where custody is contested, providing for substitute care during the marriage has been recognized as evidence of everyday parenting. Thus in states that use the "primary caretaker standard" to determine custody, "arranging for alternative care (i.e., babysitting, daycare, etc.)" has been one of the enumerated criteria for determining which parent managed parental responsibilities before the divorce and therefore should get custody after.[70] The standard explicitly recognizes that separating from a child is not inconsistent with concern about its well-being. Finally, parents may choose substitute caretakers for their children in anticipation of a permanent separation. All states now provide for the testamentary appointment of guardians and the rule is clear: "In the absence of facts or circumstances disqualifying testamentary guardians, the statutory right of the parent, duly and lawfully exercised by the execution of his or her will, must be respected and maintained by the court."[71]

All of these examples—custody, babysitting, guardianship, summer camp—reflect the law's respect for parental determinations regarding the provision of substitute care in the parent's absence, whether the arrangement is temporary, long term, or permanent. Adoption simply provides another type of separation on the spectrum of acceptable absences that necessitate a surrogate caretaker. I suspect we may be unused to thinking of adoption in the same breath with other separations. Adoption is somehow bigger, combining as it does both voluntariness *and* permanence. Nonetheless, the law has appreciated that even the decision to give up a child for adoption may be an appropriate exercise of maternal judgment in just the way I am describing. Consider a 1992 Texas case in which a birth mother, on the day her baby was born, relinquished her parental rights and handed the baby over to an adoptive couple she had earlier chosen. The next day the birth mother decided she had made a huge mistake and wanted the baby back. (The Texas revocation period had not expired.) The couple argued that by "voluntarily leaving it in the possession of another [with] an intent not to return," the birth mother had abandoned the baby and therefore no longer had any rights over the child. The trial court agreed, but the case was reversed on appeal. The appellate court held that in turning the child over to the couple under the terms of an open adoption, the birth mother was not "disregarding her parental obligations, as contemplated by [the Texas abandonment statute], but instead was attempting to affirmatively provide for [the baby's] welfare through others." Thus the court properly distinguished between disregarding a child's welfare and securing it.[72]

The argument here is not that all birth mothers must or should choose open adoption. Many prefer traditional adoption, perhaps because they desire no further contact with the child, because they trust an agency's ability to select parents, or because by relinquishing the baby to a particular agency such as Catholic Charities, they have secured for their child the essence of what they want in adoptive parents (a Catholic upbringing) without needing to know exactly who will be doing it. Birth mothers with drug or other problems may also choose a closed adoption to avoid possible rejection by couples they might choose.[73]

My argument is not even that all birth mothers will choose well. This possibility is hinted at in my earlier spite and petulance examples, though it may be difficult to know whether bad motives produce bad decisions. Certainly, data suggest that at least some teenage birth mothers choose open adoption for reasons less connected with the child's needs than with their "self-related concern about their own ability to know the child." As researchers explain, "Given the developmental status of adolescence in regard to altruism versus self-concern and the difficulty for teens to think through the long-term consequences of behavior, this finding of self-interest is not surprising."[74] It has also been suggested that because this is a final, "last-shot" decision on the birth mother's part, there is no incentive for her to choose the adoptive parents with particular care; she bears none of the consequences of a bad decision, as she need never deal with the child again.

But this game theory objection does not ring true for me. First, it is odd to imagine that a birth mother would deliberately choose against her child's interests. Just because the adoption is *good* for her—and doesn't "self-concern" motivate many/most maternal decisions to leave children, even if only temporarily?—it does not follow that she will want things to go *badly* for her child. Second, even if the birth mother might be so inclined, the law does not permit her to choose *too* poorly. All states require the judge to certify that the order of adoption is in the child's best interest and the court's determination on that point trumps whatever placement preferences a birth mother may have. In the Tennessee case discussed earlier, the court heard the grandparents' arguments against their daughter's choice of a lesbian adoptive mother, acknowledging that while Tennessee law respects "the biological parent's right to choose a prospective adoptive parent," it remains "the trial court's duty to protect the child's best interest."[75] (The court upheld the adoption.)

We might also keep in mind that there is little quality control on parental decision making outside of adoption. People have children and some raise them badly.[76] In this regard it would seem that birth mothers are perhaps ahead of the pack. They are at least *aware* that they may raise their children badly, simply by virtue of not wanting to raise them at all, and they are acting responsibly on that knowledge. What birth mothers want, and what all other parents get as a matter of course, is some recognition that they are their child's parent and have contributed to their child's life in some manner or form beyond childbirth itself: a name, a photo, securing good adoptive parents.

Open adoption in any of these variations permits the exercise of such ordinary parental authority in the context of what is never an ordinary decision. The significance of birth mother participation for adoption practices is made clear by considering the work it does for adoption vocabulary. At present, the verbs typically (awkwardly, reluctantly) used to describe what birth mothers do with their children are *surrender, relinquish,* or *give up*. Consider the difference for the mother—and for the child—when it is understood that the mother *placed* her child. Indeed, the adoptive parents too might benefit from knowing something of the birth mother, in part to satisfy their child's questions when the questions finally arise. Elyse Gasco describes an adoptive mother who, without any facts to tell her daughter, makes up what she hopes is an appealing story. But as the mother thinks of her daughter's original mother, she thinks this:

> Stupid, stupid girl. Why couldn't she have left her daughter something? A letter, a glove, a piece of her stupid hair. Was she a moron? A simpleton? Probably a cruel and reckless beauty queen. Probably an impossibly loose bully. It is as though Mother's own love is weak, watered down, muted and she is being forced into speaking like a ventriloquist through the mouth of this dummy dummy girl. Surely, thinks Mother, you were the type of person everyone followed behind picking up pieces.[77]

I therefore agree with Shanley that birth mothers should be given a voice in choosing the kind of family in which their child will be placed, though whether such preferences should be limited only to those mothers who fall within the present penumbra of embeddedness is another matter.

VI. Conclusion

Mary Shanley is after an adoption regime open enough to give adult adoptees sufficient information to "construct a coherent story of origin, an explanation of how they came into the world." This is admirable and, as Shanley explains, can be achieved by opening adoption records or by opening adoption itself through contact or communication between the family of origin and the adoptive family. Even the provision of nonidentifying birth parent information secures some of the values encompassed by the idea of embeddedness: the sense that we are not "self-made" but rather that each of us is vitally informed by our relation to a community of origin and is entitled at least to know what that community is. There are, of course, risks in all this. Ongoing or later initiated contact with birth mothers may be difficult and the release of birth records does not always result in a *pleasing* story of coherence. It may throw into disarray whatever invented story has been functioning as placeholder for the true one.[78] Consider P. D. James's novel *Innocent Blood*, in which the adopted heroine constructs a lovely story of origin for herself: her biological mother a beautiful servant girl at a country estate; her father, a handsome gentleman passing by. She is then dumbstruck to learn upon obtaining her birth records under Britain's Adoption Records Act that her father was *not* a nobleman but a child molester, still serving time for the murder of one of his hapless victims, and that her mother was his willing accomplice.

Of course, for most of us life is neither a fairy story nor a P.D. James thriller. But that all adopted children will not have been given up by Cinderella figures is not my point. It is rather to suggest that all adults desire a coherent and satisfying story of origin. I suspect that there are few among us who, if given a red pencil, would not rewrite a page or two of the original text. Even children living with their natural parents sometimes challenge the script. Many—particularly in early adolescence—entertain "adoption fantasies" as the only explanation for how they could have ended up with such awful so-called biological parents.

I want therefore to frame my conclusion around a more functional phrase that I have borrowed from Elyse Gasco. In another of Gasco's brilliant short stories about adoption, a young adopted woman describes a brief conversation with her counselor: "Finally he clasps his hands together hard and I think I can see the blood in his nails. He says: Eventually, you will find a story you can live with. And he opens his hands again, reading the lines to see if he's right."[79] It is the "story one can live with" that provides the project for many adult lives. This is not to say that adoption doesn't matter, and that the real problem is just a shortage of good therapists. Rather, in thinking about placement regimes, it seems useful not to substitute one idealized concept—here embeddedness—for the earlier fiction that if we only pretend adopted children are exactly like biological ones, everything will turn out just fine. Many aspects of an adopted child's life may change in ways that produce someone of different temperament, tastes, habits, and beliefs than the person who might otherwise have resulted. It may be impossible to know which of these attributes are essential to the construction of the self and would therefore be preserved or nurtured by a placement scheme that takes embeddedness into account.[80] Consider the matter of birth order, now understood to be a significant feature in personality development. An overburdened birth mother may relinquish her third child, who by virtue of adoption now becomes an oldest child, with all the personality peculiarities that attend that distinction. If birth order is crucial to what one becomes, should *it* be then replicated within the adoption scheme in the interest of securing a more authentic self?

This returns us to the concept of remainders. It seems likely that adoption will always produce a moral remainder. The interests of the three central parties—not to mention the complicated interests of the adoption industry, political groups, and ethnic communities for whom adoption is of symbolic as well as practical significance—are unlikely to converge. The question then, is: Who is to bear the burden of the remainder? Whose morally reasonable claim will be left unsatisfied, squeezed out of the equation, stuck forever behind a lower-case "r"? Under the regime of closed adoptions, birth mothers bore the weight. The very fact of their maternity was obliterated by the practices of traditional adoption. Thus although it was argued that the system benefited everyone (kids got parents, childless parents got kids, unwed mothers got a second chance), birth mothers as beneficiaries limped in a very poor third.

The active participation of birth mothers changes all this. The emotional complications of adoption are now distributed more evenly across the three major participants, with adoptive parents perhaps shouldering the greatest adjustment. Once secure in adoption's protective wrap, they now begin with their child's birth mother in mind, if not in sight. This may not be the burden many have feared; initial studies of open adoptions indicate that most adoptive parents do well under the new system. Many are relieved to have the rules of contact clear and established up front. Yet concern about possible entanglements with intrusive birth families cause some to pursue children by other means, such as turning to foreign adoption.[81] Of course, it is too early to know what the consequences, good and bad, of open adoption will be for the various players. Certainly, birth mothers must still come to terms with their decision and with the experience of loss that often and understandably accompanies it.

Returns on how children fare in all this are sparse. So far it appears that children in open adoptions are secure in their adoptive homes and that adoptive parents also find some relief that the terms of engagement are clearly established from the start. To be sure, empirical research findings do not always matter much with regard to family law reform. In custody law, for example, joint custody replaced a maternal presumption, which replaced a paternal presumption. In each case, it was argued that the child benefited by the change, but in fact, each shift resulted from a mix of politics with contemporary theories about families, gender roles, or children's needs. So too with adoption. The very preference for adoption (in contrast to orphanages) reflected 1950s postwar assessments about the social and political importance of the nuclear family, with as much attention given to the benefits of children for couples as to the benefits of parents for children. This is all to say that policy shifts are rarely based on the state of developmental research alone. The effects of open adoption on children's developmental well-being remain speculative and will likely take generations to measure and assess. Thus whether birth mothers should participate in placement decisions is likely to be worked out, like much else in family law, without benefit of empirical data.

In all of this, adoption law and practices are guided by enormous cultural changes in the composition and the meaning of family. As families become increasingly blended outside the context of adoption—with combinations of blood relatives, step-relatives, de facto relatives, and ex-relatives sitting down together for Thanksgiving dinner as a matter of course—birth families and adoptive families knowing one another may not seem so very strange or threatening at all. There will simply be an expectation across communities that ordinary families will be mixed and multiple. With that in mind, we should hesitate before establishing embeddedness as the source of a mother's authority over her child's placement. It is a concept that only sounds cozy in great part because it simplifies the relational complexities of the world in which we live.

NOTES

I would like to thank Albert Alschuler, Richard Briffault, John Manning, Jeremy Waldron, and participants at workshops at Columbia, Brooklyn, University of Miami, and Ohio State University law schools for their comments and Lynn Beller and Roger Heller for excellent research assistance.

1. For the idea of the encumbered self (and the opposing liberal image), see Michael Sandel, *Liberalism and the Limits of Justice* (New York: Cambridge University Press, 1982), 54–62.
2. Indian Child Welfare Act of 1978, 25 U.S.C. §§ 1901–1963 (1978).
3. See Joan H. Hollinger, *Appendix 13B: Agreements and Court Orders for Post-Adoption Contact between Adoptive Families and Birth Parents or Other Birth Relatives in Adoption Law and Practice* (New York: Matthew Bender, Update 2000).
4. This was not always adoption's purpose. Historically, adoption was used primarily to benefit the adopting male parent by providing the necessary heirs to mourn, inherit, and carry on the family line. The Ameri-

can states were among the first to "distinguish the *adoptee* as the prime beneficiary." See Jamil S. Zainaldin, "The Emergence of a Modern American Family Law: Child Custody, Adoption, and the Courts, 1796–1851," 73 *Northwestern University Law Review* 1038, 1041 at n. 42 (1979). Certainly adults continue to benefit from adoption, if perhaps secondarily; indeed, it is the competing preferences among adults that now complicate policy formation.

5. See particularly Judith Schacter Modell, *Kinship with Strangers* (Berkeley: University of California Press, 1994).

6. There is, of course, a tension between the move away from the "biologism" in the first point and honoring it through deference to the birth mother (whose ties to the child are essentially biological) in the second.

7. 42 U.S.C.A. § 5115a (West 1995).

8. The focus on birth mothers, in contrast to birth parents or birth fathers, reflects the fact that most adoptions still proceed without the participation of birth fathers. See Mary L. Shanley, "Unwed Fathers' Rights, Adoption, and Sex Equality: Gender-Neutrality and the Perpetuation of Patriarchy," 95 *Columbia Law Review* 60 (1995). Participation from the paternal side sometimes comes from grandparents seeking to block the adoption of their grandchild. While grandparents have no legal standing to intervene as progenitors, their interests might be subsumed under a group embeddedness claim.

9. Wayne Carp, *Family Matters: Secrecy and Disclosure in the History of Adoption* (Cambridge, Mass.: Harvard University Press, 1998). Thus the unhappy (and unsuccessful) opposition of several Oregon birth mothers who surrendered children over the last thirty years under a secrecy regime to recent legislation opening birth records retrospectively upon the sole request of adult adoptees. See *Jane Does 1–7 v. Oregon*, 164 Ore. App. 543, 993 P.2d 822 (Or. 1999).

10. See Michael D. Resnick et al., "Characteristics of Unmarried Adolescent Mothers: Determinants of Child Rearing Versus Adoption," 60 *American Journal of Orthopsychiatry* 577, 583 (1990).

11. Jan Waldron, *Giving Away Simone* (New York: Time Books, 1995), xvii.

12. The only place in Shanley's proposal where the interests of birth mothers are relegated regards the confidentiality of records. Shanley proposes that "except in cases in which [disclosure] would put a woman in grave danger, the adult adoptee's right to know his or her specific history overrides an adult's right to privacy."

13. Shanley notes "the web of social and economic injustice—including poverty, lack of access to birth control, and stigmatization of unwed

motherhood—that leads women both in the United States and abroad to relinquish their children for adoption." It is important to note, however, that poverty no longer so clearly leads women in the United States to choose adoption. Indeed, the higher a pregnant teenager's social-economic status, the more likely she is to place her child for adoption than to keep it. She is more likely to have plans for herself—educational, occupational, relational—that she believes early single motherhood will thwart. See Christine A. Bachrach et al., "Relinquishment of Premarital Births: Evidence from National Survey Data," 24 *Family Planning Perspectives* 27, 31 (1992).

14. *Parham v. J.R.*, 442 U.S. 584 (1979).

15. Elizabeth Bartholet, *Nobody's Children: Abuse and Neglect, Foster Drift, and the Adoption Alternative* (Boston: Beacon, 1999); Richard Banks, "The Color of Desire: Fulfilling Adoptive Parents' Racial Preferences through Discriminatory State Action," 107 *Yale Law Journal* 875 (1998).

16. Janet Farrell Smith, *The Realities of Adoption* (Lanham, Md.: Madison, 1997).

17. One ground of skepticism regarding communitarianism has been that the communities typically included within its framework are what Marilyn Friedman has called "imposed communities," such as families. These stand in contrast to communities that are *chosen*, such as friendship. See Marilyn Friedman, "Feminism and Modern Friendship: Dislocating the Community," 99 *Ethics* 275–90 (1989). We should recognize of course, that for children, *all* communities are imposed, whether they are biological or adoptive.

18. To be sure, the line between voluntary and involuntary is not always sharp. It is not always clear, for example, that a homeless mother has *voluntarily* decided to separate when she places her daughter in foster care after a social worker tells her that neglect proceedings will start if she doesn't. See Clara Hemphill, "City's Homeless Policies Create a House Divided," *Newsday*, Apr. 13, 1989, 6. Thus while certain separations are voluntary (and intended to be temporary), the circumstances that have provoked them may not be. See Somini Sengupta, "Despondent Parents See Foster Care as the Only Option," *New York Times*, Sept. 1, 2000, B1.

19. Historically, the "genetic" circumstances of a child's birth did play a determining role in adoption placements. The issue arose with regard to illegitimacy in the early decades of the twentieth century. It was considered a matter of scientific fact that unwed mothers passed their sexual deviancy to their offspring; illegitimate children were therefore "encumbered" right out of the adoption pool. By the 1950s, psychological explanations for unwed motherhood replaced biological ones, and it

was suddenly safe to adopt children no longer viewed as blighted by the circumstances of their conception. See Ricki Solinger, *Wake up Little Susie: Single Pregnancy and Race before Roe v. Wade* (New York: Routledge, 1990), 168, n. 77.

20. This is not to deny that children are born with certain traits that, at least as a starting point, we take as fixed, profoundly significant for identity, and not subject to alteration by new parents. A child's sex is an example. No matter how much adoptive parents might prefer a girl (as the majority of would-be adoptive parents do), they may not turn a boy into a girl to satisfy that preference. For an upsetting and instructive case of infant sex reassignment, see John Colapinto, *As Nature Made Him: The Boy Who Was Raised as a Girl* (New York: HarperCollins, 2000). After the baby's penis had been obliterated in a botched circumcision, his young parents were advised by doctors at the Johns Hopkins Sex Reassignment Clinic to raise the child as a girl. The child—renamed, dressed, and socialized to be sweet and feminine—struggled unknowingly against this imposed sexual identity. At the age of fourteen, he was told the truth and thereupon chose to live as a boy, a volitional and apparently successful re-reassignment. For our purposes, the case marks one extremity of an innateness spectrum on which other traits might be plotted, as we consider whether other characteristics work in the same way as sex.

21. See Karin Evans, *The Lost Daughters of China* (New York: Tarcher/Putnam, 2000).

22. And are surprised when we are wrong, as in "Funny, you don't look Jewish."

23. Linda Gordon, *The Great Arizona Orphan Abduction,* (Cambridge, Mass.: Harvard University Press, 1999); see also Matthew Frye Jacobson, *Whiteness of a Different Color: European Immigrants and the Alchemy of Race* (Cambridge, Mass.: Harvard University Press, 1998).

24. Gordon, *The Great Arizona Orphan Abduction,* 19.

25. The five racial categories are American Indian/Alaskan Native, Asian, African American, Native Hawaiian/Pacific Islander, and white. Steven A. Holmes, "New Policy on Census Says Those Listed as White and Minority Will Be Counted as Minority," *New York Times,* March 11, 2000, A9. Curiously—and of special interest to the white citizens of Arizona studied by Linda Gordon—Hispanic is considered an ethnic, not a racial, category. Thus under Directive No. 15, which establishes the federal race and ethnicity standards, Mexican Americans are presumptively white.

26. N.Y. C.L.S. Family Court Act § 116(c) and (g).

27. Ibid. Different religions have different views on the inheritability of religious affiliation. Some Christian denominations reject infant baptism on the ground that the religion must be embraced by the informed

choice of the new member. Even among denominations that allow infant baptism, it is still understood as something distinct (in theory if not in practice) from straight inheritability. It is not clear how the concept of embeddedness would help make sense of these tangles.

28. *Pope v. Department of Human Resources*, 209 Ga. App. 835, 434 S.E.2d 731 (1993)

29. Ibid., 733. The parents lost the suit against the hospital for the switch. Prior to the discovery, Pope's husband had divorced her, claiming he could not have been the father of Cameron. Pope then kept Cameron, her (nonbiological) child, and also gained permanent custody of Melvin (her biological child) following a heated custody fight and an appearance on Oprah.

30. Judith Modell and Naomi Dambacher, "Making a 'Real' Family: Matching and Cultural Biologism in American Adoption Law," 12 *Adoption Quarterly* 3, 6–7 (1997).

31. Consider, in this regard, Mark Twain's *Pudd'nhead Wilson.*

32. I put aside the question of whether "coming from a long line of Democrats/Republicans" is the same thing as "being" a Democrat/Republican. Is party embedded? Should birth mothers be permitted to request party placements? And would this apply in the case of any registered Democrat/Republican or only those who come from a long line? (I put even further aside former candidate Nader's view that the distinction is meaningless.)

33. 490 U.S. 30 (1989).

34. Thus while the claim of embeddedness is articulated as being in the child's interest, it is not always made entirely on his or her behalf. The best the Supreme Court could say in *Holyfield* was that "[i]t is not ours to say whether the trauma that might result from removing these children from their adoptive family should outweigh the interests of the Tribe—and perhaps the children themselves—in having them raised as part of the Choctaw community" (54).

35. N.Y. C.L.S. Family Court Act § 116(c) and (g).

36. The passage from *Daniel Deronda* continues:

> "I am glad of it," said Deronda, impetuously, in the veiled voice of passion. He could not have imagined beforehand how he would come to say that which he had never hitherto admitted. . . . But the mother was equally shaken by an anger differently mixed, and her frame was less equal to any repression. The shaking with her was visibly physical, and her eyes looked the larger for her pallid excitement as she said violently, "Why do you say you are glad? You are an English gentleman. I secured you that." "You did not know what you secured me. How could you choose my birthright for

me?" said Deronda, throwing himself sideways into his chair again, almost unconsciously, and leaning his arm over the back while he looked away from his mother. . . . "Ah!"—here her tone changed to one of a more bitter incisiveness—"you are glad to have been born a Jew. You say so. That is because you have not been brought up as a Jew. That separateness seems sweet to you because I saved you from it." George Eliot, *Daniel Deronda* (New York: Penguin), 689-93.

37. See Philip Roth, *The Human Stain* (New York: Houghton Mifflin, 2000). For a nonfictional account, see Gregory H. Williams, *Life on the Color Line: The True Story of a White Boy Who Discovered He Was Black* (New York: Dutton, 1995).

38. Elyse Gasco, "A Well Imagined Life," in *Can You Wave Bye Bye Baby?* (New York: Picador, 1999), 11.

39. Thus in a study of unwed mothers, a number of the young women reported that one reason for getting pregnant was "spiting their parents." See Resnick et al., "Characteristics of Unmarried Adolescent Mothers."

40. "'Mom, Dad,' says Susan when she gets home from the hospital, 'I GAVE IT TO FAGS! I HOPE YOU'RE HAPPY. YOU WOULDN'T LET ME HAVE AN ABORTION SO I GAVE YOUR GRANDCHILD TO FAGS! FAGS!'" Dan Savage, *The Kid* (New York: Dutton, 1999), 90–91. In Savage's daydream, this causes the parents to die instantly of heart attacks; Susan *and* the baby then come live with the adoptive fathers.

41. *In re Adoption of M.J.S.,* No. W1999-00197-COA-R3-CV (Oct. 5, 2000, Tenn. Ct. of App.); see http.//pub.bna.com/fl./9900197.htm.

42. "Lengthy Adoption Battle End in Gay Couple's Favor," *New York Times,* Dec. 27, 1994, A10.

43. *Loving v. Virginia* 388 U.S. 1 (1967).

44. To clarify, open adoption in general has additional bases of political support. Adult adoptees are probably the predominant force behind opening records and facilitating contact. (See Web sites of ALMA, the Adoption Liberty Movement Association, and the newer Bastard Nation, at www.bastards.org and www.almanet.com.) Their concerns, however, have focused on access to their family of origin rather than on the manner of selection of their adoptive family. The latter, and particularly the participation of the birth mother, is the focus here.

45. Robert Mnookin, "Two Puzzles," 1984 *Arizona State Law Journal* 1984 (1984): 667. Mnookin uncovered a three-way synergy among the prolife movement, advocates for the handicapped, and hospital organizations.

46. Donna Warner, "Pro-Life Approaches to Adoption," in *Adoption Factbook III* (Washington, D.C.: National Council for Adoption, 1999),

281. Several of its "facts" have been challenged as unsupported. One example is the *Factbook*'s claim that a regime of nonconfidentiality of records will increase abortion.

47. William Pierce, "Twenty-One Barriers to Adoption to Address in the Twenty-First Century" in *Adoption Factbook III*, 558.

48. See Patrick F. Fagan, "Adoption: The Best Option," in *Adoption Factbook III.*

49. Martin Olasky, "The Antiabortion Abortion Movement's Future," *Wall Street Journal*, Dec. 13, 1995, A14.

50. Until the early 1990s, prolife adoption advocates (though not necessarily adoption agencies) commonly listed themselves in the Yellow Pages under "Abortion Services." Women who sought their help were then strongly counseled not to abort but to place the child for adoption. Such misrepresentation is now prohibited as false advertising; the Yellow Pages now include a bold-faced notice that distinguishes "Abortion Alternatives" from "Abortion Providers."

See John Henderson, "Texas Official Urges U.S. to Ban Misleading Anti-Abortion Ads," *Houston Chronicle*, Sept. 21, 1991, A4; Lisa Petrillo, "Abortion-Rights Side Claims Classified Victory," *San Diego Union-Tribune*, Nov. 24, 1991, B3.

51. "'Choose Life' License Plates Cause Controversy in Florida," CNN Talkback Live, Nov. 29, 1999, Transcript No. 99112900V14. Elizabeth Toledo of the National Organization of Women responded that "[not] only [did the legislature] adopt the slogan that is often used in anti-abortion campaigns, but the moneys have to go to organizations that can't even make a referral [for an abortion]."

52. In contrast, the National Right to Life and the National Council for Adoption continue to lobby against any legislation that would disclose identifying information about the birth mother at the request of an adult adoptee. They argue that the possibility of such disclosure is so painful as to drive pregnant women into abortion. See Jonathan Riskin, "Fans, Foes, Debate Bill to Open Adoption Records," *Columbus Dispatch*, Jan. 24, 1994, 2C; Dureen Cheek, "Law Puts Adoption Privacy at Stake," *Tennessean*, Sept. 3, 1995, 1B. In this regard, consider the availability in France of *accouchement sous X*, which provides a method of anonymous childbirth. The mother signs into the hospital under the pseudonym of "X," and after delivery the baby is put immediately in the custody of social services for adoption placement. See Laura J. Schwartz, "Models for Parenthood in Adoption Law: The French Connection," 28 *Vanderbilt Journal of Transnational Law* 1069, 1106–08 (1995). The law is explicitly intended to deter illegal abortion and infanticide; about seven hundred babies a year are born *"sous X."*

53. http://www.adoptionservices.org/

54. "It's a Seller's Market," *Life*, Sept. 1988, 80.

55. Harold D. Grotevant and Ruth G. McRoy, *Openness in Adoption: Exploring Family Connections* (Thousand Oaks, Calif.: Sage, 1998), 35. Researchers Grotevant and McRoy underline what was *not* on the list: "[V]ery few agencies cited research as a factor leading to change in practice." It is unclear from their study whether the research to which they refer concerns the reported difficulties of adoptees who suffer because of not knowing of their origins or the difficulties faced by birth mothers in closed adoptions. It is noteworthy for empiricists to understand how little developmental research findings have to do with the placement of children.

56. While it appears many birth mothers prefer open adoption, "popular demand" may also have taken on a life of its own. That is, to satisfy perceived demand, all agencies offer open adoption; many that did not either went out of business or feared they would. Further, adoptive parents are informed if they will not even consider open adoption as an option, they are unlikely to be chosen. Most therefore agree. Thus open adoption may be somewhat self-fueled.

57. N.Y. Soc. Serv. Law §§ 383-c(5)(b)(ii) (Mckinney Supp. 1996).

58. Birth mother quoted in Barbara Yngvesson, "Negotiating Motherhood: Identity and Difference in 'Open' Adoptions," 31 *Law and Society Review* 53–54 (1997).

59. See Carol Sanger, "Separating from Children," 96 *Columbia Law Review* 375 (1996).

60. Resnick, "Characteristics of Unmarried Adolescent Mothers," 583.

61. Birth mother, quoted in Yngvesson, "Negotiating Motherhood," 52.

62. Unless there was an informal, or, as Barbara Yngvesson puts it, "outlaw" arrangement between birth mother and adoptive family.

63. The therapeutic model is captured in "Once-Silent Mothers Raise Voices," *New York Times*, May 8, 1994, 26 (reporting celebration by support group for birth mothers). See also the Web site of Concerned United Birthmothers at www.cubirthparents.org.

64. There is some suggestion that the birth mother is more often the party who fails to meet the terms of the agreement, not by demanding more contact than contracted for but by failing to request or participate in meetings to which she is entitled under the agreement.

65. *Weinschel v. Strople*, 466 A.2d at 1306 (Md. 1983).

66. Recognition of market forces is also found in a California statute authorizing parents to set aside an adoption if the child "shows evidence of a pre-existing developmental disability or mental illness" of which the

parents had no knowledge at the time of the adoption. Cal. Civil Code § 227b. In *Adoption of Kay C,* a fourteen-year-old adoptee whose adoptive parents sought to revoke her adoption challenged the statute on various constitutional grounds. The Court of Appeals rejected her arguments, noting that "[i]t is unquestioned that the promotion of adoptions is a legitimate state purpose. . . . Although the primary purpose of adoption is to promote the child's best interests, the adoptive parents' interests also deserve some consideration. . . . [A] couple must be allowed to consider a variety of factors, including their ability to parent a child who they believe may never form an emotional bond with them. . . . *Thus it is rational to conclude that more adoptions will occur given the alternative provided by section 227b." Adoption of Kay C.,* 228 Cal. App. 3d 741 (1991) [emphasis added.].

67. See Hollinger, *Appendix 13B,* § 13B.

68. *Parham v. J.R.,* 442 U.S. 584, 604 (1979). Parents control not only with whom their children will live but also for how long they may *visit.* In 2000, the Supreme Court reaffirmed this right even as against visitation with loving, involved grandparents. *Troxel v. Granville,* 530 U.S. 57 (2000).

69. See Sally G. Sharp, "Modification of Agreement-Based Custody Decrees," 68 *Virginia Law Review* 1263, 1264 (1982).

70. See *Garska v. McCoy,* 278 S.E.2d 357, 363 W. Va. (1981).

71. *Gardner v. Hall,* 26 A2d 799, affd. 31 A2d 805 (1942); see also *Bristol v. Brundage,* 24 Conn. App. 402, 589 A2d 1 (1991) (probate court erred in appointing orphan's grandmother as co-guardian along with child's uncle, who was sole guardian named by deceased mother; guardianship statute should be interpreted as mandating appointment of parent's choice unless the appointment would be detrimental to the child).

72. *Swinney v. Mosher,* 830 S.W.2d 187, 193–94 (1992).

73. For an excellent account of how an adoptive couple assesses whether to proceed with an adoption after learning that the birth mother drank heavily in early pregnancy, see Savage, *The Kid,* 112–27.

74. Marianne Berry, "Risks and Benefits of Open Adoption," 6 *Future of Children* 125, 130 (Spring 1983).

75. *In re Adoption of M.J.S.*

76. As Legal Services Director Danny Greenberg has observed with regard to the law's ability to fix children's lives, "Remember that some kids get the good parents and others get the sons of bitches."

77. Gasco, *Can You Wave Bye Bye Baby?* 224.

78. Birth mothers too construct stories of origin; thus the immense disruption when the story is challenged by virtue of unwelcome contact

with an adult child who has obtained records once sealed. Voluntary reunions would seem another matter, as are those that follow adoptions under a known regime of open records.

79. Gasco, *Can You Wave Bye Bye Baby?* 21.

80. See Frank J. Sulloway, *Born to Rebel: Birth Order, Family Dynamics, and Creative Lives* (New York: Pantheon Books, 1996).

81. In this regard, Joan Hollinger notes that the number of foreign adoptions has doubled from fewer than eight thousand in 1989 to over sixteen thousand in 1999. Joan H. Hollinger, "Authenticity and Identity in Contemporary Adoptive Families," *Journal of Gender Specific Medicine* (forthcoming).

3

THE CHILD WELFARE SYSTEM'S RACIAL HARM

DOROTHY E. ROBERTS

I. Introduction

One of the most striking aspects of the American child welfare system is that it is populated so heavily by black children. If an outsider visited any urban juvenile court deciding the fate of children removed from their homes, she would have to conclude that the system was designed to regulate black families. Indeed, dependency proceedings resemble criminal proceedings in many jurisdictions—the vast majority of people before the court are black. Race helps to explain both why so many children enter the foster care system and the nature of the resulting harm. Stereotypes about black family incompetence and deviance legitimate excessive intrusions into family autonomy. Excessive family disruptions, in turn, help to perpetuate the subordination of black people as a group. This essay argues that the gross disparity in the child welfare system generates serious group-based harms by reinforcing disparaging stereotypes about black families and by weakening blacks' collective ability to overcome institutionalized discrimination. I hope to illuminate the political role of the child welfare system in America, a role often obscured by the focus on its rescue of individual children from neglectful parents.

II. The Role of Race in the Child Welfare System

A. The Racial Disparity

The demographics of America's child welfare system undeniably show that race matters to state interventions in families. The number of children in foster care has doubled in the last two decades, from 262,000 in 1982 to 520,000 in 1998.[1] Black families are the most likely of any group to be disrupted by state authorities. Black children enter the child welfare system in grossly disproportionate numbers—and the racial disparity is increasing. In 1986, black children, who were only 15 percent of the population under age eighteen, made up about 26 percent of the children entering foster care and 35 percent of children in foster care at the end of that year.[2] They were three times more likely than white children to be placed in foster care.[3] By 1998, the segment of the foster care population who were black had risen to nearly half.[4] The proportion of black children in out-of-home care in the largest states ranges from three times to over ten times as high as the proportion of white children.[5] In urban centers such as Chicago and New York City only a tiny fraction of the children in foster care are white.[6]

Black children also fare the worst under the state's supervision. Child protective agencies are far more likely to place black children in foster care than to offer less traumatic assistance.[7] Indeed, foster care is the main service that state agencies provide to black children brought to their attention. Once black children enter foster care, they remain there longer, are moved more often, and receive less desirable placements than white children. A 1985 study found that the cumulative time in long-term foster care for black children (61.6 months) was nearly double that of white children (36.8 months) or Hispanic children (36 months).[8] The author concluded that "regardless of the reason for referral or problem category, black children were consistently in placement for longer periods of time than Hispanic or white children."[9] Black children, moreover, are less likely than white children to be returned home or adopted.[10] As a result, most of the 110,000 children whose family ties have been terminated and who are awaiting adoption are black.[11]

B. Reasons for the Disparity

What are the reasons for this striking racial disparity in the child welfare system? Can we attribute the high level of black children in foster care to racism? Although empirical evidence of racial bias is inconclusive, I argue that black children are disproportionately removed from their homes because of their race.

i. Poverty

First, the inequitable representation of black children in the system is largely attributable to high rates of poverty among black families. With rare exceptions, the families who become involved with child protective services are poor.[12] There is a high correlation between poverty and reported cases of child abuse and neglect.[13] State agencies are also more likely to take abused and neglected children from their parents when the family is impoverished. Parental income is a better predictor of removal from the home than is the severity of the alleged child maltreatment.[14] After reviewing numerous studies on the reasons for child removal, Duncan Lindsey concludes, "[I]nadequacy of income, more than any factor, constitutes the reason that children are removed."[15] Moreover, government authorities are more likely to detect child maltreatment in poor families because these families are more open to inspection by social and law enforcement agencies.[16] Because black children are disproportionately poor, we would expect a corresponding racial disparity in the foster care population.

There is a persistent and striking gap in the economic status of blacks and whites that shows up in unemployment, poverty, and income.[17] Black families are more than three times as likely as whites to be poor.[18] In 1993, white children lived in families with an average income that was about 80 percent higher than for blacks.[19] Almost half of black children lived in poverty, compared to 17 percent of whites.[20] Especially alarming was the number of black children raised in extreme poverty, with family incomes less than one-half of the poverty line. These are the children at the highest risk of being removed for severe neglect. More than a quarter of black children, versus only 6 percent of white children, lived in these dire circumstances.[21]

There are dramatic racial differences in a child's risk both of experiencing long-term poverty and of experiencing poverty at all. Poverty researcher Greg Duncan calculated that among children who turned eighteen between 1988 and 1990, nearly one-half of all black children were poor for six or more years, while only 8 percent of white children spent so many years in poverty.[22] The chances for black children to experience poverty only increase as they grow older.[23] In a sense, the economic fortunes of white and black children are just the opposite: the percentage of black children who *ever* lived in poverty while growing up is about the same as the percentage of nonblack children who *never* did.[24]

Moreover, black children are the most likely of any group to live in very poor neighborhoods. In 1990, nearly 20 percent of black children lived in neighborhoods where at least 40 percent of the residents lived in poor families, compared to only 1.2 percent of white children.[25] This is significant because, even after controlling for family background characteristics, researchers find that living in low-income neighborhoods negatively affects early childhood development.[26] A group of researchers found, for example, that "living in areas of localised high unemployment (particularly male) is likely to put families, otherwise vulnerable, at greater risk of child physical abuse and neglect."[27] Parents living in poor neighborhoods are also subject to greater government surveillance and therefore more likely to be reported for child maltreatment.

ii. Racial Bias

These alarming rates of black childhood poverty are directly related to the racial disparity in the foster care population. But does racial bias affect child welfare decision making, even controlling for economic status? The available data are inconclusive. Studies have reached conflicting conclusions about the strength of race as an independent variable in predicting child abuse and neglect cases.[28] Racial disparities in reported cases of maltreatment may reflect differences in the actual incidence of abuse or in the reporter's decision making. Some studies show that the actual incidence of child maltreatment among black families is no greater than the incidence among other groups.[29] Yet researchers have found that children from black families are more likely to be identified as abused than white children with similar injuries.[30] Gelles and Cornell conclude that "Blacks are more likely to be recognized and reported [but] the link between race and abuse is probably tenuous and quite limited."[31] Race appears to influence which injuries to children will be labeled child abuse or neglect. Studies have also discovered that, controlling for other variables, black women are far more likely to be reported for substance abuse during pregnancy and to have their drug-exposed newborns placed in out-of-home care.[32]

There is also scholarship that suggests that African American families are penalized by culturally biased definitions of child neglect. Child neglect is sometimes defined broadly as any parental failure that presents an imminent risk of serious harm to a child.[33] Unlike child abuse, which can often be substantiated with physical evidence, this vague definition of neglect is highly susceptible to biased evaluations of harm based on the parents' racial or class status or on cultural differences in child rearing.[34] The black community's cultural traditions of sharing parenting responsibilities among kin have been mistaken as parental neglect.[35] Black mothers who cannot afford nannies or licensed day care centers often depend on relatives and neighbors for child care. Black women share a rich tradition of women-centered, communal child care. These cooperative networks have included members of the extended family (grandmothers, sisters, aunts, and cousins), as well as non–blood kin and neighbors.[36] Their relationship with children ranges from daily assistance to long-term care or informal adoption. Carol Stack's research in the "Flats" revealed that many children there moved back and forth between households of close female relatives.[37] Three or more women related to a child often formed a cooperative domestic network, taking turns assuming parental responsibility toward the child. Because these mothers do not fit the middle-class norm of a primary caregiver supported by her husband and paid child care, they seem to have abrogated their duty toward their children.[38]

It is nevertheless difficult to establish that the overrepresentation of black children results from racially biased decisions on the part of caseworkers and judges. Racial motives are rarely articulated and may even be unconscious. Moreover, it appears that the disparity is largely related to poverty rather than racial prejudice alone. In what sense, then, are black children excessively removed from their home *because of* their race? Even if most of the racial disparity could be explained by higher poverty rates among black families, this would not negate the racial impact of system or the racist reasons for the imbalance.

Race need not be the *only* reason a child is removed from the home for the decision to be racially biased. State agents may be primarily motivated by the desire to protect children, but race may be a factor in their deliberations about which course of action to take. Legal scholar Randall Kennedy refutes a related argument that racial profiling is a defensible technique when police officers use other factors along with race to identify criminal suspects.[39] The fact that race is only a marginal factor, Kennedy argues, "cannot logically negate the *existence* of racial discrimination." He concludes, "Taking race into account at all means engaging in racial discrimination."[40]

Without evidence of this racial motivation, however, is it accurate to call the disparate outcomes for black children in the child welfare system a pattern of racial discrimination? After reviewing research on race and child welfare services, a group of researchers concluded that this characterization would be misleading "because evidence about the needs of the children and families prior to service receipt cannot be used to argue that these less favorable outcomes result from worse child welfare services for African American children than Caucasians rather than from worse initial circumstances of African American families."[41] But even if equally poor or equally wealthy families had precisely the same risk of intervention regardless of race, this would not discount the far greater risk to black families. The high level of black childhood poverty reflects systemic biases against black Americans. Being black in America means having a huge risk of experiencing poverty and little chance of ever being affluent.[42] As sociologist Dalton Conley explains, "While young African Americans may have the *opportunity* to obtain the same education, income, and wealth as whites, in actuality they are on a slippery slope, for the discrimination their parents faced in the housing and credit markets sets the stage for perpetual economic disadvantage."[43] Disruption of families is one symptom of this institutionalized discrimination. It reflects the persistent gulf between the material welfare of black and white children in America. Thus the racial disparity in the foster care system, even if related directly to poverty, ultimately results from—and results in—racial injustice.

The racial composition of the foster care population may also affect child welfare policy. It is possible that the willingness of state agencies to resort to child removal rather than less disruptive services results from the fact that so many of the affected families are black. If the rate of white children entering foster care began to approach the present rate of blacks, we might see more concern about the level of state interference in families. I suspect that race influences child welfare decision making in this insidious way as well.

Refining the precise reason for the system's racial disparity—black parents' income insecurity, caseworkers' cultural misconceptions and racist stereotypes, or policy makers' insensitivity to black families—would help to develop the most efficacious programs for reducing the disparity. But for my purposes of identifying and describing its harm, it is most helpful to attribute black family disruption to a web of racial injustice that includes all of these causes. It would be a mistake to obscure the system's racial impact by focusing solely on its connection to economic inequality. Poverty and race are so interrelated in America that it makes little sense to try to separate them in bringing attention to the racial injustice of the child welfare system.

iii. The System's Fundamental Flaw

More fundamentally, the fate of black children in the American child welfare system can be traced to a profound flaw in the system's very conception. The system is built upon the presumption that children's basic needs for sustenance and development will and can be met solely by parents.[44] The state intervenes to provide special institutionalized services—primarily placing children in foster care—only when parents fail to fulfill their child-rearing obligations.

This concept of child welfare is defective in three related ways. First, it places all responsibility for taking care of children on their parents, without taking into account the economic, political, and social constraints that prevent many parents from doing so. Most single mothers, for example, face numerous barriers to providing for their children, including a segregated job market, inadequate wages, and a dearth of affordable child care.[45] Thousands of poor families in this country lack the income to meet their children's basic needs of food, clothing, and shelter and live in a deprived environment that is dangerous for children.[46]

Second, this notion of state child protection is activated only when families are already experiencing difficulty. The role of government is limited to rescuing children who have been mistreated by parents who are considered deficient, rather than ensuring the health and welfare of all families.[47] Caseworkers perceive the family's problems as those amenable to social work intervention; they have at their disposal only tools to treat the immediate crisis. Social workers are discouraged from dealing with the systemic problems many probably know are the causes of child neglect. As Ann Hartman, a University of Michigan professor of social work, forthrightly confesses, "[T]he minute we turn around to attempt to address the system that is victimizing people, rather than making the victimization palatable, which is what our profession has done, we will have our heads in a noose."[48] It is almost inevitable that the state's solution will be inadequate, if not more damaging to the family.

Finally, because the system perceives the resulting harm to children as a parental rather than a societal failure, state intervention to protect children is punitive in nature. The state's solutions to children's deprivation involve intrusive meddling by social workers, behavioral requirements, and temporary or permanent removal of children from their homes. Child protection proceedings are more akin to criminal trials than most civil adjudications because they pit individuals against the state and involve moral condemnation of neglectful parents.[49]

This narrow concept of child welfare hurts all families in America. But it hurts black families the most. Attributing children's deprivation to parental fault falls more heavily on black parents, who are more likely to suffer the consequences of poverty and institutional discrimination. The judgmental aspect of child protection decisions, moreover, allows for intervention based on the racial biases of state agents. It fosters the widespread assumption that "the Black child's problems stem from his negatively valued family and disorganized community, and that his solutions lie in the institutions of the larger white society."[50] Child welfare interventions become a way both to punish black parents for their perceived moral depravity and to place black children in the state's superior care.

C. New Trends in Child Welfare Policy

New trends in child welfare policy are likely to intensify the racial imbalance in state interventions in families. The Personal Responsibility and Work Opportunity Reconciliation Act of 1996 (PRA) ended the federal guarantee of cash assistance to America's children and allowed the states to implement extensive welfare reform programs. Recent welfare reform measures make it more difficult for some poor mothers to take care of their children in several ways: they reduce the amount of cash assistance to families; they cut off payments altogether to some families; and they require mothers to work and to participate in job training, counseling, and other programs, often without adequate child care.[51] What will happen to the children of mothers who fail to meet new work rules because of child care or transportation problems, who are unable to find work within the two-year time limit, or who leave their children at home without adequate care while they participate in required work programs? It is likely that many of them will be removed from their mother's custody and placed in foster care.

Family integrity is jeopardized further by the interaction of the new welfare law and recent federal reforms concerning adoption. In November 1997, President Clinton signed the Adoption and Safe Families Act, aimed at doubling the number of children adopted annually by 2002.[52] The new adoption law represents a dramatic shift in federal child welfare philosophy from an emphasis on the reunification of children in foster care with their biological families toward an emphasis on the adoption of these children into new families. The retreat from family reunification is implemented through swifter timetables for state agencies to petition for termination of the rights of biological parents and the removal of other barriers to adoption. The act also gives states financial incentives to move more children into adoptive homes. The law's supporters argue that these provisions promote adoptions for the one hundred thousand children in foster care who cannot return safely to their birth families.[53]

Of course, the state should usually facilitate adoptions of children where there is no hope of family reunification. The act's impact, however, may be to permanently separate poor children from families that might have been preserved with adequate state resources. Black parents' rights are already terminated sooner than those of white parents, yet black children are less likely to be adopted. The combination of welfare reform's decimation of much of the federal safety net for children and adoption reform's abandonment of the commitment to family preservation may only intensify the permanent dismantling of poor black families. Congress misidentified the reason for the overcrowding of the foster care system: it is not that too few children are being adopted, but that too many children are removed from their homes.[54] Even if all of the black children in foster care were adopted tomorrow, it would not cure the racial injustice in the child welfare system.

III. Images of Bad Black Mothers

Constitutional jurisprudence shields family autonomy against the encroachment of the state.[55] Yet the previous discussion demonstrates a disturbing rate of government intervention in black families. Why have courts and lawmakers countenanced this excessive degree of state interference in the family? The disregard of black family autonomy is supported by the devaluation of black motherhood. The dominant American culture has perpetuated a popular mythology that degrades black women and portrays them as bad mothers. Three prominent images of black mothers cast them as pathological: the careless black mother, the matriarch, and the welfare queen.[56] These images reflect traits black women are supposed to have that are detrimental to their children. It is believed that black women neglect their children because they do not care enough about them, create a fatherless family structure that provides inadequate supervision of their children, and teach their children an attitude of dependence on government handouts. The continuity of these derogatory maternal stereotypes over centuries suggests that they have a real impact on the way many Americans view black families. All of these myths about black mothers confirm the need for the state to intervene in their homes to safeguard their children and to ensure that their children do not follow their dangerous example.

A. Careless Black Mothers

Charges of black mothers' carelessness emerge from the institution of slavery. The ideal black mother figure, Mammy, selflessly nurtured her master's children, but not her own. Mammy was both the perfect mother and the perfect slave: whites saw her as a "passive nurturer, a mother figure who gave all without expectation of return, who not only acknowledged her inferiority to whites but who loved them."[57] Mammy, however, did not reflect any virtue in black women as mothers of their *own* children. While caring for her master's children, she remained under the constant supervision of her white mistress. She had no real authority over either the white children she raised or the black children she bore.

In contrast, whites portrayed slave mothers as negligent and unable to care for their own children. Southern state officials commonly attributed the deaths of black babies to accidental suffocation by their mothers in bed.[58] When a one-month-old slave girl named Harriet died in the Abbeville District of South Carolina on December 9, 1849, for example, the census marshal reported the cause of death as "[s]mothered by carelessness of [her] mother." The census marshal explained: "I wish it to be distinctly understood that nearly all the accidents occur in the negro population, which goes clearly to prove their great carelessness & total inability to take care of themselves."[59] It now appears that the true cause of the high infant mortality rate among slaves was the hard physical labor, poor nutrition, and abuse the mothers endured during pregnancy.[60] These census reports provide an early example of the scapegoating of black mothers for the social causes of their children's poor health.

A contemporary image of the careless black mother who harms her children is the pregnant crack addict. This image arose in the late 1980s from the urban crack-cocaine epidemic and the reporting of a surge in the numbers of newborns testing positive for drugs. Despite similar rates of substance abuse during pregnancy by white and black women, the media erroneously suggested that the problem was most prevalent among blacks.[61] The pregnant crack addict was portrayed as a black woman who put her love for crack above her love for her children. News stories reported that the chemical properties of crack destroyed "maternal instinct," making women who smoked the drug incapable of nurturing their children.[62] A public health crisis that affected all communities became yet another example of black mothers' depravity that justified harsh state intervention.

B. The Matriarch, Black Unwed Mothers, and Absent Black Fathers

Modern social pundits have held black mothers responsible for the disintegration of the black family. Stereotypes about deviant black mothers and absent black fathers together form a picture of dysfunctional black families. Daniel Patrick Moynihan popularized the myth of the black matriarch, the domineering female head of the black family, in his 1965 report *The Negro Family: The Case for National Action.* Moynihan, then Assistant Secretary of Labor and Director of the Office of Policy Planning and Research under President Johnson, described black culture as a "tangle of pathology" that was "capable of *perpetuating itself* without assistance from the white world." The chief cause of this pathology, Moynihan asserted, was blacks' "matriarchal" family structure. According to Moynihan, "At the heart of the deterioration of the fabric of the Negro society is the deterioration of the Negro family. It is the fundamental cause of the weakness of the Negro community."[63]

Black families have the highest rate of unwed motherhood, with black families three times as likely as white families to be headed by a woman.[64] Most black children in America are born to unmarried mothers. But the rate among whites is rising faster. Growing from 3 percent to 25 percent since 1965, the rate of fatherlessness among whites today has reached what it was among blacks three decades ago.[65] Today, there are more white babies born to single mothers. Still, single motherhood is viewed as a *black* cultural trait that is infiltrating white homes. Charles Murray hammered in this point in his *Wall Street Journal* editorial "The Coming White Underclass," which warned white Americans that their rising illegitimacy rate threatened to spread to white neighborhoods the same crime, drugs, and "drop out from the labor force" that now infected black communities.[66]

The flip side of the rebellious black single mother is the absent black father. Black men have a hard time fitting the ideal model of the father as married breadwinner.[67] The dominant assumption is that black men have little to do with their children, providing no financial support and rarely developing any emotional attachments.

The absence of fathers in many black households has justified state intervention on the grounds that single mothers are uncooperative with government authorities or incapable of properly supervising their children. Judges and prosecutors are more likely to detain black children who are charged with crimes than white children who commit the same offenses. Caseworkers in Florida, for example, attribute the racial disparity in the state's detention of juveniles to policies that focus on family support and cooperation in disposing of delinquency cases.[68] Florida's Department of Health and Rehabilitative Services (DHRS), which initially reviews all juvenile arrests and complaints, refuses to recommend delinquent youths for diversion programs if their parents or guardians cannot be contacted, are unable to be present for an intake interview, or are perceived to be uncooperative. Black single mothers often fail this standard because they work at low-paying jobs that do not permit time off to be interviewed or because they cannot afford child care, do not have telephones, or must rely on inconvenient public transportation to get to the DHRS office.

Juvenile justice officials also resort to detention rather than informal alternatives because of stereotypes about black families.

They perceive single mothers as incapable of providing adequate supervision for their children and therefore feel justified in placing these children under state control.[69] Judges rely heavily on pre-disposition reports that disparage black children's family situations and therefore believe that the disproportionate detention of black children is warranted. One judge explained to researchers, "Inadequate family correlates with race and ethnicity. It makes sense to put delinquent kids from these circumstances in residential facilities."[70] A state's attorney defended the racial bias in similar terms:

> Detention decisions are decided on the basis of whether the home can control and supervise a child. So minorities don't go home because, unfortunately, their families are less able to control the kids. . . . I think the way the system sets up programs shows some institutional bias. If family stability was not a prerequisite to admission to less severe program options, race differences would be less.[71]

Another state's attorney likewise stated, "In black families who the dad is, is unknown, while in white families—even when divorced—dad is married or something else. The choices are limited because the black family is a multigenerational non-fathered family. You can't send the kid off to live with dad."[72] Thus myths about the inadequacies of black families headed by women have become a powerful justification for removal of children from their homes for placement in state institutions.

C. The Welfare Queen and Welfare Reform

A contemporary image of black mothers is the welfare queen, the lazy mother who refuses to work and breeds children to fatten her monthly check from the government. This mythological character was supported by conservative writers, such as Charles Murray, who argued in the 1980s that welfare induces black women to refrain from marriage and to have babies.[73] The claim that welfare creates a financial incentive for recipients to have more children is refuted by empirical studies and common sense.[74] It would be completely irrational for a mother on welfare to assume the tremendous costs and burdens of caring for an additional child given the meager increase in benefits that results. The vast majority of women on welfare have only one or two children. Yet the popular image of the welfare queen helped to drive the passage of child exclusion laws—or "family caps"—in a number of states, denying any increase in benefits to mothers who have children while already receiving public aid.[75]

The public despises this mother not only because she cheats taxpayers out of their hard-earned money but also because she uses the money selfishly. Welfare mothers cannot be trusted to spend their benefits for the care of their children instead of wasting them on drugs, fancy clothes, and entertainment for themselves. Caseworkers therefore inspect the homes of poor families in search of evidence of child maltreatment while preserving the privacy of wealthier families. Courts assume that mothers who receive public assistance require state supervision to ensure that benefits are devoted to their children's welfare.[76]

The welfare queen is guilty of a more devastating injury to her children as well. Contemporary poverty rhetoric blames poor black mothers for perpetuating welfare dependency by transmitting a deviant lifestyle to their children.[77] Part of the impetus for welfare reform was the sense that payments to black mothers merely encouraged this transgenerational pathology. Welfare reform discourse also paid little attention to the relationship between poor black mothers and their children, never questioning the impact of compelling these women to leave their young children to find work. The belief that poor black mothers have nothing beneficial to impart to their children helps to legitimate the disproportionate disruption of their family bonds.

IV. Race and The Harm in Child Welfare Interventions

I have shown a gross racial disparity in the state's interventions in families to protect children, as well as the importance of racism in explaining the reasons for this disparity. Why should we be concerned about the child welfare system's disproportionate intrusion in black families?[78] Surely parents and children who are wrongfully separated from each other suffer a terrible injury. But is it helpful to explain this injury in terms of race?

American constitutional jurisprudence defines the harm caused by state interruption of the parent-child relationship in terms of individual rights. Wrongfully removing a child from the parents' custody or terminating parental rights violates parents' due process right to liberty. In *Santosky v. Kramer*, the U.S. Supreme Court recognized parents' liberty interest in maintaining a relationship with their children:

> The fundamental liberty interest of natural parents in the care, custody, and management of their child does not evaporate simply because they have not been model parents or have lost temporary custody of their child to the state. Even when the blood relationships are strained, parents retain a vital interest in preventing the irretrievable destruction of their family life.[79]

Parents have a constitutionally protected interest in raising their children according to their own values. In *Meyer v. Nebraska*,[80] for example, the U.S. Supreme Court struck down a law that prohibited foreign language teaching as a violation of parents' liberty to direct the upbringing of their children. This legal doctrine safeguards parental authority to prevent the state from standardizing children.[81] William Galston argues in Chapter 7 of this volume that these cases recognize, as well, the "'expressive interest' of parents in raising children in a manner consistent with their understanding of what gives meaning and value to life." The ability parents have to rear their children is an expression of their freedom of conscience; it is one of the most significant ways individuals convey their values. For most people, the freedom to conduct their family life according to their personal beliefs is as meaningful and precious as the freedom to organize with others for political ends.[82] The state interferes with parents' authority to educate their children when it removes them from the home and places them in the care of others.

Unwarranted government intervention in families also has an adverse impact on children. It is psychologically damaging for children to be ripped from the relationships of intimacy and support on which they depend.[83] In addition, children flourish better in homes that enjoy expressive freedom than in state-run environments. The reason for limiting state intrusion in the home is not only a concern for parental privacy but also the recognition that children suffer harm when unnecessarily separated from their parents. When the state seeks to protect children,

> it takes on the exquisitely difficult task of deciding when intervention is reasonably necessary to the physical or emotional well-being of a child and when it is destructive, both of the bonds upon which the child depends for healthy nurturance and of the child's right to grow in a community that is open, flexible, and self-defining, rather than state-controlled.[84]

Thus, undue state intervention in families interferes with the individual interests of both parents and children.

These explanations of harm, however, do not account for the particular injury inflicted by racially disparate state intervention. Without considering race, we have not captured the full scope of the harm caused by taking relatively large numbers of black children from their families. Indeed, without considering race, we might not see any harm at all. Focusing solely on individual cases, many of which are difficult to judge, obscures the impact of state interventions taken as a whole as well as the impact on the black community. High rates of removal of black children from their homes harm black people *as a group*, as well as individual parents and children.

I argued above that the racial disparity is a group-based harm in terms of the *reasons* for racial differences in child welfare interventions. The overrepresentation of black children in foster care is not simply an accident. All those displaced children do not "just happen to be black," as color-blindness advocates are fond of saying. The disproportionate number of black children under state supervision is a consequence of discriminatory decision making within the system as well as racist institutions in the broader society. The disparity results from the high rates of poverty among black families and stereotypes about black parental fitness. Black children suffer a racial harm because their chance of being taken from their parents is far greater than that of white children. Without claiming racial motivation, one can still accurately say that the risk of entering foster care differs according to a child's race.

The system's racial disparity also *inflicts* a group-based harm. Disrupting large numbers of black families negatively affects black people's status and welfare as a group. Explaining the racial injustice of the child welfare system is part of the inquiry into the role of group identity in conceptions of justice. As Jurgen Habermas framed the broader question: "Should citizens' identities as members of ethnic, cultural, or religious groups *publicly* matter, and if so, how can collective identities make a difference with the framework of constitutional democracy? Are collective identities and cultural membership politically relevant, and if so, how can they legitimately affect the distribution of rights and the recognition of legal claims?"[85] The racial gap in state intervention in families creates a political harm that gives rise to a group-based claim of racial injustice. I will explicate this claim in three parts. First, I argue that there is a relationship between the welfare of individual black children and parents and welfare of blacks as a group. Second, I discuss power of state supervision of families to influence the political status of groups. Finally, I present the specific ways the child welfare system creates group-based harms and address potential objections to this approach. In sum, I hope to show that the child welfare system's racial disparity has negative material and ideological consequences for black families that affect the status of blacks in America as a whole and consequently the welfare of black children.

A. Connecting Black Individual and Group Interests

Black Americans' welfare is determined not only by the atomistic decisions of each individual but also by the condition of the entire community. According to the American system of racial classification, individuals are born into racial categories that determine their status in society.[86] By the eighteenth century, African chattel slavery constituted a perpetual, lifelong condition passed on to the next generation. Whites established a racial caste system that required a clear racial demarcation between slaves and their masters. An official rule of racial purity based on the natural separation of the races survived emancipation and was not abolished until 1965.[87]

America's racial hierarchy continues to accord automatic benefits and privileges to people who are born white and automatic disadvantages to others.[88] Powerful racist imagery portrays black bodies, intellect, character, and culture as inherently inferior and vulgar.[89] Demeaning racial stereotypes judge African American individuals according to assumed group traits. The criminal behavior of a minority of individual blacks makes all blacks seem suspicious. This negative group treatment is exemplified by racial profiling, the routine use of race by police in deciding whom to stop and question, as well as by actor Danny Glover's inability to catch a taxi.[90]

Moreover, black Americans have been subjected to discrimination on the basis of their race in the political, economic, and social realms. Although racism is not as blatant or brutal as during the periods of slavery and Jim Crow laws, it continues through practices such as employment discrimination, neighborhood segregation, and police abuse. The eradication of overt barriers to equal opportunity has not equalized the condition of black and white Americans.[91] Past barriers to black property accumulation, for example, produced a huge racial gap in wealth generations later.[92] In short, "In African Americans' historical experience, life chances have been linked to the ascriptive feature of race in all spheres of life."[93]

Most African Americans also identify themselves as part of a group whose members are tied together by a common heritage, culture, and social experience.[94] By the turn of the twentieth century, blacks had developed a race consciousness rooted in a sense of shared destiny that laid the foundation for later civil rights struggles.[95] Political scientist Michael C. Dawson has highlighted the critical role of racial group interests in explaining black Americans' relatively unified political behavior.[96] Blacks' political beliefs and actions as *individuals* are strongly related to their sense of racial *group* interests.[97] Thus a critical aspect of the racial identity of African Americans is "the perceived link between one's own fate and that of the race."[98] A 1988 national survey of African Americans, for example, found that 64 percent responded affirmatively to the question "Do you think that whatever happens generally to the black people in this country will have something to do with what happens in your life?"[99] Most African Americans are well aware that, whatever their individual character and efforts, their personal welfare is inextricably tied to the welfare of African Americans as a group. What happens to individual black parents and children affects the entire group and vice versa.

B. The Political Impact of Family Disruption

Family disruption has historically served as a chief tool of group oppression. Examining the importance of race in state interventions in the family illuminates the reasons for safeguarding family autonomy. Parents' freedom to raise their children is important not only to individuals but also to the welfare or even survival of ethnic, cultural, and religious groups. Disintegrating families and weakening the parent-child bond among people within a group are means of subordinating the entire group. The individualized focus on preserving personal choice in the private sphere of family life fails to recognize the family's *political* role. We must understand the family not strictly as the expression of individual choice but as a social institution serving political ends.

The American regime of slavery reveals the political function of repressing family autonomy. Slave law installed white masters as the head of an extended plantation family that included their slaves. The plantation family ruled by white men was considered the best institution to transmit moral values to uncivilized Africans.[100] Courts reasoned that the slave owner's moral authority over the family was ordained by divine imperative. Slaves, on the other hand, had no legal authority over their children. Naming a slave after his or her owner reinforced the child's ultimate subservience to his or her white master rather than to his or her parents. Malcolm X, describing the disruption of his own family by child welfare workers, noted the contemporary parallels to slavery: "A Judge . . . had authority over me and all my brothers and sisters. We were 'state children,' court wards; he had the full say-so over us. A white man in charge of a Black man's children! Nothing but legal, modern slavery."[101]

Legal scholar Peggy Cooper Davis powerfully reveals that a critical aspect of slave masters' control of their slaves was the restriction of slaves' capacity to educate and socialize their children.[102] In this way, whites attempted to prevent slaves from constructing their own system of morals and from acting according to their own chosen values. Slaveholders proclaimed their moral authority by reinforcing the message of parental helplessness, frequently whipping adult slaves in front of their children. The sale of children apart from their parents was another brutal incarnation of this power. According to Davis, the tragic stories of family disruption generated the Fourteenth Amendment rights "to maintain a parental relationship, to have a measure of liberty in child rearing, and, some would argue, to expect a measure of public responsibility for children."[103] Thus contemporary notions of family liberty, typically interpreted as individual rights, can trace their origins to the effort to eradicate racial oppression.

C. The Child Welfare System's Group-Based Harms

The linked fate of all black Americans and the political impact of family disruption help to explain the child welfare system's racial harm. The disproportionate removal of individual black children from their homes has a detrimental impact on the status of blacks as a group because it weakens their collective ability to overcome institutionalized discrimination and because it reinforces stereotypes about black people's need for government supervision.

The excessive disruption of black families affects the stability of the group as a whole, weakening its ability to struggle against the many forms of institutional discrimination that persist in this country and to improve the welfare of community. The material impact of family disruption and supervision is intensified when concentrated in inner-city neighborhoods. In Chicago, for example, almost all child protection cases are clustered in two zip code areas, which are almost exclusively African American.[104] Most of the families in the city's poorest neighborhood are involved with state protective services.[105] Family integrity is crucial to group welfare because of the role parents and other relatives play in transmitting survival skills, values, and self-esteem. Families are a principal form of the oppositional enclaves that Jane Mansbridge identifies as essential to democracy: "The goals of these counterpublics include understanding themselves better, forging bonds of solidarity, preserving the memories of past injustices, interpreting and reinterpreting the meanings of those injustices, working out alternative conceptions of self, community, of justice, of universality."[106]

Just as whites have made family disruption a tool of racial oppression, so blacks have made family solidarity a tool of resistance. For slaves, the family was a site of solace from white oppression.[107] Their care for their families defied the expectation of total service to whites. Angela Davis observes that "slave women perform[ed] the only labor of the slave community which could not be directly and immediately claimed by the oppressor."[108] Although some slave mothers opposed slavery by abandoning or even killing their children, the vast majority defied bondage by caring for their children. Thus blacks have had a political interpretation of the home as a site of resistance against outside oppression.

The mother-child relationship continues to have political significance for black women. Black women historically have experienced motherhood as an empowering denial of the dominant society's denigration of their humanity. Alice Walker described her relationship with her child in terms of their political solidarity: "We are together, my child and I. Mother and child, yes, but *sisters* really, against whatever denied us all that we are."[109] Black women have seen their children as the source of motivation, courage, and insight to resist oppression.[110] Concern for children has often served as the foundation for formal collective struggles among black women, such as the Sisterhood of Black Single Mothers in Brooklyn and the Welfare Mothers' Movement. Black women often explain their involvement in social activism as an outgrowth of their experience as mothers and use their mothering skills in their political work. The black women involved in a union organizing drive at a local medical center, for example, brought family events into the workplace to create unity among workers and shared a family idiom that conceptualized their relationships with their coworkers.[111]

The disproportionate shattering of black family ties also reinforces stereotypes that negatively affect every member of the group. Placing so many black children in the state's care expresses the quintessential racist insult that black people are irresponsible and continue to need white supervision. Disparate state intervention and the devaluation of black families' autonomy send a message of inferiority that rebounds on the perceived character and the opportunities of individual African Americans.

My arguments based on a political harm to blacks as a group can be distinguished both from traditional legal claims of individual discrimination and from claims based on an essential biological or cultural black identity.[112] My approach recognizes that individual parents and children are harmed by discriminatory child welfare practices while recognizing that this harm is tied inextricably to their group status. Under the dominant individualistic model of justice, individuals bring lawsuits to enforce their rights and to redress the harm they have suffered. Although the individual discrimination claims of many black families have merit, this is not the type of argument I make here. My claim of group harm does not depend on evidence that decisions in individual cases were motivated by racial bigotry or would not have been made if the parents were white.

My argument also differs from the group-based characterization of the harm to black children presented in the National Association of Black Social Workers' position paper on transracial adoption. The organization conducted a workshop in 1972 on placement of black children in white adoptive homes that culminated in their stand against the practice. The NABSW called transracial adoptions a form of "genocide," explaining:

> Black children should be placed only with Black families whether in foster care or adoption. Black children belong physically, psychologically and culturally in Black families in order that they receive the total sense of themselves and develop a sound projection of their future. . . . Black children in white homes are cut off from the healthy development of themselves as Black people.[113]

The NABSW's position revolved in part around the need of black children to learn specialized skills to survive in a racist society, something the organization argued white parents were not equipped to impart. The NABSW also asserted that a black cultural environment was crucial for the development of black children's racial and cultural identity.

Although the U.S. government has rejected this notion of black cultural injury, Congress recognized such a claim when it passed the Indian Child Welfare Act in 1978.[114] The federal lawmakers acknowledged a deliberate government campaign to wrongfully remove Indian children from their parents to place them in white adoptive homes and its devastating impact on Indian culture.[115] The Indian Child Welfare Act gives sovereign Indian tribes jurisdiction over child welfare decisions involving tribal members.

Aborigines in Australia made a similar argument about the removal of indigenous children from their families.[116] From the turn of the twentieth century until the 1960s, Aboriginal children were systematically taken from their parents and placed in white-controlled institutions and foster care.[117] This practice was part of a deliberate, government-sponsored attempt to absorb the indigenous population biologically into the white population as well as to assimilate them into the dominant culture. In *In re Marriage of B and R*, the court acknowledged that the Australian removal policies were motivated by "the belief that the indigenous people of this country would die out and their young children would be better served by occupying (lowly) places in a dominate white society."[118] This policy not only injured the removed children, who today suffer from psychological and social problems, but also helped to destroy the Aboriginal culture.

Claims of cultural genocide have been less persuasive in the case of black children supervised by white-dominated child protective services. This approach to the proper placement of black children has been vehemently criticized both as factually unsound and as essentialist. Supporters of transracial adoption argue that white parents can be just as successful as black parents at raising healthy black children in American society. They point to studies showing that transracial parenting has not adversely affected adopted children.[119] Supporters of transracial adoption have also criticized the notion of an essential and uniform black identity that must be transmitted to black children. The harm to black children caused by languishing in foster care, they argue, outweighs any disadvantage in being raised in a culturally unfamiliar but loving home. In response to these criticisms, recent federal legislation has prohibited race matching in adoptions supported by federal funds.[120]

In addition, it seems unlikely that transracial adoption will perpetrate a literal decimation of black culture, as was threatened in the case of indigenous peoples in the United States and Australia. Adoptions of black children by white parents are still relatively rare (although they may increase dramatically with new federal incentives).[121] An increasing number of black children, moreover, are placed with kin when removed from their parents' care.[122]

None of these criticisms, however, refutes the importance of attending to the racial impact of child welfare interventions. My assertion of group-based harm does not posit an essential black identity or way of raising children; nor does it warn of the total obliteration of blacks as a cultural group. I argue instead that disproportionate state intervention in black families reinforces the continued political subordination of blacks as a group. Another aspect of the NABSW's position is relevant to this point. The organization argued that black people were hurt as a political entity by the loss of such a large portion of their children. The position paper referred to "the necessity of self-determination from birth to death, of all Black people" and "the philosophy that we need our own to build a strong nation."[123] Law professor Twila Perry observes that the opposing views on transracial adoption reflect two very distinct perspectives on the analysis of race and racism in America.[124] Support for transracial adoption often reflects a "liberal colorblind individualism," while opposition to transracial adoption often reflects a "community consciousness." The group-based perspective "sees the individual Black child as inextricably linked to the Black community and inevitably identified with that community."[125] Although this perspective opposes the placement of black children in white homes, it also condemns the large-scale removal of black children from their families. Concerns about cultural transmission might be allayed if the state placed more black children in black foster or adoptive homes. But the political harms created by racially disparate family disruption and state supervision of children remain.

Recognizing the system's racial impact does not necessarily establish that the system causes a net group harm. The state might be charged with racism if it failed to rescue black children from dangerous parents. As a group of social work researchers noted, "[I]n the absence of efforts to improve the lot of impoverished families, it might be justifiable cause for concern if the children of such families were *not* overrepresented in child welfare services caseloads."[126] Responding to my argument, philosopher and adoptive parent Larry May argues that black children suffer a group-based harm different from the one I have described—"[t]he insecurity of Black children, who go back and forth between abusive or neglectful homes and unstable foster care."[127] This harm, May asserts, is also having a devastating impact on black community life and might be abated through programs that free these children for adoption. May offers a powerful rejoinder to my claim of group harm caused by high rates of family disruption by the state:

> Black children are harmed by the continued disintegration of Black family life, which results from the removal of children from their families. But some Black children are harmed much more by their own biological families and by the systemic deprivation they suffer by never having a stable, loving home life. Black children are also harmed by the deterioration of Black communities that results from so many Black children remaining in unstable homes during their most formative years.[128]

Taking into account the serious individual and group injuries caused by child maltreatment, however, does not offset the harms caused by the racial disparity in the system. I do not argue that black children who are abused and neglected should never be removed from their parents. Surely black children deserve the same protection from injury as others. Acknowledging the problem of child maltreatment, however, does not resolve the question of how the problem should be addressed. The racial disparity in the foster care population should cause us to reconsider the state's current response. The enormity of the racial gap suggests that at least some significant portion of children are removed from their homes unnecessarily. There is evidence of irrationality in child welfare decision making whose detrimental effects fall disproportionately on black children. Moreover, the state could address the group harms caused by both neglectful parents and the disruption of families by doing more to improve the material circumstances of families. The strategy of moving more black children in foster care into adoptive homes may improve the well-being of a fraction of the population, but it will not solve the group-based harms I have identified. Indeed, the adoption strategy bolsters the stereotype of black family incompetence.[129] I see the child welfare system's racial harms as a powerful argument in favor of policies that are more supportive of struggling families. The price of present policies that rely on child removal rather than family support falls unjustly on black families.

V. Conclusion

Race helps to determine the fate of the largest group of children removed from their homes and placed under state supervision. Given the disproportionate impact of state interventions on black families, race must be a central part of our explanation of the harm caused by family disruption. Only by focusing on group-based racial injustice can we understand the harm inflicted on children by the child welfare system and take the right steps to solve it. The connection between group status and family autonomy helps us to understand the political role of families and the reasons for safeguarding family rights. Finally, the racial disparity suggests that we must do more than devote greater resources to services and improve the management of the present system. Ending this racial harm will require addressing the systemic deprivation of poor and minority families, as well as the coercive and punitive function of a system that is supposed to serve them. These changes would improve child protective services for all families.

NOTES

This paper was presented at the 44th Annual Meeting of the American Society for Political and Legal Philosophy at the program "Child, Family, and the State," and I thank the participants for their comments. It is part of a larger paper, "Why Race Matters to Child Welfare Interventions," that I am preparing for the Center for Families in an Open Society.

1. U.S. Department of Health and Human Services, Office of the Assistant Secretary for Planning Evaluation, *Trends in the Well-Being of Children and Youth: 1996* (Washington, D.C.: U.S. Department of Health and Human Services, 1996), 26; Children's Defense Fund, *The State of America's Children: Yearbook 1999* (Washington, D.C.: Children's Defense Fund, 1999), 86.

2. House Select Committee on Children, Youth and Families, *U.S. Children and Their Families: Current Conditions and Recent Trends* (Washington, D.C.: U.S. House of Representatives, 1989).

3. Children's Defense Fund, *Black and White Children in America: Key Facts* (Washington, D.C.: Children's Defense Fund, 1985).

4. U.S. Department of Health and Human Services, Administration for Children and Families, Children's Bureau, "Foster Care and Adoption Statistics" (Jan. 1999), available at www.acf.dhhs.gov/programs/cb/stats/afcars/rpt0199/ar0199a.htm (reporting that 45 percent of children in foster care are black).

5. R. M. George, F. S. Wulczyn, and A. Harden, *Foster Care Dynamics: California, Illinois, Michigan, New York, and Texas—A First-Year Report from the Multi-State Foster Care Data Archive* (Chicago: Chapin Hall Center for Children, 1994).

6. Patrick Murphy, *Wasted: The Plight of America's Unwanted Children* (Chicago: Ivan R. Dee, 1997) (almost 90 percent of children in Chicago foster care are black); Martin Guggenheim, "Somebody's Children: Sustaining the Family's Place in Child Welfare Policy," *Harvard Law Review* 113 (2000): 1716, 1718, n. 11, citing New York City Administration for Children's Services, *Selected Child Welfare Trends* 81 (1998) (of forty-two thousand children in New York City's foster care system, fewer than two thousand are white).

7. "Fifty-six percent of the Black children receiving child welfare services are in foster care placement—twice the percentage for White children." U.S. Department of Health and Human Services, Children's Bureau, *National Study of Protective, Preventive, and Reunification Services Delivered to Children and Their Families* (Washington, D.C.: U.S. Government Printing Office, 1997).

8. E. V. Mech, "Public Social Services to Minority Children and Their Families," in R. O. Washington and J. Boros-Van Hull, eds., *Children in Need of Roots* (Davis, Calif.: International Dialogue Press).

9. Ibid., 164.

10. Joyce E. Everett, "Introduction: Children in Crisis," in Joyce E. Everett, Sandra S. Chipungu, and Bogart R. Leashore, eds., *Child Welfare: An Africentric Perspective* (New Brunswick, N.J.: Rutgers University Press, 1991), 1, 3; Sylvia S. Gray and Lynn M. Nybell, "Issues in African-American Family Preservation," *Child Welfare* 69 (1990): 513, 513–14; Sandra M. Stehno, "Differential Treatment of Minority Children in Service Systems," *Social Work* 27 (1982): 39, 39–41.

11. U.S. Department of Health and Human Services, Administration for Children and Families, Children's Bureau, "Foster Care and Adoption Statistics" (Jan. 1999), available at www.acdf.dhhs.gov/programs

/cb. Black children receive inferior services according to every measure, such as provision of both in-home and adoption services, recommended versus actual length of placement, and worker contact with the child and caregivers. They are also more likely to live in institutions or group homes. Ketayun H. Gould, "Limiting Damage Is Not Enough: A Minority Perspective on Child Welfare Issues," in Everett et al., *Child Welfare,* 58, 59; Mech, "Public Social Services"; M. M. Close, "Child Welfare and People of Color: Denial of Equal Access," *Social Work Research Abstracts* 19, no. 4 (1983): 13.

12. LeRoy Pelton, *For Reasons of Poverty: A Critical Analysis of the Public Child Welfare System in the United States* (Westport, Conn.: Greenwood, 1989).

13. Kristine E. Nelson, Edward J. Saunders, and Miriam J. Landsman, "Chronic Child Neglect in Perspective," *Social Work* 38 (1993): 661; Richard J. Gelles, "Child Abuse and Violence in Single-Parent Families: Parent Absence and Economic Deprivation," *American Journal of Orthopsychiatry* 59 (1988): 492; Leroy H. Pelton, "Child Abuse and Neglect: The Myth of Classlessness," *American Journal of Orthopsychiatry* 48 (1978): 608. The 1988 National Study of Incidence and Severity of Child Abuse and Neglect found that families who earned less than $15,000 annually were four and a half times more likely to be reported for child maltreatment than those with higher incomes. National Center on Child Abuse and Neglect, *Study Findings: Study of the National Incidence and Prevalence of Child Abuse and Neglect* (Washington, D.C.: U.S. Department of Health and Human Services, 1988).

14. Duncan Lindsey, *The Welfare of Children* (New York: Oxford University Press, 1994), 139–54. See also Everett et al., *Child Welfare,* 184 ("Studies indicate strong correlations between the incidence of child neglect and lack of the basic elements of what is considered a minimal standard of living for all Americans and less correlation with the psychological makeup of the caretaker").

15. Lindsey, *The Welfare of Children,* 155. In 1996, 52 percent of the one million cases of confirmed child maltreatment involved neglect rather than physical or sexual abuse. Children's Defense Fund, *The State of America's Children,* 85.

16. Annette R. Appell, "Protecting Children or Punishing Mothers: Gender, Race, and Class in the Child Protection System," *South Carolina Law Review* 48 (1997): 577, 584; Robert L. Hampton, "Child Abuse in the African American Community," in Everett et al., *Child Welfare,* 229.

17. Michael C. Dawson, *Behind the Mule: Race and Class in African-American Politics* (Princeton, N.J.: Princeton University Press, 1994), 15–34.

18. Ibid., 28.

19. Roger P. Weissberg, ed., *Trends in the Well-Being of America's Children and Youth* (Washington, D.C.: CWLA Press, 1996), 36.

20. Ibid., 39.

21. Ibid.

22. Ibid., 48, citing calculations by Greg J. Duncan, based on data from the Panel Study of Income Dynamics (PSID), Survey Research Center, University of Michigan.

23. Social work professor Mark Rank summarizes the alarming trajectory of black childhood poverty:

By the age of six, fifty-seven percent of black children will experience at least one year of life below the poverty line as compared with fifteen percent for white children. By age twelve the percentages rise to sixty-seven percent for black children versus twenty-one percent for white children, and by age seventeen, sixty-nine percent of black children versus twenty-six percent of white children will experience at least one year of life below the poverty line.

Mark R. Rank, "The Racial Injustice of Poverty," *Washington University Journal of Law and Policy* 1 (1999): 95, 96.

24. Weissberg, *Trends of America*, 49, figure E S1.5.B, "Percent of Children in Poverty by Number of Years in Poverty by Race, for Cohort Age 18 in 1988–90" (showing that 72 percent of black children versus 27 percent of white children had ever experienced poverty and that 73 percent of non-black children versus 28 percent of black children had ever experienced poverty).

25. Ibid., 30.

26. Jeanne Brooks-Gunn et al., "Do Neighborhoods Influence Child Adolescent Behavior?" *American Journal of Sociology* 99 (1994): 353. See generally Jeanne Brooks-Gunn, Greg J. Duncan, and J. Lawrence Aber, eds., *Neighborhood Poverty* (New York: Russell Sage, 1997).

27. Bill Gillham et al., "Unemployment Rates, Single Parent Density, and Indices of Child Poverty: Their Relationship to Different Categories of Child Abuse and Neglect," *Child Abuse and Neglect* 22 (1998): 88.

28. See Mark E. Courtney et al., "Race and Child Welfare Services: Past Research and Future Directions," *Child Welfare* 75 (1998): 99, 101–07.

29. Toshio Tatara, "Overview of Child Abuse and Neglect," in Everett et al., *Child Welfare*, 187, 190.

30. Hampton, "Child Abuse," 222; Robert L. Hampton, "Race, Ethnicity, and Child Maltreatment: An Analysis of Cases Recognized and Reported by Hospitals," in Robert R. Staples, ed., *The Black Family: Essays and Studies*, 3d ed. (Belmont, Calif.: Wadsworth, 1986), 172.

31. R. J. Gelles and C. P. Cornell, *Intimate Violence in Families* (Beverly Hills, Calif.: Sage, 1985), 56.

32. Courtney et al., "Race and Child Welfare Services," 105–7.

33. National Association of Public Child Welfare Administrators, *Guidelines for a Model System of Child Protective Services for Abused and Neglected Children and Their Families* (Washington, D.C.: American Public Welfare Association, 1988), 23.

34. Carol C. Williams, "Expanding the Options in the Quest for Permanence," in Everett et al., *Child Welfare*, 266, 273.

35. Carol B. Stack, "Cultural Perspectives on Child Welfare," *New York University Review of Law and Social Change* 12 (1983–84): 539, 541.

36. E. P. Martin and J. M. Martin, *The Black Extended Family* (Chicago: University of Chicago Press, 1978).

37. Stack, "Cultural Perspectives," 12.

38. Appell, "Protecting Children," 586. See also James Goodman, ed., *Dynamics of Racism in Social Work Practice* (Washington, D.C.: National Association of Social Workers, 1973).

39. Randall Kennedy, "Suspect Policy," *New Republic*, Sept. 13 & 20, 1999, 30, 32–33.

40. Ibid., 33.

41. Courtney et al., "Race and Child Welfare Services," 130.

42. Rank, "The Racial Injustice of Poverty," 97 (noting that "[t]he odds of black Americans experiencing affluence versus poverty are approximately one to twenty-five versus the one to one odds of all Americans").

43. Dalton Conley, *Being Black, Living in the Red: Race, Wealth, and Social Policy in America* (Berkeley: University of California Press, 1999), 152.

44. Andrew Billingsley and Jeanne M. Giovannoni, *Children of the Storm: Black Children and American Child Welfare* (New York: Harcourt Brace Jovanovich, 1972), 4.

45. Martha A. Fineman, *The Neutered Mother, The Sexual Family, and Other Twentieth Century Tragedies* (New York: Routledge, 1995); Gwendolyn Mink, *Welfare's End* (Ithaca, N.Y.: Cornell University Press, 1998).

46. Children's Defense Fund, *Black and White Children.*

47. Billingsley and Giovannoni, *Children of the Storm*, 5; Lindsey, *The Welfare of Children.*

48. Comments of Ann Hartman to Carol B. Stack, "Social Policy and Practice," in Sylvia Sims Gray, Ann Hartman, and Ellen S. Saalberg, eds., *Empowering the Black Family: A Roundtable Discussion with Ann Hartman, James Leigh, Jacquelynn Moffett, Elaine Pinderhughes, Barbara Solomon, and Carol Stack* (Ann Arbor, Mich.: National Child Welfare Training Center, 1985), 21, 26.

49. The U.S. Supreme Court recognized similarities between proceedings to terminate parental rights and criminal trials. See *Lassiter v. Dep't of Social Services,* 452 U.S. 18 (1981) (holding that parents have a due process right to counsel in complex proceedings to terminate parental rights); *Santosky v. Kramer,* 455 U.S. 745 (1982) (holding that termination of parental rights must be justified by clear and convincing evidence). See also Pelton, "Child Abuse and Neglect," 118–25 (criticizing the dual role of child protection services, which are directed to both investigate and help impoverished families).

50. Billingsley and Giovannoni, *Children of the Storm,* 215.

51. See generally Gwendolyn Mink, ed., *Whose Welfare?* (Ithaca, N.Y.: Cornell University Press, 1999).

52. Adoption and Safe Families Act of 1997, Pub. L. No. 105-89, 111 Stat. 2115 (1997) (codified in scattered sections of 42 U.S.C.). See "Cheers for New Law on Adoptions," *New York Times,* Nov. 20, 1997, A27.

53. See Children's Defense Fund, *The State of America's Children* (Boston: Beacon, 1998), 66.

54. I elaborate this argument in Dorothy E. Roberts, "Is There Justice in Children's Rights? The Critique of Federal Family Preservation Policy," *University of Pennsylvania Journal of Constitutional Law* 2 (Dec. 1999): 112–40.

55. See, e.g., *Santosky v. Kramer,* 455 U.S. 745, 753 (1982).

56. I discuss degrading images of black mothers more fully in Dorothy Roberts, *Killing the Black Body: Race, Reproduction, and the Meaning of Liberty* (New York: Pantheon, 1997), 8–21.

57. bell hooks, *Ain't I a Woman: Black Women and Feminism* (Boston: South End, 1981), 84–85. See also Deborah Gray White, *Ar'n't I a Woman? Female Slaves in the Plantation South* (New York: Norton, 1985), 46–61 (describing the image of Mammy and how it fit within the cult of domesticity).

58. Michael P. Johnson, "Smothered Slave Infants: Were Slave Mothers at Fault?" *Journal of Southern History* 47 (1981): 493.

59. Ibid., 493 (quoting South Carolina Mortality Schedules, 1850, Abbeville District).

60. Ibid., 508–20.

61. Roberts, *Killing the Black Body,* 154–59.

62. See, e.g., Cathy Trost, "Born to Lose: Babies of Crack Users Crowd Hospitals, Break Everybody's Heart," *Wall Street Journal,* July 18, 1989, A1.

63. Office of Planning and Policy Research, U.S. Dept of Labor, *The Negro Family: The Case for National Action* (Washington, D.C.: Office of Planning and Policy Research, U.S. Dept of Labor, 1965), 5, 29.

64. Carrie Teegardin, "Single with Children," *Atlanta Journal and Constitution,* May 7, 1995, 6G.

65. Lee Smith, "The New Wave of Illegitimacy," *Fortune,* April 18, 1994, 81; Tamar Lewin, "Creating Fathers out of Men with Children," *New York Times,* June 18, 1995, A1.

66. Charles Murray, "The Coming White Underclass," *Wall Street Journal,* Oct. 29, 1993, A14.

67. William Julius Wilson, *The Truly Disadvantaged: The Inner City, the Underclass, and Public Policy* (Chicago: University of Chicago Press, 1987).

68. Donna M. Bishop and Charles E. Frazier, "Race Effects on Juvenile Justice Decision-Making: Findings of a Statewide Analysis," *Journal of Criminal Law and Criminology* 86 (1996): 407.

69. Ibid., 409.

70. Ibid.

71. Ibid.

72. Ibid., 409–10.

73. Charles Murray, *Losing Ground: American Social Policy, 1950–1980* (New York: Basic Books, 1984), 154–66.

74. See Dorothy E. Roberts, "Irrationality and Sacrifice in the Welfare Reform Consensus," *Virginia Law Review* 81 (1995): 2607.

75. See Roberts, *Killing the Black Body,* 202–45.

76. See *Wyman v. James,* 400 U.S. 309 (1971) (holding that the Fourth Amendment does not protect welfare recipients from mandatory, unannounced home inspections by government caseworkers).

77. Martha L. Fineman, "Images of Mothers in Poverty Discourses," *Duke Law Journal* 1991 (1991): 274; Dorothy E. Roberts, "The Value of Black Mothers' Work," *Connecticut Law Review* 26 (1994): 871, 873–74.

78. Contrary to Larry Mead's interpretation of my argument in Chapter 4 of this volume, I am asking a moral question about undisputed empirical evidence of a gross racial disparity in the child welfare system. Although this racial discrimination may not be as intentional as Jim Crow laws, it nevertheless inflicts a group-based harm on black Americans. The disproportionate number of black children in foster care is the "smoking gun"; my objective is to demonstrate its injustice.

79. *Santosky v. Kramer.*

80. 262 U.S. 400 (1923).

81. See *Pierce v. Society of Sisters,* 268 U.S. 510, 534 (1925) (invalidating an Oregon law that required parents to send their children to public school because it "unreasonably interferes with the liberty of parents and guardians to direct the upbringing and education of children under their control").

82. See Eamonn Callan, *Creating Citizens: Political Education and Liberal Democracy* (New York: Clarendon, 1997), 143.

83. See Joseph Goldstein, Anna Freud, and Albert J. Solnit, *Beyond the Best Interests of the Child* (New York: Free Press, 1979), 32–34.

84. Peggy Cooper Davis and Gautum Barua, "Custodial Choices for Children at Risk: Bias, Sequentiality, and the Law," *University of Chicago Law School Roundtable* 2 (1995): 139, 141–42.

85. Jurgen Habermas, "Multiculturalism and the Liberal State," *Stanford Law Review* 47 (1995): 849.

86. See Stephen Jay Gould, *The Mismeasure of Man* (New York: Norton, 1981); A. Leon Higginbotham, Jr., *In the Matter of Color: Race and the American Legal Process* (New York: Oxford University Press, 1978); Arthur K. Spears, *Race and Ideology: Language, Symbolism and Popular Culture* (Detroit, Mich.: Wayne State University Press, 1999).

87. See *Loving v. Virginia,* 388 U.S. 1 (1967) (holding laws forbidding interracial marriage unconstitutional).

88. See Cheryl Harris, "Whiteness as Property," *Harvard Law Review* 106 (1993): 1707 (detailing the evolution of the concept of whiteness as a valuable property interest).

89. Cornel West, *Race Matters* (Boston: Beacon, 1993), 85–86.

90. "Angry Father Danny Glover Files Complaint against Taxis," *Chicago Tribune,* Nov. 4, 1999, C2.

91. Conley, *Being Black,* 7–13.

92. Ibid., 25–53.

93. Dawson, *Behind the Mule,* 56.

94. See generally Gerald Early, ed., *Lure and Loathing: Essays on Race, Identity, and the Ambivalence of Assimilation* (New York: Allen Lane, 1994) (a collection of essays by twenty black intellectuals pondering the shaping of black Americans' identity).

95. David Gordon Nielson, *Black Ethos: Northern Urban Negro Life and Thought,* 1890–1930 (Westport, Conn.: Greenwood, 1977).

96. Dawson, *Behind the Mule,* 45–68.

97. Ibid., 45.

98. Ibid., 61.

99. Ibid., 77–78.

100. Orlando Patterson, *Slavery and Social Death: A Comparative Study* (Cambridge, Mass.: Harvard University Press, 1982), 189–90.

101. Malcolm X and Alex Haley, *The Autobiography of Malcolm X* (New York: Grove, 1965), 21–22.

102. Peggy Cooper Davis, *Neglected Stories: The Constitution and Family Values* (New York: Hill and Wang, 1997), 81–166.

103. Ibid., 82.

104. Presentation by Maisha Hamilton Bennett, Seminar on Current Controversies in Child Welfare Policy, Northwestern University School of Law, Chicago, Sept. 7, 1999.

105. Ibid.

106. Jane Mansbridge, "Using Power/Fighting Power: The Polity," in Seyla Benhabib, ed., *Democracy and Difference: Contesting the Boundaries of the Political* (Princeton, N.J.: Princeton University Press, 1996), 46, 58.

107. Jacqueline Jones, *Labor of Love, Labor of Sorrow: Black Women, Work, and the Family from Slavery to the Present* (New York: Vintage, 1986), 12–13.

108. Angela Y. Davis, *Women, Race and Class* (New York: Vintage, 1983), 17, quoting Angela Y. Davis, "The Black Woman's Role in the Community of Slaves," *Black Scholar* 3 (Dec. 1971). Davis amended this statement to acknowledge that men also performed domestic tasks important to the slave community.

109. Alice Walker, "One Child of One's Own: A Meaningful Digression within the Work(s)," *Ms.*, Aug. 1979, 47, 75.

110. Dorothy E. Roberts, "Motherhood and Crime," *Iowa Law Review* 95 (1993): 130–6.

111. Ibid., 133–34.

112. For a similar point, see Larry May, *The Morality of Groups: Collective Responsibility, Group-Based Harm, and Corporate Rights* (Notre Dame, Ind.: Notre Dame University Press, 1987). Philosopher Larry May criticizes the dualistic conception of rights and justice that divides into two models—an individualistic model that sees only harms to individuals and a collectivist model that attaches rights to groups, with individuals holding only derivative rights. He develops an intermediate category of group-based rights, which are rights the individual obtains by virtue of being a member of a group.

113. National Association of Black Social Workers, "Position Paper Developed from Workshops Concerning Transracial Adoption," reprinted in Rita J. Simon and Howard Alstein, *Transracial Adoption* (New York: John Wiley, 1977), 50. See also National Black Heritage Child Welfare Act proposed in 1986 as amendment to Indian Child Welfare Act of 1978.

114. 25 U.S.C.S. § 1911.

115. Bruce A. Boyer and Steven Lubet, "The Kidnapping of Edgardo Mortara: Contemporary Lessons in the Child Welfare Wars," *Villanova Law Review* 45 (2000): 245, 269–70; *Mississippi Band of Choctaw Indians v. Holyfield*, 490 U.S. 30 (1989).

116. Tony Buti, "Removal of Indigenous Children from Their Families in Australia: The History" (paper presented at the conference "Fam-

ilies in an Open Society: A Proposal to Develop the Theoretical Foundations," New York University, New York, May 7, 1999); Philip Shenon, "Bitter Aborigines Are Suing for Stolen Childhoods," *New York Times,* July 20, 1995, A4.

117. A. Haebich, *For Their Own Good* (Perth: University of Western Australia Press, 1988); Human Rights and Equal Opportunity Commission, *Bringing Them Home: National Inquiry into the Separation of Aboriginal and Torres Strait Islander Children from Their Families* (Canberra: Australian Government Printing Service, April 1997).

118. *Family Law Review* 19 (1995): 594, 602.

119. See, e.g., Rita J. Simon and Howard Altstein, *Transracial Adoptees and Their Families* (New York: Praeger, 1987); Elizabeth Bartholet, *Family Bonds: Adoption and the Politics of Parenting* (Boston: Houghton Mifflin, 1993).

120. 42 U.S.C.S. § 622.

121. Elizabeth Bartholet, "Where Do Black Children Belong? The Politics of Race Matching in Adoption," *University of Pennsylvania Law Review* 139 (1991): 1163, 1180.

122. Dorothy E. Roberts, "Kinship and the Price of State Support for Children," *Chicago-Kent Law Review* 76 (2001): 1619, 1620.

123. National Association of Black Social Workers, "Position Paper."

124. See Twila L. Perry, "The Transracial Adoption Controversy: An Analysis of Discourse and Subordination," *Review of Law and Social Change* 21 (1993–94): 33.

125. Ibid., 53.

126. Courtney et al., "Race and Child Welfare Services," 130.

127. Larry May, "Adoption, Race, and Group-Based Harm," *Washington University Journal of Law and Policy* 1 (1999): 77, 82. This essay is a response to my presentation "Poverty, Race, and New Directions in Child Welfare Policy," *Washington University Journal of Law and Policy* 1 (1999): 63.

128. May, "Adoption, Race," 82–83.

129. I am not arguing that the state should refrain from facilitating adoptions of black children in foster care, but rather that these adoptions do not correct the child welfare system's most serious racial harms.

4

IS COMPLAINT A MORAL ARGUMENT?

LAWRENCE M. MEAD

In her essay "The Child Welfare System's Racial Harm," Roberts attacks the fairness of the child welfare system. She starts with the fact that the families involved in this system are disproportionately black. That is, more black parents have their children taken away by the authorities on grounds of child abuse or neglect than parents from other racial groups. The disproportion, Roberts claims, reflects racism. Either black families are unfairly accused of child abuse, or they are driven into it by unusual levels of poverty. Their economic need is itself due to the background racism of the society. Aside from the harm to individuals, the black face of child welfare damages the standing of blacks as a group, thus weakening their ability to resist racism. So society should take steps to reduce this unequal intervention in black families.

As a specialist in social policy, I often read arguments like this. A substantial group of scholars in such fields as public policy, social work, and law-and-society makes cases like Roberts's, although they may write about some other disadvantaged group, such as Hispanics, women, or the poor. Their argument proceeds in the same three steps. Identify a condition where the group in question has unusually bad outcomes, for instance in education, income, or access to desirable jobs. Attribute the disadvantage to social unfairness, either racism, sexism, or indifference to the needy. Then call for redress in the name of equality. Roberts's essay is actually quite a good example of this genre. It is well written and interesting.

But I have a problem with the genre. The authors of such papers imagine, like Roberts, that they are making a moral indictment that deserves political attention. I don't think they are. What does it take to argue for redress of a social inequity in a manner relevant to politics? One has to show that (1) the inequity actually occurred, (2) doing something about it is in the general interest, and (3) government is able to do something about it. In my view, Roberts doesn't do any of these things. Indeed, she doesn't seriously try to do them. So this is not a moral argument relevant to politics or academic discourse. It is instead a complaint that belongs in the courts or private life.

Consider in turn the three standards I have suggested for a moral argument.[1]

I. The Reality Test

The most important test is the first. Are blacks actually wronged by the current child welfare system? Nobody doubts that they are overrepresented in it, as they are also in the criminal justice system and in society's other remedial institutions. That fact raises a political issue, however, only if some mistreatment by the society is to blame. Roberts says racism is to blame, and her argument depends on that assertion. For suppose that the overinvolvement of blacks in child welfare were *not* caused by racism. That would imply that black families actually do abuse or neglect their families more often than other parents. There would then be no serious case to reduce the black presence. For to do this would imply that black parents who mistreated their children should not be held to the normal standards of the society and that their children should not get the normal protection.

Roberts offers no serious evidence that inequity occurs. She does not show that child welfare authorities discriminate against blacks. She rehearses the invidious images of black mothers that she says prevail in the culture, but she does not show that child welfare officials think this way. We do not know that they take black children away without cause or that they believe that blacks are incompetent parents. Nor can she show clear statistical evidence that race influences whether a family loses its children, controlling for other factors; the studies, she says, are equivocal. So she never proves that child welfare actually wrongs blacks—at least at the level of individual cases.

Some of what Roberts says is clearly false, and this weakens her case. For instance, she says that the recent national welfare reform cut benefits to the recipients and caused harm to families by demanding that mothers work. Indeed, more mothers have had to work, but the cuts were mainly in benefits for aliens, and most of these were later reversed. The cash benefits families receive were not cut; many states have actually raised them, by raising work incentives. They do this because, when more recipients work, they appear more deserving. While the recent fall in the caseload has cut spending on welfare overall, it has sharply increased the amount states can spend on the remaining cases. Welfare mothers who go to work usually have higher incomes than before. More limited evidence suggests that families and children are usually better off too. While there are some hardship cases, the consequences of the reform overall have been remarkably positive.[2]

Roberts's case is also weakened by the limited research behind it. She has apparently not done her own studies of why blacks are overrepresented in child welfare. Rather, she cites the studies of others, and they do not clearly support her. When she quotes child welfare officials, they do not sound like racists. They say, more in sorrow than anger, that they cannot locate families able to take care of many black children, so they have to take them into custody. Roberts dismisses views that black families neglect children as "myths." She quotes scholars who believe that the authorities overlook the shared parenting that occurs among black adults, in and out of a family. Thus black children who appear to lack parenting actually are taken care of. How do we know who is right here? I am inclined to believe the officials because they operate closer to reality than academic critics. But we do not know.

A. Why There Is Doubt

It is a mistake to believe that Roberts ever could establish racism as the cause of the black predominance in child welfare. Nor can conservatives, as they sometimes think, disprove the charges of mistreatment brought by Roberts and others on the left. I have spent years trying to prove that social barriers do not prevent adults on welfare from working. I think the literature on poverty implies this, and I have done my own studies of welfare work programs to demonstrate it. My results show that whether welfare mothers work depends mainly on whether they are expected to work, not on their employability or the labor market.[3] But I obtain only grudging agreement from other experts who believe in barriers.

The reason is that the causes of social problems today are deeply contestable. That is true of all the problems in which blacks are heavily involved—not only child abuse but homelessness, drug addiction, and school failure. In all these cases, all we know for sure is that racial groups are involved in these problems at very different rates. We do not know why. Is it because the groups actually behave differently, causing some to fall foul of social authority more often than others? Or is it because of bias hidden in the institutions? And even if lifestyle differences are the immediate cause, these may themselves be traceable to the background unfairness of the society. Roberts tacitly concedes that many black parents who lose their children do abuse or neglect them. But she blames this mostly on the fact that they are poor, because poor people encounter child welfare more often than the better-off. And black poverty she blames in turn on the society. It is the result of centuries of denial of equal opportunity to blacks.

Others easily take a different view. Social problems today may have multiple causes, and the priority among them is unclear. Roberts posits that racism leads to black poverty, which in turn raises black exposure to child welfare. But one could equally argue that both poverty and child abuse result from the family's inability to cope. If that trait is more common among blacks than other groups, then more blacks than others will have social problems. Racist reactions in the society might then be the *result* of unusual social problems among blacks, rather than the cause.

Social scientists claim to research these issues quantitatively, but numbers do not yield agreement. Not all forces bearing on disadvantaged groups can be quantified. Even if they could be, all one knows for sure is that various influences are correlated with the problem. Which ones are causal, and in what sequence, must be settled on theoretical grounds. Thus any statistical model can be challenged. If one is determined, there is always some way to project the causes of social problems onto the environment. And again, even if one admits that people are poor or dependent initially because of behavior (e.g., unwed pregnancy, nonwork), one can refer these patterns back to social deprivations in prior generations, as Roberts and others do. But the contrary reading, where behavioral problems cause social problems and hence racism, is also plausible.

Please note: I am not saying that the black disproportion in child welfare is *not* due to racism, as Roberts claims. I am not making a counterclaim. I am simply saying that, in the nature of things, cases like this cannot be proven, so they cannot be a fair basis for a general moral argument.

B. Identity-Neutral Evidence

The causes of injustice used to be clearer. To say that the facts about a social condition are clear means not only that the condition itself is apparent but that at least its immediate causes are agreed. Under Jim Crow, for instance, dual water fountains used to stand in southern towns, one for each race. It was clear not only that the fountains existed but who put them there—segregationist local authorities. Similarly, it is clear today that the military discriminates against gay soldiers, and who is responsible for that. In these cases, the evidence for discrimination is what I call identity-neutral. That is, it is clear that bias has occurred, *whatever one assumes about the behavior* of the victims or oppressors.

But in today's society, obvious oppressions like this have largely been reformed away. It is now much harder to establish that injustices occur without making contestable presumptions about behavior. In the child welfare case, the evidence for inequity is not at all identity-neutral, and the same is true of other social problems. The condition of black overrepresentation is clear, but the causes, even the most immediate, are not. The racial disproportion might be due to inequity by the authorities, but it may also reflect an actual problem in black behavior. The same is true for other social problems in which blacks are disproportionately involved.

To prove an inequity, one needs a "smoking gun"—evidence that clearly fixes responsibility without a need for behavioral assumptions. For Roberts and others like her, that means evidence that the authorities discriminate independent of actual misbehavior by the victims. That is the evidence that the dual water fountains used to provide. For their part, conservatives who defend the society look for signs that people who misbehave "choose" to do so from a position of autonomy, rather than being pushed into it by adverse social forces. But smoking guns are scarce. Generally, either side has to infer behavior from the evidence in contestable ways. Positions cannot be called clearly true or false. One can only say that they are reasonable or unreasonable.

I think that these opposed interpretations ultimately hinge on different views of the identity of the disadvantaged group in question. Are they vulnerable sufferers who are overwhelmed by an unjust society, as the left assumes, a view that minimizes their own agency and responsibility for their predicament? Or are they amoral calculators who exploit the society and only pose as victims, as conservatives assume, a view that maximizes their agency and responsibility?[4] All we know for sure is that people have behaved dysfunctionally in the face of social pressures. We cannot from this fact alone determine the psychology that produced the behavior, or whether the pressures were normal or extreme. So social problems can always be blamed on either the society or the individual.

C. Incivility

I think this sort of argument ought to be excluded from moral and political discourse, whatever view one takes of the merits. The reason is that dispute over the facts defeats all dialogue.

Arguments like Roberts's may or may not be true, but they are certainly abusive. They are contestable at such a level that they become uncivil. A civil argument is one to which one's hearers have a reasonable chance to respond. To claim racism is a trump card to which a civil reply is impossible. It creates an intellectual fait accompli that forecloses challenge. This spares Roberts the burden of making any serious case for her conclusion.

Only when the present facts are agreed is it possible to have a truly moral or political discussion of a social problem. In the cases of Jim Crow or gays in the military, the facts of discrimination are indeed clear. The issue then is not what is happening or why but whether it is moral or constitutional. That is a debate in which an author and his or her audience could fairly engage. In disputes about contemporary racism and equal opportunity, however, the facts are decidedly unclear. One side claims that there is racism, the other not, and a moral discourse can never even begin.[5] So far as Roberts appeals to ordinary discrimination, that is reason enough to keep her argument, and others like it, out of the public forum.

To make a civil argument, Roberts would have to argue on some basis that did not require contestable presumptions about bias. In the latter part of her essay, she begins to do this. She says (note 78) that her "smoking gun" is simply black overrepresentation in the child welfare system. This fact alone, she says, establishes a "group-based harm" that exists even if no inequity in individual cases can be shown. Disproportionate intervention in black families denies them essential rights and impugns their reputation in the society, thus undercutting their resistance to racism. Roberts makes no contestable assumptions here, about either black parents or the authorities. The racial disproportion may not be identity-neutral evidence for inequitable treatment, but it is identity-neutral evidence for unequal group outcomes.

This argument does not create a fait accompli. Roberts's hearers can respond by making different *moral* judgments, as against reading the facts differently. For this reason, she now has to bear the burden of an argument. But are her assertions about group-based rights reasonable? This leads to my second test.

II. The Generality Test

Even if an injury is shown, is there a general interest in doing anything about it? A moral argument must show this if it is to be relevant to politics. We would readily see a broad interest in changing the black face of child welfare if it reflected racism at the individual level. Society has already decided that bias in this sense is wrong. In that case, to give blacks redress is only to implement that judgment. This vindicates norms of impartiality in which everyone has an interest. If redress depends on asserting group rights for blacks, however, the case is untenable. For this seems to say that the authorities should treat blacks no worse than other groups whether they mistreat their children worse or not. That appears to argue for black privilege rather than redress.

In arguing that the black disproportion violates essential rights, Roberts offers Supreme Court cases and constitutional reasonings that reject "undue" interference in black families. But the intervention is "undue," presumably, only if children are taken away without cause. That takes us back to the claims of specific mistreatment that Roberts cannot prove. She admits that to limit intervention might expose some black children to danger, a fear raised by Larry May. She then can defend her case only by claiming that some black children are taken from homes "unnecessarily," which again resurrects contestable claims of individual mistreatment.

The argument that blacks deserve an unsullied reputation to strengthen their political standing is equally dubious. Perhaps lightening the face of child welfare would be in the interests of blacks. But why should it be in the general interest? *General* here implies a community including people besides blacks. What do *they* gain from privileging the black group in this way? Roberts offers no answer. I am not saying that it would *not* be in the general interest to help blacks, but one cannot just assume this. Blacks cannot just appropriate the interests of whites as if they were the same as their own. Whites are entitled to some appeal to *their* interests, apart from the benefits to blacks. That case might be that helping blacks would reduce other social problems.

Academic claims on behalf of other disadvantaged groups—other minorities, women, the poor—often have this same narrow character. In judging the morality of actions, only the interests of the victims count for anything. There is no moral argument of the kind that politics should involve an attempt to redefine and elevate the entire community. Such confined discourse makes moral sense only if the nonvictims are clearly responsible for the disadvantage. Again, under current conditions, that might be true, but it cannot be shown. Such an appeal also makes no political sense, for it involves calling on the oppressors themselves to undo oppression. If whites are racists, there is no point in appealing to them for redress; if they are not, then blacks probably have not suffered any inequity in the first place.

III. The Policy Test

A serious moral argument, finally, must show that there is something government could do to accomplish redress. In this instance, is there some practical way to reduce the current disproportion of blacks in child welfare? Roberts is sure that the predominance ought to be reduced, but not sure of how. She recognizes that it will not do simply to stop enforcing child welfare standards—black children would be too much at risk.

Instead, she speaks vaguely of how society should spend more "state resources" on the victims. If poverty is the immediate cause of black overexposure to child welfare, the solution is to make black families less poor. Roberts alleges that some children are taken away solely because the family is needy. Rather than disrupting families, government should be "ensuring the health and welfare of families" and also "dealing with the systemic problems" that are the real "causes of child neglect." This suggests enriching the income and benefits that many black families already draw from social programs.

Roberts, like many theorists on the left, imagines that the main barrier to a better social policy is public indifference. Comfortable white America doesn't want to spend money on poor blacks, whom it considers "undeserving." Public opinion studies suggest, rather, that the main impediment is getting the poor who receive aid to make more effort on their own behalf. The public wants government to help the poor, but it also wants poor adults to help themselves. Public effort and individual effort are seen as complements, not opposites as intellectuals tend to see them. If poor adults work, they are seen as more deserving of public support, not less. That feeling explains why stronger work requirements are the main theme of recent welfare reforms.[6] Helping the *working* poor is popular. Aid is not eliminated but refounded on a new social contract.[7]

The last thirty years make clear that merely to spend more money on the poor accomplishes little. Poverty is rarely, as Roberts implies, simply imposed on blacks by an unjust society. While social factors play a role, poverty among the working-aged and their children is usually due in the first instance to single parenthood and low work levels among poor parents, both the mothers and absent fathers. This is true even if, again, one refers these behaviors back to social causes. Even if society were willing simply to give money to the poor, that would do little to assuage the family problems Roberts is talking about. Instead, aid must be combined with structure—demands that aided families adopt constructive behaviors as a condition of support. Directive programs that do this have appeared in several areas of antipoverty policy—child support enforcement, homelessness, education, drug addiction. Work tests in welfare are only the most visible instance.[8]

Roberts seems to know nothing of this. She wants to resurrect the failed social policy of the 1960s and 1970s. The main problem with the Great Society was not that it spent too much on the poor but that it did so permissively, expecting next to no effort from them in return. If government did what Roberts wants, it would probably have to take away nearly as many black children from families as it does now, and the black face of child welfare would endure. In contrast, the current, more directive welfare policies appear to have *reduced* child abuse.[9]

IV. A Complaint, Not a Judgment

By my standards, Roberts has made no serious moral case for her position. There is no way she could have. All arguments of this kind face serious difficulties today. The standards I have suggested for moral argument are only common sense, but they have become tough to satisfy. I do not deny that, in the current society, some individuals still suffer injustice, in child welfare and elsewhere. They should obtain redress. But it is very difficult to prove that an entire group suffers inequity without assuming things about behavior and asserting values that can be dismissed out of hand.

We should instead see Roberts's argument as a complaint. By this I mean a simple appeal to some trusted authority to save the complainant from an adversity. Such appeals rest not on moral argument but on the complainant's relationship with the authority. Roberts says in essence that society is hurting blacks in child welfare, and that it should stop. That statement makes no moral argument; instead, it *presumes* such an argument. A true moral argument establishes a new order. Roberts, rather, takes for granted an old order—the regime of racial protection that was established by civil rights.

In a moral argument, the philosopher bears the burden of establishing the new value. With a complaint, rather, the onus shifts to him or her to whom the complaint is brought. This authority is supposed to solve the problem *for* the victims. Roberts uses cynical, antigovernment rhetoric, but in truth she trusts the regime. So do most blacks, and they have reason to. Government has been the main instrument of their advancement ever since emancipation. Roberts calls the authorities oppressors, but her demands on them imply the opposite. She ridicules the presumption of child welfare, that the solutions to black family problems "lie in the institutions of the larger white society." But she makes exactly the same presumption.

She could hardly do otherwise. The United States has already reformed away the most obvious social inequities of the past, including those surrounding race. We already have civil rights—even affirmative action—and a welfare state. So it is inevitable today that reformers find fewer new moral purposes to proclaim than they did forty or fifty years ago. Their claims become more limited. Groups that already have protections ask for better implementation of their rights. That is what Roberts wants. New groups—gays, the handicapped—demand the same rights.

Injustices today will seldom be obvious in the manner of the dual water fountains. When they occur, they will be buried in the bowels of bureaucracies that, in their formal purposes, are enlightened. The evidence for mistreatment will seldom be identity-neutral. Every outcome that one might attribute to racism or sexism can also be attributed to the behavior of the victims. This is the kind of inequity Roberts is talking about. The denials of the child welfare system simply are not of the same order as keeping blacks from registering to vote in Selma. It will be easy to contest the reality of injustice and the wisdom or the practicality of redress.

The claims are more and more empirical, less and less about principle. Roberts's case turns mostly on whether there actually is mistreatment in black child welfare. All other issues pale in comparison. That is why such disputes are inappropriate for settings keyed to general discussion. Since they present no serious argument about morals or utility, they deserve no place in an academic forum or political debate. There is no large issue here that citizens, legislators, or philosophers need to discuss. The issue comes down simply and only to whether black families actually are abused.

Such questions are private, not public. They belong in the courts, not in politics or the academic world. Here is where their truth can be tested, as it cannot be in the academic forum. Political or moral debate works best when the facts are clear and values in dispute. The judicial system presumes, on the contrary, that facts are in question rather than values. The courts are designed precisely to determine whether *in fact* agreed values have been infringed. The law states standards, and trials address whether defendants have violated them. Roberts's complaint is already suitlike in character. She has not made a moral judgment against the society. Rather, she has libeled it. She alleges that it violates norms of fairness that it has already accepted. No political or academic setting is likely to push her to prove her case. In court, she would have to.

It is not an accident that many allegations of injustice that have this concrete character begin or end up as lawsuits. If the charges are proven, they become more credible. Verdicts in courts establish the evidence for actual mistreatment as general argument or research can never do. The limitation is that verdicts apply only to individual cases. It takes many such cases to build an identity-neutral argument to change policy. And even when policy is changed, the effect is largely to affirm old public values, not to establish new ones. Institutions and practices are reformed, but the role of government is unlikely to change.

The other proper arena for complaint is simply private life. When friends or family members come into conflict, the reason is almost always some concrete friction, not great issues of principle. People allege damage and demand redress in the same tone as Roberts's, absent the moral pretenses. And this is appropriate. The feature of private life is that people know each other well. They are able to assess the empirical claims that complaint involves. In public life, however, such claims are disruptive. Citizens rarely know each other well, so they cannot assess the sort of concrete charges that Roberts makes. Such claims only become an apple of discord, rendering discourse impossible.

I don't mean that complaint has no place in the political order. Courts and legislative committees legitimately ask whether the nation's principles are fully implemented. They might well be interested in the sort of claims Roberts makes. She ought to write a brief for them. But hers is not a general argument that is worthy of academic or political attention.

NOTES

1. The following summarizes a longer argument that I make in "The Politics of Complaint," a paper that I recently presented at Boston University and Yale and, in an earlier form, at Princeton. For a preliminary statement, see Lawrence M. Mead, "The Politics of Disadvantage," *Society* 35, no. 5 (1998): 72-76.

2. For a summary, see Ron Haskins, "Effects of Welfare Reform on Family Income and Poverty," in *The New World of Welfare,* ed. Rebecca Blanka and Ron Haskins (Washington, D.C.: Brookings, 2001), chap. 4.

3. Lawrence M. Mead, *The New Politics of Poverty: The Nonworking Poor in America* (New York: Basic Books, 1992).

4. Lawrence M. Mead, "Conflicting Worlds of Welfare Reform," *First Things,* no. 75 (August/September 1997): 15-17.

5. Amy Gutmann and Dennis Thompson, *Democracy and Disagreement* (Cambridge, Mass.: Harvard University Press, 1996), discuss moral conflict in democratic politics persuasively, but they downplay conflict over social facts, which I find more intractable and uncivil.

6. Martin Gilens, *Why Americans Hate Welfare: Race, Media, and the Politics of Antipoverty Policy* (Chicago: University of Chicago Press, 1999), chaps. 2, 8-9.

7. Lawrence M. Mead, *Beyond Entitlement: The Social Obligations of Citizenship* (New York: Free Press, 1986).

8. Lawrence M. Mead, ed., *The New Paternalism: Supervisory Approaches to Poverty* (Washington, D.C.: Brookings, 1997).

9. Somini Sengupta, "No Rise in Child Abuse Seen in Welfare Shift," *New York Times,* August 10, 2000, A1, B8.

5

COMMENTS ON DOROTHY ROBERTS'S "THE CHILD WELFARE SYSTEM'S RACIAL HARM"

EVA FEDER KITTAY

I. Prologue

As I compose my thoughts concerning Dorothy Roberts's article "The Child Welfare System's Racial Harm," I spy two robins who hover over a nest they have built outside my window in the pergola that frames my garden. These two shuttle back and forth unceasingly procuring food and carrying it in their beaks for their new offspring. It seems odd that these benighted robins can take such good care of their young while we humans need a child welfare system to ensure that our own progeny are properly cared for.

My reveries recall to me a recurrent dream. I have given birth. The newborn of my dream looks more like a miniature child or adult than like a real baby. I resume my busy life, forget about the newborn, then suddenly remember that I neglected to feed the baby. I approach her and find that she's shrunk, becoming more like a small doll than a real infant. She is—or appears—lifeless. Distressed, I try to nurse her, to breathe life into her, but with each effort she grows smaller and still more lifeless until I abandon the effort altogether. She never actually dies—she just becomes a sad inert thing.

Commenting on this dream—not as a psychoanalyst, but as a reflective, coolly rational philosopher might—one could say that it is, in fact, remarkable that infants don't generally suffer the fate of my nocturnal-brain child. The young are a great deal of trouble, consuming much time and resources, as even the efforts of my robins attest. Without the active intervention of adults, they almost invariably die. When all available adults are consumed with other labor, rates of child mortality are shockingly high, as in prerevolutionary China, among African Americans under slavery, in South African townships under apartheid, and among the impoverished sugarcane workers of northeastern Brazil.[1]

When adults are available they do generally respond appropriately and effectively to the neediness of these helpless beings. Viewed in a certain light, this seems to be a miracle, for unlike interactions with peers, these interactions involve no give and take, no reciprocity or even expectation of reciprocity (except in some indefinite future). And unlike interactions with our superiors, they involve no compulsion: these small beings have no power to withhold goods or punish us. Yet we go to extraordinary lengths to accommodate them. Moreover, we suffer if we are denied the opportunity to do so.

In my dream, the miracle doesn't happen—I have other things to do and they take priority, with catastrophic consequences. In the waking nightmares of many women, the miracle is not permitted to happen: mothers are compelled to direct their labor elsewhere; mothers have their children taken from them; mothers are denied the means by which to respond or respond adequately.

Watching the robins, one could suppose that they respond by the unimpeded realization of their nature. Can we similarly point to nature as the reason we respond? The answer is inadequate for humans. Humans also abuse and neglect their children in conditions of relative freedom, and humans also care for and nurture children, their own and those of others, under conditions of relative unfreedom.

Neglect is a failure to respond—abuse is the wrong response—to the vulnerability of another. Care, neglect, and abuse, are, we might say, the three ethical possibilities in the face of dependent others. The dependent is vulnerable to my actions. What I would call the miracle of response, or we should say of a caring response, is an ethical possibility to respond to a dependent's vulnerability with care—a vulnerability that some experience as a call for their caring. Whether child abuse and neglect are universal features of human existence or are cultural constructs, like so much we once took to be "natural" or "universal," it is clear that when we speak of human response to vulnerable young beings, we, unlike my robins, are always in the realms of the ethical and social.

II. The Troubled Relation of Dependency and Racist Stereotypes

The historical record suggests that child abuse and neglect are cultural constructions.[2] Should we then conclude that there are different cultural conceptions of what constitutes neglect or abuse? Roberts's essay offers another understanding. On the one hand, there are social conditions under which child abuse and neglect, especially neglect, are more likely. This suggests that the behavior that comes to the attention of the authorities is in fact abusive or neglectful but would be avoidable, were the social conditions that facilitated the harm addressed adequately. On the other hand, cultural constructions regarding the mothering behavior of a subordinated group are imbricated in the judgments of the dominant group. It may be not the behavior of the mother but the interventions that are harmful to the child. Roberts argues that both situations pertain at once in the case of African American children who are brought into the child welfare system. Either way, harm is done to the children and the families whose lives are blighted by the experience of abuse or neglect, or the perception of such, that brings them into the system. Moreover the harm is not only to individuals or families; damage is also done to a group when that group is disproportionately represented in the child welfare system, as are African Americans. African Americans' history of slavery has been one in which families were disrupted, men and women were not permitted a legal union, and children were torn from their parents. Women mothered the children of other women, but were forced to part from their own. As Peggy Cooper Davis argues in *Neglected Stories,*[3] and as readings of slave narratives such as Harriet Jacobs's *Incidents in the Life of a Slave Girl*[4] confirm, the forceful separation of families, and especially of mothers and their children, may have been the single most vicious aspect of slavery.

The centrality of relations between an adult and a dependent child who is in their care is rarely countenanced by our political philosophies. Those who are denied the possibility of such relations perhaps most acutely feel its significance. Indeed, Roberts and Davis point out that the right to form autonomous families, inscribed in the Constitution through the Fourteenth Amendment, derives primarily from the denial of this right to slaves. Yet, as Roberts shows, the sad irony is that African Americans still face the disruption of family life, now in the guise of attending to the welfare of children. The twin evils of the increased likelihood of poverty for African American families and the stereotyping of black mothers as bad mothers combine with a problematic system of child welfare to bring about this result. I will suggest that our system of child welfare as well as its special impact on African Americans derives from a conception of dependency that obfuscates real relations to others and that fails African American families especially but also ill serves a society that holds fast to a fiction of the independence of the individual.

A child is a dependent—one dependent on the care of another with whom a sustained relation is not merely desirable, but necessary. Most modern political theories (and the actual systems they reflect in an idealized form) begin with an understanding of humans as independent of one another, held together primarily by advantageous alliances and by laws that prevent inevitable clashes of self-interest from erupting into violence. They do not take the inevitable dependency we have on one another, especially when we are in need of care, as a political matter. The subject of laws and of political theory is therefore the independent individual celebrated in liberal theory. But the child fits poorly into this picture. Is the child to be treated as a member of a unit or as an individual? Is its mother to be treated as an individual or as part of a unit?

A right of individuals to form autonomous families is one that embraces the child as well as the adult(s) in question. Taking the

Fourteenth Amendment seriously in conjunction with the belief that the child's fate needs to be tied to that of the family means treating the family as a whole and trying to keep the family together at all costs. Yet combining a child's vulnerability with a moralistic attitude toward the mother who is unable to sustain an economically viable autonomous family, and with a historic suspicion of the African American family, results in treating the child's welfare as independent of that of the mother (or other relative that takes primarily responsibility for the child's well-being), especially when the family in question is black. This has meant that the child welfare system has "whipsawed" between considering "the inordinate risks that children will be abused at the hands of their parents and inordinate risks that children will be subjected unnecessarily to the traumas of family separation and the inevitable deficiencies of public care."[5]

Addressing these conflicting demands, Professor Roberts points out that they can be related to three flaws in the system of child protection:

1. It places all responsibility for taking care of children on their parents, without taking into account the economic, political, and social constraints that prevent many parents from doing so.
2. This notion of state protection is activated only when families are already experiencing difficulty. The system is not designed to ensure the health and welfare of all families in the first place.
3. Because the system perceives the resulting harms to children as parental rather than societal failures, state intervention to protect children is punitive in nature.

Each of these flaws, I would claim, reflects the problematic nature of dependency. The question of dependency enters here in at least three ways. First, the child welfare system is about a dependent, for children are dependents—dependent on at least one caring adult. Second, as I argue at length elsewhere,[6] caring for those who are inevitably dependent (children, the significantly ill or impaired, the frail elderly) makes those who do the caring dependent on others for some degree of support. In devoting one's attention and resources to another who cannot care for him- or herself, one comes to be less capable of meeting one's own needs and requires a third party to help supply resources and effort to sustain both oneself and the one for whom one cares. Therefore those who care for persons who are *inevitably* dependent (dependency workers, as I call them) themselves become *derivatively* dependent on a larger social group to support them in their work caring for dependents. Finally, we are importantly and ineluctably interdependent economically once we are part of a society with any significant degree of complexity.

But this material interdependence is not the only way in which dependency pervades the life of even the most independently functioning adult. Our very identity is dependent not only on the definitions others force on us but also on the definitions placed on others by us and social groups with which we interact. It is well recognized that we cannot entirely escape the identities third persons attach to us, especially when these are given social and legal sanction. (Blacks could not dodge a black identity in the Jim Crow South, nor could Jews evade a Jewish identity under Nazism, regardless of what their choice of self-identification might have been.) But the importance of how the identity of the Other serves to form that of a dominant group is less well appreciated, especially by dominant groups themselves. Race theorists have begun to explore the ways in which white identity in the United States has been shaped by the "dreams, fears and idols" whites have projected onto blacks.[7] In this way, blacks have engaged in a particular kind of dependency work for whites.[8] The load of stereotypes African Americans have shouldered have permitted white Americans to congratulate themselves on being, if men, productive, hardworking, and virtuous citizens and, if women, sexually virtuous wives and good mothers. These three forms of dependency, the inevitable dependency of children, the derivative dependency of caregivers, and the dependency of identity, interact and come into play in all the flaws that Roberts spots.

Dependency also plays a prominent role in stereotypes of blacks. Above I did not mention the dependency that comes most readily to mind when the term *welfare* is uttered, and that is the presumably pernicious "welfare dependency" of the welfare queen. The term is infused with a racist stereotype of a black woman with multiple children parasitic on the hard-earned taxes of good working people. Nor have I mentioned the dependency of the slave on his master, a dependency used by whites to render slaves and later freed African Americans "childlike" and incapable of taking care of themselves without the intervention of whites. These can be seen as figuring prominently in the saga of the child welfare system and the group harm it effects.

These racial stereotypes along with the public's failure to acknowledge the multiple interdependencies that render "the independent individual" a chimera and the ways in which white identity depends on that foisted on blacks form a tangled set of (mis)understandings of dependency. A program geared to the welfare of dependents must be wary to steer clear of the distortions such ideas of dependence are likely to yield. If we look at the flaws Roberts identifies and the way in which the child welfare system interacts with the welfare system intended to offer Aid to Families with Dependent Children (AFDC), it is clear that the child welfare system only compounds the distortions.

III. The System's Failure to Consider Constraints on Families

To place all responsibility for caring for children on parents without regard for economic, social, and political constraints disregards the ways in which we are all interdependent—economically, politically, and socially. A family barred from achieving economic stability through racist policies and behaviors, whether these are socially maintained or politically enforced, cannot provide economic stability for their child.

Poverty statistics of African Americans are portentous indicators of conditions unfavorable to caring for dependent others. Poverty is associated not only with material deprivations but with crises that deepen the despair and the stigma: self-medication through substance abuse, violent and crime-ridden neighborhoods, inadequate medical services, lack of familial and community support, a sense of being overwhelmed and depression resulting from a life out of control. Add to these the frustration and rage of a pervasive racism and we have to marvel at the vast majority of black mothers whose ethical response remains intact.

While AFDC retained some understanding that the welfare of a child was bound to economic constraints of the family, neither that program nor its successor, Temporary Assistance for Needy Families (TANF), nor child welfare addresses the racism that prevents many African Americans from providing for their children. Worse still, the meager aid provided is seen as a "handout" and not as one of many structures by which our interdependence manifests itself. The labor of mothers is not understood to be a labor that contributes crucially to the well-being of society and that deserves in itself to be well compensated by society at large. The work of one raising a child is viewed rather as a "private" matter, where the only acceptable arrangement is one where this undertaking is "privately" financed—preferably in a nuclear family. The ability or inability of a private provider to finance this project is outside of the sphere of welfare arrangements.

Should a designated provider not find gainful employment or lose a job, the dependency worker and dependent alike are at risk of being thrust into the unwelcoming embrace of the welfare system and suffering the ignominy of being "dependents of the state." In truth they are dependent on the state even prior to accepting a welfare check—as are we all. Whether we benefit from tax deductions, mortgage loans, Social Security payments, or employment that hinges on government fiscal policy, services, and infrastructures, we are dependent on the state. Even worse, our dependency extends to state policies and laws that enable or exclude our participation in social and economic life: for example, Jim Crow was enforced by law and removed by law, as have been other forms of discrimination and segregation. We depend on the state to provide us essential tools such as education on which our ability to earn an income depends. In more ways than we can count, we all are dependents of the state. Yet to be called a dependent of the state refers to only one of these forms of dependency. Through this careful manipulation of language, all the rest of us acquire the valued status of independence, while a few are rendered parasitic dependents.

Professor Mead (Chapter 4 of this volume) will tell us that good citizens pay back their due. Thus they retrieve their status as independents, not through verbal shenanigans, but through honest hard work. But the welfare mothers who raise children to be citizens and care for the needs of even those who will never be able to reciprocate also work hard, often with scarcely any remuneration. The distinction of status is made without a difference to warrant it.

Were the interdependence of all fully acknowledged, it would be much easier to see that social, political, and economic forces operate on all families and that these are no less responsible for the economic and social viability of a family than the actions of the family members themselves.

IV. Interventions Are (Too) Late

Roberts observes that state protection of a child is brought into play only when families are already having serious troubles and that it does not take as its task ensuring the health and welfare of families in the first place. This fact is a direct consequence of the first flaw she identifies. It also issues from a failure to acknowledge the extent to which any person who cares for a dependent becomes dependent, at least to some degree (and the greater the dependency of the charge, the greater the derived dependency of the caregiver). A family is the place where dependents are cared for, and it is a fine social technology for raising dependents. Dependents, particularly young children, require intimate contact with persons (usually just a few persons) who will focus their attention on responding to the needs that they cannot fulfill, or even articulate, themselves, and who will form the affective bonds that are so necessary for this degree of responsiveness. But a family in which there is only one adult is severely disadvantaged when there is no one who can support the caregiver financially, emotionally, or socially. I just spoke of the multiple ways we are all dependents of the state. Beyond this, even in families where there are two adults, a wider community is needed, if not for financial support, then for guidance, emotional support, and respite, especially when families are financially precarious and isolated from larger groups of kin.

Insofar as children are raised well, they are a resource for the entire community, and insofar as each of us would want to be cared for if we were to become dependent, it is not at all clear why caring for dependents is viewed as the responsibility solely of a family. Nor is it understandable, in the abstract at least, why a sole parent with young and highly dependent children should be expected, or, as the new welfare law has it, *required,* to hand over the care of the child to another so that the parent can earn a wage. Why is the care of children not seen to be the labor it is and remunerated adequately by the larger society?

To understand why, I believe we have to note that the world of inevitable dependence is hidden from view. Public policies shaped by a view of society as composed first and foremost of independent individuals who are able to be self-sustaining pay little attention to the place of children and others who are not able to care for their own needs because of age, illness, or impairment. When society is viewed as an association of independent individuals, there is no well-formulated notion of the role played by *relationships* between dependents and those for whom the well-being of the dependent is of prime importance. Neither is there recognition of the state's role in supporting the relationship and thus enabling the giving and receiving of care.

In my book *Love's Labor* I argue that the care of children and other dependents is a responsibility that must be shared societally. The argument in the book centers on women's aspirations for equality. But after considering the arguments in Roberts's essay, I now believe it has bearing on equality aspirations of racial groups such as African Americans, where mechanisms of social oppression extend into the family and are aggravated by a lack of material resources.

A concept of equality that takes dependency seriously requires a conception of reciprocity different from that generally understood as required for social cooperation. Rawls writes, "Those who can take part in social cooperation over a complete life, and who are willing to honor the appropriate fair terms of agreement are regarded as equal citizens."[9] This concept of social cooperation spans the left-right continuum. The Communitarian Platform asserts: "At the heart of the communitarian understanding of social justice is the idea of reciprocity: each member of the community owes something to all the rest, and the community owes something to each of its members."[10] When Professor Mead speaks of the "social obligations of citizenship," he writes that "government is really a mechanism by which people force themselves to serve and obey each other in necessary ways."[11]

This understanding of reciprocity is limited to interactions between independent and fully functioning persons. To understand social cooperation that takes into account interactions with dependents, I suggest a notion of reciprocity I term *doulia,* by which I mean that those who care for dependents need in turn to be tended to and supported in their efforts by others.[12]

I have argued for a public conception of doulia (service) by which we acknowledge the social responsibility to care for the caretaker so that he or she and the dependent can both receive the care they require. Those who benefit from the dependency workers' care of dependents—society at large as well as those more intimately involved—are morally obligated to attend to the caretaker because, I want to insist, at the heart of our notion of equality is the idea that we are "all some mother's child"—we are each persons who have benefited from the care of another, who have been seen as worthy of an investment of care and attention merely to survive, much less thrive, as we grow into adults. The mother too is a "mother's child"—also someone who is worthy of care and attention when it is needed by her. This is a notion of fairness and reciprocity that is not dyadic; rather, it spirals out to relationships that both reach into our past and project into future generations. It calls for a collective, social responsibility for care, but one that doesn't dilute relationships between dependent and caregiver, between dependent and dependency worker. The vulnerabilities created by the care of a fully dependent charge create a set of obligations that in turn is nested within the scope of responsibilities of another. Eventually the responsibility spills out to the larger social order of which the dependent and dependency worker are a part. The well-being of the family depends on the economic and social well-being of the larger society.

Because a long history already identifies African Americans as dependents, particularly if they are poor, and particularly if they are women (especially, but not only, when they receive public assistance), it is not difficult for the state to assume a presumptive authority that it exercises directly over the children of these women. Because the parents are themselves seen as dependent, bypassing the dependency of the children on their parents is more easily justified than where the independence of the adults is presumed. Rather than respecting the dependency relation between children and their mothers (or the kinship systems that sometimes function with, or in lieu of, maternal relations), the state appropriates that relationship. To maintain the integrity of the family—that is, to respect and acknowledge the dependency relation—would require state intervention not when families are already in trouble but before, when intervention can ensure family well-being in the first place.

V. The Punitive Character of Child Welfare Interventions

Because the entire responsibility for the care of dependents is assumed to be the family's, Roberts observes, evidence of a failure evokes a punitive response. Without a doubt, reconciling a healthy respect for family integrity with the public interest to keep children safe and flourishing can be very difficult, especially where families are already in trouble. Dependents are indeed vulnerable and adults are less so. Once the family is in trouble, an effort to save children may inflict a punitive consequence on the adults.

Nonetheless the punitive approach to the adult, as well as the disproportionate impact of the system on African Americans, is a legacy of a welfare system mired in racism and moralism. Worse still, it is a living legacy, one that has found renewed strength in the welfare reform policies of 1996. It is a legacy of a welfare system in which being dependent on the state makes one suspect. But although the stigmatization of welfare dependency tars whites and blacks with same brush, welfare historians have documented that black women were intentionally excluded from even this insufficient aid. Only in the 1960s, after considerable federal intervention and attention paid to battling Jim Crow, did African American women gain access to public aid in significant numbers. Even then, "home suitability clauses" were used extensively to drop African Americans from the rolls until the intervention of the "Flemming Rule," which held that if a state believed a particular home was "unsuitable," it had to provide due process for the family, and it could not merely drop families off the roster, but had to provide service interventions for them.[13] Unsuitability requirements as set by the states were still permitted, but it became impermissible to forfeit benefits for the child because the behavior of the relative was deemed unsuitable. If a home was found to be unsuitable and the unsuitability was a consequence of extreme poverty or other social situations in which social workers were unprepared to intervene, the duty of the social worker was to remove the child from these unsuitable conditions rather than withhold material necessities from the child.

In many ways the Flemming Rule was a progressive measure intended to respond to discriminatory behavior on the part of the states. But because the child welfare system was not intended to shore up a family at risk due to societal problems (such as lack of decent affordable housing or extreme poverty) the Flemming Rule shifted the language of "unsuitability" to one of "neglect."[14] The former focused attention on the adult, the latter on the child. In the process, the well-being of the child became theoretically, and all too often actually, decoupled from the well-being of the adult charged with his or her care. If the life of the parent or relative could not be salvaged, it seemed that at least the well-being of the child should be secured. To treat African American children differently from white children in this regard is, as Larry May and others have pointed out, surely racial discrimination at its worst. Here, apparently, begins the whipsawing that ultimately tears at the fabric of the African American community.

The point that Roberts makes is that by failure to take into account the economic, political, and social constraints that prevent parents from properly assuming care of their children, and specifically by indifference to the pervasive poverty experienced by African Americans, racism enters into the system and serves its punitive function. Roberts also emphasizes that the punishment is most readily meted out in response to the negative stereotypes that attach to the black mother, in that there is a presumption in favor of "saving the child" from the "depravity" of its mother.

The devaluation of black motherhood is evident in the maternal labor stolen from her under slavery, in her exclusion, prior to the 1960s, from welfare benefits that white poor women received, in the intrusive and disrespectful ways in which those benefits were finally meted out, and in the recent cruel stereotypes of welfare mothers that Roberts rehearses for us. Yet there is a paradox: the very black women whose mothering has been maligned are the women enlisted to care for white people's children and elderly. If they are such worthless mothers to their own children, why are they assumed to be the appropriate caregivers to others' children and dependent adults? The Mammy of the American South was presumed to be loving and caring by nature. But the presumption of the naturalness of her caring can also account for the rationalization that black mothers are irresponsible, neglectful of their own children, and so on. If the black Mammy's caring is "natural," then, like any force of nature, it must be contained and subjected to a "rational" and "civilized" supervision, or it will miss its mark. Attributing many black infant deaths to black mothers' negligently smothering their babies as they slept with them ("smothering them with love"?) surely provides an image of caring gone astray.

White mothers too are traditionally viewed as requiring the supervision of men to mother adequately—witness the overwhelming concern with the evils of single parenthood.[15] The patriarchal understanding that women are (or ought to be) subordinate to men renders women dependent on men, just as the white patriarchal view that blacks are (or ought to be) subordinate to whites renders blacks dependent on whites. Women, on this view, are appropriately dependent on men insofar as they are associated with properties of nature, such as irrationality, sexuality, lack of judgment, and wildness. Because not only femaleness but also blackness is figuratively associated with what is irrational, natural, and so on, the black mother is doubly untamed, twice in need of control and supervision. While a white woman's motherhood ties her to a (white) man who has authority, at least by virtue of her economic dependency on him, a dependency that is then laudable, motherhood in a black woman presents a double threat: the loss of a worker if she is provided economic support, and a mother not under the control of a white man.[16]

Contrary pulls here establish a tension. Guilt and fear are projected onto the black mother. Her caring is to be harnessed as labor, not released as maternal love. Yet this forms a woman who has a degree of economic self-sufficiency. As such she becomes the powerful black matriarch, who, if permitted control over her children, can lead them astray. But as a woman who can be a worker and hence not under the direct economic control of a spouse, she also can serve as a model for white women and hence lead white women astray. White mothers could do what she is doing. White racist society already sees blackness as a contaminant.[17] The "one drop of blood" rule is both metaphorically and literally an apt expression of that fear of contamination. The contagion of blackness now expresses itself in the views such as those of Charles Murray, cited in Roberts's essay.[18] Blackness today contaminates by promulgating a "deviant" family form—mothers raising children on their own. The black mother must be constrained and punished for her deviance lest white women follow her example. Thus not only are the changes in welfare and child welfare, as Roberts maintains, "likely to intensify the racial imbalance in state interventions in families"; they also reinforce the message that attempting to raise a child on your own subjects a woman to the threat that she will lose the child entirely. The racism that fuels the attempt to control and regulate black families is not directed only against blacks. It is also deployed in the service of controlling and regulating the sexuality, reproductive capacities, and caring of white women, pushing them toward traditional marital arrangements—toward their "proper" and "natural" dependency.[19]

I spoke earlier of a dependency of identity—namely, that there are important ways in which the identity of white Americans depends on an identity whites have thrust on African Americans. If black women are independent of the income of a man and dependent on that of the state, what is appropriate for white women is that they, in contrast, be dependent (partially at least) on the income of a man and independent of state support. Just as the southern belle in her "purity" and sexlessness was defined in contrast to the black female slave, who was "impure" and an always accessible vehicle for male lust, so the proper mother (from the perspective of the U.S. conservative) today is to be always available to child and husband, in contrast to the black mother, who is to be always available to her employer and whose child is always a potential state ward. When the white mother acts as the black mother does, the potential for a confusion of identity poses a serious threat to the social order. State support for mothers needs to be withdrawn from black women so that they will be available for employment, and from white women so that their opportunities for employment will not preclude their availability to white men. This perhaps sounds like only a conservative or even far right perspective. But we must recall that the conservative piece of legislation known as welfare reform was signed by a Democratic "centrist" president who seemingly did not himself hold these views. Yet as the literature from the right around the time of the "welfare debates" and the welfare reform legislation itself—which sees as its first raison d'être the preservation of the institution of marriage[20]—indicates, welfare reform was not about getting people out of poverty, or even about saving money. It was much more about the social changes that had occurred in the light of women's liberation and the constriction of the already narrow bounds of the U.S. welfare state. The identities of black women and white women and the danger that the boundaries between them will break down are central to the scenario motivating the welfare changes.

VI. Taking Seriously the Community's Responsibility in Caring for Children

The first and third flaws identified by Roberts are, I believe, corollaries of the second. If all the responsibility for taking care of children is the family's, then failures are parental, and a punitive policy makes sense insofar as one believes that irresponsible behavior that damages another should be punished. And if all the responsibility for taking care of children is the family's, then the state has no business interceding until families fail in that responsibility—that is, when they are already experiencing difficulty. At the heart of the matter, then, is the question of whether all responsibility for taking care of children should fall to parents——whether there are not societal responsibilities to children and societal responsibilities to families in which there are children and other vulnerable dependent persons.

If we adopt the conception of doulia of which I spoke earlier, then we grant that obligations to children take the form of a set of nested responsibilities to dependents. While the caregiver cares for the dependent, a provider is obliged to support the caregiver in his or her relationship with the dependent. As the provider fulfills its obligation to the caregiver/cared-for dyad, obligations devolve on a larger social entity. Where the provider is the larger family, the community or an employer or the state is obliged to enable the provider to provide for the caregiver. Where the provider is the state itself, the obligation is on the citizenry to provide the taxes to the state. Citizens in this way return the debt they incurred when they were dependent. Moreover, any citizen, even when an adult, can always, through illness, injury, or frail old age, once again be in need of a caregiver. Similarly, any citizen can find him- or herself with responsibilities of care and with the need of support in that caring labor. With an awareness of our own history of past dependence and possibility of future dependence, with an acknowledgment that the inner and outer ends of the spiral return to one another, we can keep alive an understanding that the responsibility for the well-being of children is not the parents' alone. It is one we all have obligations to share, an obligation that arises out of our common good. That is the nature of social obligations that begin with our dependency.

What are some consequences of this view?

On this view, the relationship between the dependency worker and the charge itself must be respected as nonfungible and of inherent value. The obligations of those in the outer circles are discharged through support of those of the inner circles so that the dependent retains the intimate relation to the caregiver who is directly responsible for his or her well-being. The answer to whether a decision should be "child focused" or "parent focused" should be "relationship focused."[21] Only when there is no other way to avoid damage to either the dependent or the dependency worker should these relations be forcibly severed.

Furthermore, on this view, the traditional nuclear family is only one possible social technology among many for ensuring the well-being of the dependent and dependency worker, for the role of provider need not be played by the father/husband but can as legitimately be played by a different or wider nesting circle.

And on this view, the responsibility and care of dependents must not fall to the dependency worker alone—even the family unit is inadequate as the sole context for dependency care and dependency relations. Various elements of the community, employers, local communities, and the state have a role to play in supporting dependency workers in their effort to care for their charges.

What are the implications of such a conception for the vexing problem of child welfare and its racialized dimensions? First, there is indeed a social responsibility for the raising of children, but it is a responsibility that must primarily work through the family—through the dependent/dependency worker relation and the nested systems of support that enable the proper functioning of that relationship. The state needs first of all to serve as a doula to the family—to support family caretakers so that they can provide care for dependents in the family—and a good place to start would be to provide doulas for new mothers who are at risk or who do not have familial support. This should not be a means-tested program but a service available to all mothers.

The principle of doulia would further require that dependency work be compensated, that the labor be recognized as such, and that material resources be devoted to recognizing that labor. This would go a long way to ensuring that families raising children are not languishing in poverty. Workfare has not accomplished what it was never really designed to do: move families out of poverty. By providing compensation for the time mothers spend raising their children (or caring for ill or incapacitated family members) or allowing them to use such monies for child care so that they can earn additional income—determined by a schedule of payment that varies with the dependency of the charge—the state/community/employers serve the function of the doula who aids the new mother so she can care for her child. In the process, they fulfill their obligation to pay back to mothers the service the mothers or other persons responsible for dependents perform for the community, and they help to ensure that the young children will emerge from home sufficiently unscathed by the ravages of poverty to participate in their turn as dependency workers, providers, and taxpayers.

But disturbingly, or perhaps not, we have moved away from the question of race. In fact, I do not seem to be recommending programs targeted to racial minorities; I am not even advocating more means-tested programs. The obligation of the state to serve as a doula for the family is a universal one—meant to serve all families, all dependency workers, all children. How are we to be sure that the poor and the racially marked members of our society will not once again be ill served? By orienting universal policies first around the needs of those most vulnerable, those least well served by the current arrangement. Unless the policies are universal, they will be stigmatized, underfunded (as all means-tested programs are), and the object of resentment of those just above the mark and those who think that "their taxpayer dollars" serve not themselves but others. Instead, we all throw our hats in the ring together, but policies are shaped first, though not only, by the needs of the neediest.

The end of Roberts's paper spells out for us the many ways in which the fate of a single disrupted black family injures an entire segment of our population. In doing so she reminds us that a society is not only not an association of independent, equally functioning, and equally empowered individuals. It is also not merely an association whose parts include the dependent and the dependency worker or family and state: there are also intervening intermediate communities. When those communities are racial minorities who have the long and twisted history of oppression that African Americans have had in the United States, the interests of the different components do not all fall easily in line. While a part of the larger U.S. "community," racial minorities also stand outside it. The dependent whose life, and whose continued existence and thriving, is at the center of the spiral of social obligations is the subject of contesting authorities and communities. Peggy Cooper Davis describes scenes during Reconstruction where African American children stood at the center of disputes between parents and their former white masters.[22] With whiteness, money, power, and influence on their side, the former masters could argue that the child was better off with them. While some former masters may have had genuine feelings of concern for the children, most saw the child as the object of instrumental value (or a servant in the making) well suited to attend to their own needs. The fear heard in the National Association of Black Social Workers' disavowal of cross-race adoptions—that the African American community will be further eviscerated by the contemporary means of severing its ties to its children—has its source in a not very distant history. Communities are important mediators between the vulnerable individual and the state, just as families are. Each of the nesting vessels needs support and strengthening so that the entire society will be the product of good solid structures of trust and care. Only then will all our children be safe.

NOTES

1. See Nancy Scheper-Hughes, *Death without Weeping: The Violence of Everyday Life in Brazil* (Berkeley: University of California Press, 1992).

2. Of the two, child abuse and child neglect, neglect is the older recognized social problem. Adam M. Tomison writes: "Child neglect became recognized as a societal concern throughout much of the western world during the industrial revolution of the late nineteenth century . . . with initial concerns for abandoned and physically neglected children resulting in the formation of the first child protection societies and the first child protection legislation." Adam M. Tomison, "Spotlight on Child Neglect," *Issues in Child Abuse Prevention*, no. 4 (Winter 1995). Child maltreatment was "discovered" in the early 1960s in the United States by a group of medical professionals led by Henry Kempe, who constructed the "battered child syndrome" as a medical interpretation. Its recognition dates to the industrial revolution, a time of significant displacement of workers, as well as upheavals in family organization and labor, a period marked by poverty and mothers employed outside the home.

3. Peggy Cooper Davis, *Neglected Stories: The Constitution and Family Values* (New York: Farrar, Strauss and Giroux, 1997).

4. Harriet Jacobs, *Incidents in the Life of a Slave Girl, Written by Herself* (New York: Anchor, 1987).

5. Davis, *Neglected Stories*, 138.

6. Eva F. Kittay, *Love's Labor: Essays on Women, Equality and Dependency* (New York: Routledge, 1999).

7. Simone de Beauvoir, *The Second Sex* (New York: Vintage, 1989). Beauvoir spoke of men projecting their "dreams, fears and idols" unto women and so entitled one of the chapters in her classic work.

8. Elizabeth Spelman, "'Race' and the Labor of Identity," in *Racism and Philosophy*, ed. Susan Babbitt and Sue Campbell (Ithaca, N.Y.: Cornell University Press, 1999), 202–15.

9. John Rawls, *Political Liberalism* (New York: Columbia University Press, 1992), 302.

10. Amitai Etzioni et al., "The Responsive Communitarian Platform: Rights and Responsibilities," in *The Essential Communitarian Reader,* ed. Amitai Etzioni (Lanham, Md.: Rowman and Littlefield, 1998), xxxiv.

11. Lawrence Mead, *Beyond Entitlement: The Social Obligations of Citizenship* (New York: Free Press, 1986).

12. I adopt the term from the postpartum caretaker, the *doula,* who assists the mother who has just given birth, not by caring for the infant as much as by caring for the mother so that the mother can herself care for the infant. See Kittay, *Love's Labor.*

13. Claudia Lawrence-Webb, "African American Children in the Modern Welfare System: A Legacy of the Flemming Rule," in *Serving African American Children,* ed. Sondra Jackson and Sheryl Brissett-Chapman (New Brunswick, N.J.: Transaction, 1997), 12.

14. Ibid., 17.

15. Many of the difficulties faced by solo mothering are traceable to the poverty of families in which there is only one adult. In that case, there is no reason to presume that heterosexual two-adult parenting is the only or best remedy for the hardships faced by both mothers and children. See Eva F. Kittay, "A Feminist Public Ethic of Care Meets the New Communitarian Family Policy," *Ethics* 111 (April 2001): 523–47.

16. Ricki Solinger, "Dependency and Choice: The Two Faces of Eve," in *Whose Welfare,* ed. Gwendolyn Mink (Ithaca, N.Y.: Cornell University Press, 1999), 7–35.

17. See Dorothy E. Roberts, "The Genetic Tie," *University of Chicago Law Review* 62 (1995): 209, for a discussion of the significance of blood ties.

18. Charles Murray, "The Coming White Underclass," *Wall Street Journal,* Oct. 29, 1993, A14.

19. The dual aims are served not only by child welfare laws but also by custody rulings that punish women who work outside the home. Legal theorist Cheri Wood writes: "In an era when over fifty percent of all mothers and almost eighty percent of divorced mothers are working outside the home, media accounts of women losing custody of their children because of their working-mother status abound. Working mothers appear to be in a lose-lose situation." Wood quotes Roberta Cooper Ramo, speaking in 1995 as president-elect of the American Bar Association: "Either you're a bad mother because you work and are away from your children, or you're a bad mother because you haven't taken sufficient financial responsibility for yourself and your family. . . . It's a crazy double standard. . . . The . . . bizarre thing is that while we're telling wel-

fare mothers to work, we're also telling professional women not to. I haven't figured this out.'" Cheri L. Wood, "Childless Mothers? The New Catch-22: You Can't Have Your Kids and Work for Them Too," *Loyola of Los Angeles Law Review* 29 (November 1995): 383. The interjection of race considerations makes this far less puzzling. As many scholars have pointed out, white Americans have never presumed that there was a conflict of work and family for black mothers—they have always been compelled by law or circumstance to do work additional to familial labor. The conflict has been presumed only for white women. It is not some new double bind to which women are being subjected but the old bindings of the patriarchal family applied to white women.

20. The Personal Responsibility Act, 104th Cong., H.R. 4, was slated as a bill "[t]o restore the American family, reduce illegitimacy, control welfare spending and reduce welfare dependence." "Title 1—Reducing Illegitimacy . . . It is the sense of the Congress that: (1) marriage is the foundation of a successful society; (2) marriage is an essential social institution which promotes the interests of children and society at large; (3) the negative consequences of an out-of-wedlock birth on child, the mother, and society are well documented."

21. See also Annette R. Appell, "Protecting Children or Punishing Mothers: Gender, Race, and Class in the Child Protection System," *South Carolina Law Review* 48 (Spring 1997): 577.

22. Peggy Cooper Davis, *Neglected Stories.*

6

LEGAL FICTIONS AND FAMILY ROMANCES: CONTESTING PARADIGMS OF CHILD PLACEMENT

MORRIS B. KAPLAN

The purpose of adoption is to provide care to children.
—Mary Lyndon Shanley

I. Denaturalizing the Family

Mary Shanley provides a thoughtful, intelligent, and sensible review of two recent controversies in adoption law and policy, regarding secrecy about birth parents and cross-racial adoption. She effectively parses the issues in these debates, relating them to differing conceptions of the individual as an "unencumbered self" bearing abstract rights protected by the state or as a "relational" being defined by historical ties to family, community, and race. In analyzing particular policy issues, Shanley shows how both debates implicate a specific paradigm of the adoption process: its aim is to provide "parentless" children with "as if" families. She recognizes that family and kinship relations, and perhaps individuality itself, are culturally constructed and open to political contestation. In this essay, I will review some of Shanley's arguments and explore their broader implications for thinking about social policies governing the provision of care for children in need. I will build on Shanley's discussion to explicate more fully the historical and theoretical contexts of child placement. The family is a subject infused with personal and collective fantasies of longing and belonging. As a site of intimate association and child rearing, it has had diverse social forms and undergone many changes over time. Institutions of domesticity are linked to the organization of gender and sexuality and are invested with important educational, ethical, and ideological functions. In modernity, "the transformations of intimacy" have occasioned ongoing cultural struggle and political conflict.

Thinking critically about the practice of adoption focuses sharply many of these theoretical issues because of its manifestly constructed character. Although comparatively few people have been adopted as children or seek to adopt as adults, most of us are touched by questions about children and those who bear and raise them. The raising of children by others than their biological progenitors has been known throughout history and has been a favored subject in myth, folklore, literature, drama, and film. Something like adoption is central to some of the founding texts in Western culture. Most famously, Oedipus and Moses were "surrendered" by the women who bore them and brought up by others, with or without their knowledge, with fateful consequences for all concerned, including their communities. In Plato's *Republic,* Socrates (perhaps ironically) argues that in a city organized in accordance with justice, *all* children would be removed from their mothers shortly after birth and raised by those whose "nature" and training best equipped them for the task.[1] European literature is replete with tales of "parentless" children and the adults who take them up: from Shakespeare's Imogen in *The Winter's Tale* and the eponymous heroes of Fielding's *Tom Jones* and Dickens's *Oliver Twist,* right up through the comic strip and musical-theater heroine "Little Orphan Annie" and Mike Leigh's film *Secrets and Lies.* Often linked with illicit couplings, parental deaths, wicked stepparents, switched babies, and class or racial crossings, these "family romances" engage us at a fairly deep level of personal and cultural fantasy.

These tales also reflect social realities: relations like those in adoptive families have been widespread historically, especially in earlier times of extended families and frequent maternal death in childbirth. In *The Kindness of Strangers*, John Boswell provides an unsettling chronicle of children offered or simply abandoned to church or charity in the early modern period.[2] "Fostering" exchanges of children among aristocratic families were a practice among ancient Greeks and medieval Europeans. Toni Morrison's *Beloved* offers a powerful reminder of the absence of legally recognized families among slaves in the United States and the tragic losses suffered by parents and children alike. For much of human history, children have been raised by people other than their biological parents, as a result of social organization or sheer contingency. Since Plato, theorists of the first magnitude have delineated the relationships between the domain where children are reared and a space where adults interact in public. Political philosophy may be formally initiated by Aristotle's distinction in the *Politics* between the *oikos* or household, devoted to the maintenance of life, and the *polis*, where citizens pursue, not life alone, but a good life. Modern theorists have continued to delineate separate spheres of public and private life, with marriage and the family assigned to a naturalized prepolitical domain. As several decades of feminist scholarship have demonstrated, and as Plato explicitly acknowledged in Book V of the *Republic*, these analyses are entangled with conceptions of sexual difference that assign specific roles to women and to men allegedly based on their natural capacities.

The issues that Shanley considers differ from such classic analyses in that adoption as a formal legal status is mediated, often totally constructed, by the state and its agencies. As she writes, modern adoption is "the conscious severing of the legal ties between biologically related persons and the creation of legal ties between biologically unrelated persons." Adoptive families are distinguished not only from "natural" families but also from informal sharing of child-rearing responsibilities, from temporary "foster" homes, and from the manifold institutions in the welfare system that care for children whose biological parents cannot do so. The deliberate construction of families by the state and its diffuse agencies is an exercise in what Michel Foucault calls "biopower."[3] In the United States, state law defines adoptive relationships and the procedures necessary to establish them, sometimes subject to federal constraints; courts apply these laws to particular individuals and families, usually with the assistance of social workers from state or municipal child welfare departments or private, often religious, charities. The vast apparatus of the modern state and its adjacent bureaucracies may be implicated in the decision-making processes by which children are detached from biological forebears and incorporated into newly made "adoptive" families. Shanley's historical and conceptual analysis of adoption practice and policy during the twentieth century in the United States shows how issues about both race and secrecy were resolved in the context of a dominant paradigm in which the process was understood as establishing an "as if" family in which to incorporate allegedly "parentless" children. Adoption as a social practice and legal status emerged against a background of deep-seated cultural assumptions regarding the "natural" character of familial relationships. The connection between parents and children was regarded as biological and involuntary: although the law might intervene, its primary role was to "recognize" what was already given or to alter the legal consequences of these facts, as when parents divorced, died, or abandoned or abused a child. Social realities and political conditions might well depart dramatically from this governing set of assumptions. Notoriously, slaves were denied legal recognition of their familial relations. The children of slaves belonged to the "owners" of the biological mother and could be disposed of at their will. Similarly, children born out of wedlock were branded "illegitimate," and neither they nor their parents were entitled to the full scope of rights and responsibilities that accompanied "legitimate" births. Hobbes in the seventeenth century had already contended that the only observably "natural" familial relationship was that between a woman and the child she bore, since paternity could be established only on the word of the mother.[4] His point was that family relations with legal implications were conventional, derived from social practices and legal enactments about marriage and child rearing. Hobbes's analysis implies that family relationships are social constructions that ascribe meaning and effect, mostly through marriage, to heterosexual intercourse and childbearing. "Marriage" as a legal and civil status grows out of the state's recognition of decisions by individual men and women or their families. The legitimacy of children is established as much by legal fiat as by biological fact: lawyers, novelists, and errant wives have always known that the husband's paternity of his wife's children is a rebuttable juridical assumption rather than a natural outcome of sexual practice. Even where spousal paternity is not an issue, marriage situates children within a context of kinship relations that join groups of people only some of whom are related by "blood," or genetically, as we would say today. The genealogical location of a child is never simply natural.

The development of adoption as a set of legal relationships exposes the "dirty little secret" that while children may simply be born, parents are always to some extent "made" by the law. However, as Shanley shows, this situation is obscured by the deployment of social norms that construct adoptive families as imitations of what is taken to be the natural order of things, as if the children had been produced by sexual intercourse between the adoptive parents. Thus, those eligible to adopt have been severely limited to heterosexual couples of childbearing age of the same race and, if possible, nationality and religion as the child: "Adoptive families reflected the assumption that constructed families should imitate what was seen as a norm given by nature." Still, social convention played an important role: the stigma attached to childbearing outside marriage was among the most powerful pressures leading women to give up their children. Most jurisdictions permitted adoption only by couples who were legally married. Further, the construction of a virtually natural family required the effacement of an alternative "birth" parentage. Adoption has been from the start a two-stage process: first severing the ties with biological parents, then establishing new ties with adoptive ones. The modern legal status of adoption contrasts sharply with informal child care arrangements among members of extended families or local communities:

> Although members of a child's extended family sometimes adopted the child, the paradigmatic model of formal adoption was "stranger adoption." . . . Statutes allowing legal adoption disrupted the traditional understanding of the indestructible and involuntary nature of family bonds by severing the legal tie between origi-

> nal parents and offspring and then by creating a new legal tie by convention and choice.

As Shanley neatly puts it, parenting was taken to be an *exclusive* relationship. The recognition of more than two parents—one male, one female, preferably married to each other—would challenge the fiction of a "natural" (and monogamous) family. Thus potential adoptive parents were carefully vetted for their roles, and biological forebears lost all parental status. The legal language reveals the underlying personal drama: a mother was said to "surrender" parental rights or have them "terminated." The child, "freed" for adoption, was understood to be unencumbered by previous genetic or historical ties. However, the transfer of children from one family to another could be accomplished only with the mediation of social agencies: "The intermediary role performed by the adoption agency that accepted the child from the birth parents and then placed the child with adoptive parents reflected the fact that for a moment the child was a ward of the state not bound to any other specific persons, an individual awaiting the creation of lasting family ties by an adoption decree." The conception of "the unencumbered individual," linked as it is to personal autonomy, can be applied to a child only with difficulty. To be a child is to be dependent on adults for physical sustenance and emotional support. Adoption must be mediated by child care institutions and the rights of children guaranteed by the state. "Parentless" children available for incorporation into "as if" families are, in part, effects of judicial decision. The state's capacity to deliver on its promise of providing a permanent home and caring parents may be severely tested by the intensity of children's needs and the exigencies of their development.

Shanley sketches the social background against which this dance of legal fictions was enacted. Middle-class white women who became pregnant without being married were seriously stigmatized, encouraged to surrender their children and "get on with their lives." In fact, adoption was enabled by a double stigmatization, for married couples unable to conceive also deviated from the norms of "natural" family life. The acceptance of a child who appeared "as if" he or she could have been the progeny of the adoptive parents helped them to conform socially at the same time it satisfied personal desires to raise children. The "clean break" that both facilitated the legal construction of an "as if" family and helped the woman put behind her the birth of an illegitimate child removed the birth mother as a dissonant figure in the new family constellation. Shanley argues that condemnation of out-of-wedlock birth has been inflected importantly by race and social class. Within the black community, family disruption had been the rule under slavery. Subsequently, too, "there was a long history of informal adoption in black communities." Responsibility for child rearing was shared by extended families and the broader community. Such arrangements, persisting outside the allegedly dominant norms of monogamous marriage, became the vehicle for pathologizing the black family: while white women might err on the way to a respectable maturity, with the prospect of marriage and "legitimate" children, black single mothers were increasingly attacked as irresponsible "welfare queens" mired in a "culture of poverty" and dependency. Dorothy Roberts shows in considerable and convincing detail the racism that pervades the child care system. While healthy white babies available for adoption have become a "scarce commodity," black children in large numbers have remained without adoptive homes. The legal fiction of "as if" families, while apparently neutral regarding race, works against a background of race relations in the United States to reinforce social inequality and consign many black children to the limbo of foster and institutional care. The practice of adoption, with its dominant myth of imitating "natural" families, has resulted in a two-tiered system of child placement, with an elite of "adoptable" children and "suitable" parents at the top and a mass of others in "temporary" but long-term care dispensed by a patchwork of individuals and agencies below.

Shanley's conjunction of developing notions of "open" adoption with the debates about cross-racial adoption illuminates the transformation of governing paradigms and of the social contexts in which they are deployed. The paradigm of "as if" families works to preclude cross-racial adoption. Further, the exclusivity of parental status has supported secrecy about biological parents, termination of all "parental rights," and the enforcement of a "clean break" between those whose children are adopted and their progeny. Perhaps the most telling evidence of the hold exercised by the paradigm of "as if" families is the practice, after an adoption has become final, of sealing the child's original birth certificate and issuing a new one with only the adoptive parents' names on it. The debates about cross-racial and "open" adoption expose the precariousness of many assumptions underlying the adoption paradigm. As Carol Sanger argues, the increased frequency and social acceptability of divorce and remarriage have already undermined the norm of the monogamous family. Even within the context of "legitimate" relationships, many children find themselves in complex family configurations with "step" parents and siblings abounding and "custody" often divided or shared. Parental rights and responsibilities are no longer exclusively enjoyed by a child's biological progenitors. The increased willingness of women to bear children outside marriage further complicates the picture: single mothers may raise their children alone or in company with friends or relatives; couples may share parental responsibilities without marrying and may change partners without divorcing. Lesbians bear children through alternative insemination, raising them with or without partners. Gay or other unmarried couples seek to adopt, as do single people of all sorts. Both legally recognized and informal forms of family life proliferate. In this broader context, proposals for "open" and cross-racial adoption only mirror broader changes in social organization and political attitudes.

II. Creating Contexts of Care

Shanley shows that the contestation of norms governing child placement cannot be viewed as an external "politicizing" of a natural process. Child placement decisions always invoke "the best interests of the child," often taking for granted that this encompasses incorporation into an "as if" family. The erosion of that paradigm implicates different conceptions of the child and his or her interests and points toward a more radical understanding of individuality and familial relations as social and cultural constructions. Defining the "interests" of a child requires reference to norms of a good life and nurturing family that may be politically contested; they may also be fraught with fantasy at both the individual and social level. What are the interests of a "parentless" child? How can a system of child placement best satisfy them? Is the dominant paradigm of an "as if" family adequate to comprehend them? Shanley shows how the differing sides in each debate construct the child as either an unencumbered individual available to be incorporated in a new family or a relational entity with ties to already existing families and communities. She recommends a shift in focus toward understanding the child as having "multiple needs for security and identity." Rather than adjudicating the claims of birth parents or racial groups to connection with an adopted child, Shanley reflects on the ways these preexisting relationships may be crucial for individuals trying "to construct a coherent story of origin, an explanation of how they came into the world." Although specifically referring to information about birth families, Shanley's emphasis on historically situating the individual pertains equally to national or racial origins:

> We humans think of ourselves as temporal beings, as coming out of a past and being formed by what has gone before us, and of having a connection with the future. We are shaped by and shape the world in many ways, including physical procreation, works of craftsmanship and art, friendships, and material or spiritual legacies. Our sense of history and continuity, extending back into the past and forward into the future, is part of what gives a sense of meaning to our existence and our works. It is this experience of ourselves as beings in time that underpins a person's right to specific knowledge of his or her origins.

Shanley eloquently articulates a persuasive and useful perspective on individuality, seeing identity not as a given and fixed character but as an effect of agency, of projects through which selves are made from the historical and social circumstances in which persons find themselves. I shall call this perspective "ethical," drawing on a Hegelian conception of *sittlichkeit* or "ethical life" in which social structure and individual freedom are mutually implicated. Such a linkage resonates with contemporary appropriations of the "ethical" by such thinkers as Bernard Williams and the later Foucault as well as with the expanded conception of eros in Plato's *Symposium* and feminist conceptions of a "situated self." Judith Butler defines *sittlichkeit* as "the shared set of norms, conventions and values that constitute the cultural horizon in which the subject emerges into self-consciousness—that is, a cultural realm which both constitutes and mediates the subject's relation to itself."[5] In terms of Shanley's analysis, the ethical includes both the individual's effort to construct a meaningful story by which to give meaning to his or her life and the historical context against which that effort unfolds. An ethical perspective sees the individual both as situated in a wide range of social relations and as actively shaping a life through his or her own agency. While recognizing that ancestry plays a role in defining one's situation, ethical analysis does not privilege a biological model of genealogy: not genetics but history provides the context of individual self making. The need of a child for "identity" becomes the right to engage freely in an ongoing project of self-definition. Psychologists debate the conditions necessary for children to develop such a capacity. Rather than entering that thicket, I shall focus on the twin poles of security and identity that Shanley identifies. For adopted children, information about one's birth family may be very important for developing a sense of oneself. Importantly, the movement to dispel the secrecy attached to birth records was driven by the organized efforts of adult adoptees. Those to whom such information seems unhelpful or potentially harmful may choose not to pursue it. As Shanley points out, there may be a conflict between the perceived needs of the adoptee and the privacy interests of the birth parents, but the balance would seem to favor the former. Individuals may be unsettled by what they discover, or by the difficulties of establishing relations with newfound "families," or by the lack of reciprocal interest on the part of "real" parents. However serious, these hazards are not different in kind from other vicissitudes of adult life. Focusing on personal development and the conditions of agency also helps with some of the issues in cross-racial adoption. Opponents of the practice broaden the conception of origins to include the racial groups to which parents belong, whereas its defenders ground individuality in the fact of being human and of citizenship in a democratic polity for which racial differences are said to be unimportant. In both cases, policy positions turn on the different meanings ascribed to facts about a child's birth and historical situation.

Adoption interrupts the apparent naturalness of a process in which parental decisions shape the conditions under which an individual emerges who will eventually make decisions for him- or herself. Personal and familial choices are made instead by the state and its agents—legislatures, judges, social workers. In controversies about secrecy and cross-racial adoption, such matters have become politically contested at a variety of social, legal, and governmental levels. Although Shanley negotiates these disputes with theoretical subtlety, the law is a gross instrument. It was not designed to make nuanced evaluations of complex familial situations and determine how best to shape a child's future. Such decisions require the exercise of judgment in individual cases, whereas both law and policy operate at high levels of generality. In practice, our society generally leaves such decisions to those closest to the children, usually their parents. However, adoption becomes an issue just where that option has been foreclosed, either because the parents have decided that they are not up to it or because a court has determined that they are not competent. Faced with such sensitive decisions, legislatures paint with a very broad brush, leaving much to the discretion of individual judges. Mostly trained as lawyers, family court judges turn for assistance to experts in child development or family dynamics: psychiatrists, psychologists, social workers, or other professionals.

In *Beyond the Best Interests of the Child*, law professor Joseph Goldstein, psychoanalyst Anna Freud, and child psychiatrist Albert Solnit bring psychological perspectives on child development to bear on the choices facing legislators and judges about child placement. In summary, they distinguish between biological and psychological parenthood; argue that children have a profound need for a continuous relationship with at least one adult who provides physical security and emotional support; and insist that the child's perspective, especially his or her sense of time, renders placement decisions urgent matters. They propose that limits on the capacity of experts to predict—and courts to provide—"the best interests of the child" require adopting a more modest standard that seeks "the least detrimental alternative." Although some of these points coincide with common sense, they nonetheless provide critical perspectives on the actual processes of child placement. For instance, statutory waiting periods before adoptions become final or adjournments necessary to guarantee due process to parents whose parental rights are contested may appear reasonable to adults but generate severe strains for children. Any delay may be harmful to newborns: "Unlike adults, who measure the passing of time by clock and calendar, children have their own built-in time sense, based on the urgency of their instinctual needs. This results in their marked intolerance for postponement of gratification or frustration, and an intense sensitivity to the length of separations."[6] Changes in custody may disrupt nurturing attachments and interfere with the child's sense of security. Policies designed to facilitate adoption by couples who will provide an "as if" family configuration may lead to delays in matching a child with "appropriate" parents. Potential adoptive parents are subjected to intensive vetting by both state and private child care agencies; their assessments may be reviewed by courts. All of this takes time during which the child may remain in a temporary foster home, a succession of such homes, or institutional settings. Such circumstances may leave the child truly "parentless," unable to form ongoing ties with at least one adult charged with providing his or her care:

> The crucial problem is how and to what extent the law can, through the manipulation of a child's external environment, protect his physical growth and emotional development. How, the question then becomes, can the law insure for each child a chance to be a member of a family where he feels wanted and where he will have the opportunity, on a continuing basis, not only to receive and return affection, but also to express anger and to learn to manage his aggression?[7]

It is crucial for children to form ties to adults who want them. They may suffer considerably from the absence of at least one person with a continuous role during the early months and years of life: "[Psychoanalysis] establishes, as do developmental studies by students of other orientations, the need of every child for unbroken continuity of affectionate and stimulating relationships with an adult."[8] The harm resulting from delays and interruptions in care may far outweigh any advantage provided by an ostensibly "better" family situation. Neither genetic inheritance nor social role defines the psychological parent; rather, it is the ongoing relationship established by the giving of care:

> Unlike adults, children have no psychological conception of relationship by blood-tie until quite late in their development. For the biological parents, the facts of having engendered, borne, or given birth to a child produce an understandable sense of preparedness for proprietorship and possessiveness. These considerations carry no weight with children who are emotionally unaware of the events leading to their birth. What registers in their minds are the day-to-day interchanges with the adults who take care of them and who, on the strength of these, become the parent figures to whom they are attached.[9]

This relationship entails provision not only for the child's needs but also for the complex playing out of emotions and the development of trust. Infants are easily frustrated and may be subject to intense bouts of anger; psychological health depends on learning that connections with a parental figure will survive these powerful moments of negativity. Again the child's perspective is decisive: "He needs people to love, receive affection from, and to serve as safe targets for his infantile anger and aggression. He needs assistance from the adults in curbing and modifying his primitive drives (sex and aggression). He needs patterns for identification supplied by the parents."[10] The dynamic of adoption through which one set of ties is severed and another established requires a time in which the child is a "ward of the state." But the state and its agents cannot function as a "psychological parent": "Only a child who has at least one person whom he can love, and who also feels loved, valued and wanted by that person, will develop a healthy self-esteem. He can then become confident of his own chances of achievement in life and convinced of his own human value."[11] Even short delays may feel like abandonment to the child.

Goldstein, Freud, and Solnit offer an abstract template for thinking about child placement. Their insistence on the necessity of at least one continuing psychological parent for the development of a child is compatible with a plurality of forms of family life, although their emphasis on continuity and the distinct vicissitudes of children's time alerts one to the risks of change and to the dangers of delay. However, their brief account also acknowledges the role that fantasy may play in mediating the relations between a child's needs and the adults who care for him or her. The mechanism of phantasmatic projection becomes evident in their discussion of the impact on children of being told that they had been adopted. Goldstein and his colleagues point out that the interpretation of this information will reflect the child's own developmental state and needs:

> The young child tends to ignore it even if informed repeatedly, and to develop his attachments as wanted child to his psychological parents. The older child uses the information to a greater or lesser extent, depending on his developmental conflicts with his parents. Whenever he is disappointed in them or as he learns to appraise them realistically, the adoptive parents are compared with a fantasy image of the biological parents, however little these figured earlier in the child's mind. Adolescents frequently institute a search for the lost and unknown parents, as a step preliminary to achieving independence from any parental authority and reaching maturity.[12]

It should not be surprising that those young adults who actually meet their biological parents for the first time may be disappointed that they fail to live up to expectations or behave "just like parents" by limiting the child's independence.

III. Searching for Origins and the Imaginary Domain

The "real" parents for whom a child may search turn out to be as much constructions of fantasy as bearers of genetic material. In "Moses and Monotheism," Sigmund Freud discusses tales in which heroes (e.g., Oedipus, Moses more problematically) are imagined to have been abandoned by their highly placed biological parents and raised by others:

> [T]he source of the whole poetic fiction is what is known as a child's "family romance," in which the son reacts to a change in his emotional relation to his parents, and in particular to his father. A

> child's earliest years are dominated by an enormous overvaluation of his father. . . . Later, under the influence of rivalry and disappointment in real life, the child begins to detach himself from his parents and to adopt a critical attitude towards his father. Thus the two families in the myth—the aristocratic one and the humble one—are both of them reflections of the child's own family as they appeared to him in successive periods of his life.[13]

In an earlier essay, "Family Romances," Freud analyzes more fully how these fantasies reflect the dynamics within actual families:

> There are only too many occasions on which a child is slighted, or at least feels he has been slighted, on which he feels he is not receiving the whole of his parents' love, and, most of all, on which he feels regret at having to share it with brothers and sisters. His sense that his own affection is not being reciprocated then finds a vent in the idea, often consciously recollected later from early childhood, of being a step-child or an adopted child.[14]

Sometimes too, such fantasies may be aspects of the effort of the child to separate from parental influence: "They are found to serve as the fulfillment of wishes and as a correction of actual life. They have two principal aims, an erotic and an ambitious one."[15] For the child who has glimpsed the role of sexual intercourse in reproduction, the primary erotic object may be the mother: "The child . . . tends to picture to himself erotic situations and relations, the motive force behind this being his desire to bring his mother (who is the subject of the most intense sexual curiosity) into situations of secret infidelity and into secret love affairs."[16] This dynamic leads to fantasies of the child's secret illegitimacy. Ambition comes into play with sibling rivalry: "A younger child is very especially inclined to use imaginative stories such as these in order to rob those born before him of their prerogatives . . . and he often has no hesitation in attributing to his mother as many fictitious love-affairs as he himself has competitors."[17] However, these fantasies may also reflect the family's social status: "[T]he child's imagination becomes engaged in the task of getting free from the parents of whom he now has a low opinion and of replacing them by others, who as a rule, are of higher social standing.[18] Freud argues that these social-climbing wishes may actually reveal nostalgia for early childhood:

> [T]hese new and aristocratic parents are equipped with attributes that are derived entirely from real recollections of the actual and humble ones; so that in fact the child is not getting rid of his father but exalting him. Indeed the whole effort at replacing the real father by a superior one is only an expression of the child's longing for the happy, vanished days when his father seemed to him the noblest and strongest of men and his mother the dearest and loveliest of women.[19]

Thus Freud introduces the theme of social inequality only to vanquish it in his own fantasy of a universal moment in which the happiest of children enjoys the total and unconditional love of two parents: "[E]ven in later years, if the Emperor and Empress appear in dreams, those exalted personages stand for the dreamer's father and mother."[20] We need not follow Freud in the details of his analyses or to his proposed happy endings. However, he sheds light on the extent to which "family romances" that conjure one's "real" parents do multiple work for both children and adults, adopted or not, reflecting the dynamics of family life, the complexity of emerging desires, and discontent with one's social location. Children who "in fact" have been adopted may be more or less well served by having another set of parents on whom to project their fantasies. The crucial point is to realize the extent to which the "search for origins" is always already an imaginary enterprise.

Psychoanalytic attention to the pervasiveness of fantasy in one's conception of one's origins complements Shanley's attention to the construction of historical narratives as an aspect of ethical self making. In a series of books, Drucilla Cornell has charted "the imaginary domain" where individuals are free to connect up the multiple aspects of lived life into more or less coherent versions of a self. She argues that the capacity for self making is inherent to human existence: legal and social orders committed to equality must provide all persons the space within which to construct such meanings, regardless of gender or sexuality and without coercive determination by the state. In her essay

"Adoption and Its Progeny: Rethinking Family Law, Gender and Sexual Difference," Cornell considers the difficulties of providing a distinctively feminist account of adoption. She traces this problem to the fact that the adoption process has been traditionally treated as one in which the interests of two women—adoptive and birth mothers—are opposed to each other in a conflict marked by social inequality: "Adoption is fraught with issues of race, class, and imperialist domination. . . . The language of adoption is the language of war. In most states the 'birth mother' surrenders her child to the state, which then transfers the child to the adopting, predominantly white, middle-class, heterosexual parents."[21]

Cornell identifies the ways that adoption as a legal construction is bound up with more pervasive attitudes toward women, maternity, sexuality, and social equality. She argues that birth mothers should have access to information about, and potential contact with, their children, much as adoptees should have such rights regarding their biological parents. She argues that the fact of having borne a child and placed it for adoption may figure importantly in constructing a meaningful life. Like Shanley, Cornell downplays biology as such in favor of an ethical conception of transforming past experience in the ongoing project of making one's self in time. Cornell supports the rights of birth mothers against the state's authority to stand between them and children who may seek each other out, whatever the risks:

> Many birth mothers who have given up their children for adoption have undergone a trauma. A legal system that makes the cut from her child absolute blocks any hope for the recovery from this trauma, for the mother certainly, and maybe for the child. The best law can do for adopted children and birth mothers who feel compelled to seek out one another is to provide them with the space to work through the traumatic event that has to some extent formed them. . . . Some adopted children will want to search for their birth parents and some will not. Some will want to be found; others will not.[22]

Cornell argues that the right of birth mothers is especially important given how women's legal status has been defined in terms of marriage and parenting:

> Could a birth mother who chose or was forced to give up primary custody still know herself in the deepest recesses of her person to be a mother? . . . To rob her of her chance to struggle through what meaning being a mother still has for her is to put the state, and not the woman, as the master over the construction of her sense of who she is. Birth mothers . . . must be allowed the space to come to terms with their own life-defining decisions about sexuality and family.[23]

Cornell defends birth mothers' rights as part of a more radical reform of the adoption process: "What should a birth mother relinquish when she relinquishes primary custody of her child? Just that—primary custody. The equal protection of the birth mother's imaginary domain at least demands that she be allowed access to any information she desires to have about her child, and the chance to meet and explore with the child what kind of relationship they might develop."[24]

The effacement of the birth mother and elimination of all her parental rights is linked to the law's incapacity to imagine that a child could have more than one mother. When the state identifies the adoptive mother as the "real" mother, the woman who actually gave birth to the child must disappear from the scene. Here Cornell's argument intersects with Shanley's analysis of traditional adoption as the construction of "as if" natural families. For Cornell, this paradigm facilitates the state's efforts to enforce monogamous marital heterosexuality; its dominance as the exclusive form of legitimate family life is a denial of equal protection to all of those who seek pleasure and intimate association outside the conjugal household. State enforcement of heterosexual marriage as the exclusive site of legitimate relations denies individuals' freedom to construct their lives in accordance with their own imaginary ideals. Gay men, lesbians, and other independent women are denied recognition of their intimate associations and forced either to forego the raising of children or to deny important aspects of themselves. Cornell focuses on the increasing number of lesbians who are bearing children and raising them with their partners to show the contradictions that arise within the paradigm of "as if" families. The last thing that a lesbian mother wants is to terminate her own parental rights to "free" her child for adoption by her partner. Her household, the family she and her partner have chosen, directly challenges the assumption that a child can have only one mother.

Many advocates of lesbian and gay equality see the legalization of same-sex marriage or civil unions as the route to legitimizing the sharing of responsibility for children as well. Cornell takes the argument in a different direction: the denaturalization of child care by shared lesbian parenting reinforces her earlier insistence that birth mothers who give up their children for adoption forfeit primary custody rights rather than completely extinguishing all parental status. Going beyond the specifics of adoption, Cornell proposes a radical revision of family law that disarticulates parental roles and responsibilities from sexual ties among adults. For her, caregiving should be an arrangement among adults binding them to a child; the child is entitled to at least one primary parent, who may share responsibilities with others. These shared parental ties should be independent of the intimate relationships of adults to each other or to others who may not share in child care. Thus the needs of children for emotional bonding and continuity of support may be secured without compromising the freedom of those who raise them to engage erotically in ways that they choose. Cornell argues that same-sex couples who seek it are entitled to the same legal recognition as heterosexual partners, whether in marriage or some other form. But she insists that the erotic pair should not be treated as the exclusive vehicle for intimate association or for parenting. Cornell has the courage to follow the logic of her analysis to unconventional conclusions, acknowledging the claims of polygamous and polyandrous relationships, of a plurality of forms of intimacy involving members of the same and of different sexes. The distinct ties of adults with children and with each other to share responsibility for these children should be similarly pluralized. Cornell's proposal is a radical and utopian departure from the current legal situation, which grants heterosexual monogamy a monopoly on legitimate intimacy, insisting on its imitation through divorce and remarriage and the construction of "as if" adoptive families. She offers an alternative fantasy to that embedded in the discourse of traditional family values. We might even understand the persistence of the myth of a monogamous natural family as collective nostalgia for a phantasmatic golden age before the fall into divorce, unmarried coupling, single motherhood, and queer parenting. At the same time, Cornell's affirmation of a multiplicity of forms of erotic intimacy and of familial care that may change over time is not so far from the realities of contemporary social life.

IV. Opening Adoption and Families We Choose

Family law in the United States is ostensibly pluralistic, primarily determined by fifty separate states. Although only Vermont recognizes a legal status for same-sex couples, other states have experimented with reform in the laws governing adoption. In addition to states that have permitted access to birth records for adult adoptees, Washington State and Oregon have instituted "open adoption" practices that envision ongoing relations among birth parents, adoptive parents, and their children. These states acknowledge the interest that birth mothers may have in maintaining contact with children they place for adoption, the potential benefit of such contact for both, and the capacity of adoptive parents to forego their exclusive status and open their families to include the biological parents of their adopted children. Open adoption anticipates that the child may someday be interested in his or her origins and provides not only access to information but the promise of a more complex relationship to the facts and persons involved. This statutory scheme goes beyond unsettling the paradigm of "as if" families to create a new configuration of family relations.

In a moving memoir, *The Kid*, Daniel Savage recounts his own experience of the open adoption process.[25] His story pushes the envelope of new paradigms even further in that his partner is another man. Savage is the very out-of-the-closet gay author of a sexually explicit advice-to-the-lovelorn column that appears in both conventional and gay newspapers. The open adoption of a child by a gay male couple appears as one more new family form at a time when same-sex civil unions have been established in Vermont and in several European nations and when childbearing by lesbians has resulted in a proliferation of queer households with two mothers. In the 1997 preface to the paperback edition of

Families We Choose, the landmark study of "lesbians, gays, kinship," first published in 1991, anthropologist Kath Weston writes:

> Over the past decade family issues have moved to the center of lesbian, gay, and bisexual lives in ways I never could have foreseen. . . . "Are you planning to have kids?" has become a routine question directed at lesbian couples, even by heterosexual friends. Advocacy organizations have turned to the courts in an effort to gain legal recognition for "our families." Wedding ceremonies have become a staple of lesbian/bisexual/gay events, including the 1993 March on Washington and a 1996 group ceremony at San Francisco City hall officiated by Mayor Willie Brown. PFLAG (Parents and Friends of Lesbians and Gays) chapters have flourished in localities across the country, with groups organized by people of color to explore cultural differences in family relations. Studies of lesbian/gay families have even helped rehabilitate kinship as a fit subject for anthropological inquiry.[26]

As this summary reveals, the development of queer families of choice has proceeded both with and without the recognition of the state. Marriage ceremonies of members of the same sex have no legal impact and may even be understood as a form of civil disobedience calling attention to the injustice of denying basic partnership rights.[27] Although child rearing, like intimacy, may be carried out by informal arrangements among friends, parental status is legally recognized through birth certificates, marriage, paternity or custody judgments—or adoption.

Savage's work allows us to think further about both the desires that lead adults to raise children and the institutional contexts within which these desires may be frustrated or fulfilled. He is a close observer of himself and others, and his story is rich with insight into human motivation and interaction. *The Kid* boasts two subtitles: "What Happened after My Boyfriend and I Decided to Go Get Pregnant" and "An Adoption Story." Although one may be drawn to it as a take on gay life and queer parenting, the book turns out to be far more generally applicable as an account of this new version of open adoption, the procedures through which it has been implemented, and its complex intervention in social fantasies of family life.

Initially Savage emphasizes the differences between the two gay men and the straight couples with whom they undergo a two-day seminar on "Adoption: A Lifelong Process":

> Heterosexual identity is all wrapped up in the ability of heterosexuals to make babies. Straight sex can do what gay sex cannot, make "miracles." The straights at our seminar had expected to grow up, fall in love, get married, make love for fun, and sooner or later make love to make life. Infertility did more than shatter their expectations; it undermined their sexual identities.[28]

However, as they get more and more involved with the process, and Savage finds himself reflecting more honestly on "the real reasons" leading him and his partner to adopt, their difference seems less important: "The real reason people in general (by which I mean straight people, since people in general are straight) have kids today is to give themselves something real and meaningful and important to do. Having children is no longer about propagating the species or having someone to leave your lands to, but about self-fulfillment."[29] However, the specificity of their situation as gay men reasserts itself through the self-examination that such a deliberate undertaking involves. Neither Savage nor his boyfriend Terry understood himself to be a gay activist, but a political context seemed to impose itself: "Public displays of affection for gays and lesbians are political acts, and what could be a larger public display of affection than the two of us adopting a kid together."[30]

Initially they sought to work out an informal arrangement with people they knew, envisioning a more extended family constellation. Their talks with a lesbian couple, a single lesbian, and a single straight woman broke down for a variety of reasons, both personal and political. The advice of an attorney friend led to the collapse of negotiations for Savage to act as "sperm donor" to the lesbian couple: "When he got it out of me that I wouldn't be the legal parent, just a donor-dad, that the lesbians would have custody but that I would get to be 'involved,' Bob promised me we would all end up in court."[31] This conversation points up the importance of legal status even for people who see themselves and their interests as lying outside the mainstream. Without even raising the issue of personal conflict among the parties, the lawyer enumerated the contexts in which the care of the child might come to be a matter for adjudication: one of them could decide to move, the couple could separate, one or another of them could become incapacitated or die. In the legal crunch, outside of marriage, only legally established paternity or adoptive parental status would give him standing even to be heard on the issue of custody. Reasons like these lead lesbian couples, often vigorously opposed to anything like marriage, to have their children legally adopted by the partner who is not the biological mother.

When Savage and Terry finally decided to explore adoption, they quickly discovered the complexity of that situation as well: not only differences in the law between states but also the variety of child care agencies involved in the evaluation of prospective parents and the placement of children. Attitudes toward homosexual parenting would figure importantly in all such determinations. Open adoption as permitted in Oregon and Washington promised a more personal process:

> [T]he birth mother selects the family her kid will be placed with out [of] a pool of prescreened couples. Then the agency introduces the birth mom and the couple. If they hit it off, the agency helps them come to an agreement about the amount of contact they're going to have after the adoption takes place. Everything is negotiable.[32]

Savage meets two children, a three-year-old and a five-year-old, who had been adopted under this regime: "[T]hey weren't confused. They knew they were adopted. They knew who their birth parents were. They knew who their real parents were. And they knew the difference."[33] (Notice the naturalness with Savage characterizes the "psychological parents" as the "real" ones.)

Whether open or closed, adoption as a process subjects potential parents to the kind of surveillance and evaluation by agency and state functionaries that middle-class people rarely encounter in a liberal society: "Before the adoption goes forward, the agency makes sure the birth mother and the adoptive couple are on the same page."[34] Savage and Terry had joined several other couples for the preliminary orientation, and the group continued to meet for support and guidance as they moved through the various stages of application. They were asked to prepare a letter of introduction to birth parents who might consider their applications and to make themselves available for a home study by social workers attached to the agency. This process brought home the differences between acquiring a child through adoption or as the consequence of sexual intercourse:

> But the straight couples had expected to make the decision to have kids with absolute autonomy. . . . When they gave up on biokids and started the process of adoption, the loss of any sense of autonomy must have come as something of a shock. The agency called all the shots and . . . made you prove you were fit to raise children before they'd help you have a baby. You had to open your home, your bank accounts, your criminal record, and your skulls for agency inspection. And in open adoption, the birth mother called the final and most important shot: she decided who got her baby.[35]

This latter aspect of open adoption addresses the drastic imbalance in power between birth mother and adoptive couple while providing her a continuing relationship with the child: "She doesn't have to pretend she never had a baby or that her baby died, as birth moms who do closed adoptions are still encouraged to do."[36] However, even open adoption requires the mediation of bureaucracy. Whereas fertile heterosexual couples could have children without anyone's prior approval, all potential adoptive parents must be screened. Savage observes that "[f]or the couples at the seminar, this double standard heaped one more insult on the pile of injuries and indignities of infertility."[37] The home study turned out to be "more complicated" than Savage and Terry had expected, involving four visits with interviews of each alone and then together. As it turned out, the social worker assigned to their case was warm and congenial. They passed with flying colors. Then they tried to settle into a long wait without letting their hopes get too high. After all, they asked, what expectant mother was likely to see a pair of gay men as the ideal parents for the child she herself would be unable to raise? One young woman, a street kid from Seattle that Savage calls "Melissa," had no hesitation in doing so. Terry and Savage were the first in their group to be selected. There began another sort of negotiation and evaluation through which both Melissa and the gay couple sought to size each other up and see whether they could work out the terms of an adoption. Savage is both funny and humane in portraying the complex interaction among the three—the progress from wariness and distrust toward an acceptance of the role that each might play in the life of Melissa's child. He sensitively charts the uncertain vacillations between fantasy and realism that the arrival of the child could provoke. There were frequent meetings during Melissa's pregnancy. They provided her prenatal care, working not to become overbearing in their solicitude for her maternal health. However they could not avoid fretting about the impact of her street life on the baby; every beer she drank evoked worries about fetal alcohol syndrome. Melissa defended her independence while confirming her initial hunch that a pair of gay men who wanted to raise a child might do very well by the one they got. They reached agreement on the terms for future visits in time for the couple to be at her bedside shortly after she gave birth. Although Savage and Terry developed considerable anxiety that Melissa might, as she was entitled to do, change her mind at the very last minute, she did not. They found themselves the proud parents of a healthy baby boy.

Although his own story has a happy ending, Savage finds himself drawn into discussion of the politics of adoption. Opposition to lesbian and gay couples as parents, whether adoptive or otherwise, has become increasingly vocal. Even more than gay marriage, queer families have become the site of resistance by proponents of "traditional family values." Many states explicitly prohibit same-sex couples from adopting. Savage quotes the conservative Family Research Council on the efforts of a gay male couple to adopt a seriously damaged child: "'A child placed with two fathers will never be able to call out the word, "Mom." . . . The state is abrogating the child's right to a mother for the rest of his life.'"[38] The would-be father of a child with two dads observes that conservatives who generally oppose the creation of new rights did not hesitate in this context to proclaim "the right to a mommy."[39] Savage does not comment on the fact that for "a child no one wanted," asserting such a right is especially empty: those consigned to live out their childhoods in institutions have neither mother nor father to call upon. When a lesbian couple succeeded in adopting twins, the Family Research Council was equally vehement: "'What kind of image of manhood and fatherhood will little Jacob obtain being raised by two lesbians? How will little Anna, who will never know the love of a father, relate to men some day?'"[40] Permitting lesbians and gay men to adopt poses a challenge to the paradigm of "as if" adoptive families that reinforces norms of heterosexual monogamy. The intensity of feeling around this issue cannot be overestimated. Even in Vermont and those European countries that recognize same-sex civil unions, the new status explicitly excludes any rights to child custody or adoption.

The range and depth of opposition to queer families is well displayed in the recent debate in France about establishing civil unions (PACS) for couples who cannot or do not want to marry, including but not limited to those involving partners of the same sex. In addition to predictable opposition from the Roman Catholic Church, a number of intellectuals weighed in, deploying the resources of psychoanalysis and structuralist anthropology. Their position was distinct from more widespread defenses of the monogamous heterosexual family as grounded in "nature." Indeed, they insisted that kinship relations are culturally constructed: same-sex couples must be excluded from marriage because families composed of adults of different sexes are essential to initiate the young into the "symbolic order." They argued that preservation of the heterosexual family as the privileged site for child rearing is essential to the very existence of culture. Judith Butler summarizes their intervention in these terms:

> [Sylviane] Agacinski notes that precisely because no culture can emerge without the presumption of sexual difference (as its ground and condition and occasion), such legislation must be opposed, because it is at war with the fundamental presuppositions of culture itself. [Francoise] Heritier makes the same argument from the perspective of Levi-Straussian anthropology, arguing that efforts to counter nature in this regard will produce psychotic consequences.[41]

Heritier argued that "heterosexuality is coextensive with the symbolic order, that no culture can emerge without this particular formation of sexual difference as its foundation, and that the PACS and other such efforts seek to undo culture itself."[42] In addition, the Lacanian psychoanalyst Jacques-Alain Miller claimed that whereas gay men may well form long-term emotional relationships that should be legally recognized, these associations should not be regarded as equivalent to heterosexual marriages because they lack the element of "sexual fidelity" introduced by the "feminine presence."[43] Butler argues that such abstract conceptions of "sexual difference" as integral to the "symbolic order" are marked by the assumptions of actually existing systems governing sexuality and gender.

The convergence of the French theorists with the views of proponents of "traditional family values" in the United States suggests that ostensibly liberal societies may depend on quite specific forms of intimate association and domestic order. As Don Westervelt has shown in considerable detail, members of the U.S. Congress deployed a similar rhetoric during debates on the Defense of Marriage Act, which sought to outlaw same-sex marriages and was adopted by an overwhelming majority in 1996.[44] They claimed that heterosexual marriage is the very foundation of Western civilization; without the psychoanalytic overlay, they also made much of the deleterious effects of same-sex couples on the gender identities and mental health of children. Given the massive transformations in family life during the last several decades, there is something profoundly out of touch about the notion that the greatest threat to traditional marriage (and Western civilization) comes from those lesbians and gay men to wish to marry and perhaps raise children together. It would seem that the question of same-sex marriage does indeed have "symbolic" resonance far beyond its material effects.

Even more important here, the controversy about lesbian and gay adoption is conducted in complete abstraction from the social and institutional realities confronting children in need of care. Although open adoption offers a promising alternative, practically its reach is limited to those biological parents who recognize in advance the desirability of having a child adopted. Savage and Terry rejected one possible route: "[W]e could adopt an abused or neglected kid from the state, some poor kid languishing in foster care, and attempt to undo the damage done by the kid's biological family."[45] Many same-sex couples manage to adopt because of their willingness to accept "hard-to-place" children with "special needs." The existence of such children, in great numbers, further complicates the paradigm of "as if" families, which imagines the adoption of an infant unencumbered by its history and a voluntary surrender by biological parents. The welfare system is filled with children already marked and removed against their parents' will: "They are hard-to-place because most couples doing adoptions want the same thing: the Great White Infant. Couples want a healthy baby, one without emotional and physical scars."[46] By the time parents have been judged inadequate and unable to respond to assistance, their children may be badly affected and are no longer infants. Worse yet, they may be further injured by the state's temporary care while they wait for adoptive parents who may never appear.

V. "Sometimes I Feel Like a Motherless Child": Racial Harm and the Adoption Paradigm

The debate about cross-racial adoption requires us to broaden our horizon to include the institutional contexts of child welfare systems and the historical struggles of Native and African American communities. Many of the children of color who come into care are older, with stories and memories of their own. Some biological parents may come late to a placement decision because of growing insight or changed circumstances, but others lose custody of their children as result of judicial determinations of neglect or abuse. Equally important, large numbers of children "freed" for adoption are never placed in permanent homes and grow up in a limbo of "temporary" care as "wards of the state." Proponents of cross-racial adoption have often been motivated by the plight of such children as well as by ideals of equality and integration, whereas its critics have responded to the disproportionate removal of children of color from their communities of origin, defending ideals of group solidarity and multiculturalism. If we juxtapose Shanley's dissection of adoption paradigms with Dorothy Roberts's analysis of the pervasiveness of race in the welfare system, we are forced to interrogate the ways that the state intervenes in black families and the actual alternatives that it offers children whom it displaces. The situation of African and Native American children must be related to efforts by these groups to secure equality, especially through the civil rights movement of the 1960s and its aftermath. The norms invoked in the controversy are embodied in competing narratives of collective history and projections of ideal community. Powerful fantasies of belonging and aspiration are at work against a background of material inequality and racial stigma.

The debate has been couched in terms of the conflict between equality, understood as the child's right to the best and speediest placement available regardless of race, and the cohesion or even survival of historically oppressed minority groups, taken to require that children be placed with families who share their racial affiliation. In terms of the general paradigms governing adoption policy, the placement of children with members of their "own" race would seem necessary to reinforce the fiction of "as if" natural families. However, the displacement of that paradigm through abandoning the secrecy of birth records and opening up the possibility of contact between adoptees and their biological parents does not simply lead to the acceptance of a "race-neutral" principle. Rather, it requires acknowledgment of the role that the race of one's ancestors may play in the construction of individual identity. Certainly, in the imaginary project of searching for one's origins and telling a story that gives meaning to an individual life, the communities—racial, national, religious—from which one's parents emerged may be significant factors. It is hard to spell out in advance the child's interest without what appear to be external judgments about the importance of race in individual self making. Does a child have a right to be raised within a family of the same race as him- or herself, or, more accurately, his or her parents? Or does the child have a right to be placed within the "best" available family as quickly as possible without regard to race? Thus formulated, the balance would seem to lie with the latter. After all, without the security of an early placement, the child's subsequent capacity to construct a coherent life story, including his or her racial origins, may be jeopardized. However, the advocates of cross-racial adoption and recent federal law go beyond this pragmatic point to rule out any consideration of race in the child placement process. Even if a family of the same race as the child's parent is available, that cannot be a sufficient reason for the placement. The extremes on both sides of the debate do indeed import political aims beyond the interests of the child: racial integration is opposed to group solidarity. Native American groups did not hesitate to invoke the survival of the tribe as a value worth preserving, especially given the history of domination by non-native cultures. However, the opposition of the National Association of Black Social Workers to cross-racial adoption invoked the needs of children of color for the guidance of similarly situated adults to learn how to cope with a racist culture. Neither an abstract appeal to "the interests of the child" nor an ethical conception of individuality simply resolves the dispute: one may construct a meaningful life around ties of affiliation with a specific racial group or as a democratic citizen claiming equal treatment regardless of his or her race. Shanley's proposal that the birth parents' preference (if any) should be decisive if it does not require inordinate delay in placing the child seems eminently reasonable. As she points out, these differences are entangled with questions about power: "And who should have a say concerning whether race should play any part in placing the child: the birth parents, the adoptive parents, the adoption agency, the child's racial community of origin, and in the case of Native American children, the tribe?" To which list we might add family court judges, state legislatures, federal courts, the U.S. Congress, and, finally, perhaps even the child.

Questions about race sharply focus the historical dimensions of the politics of adoption at both a collective and a personal level. Consider the differences in federal law between the treatment of Native American adoptions and those of other racial groups. Historically, American law (not only U.S. but Canadian as well) has recognized group rights for indigenous peoples that are not otherwise acceptable within the individualist paradigms of liberal constitutions. The reasons for this are rooted in a history of conquest of the North American continent by European nations that negotiated treaties with the tribal groups already living here. These treaties, partially enacted in subsequent legislation, accorded collective rights to the peoples concerned, touching on language, culture, and property.[47] Shanley reminds us of these differences in legal status: the Indian Child Welfare Act of 1978

(ICWA) gave tribes jurisdiction over adoptions involving children of the tribe, requiring them to seek placement successively with members of the child's extended family, her tribe, or other Indian families, with non-Indian families a last resort. This legislation was passed when a high percentage of Native American children had been removed from their birth families and placed in foster or adoptive homes, mostly non-Indian, or in institutions, some run by the Bureau of Indian Affairs. The emergence of political movements among Native Americans and growing awareness of the threat to cultural survival led the U.S. Congress to reinforce the tribe's legal status with the ICWA and its hierarchy of ethnically defined preferences.

The history of Native Americans differs significantly from that of African Americans, where the traumatic and decisive events were most often the Middle Passage of involuntary immigration and generations of enslavement, followed by an incomplete emancipation and further generations of racial segregation and subordination. The civil rights movement of the mid-twentieth century and since, by which African Americans have sought to overcome this sorry history, emphasized the "equal protection of the laws" and the promise of democratic citizenship rather than their collective situation. As a result, court decisions and legislative schemes such as the federal Civil Rights Acts of 1964 and 1965 and similar state laws have banned discrimination against individuals on account of their race rather than recognizing any group status for African Americans. The principle of nondiscrimination has also been extended to include religion, sex, gender, and disability (and in some states sexual orientation) in a system of "equal opportunity." The articulation of general principles of equality grounded on the right of individuals to be treated on their merits leaves little room for the specific concerns of African American communities as such. In the child care area, the application of "neutral" standards led first to the Multiethnic Placement Act of 1994 (MEPA), which permitted race to be considered only as one of a number of factors in child placement if that did not unduly delay the process. However, by 1996, in the Interethnic Placement Act (IEPA), Congress denied federal funds to any state or private agency that used race as a criterion of placement. IEPA explicitly excluded Native American children.

As Shanley persuasively argues, the conception of equality applied here works in tandem with an image of the child as a "parentless" individual (at worst, a commodity) available for incorporation into any family that desires him or her. The potential conflict between applications of general principle and judgments of a particular child's interest becomes apparent if we recognize that Shanley's proposal to consider the racial preferences of birth parents is probably precluded by the IEPA. The opponents of cross-racial adoption could tell the story of African Americans and the struggle of the civil rights movement differently, emphasizing the importance of collective action rooted in black churches and political organizations, informed by attitudes of racial pride and aspirations to black power. They could point to the origins of "equal protection" in the Civil War Amendments to the U.S. Constitution and prohibition of "badges of slavery" designed to promote the aims of black emancipation. From that perspective, the systematic denial of parental rights to slaves is an important dimension of the subsequent history of African American families. That history underwrites claims that the state's removal of their children denigrates the capacity of black parents to care for their own. In the context of the history of slavery and its aftermath, against a background of continuing racial subordination, the application of a formal principle of equal treatment to African American families works to maintain substantial inequalities.

Dorothy Roberts's argument that the child welfare system in the United States perpetuates racial harm complicates the picture: "Black children enter the child welfare system in grossly disproportionate numbers—and the racial disparity is increasing." The system licenses the removal of black children from their parents but fails to provide adequate care for the many tens of thousands who are neither adopted nor returned to their families. Roberts agrees with opponents of cross-racial adoption that the discourse of child welfare reinforces negative stereotypes of black parenting, such as the matriarch, the careless mother, the welfare queen, and the absent father. However, she shifts the focus from final placement to the initiation of proceedings by which children are taken from parents alleged to be incapable of providing care. Roberts argues that racial stereotypes operate throughout the system, distorting the judgments of social workers and judges who fail to understand the organization of child rearing within black communities and are quick to remove children from their homes. The harm caused by the state's intervention in black familial arrangements is compounded by its failure to provide better alternatives: "Child protective agencies are far more likely to place black children in foster care than to provide less traumatic assistance. . . . Black children, moreover, are less likely than white children to be returned home or adopted. As a result, most of the 110,000 children whose family ties have been terminated and who are awaiting adoption are black." As Goldstein, Freud, and Solnit forcefully remind us, children experience time differently than adults. Their overriding need for a secure connection with at least one caring adult is thwarted by disruptions in continuity and frustrated by changes in custody. Removal from familiar contexts, however inadequate they may appear to outsiders, itself causes harm. Children who are not adopted may suffer frequent changes of foster care or end up in institutions. Their history in placement may only aggravate the effects of often fraught experience of early life. Sometimes children are also separated from siblings to whom they have already formed strong attachments. The treatment of black children within welfare systems contravenes the state's claim to be acting in their interest while undermining the black community's efforts to care for their own: "The enormity of the racial gap suggests that at least some significant portion of children are removed from their homes unnecessarily. . . . The state could address the group harms caused by both neglectful parents and the disruption of families by doing more to improve the material circumstances of families." The situation of black children may be most seriously endangered by the poverty of their families.

Roberts argues persuasively that recent "reforms" in federal law that require mothers to work to remain eligible for child assistance and make it easier for the state to terminate parental rights will only make matters worse: "The combination of welfare reform's decimation of much of the federal safety net for children and adoption reform's abandonment of the commitment to family preservation may only intensify the dismantling of poor black families." She argues that such institutionalized racism operates in tandem with cultural assumptions that assign responsibility for children to their parents alone without providing social support:

> More fundamentally, the fate of black children in the American child welfare system can be traced to a profound flaw in the system's very conception. The system is built upon the presumption that children's basic needs for sustenance and development will and can be met solely by parents. The state intervenes to provide special institutionalized services—primarily placing children in foster care—only when parents fail to fulfill their child-rearing obligations.

The dominant paradigm of adoption, closed or open, contributes to this harm. Governed by the norm of creating "as if" families for some, the system not only fails to deliver on its promise for many who remain in long-term care but also reinforces the norm that children are solely the responsibility of parents, whether biological or adoptive: "The strategy of moving more black children in foster care into adoptive homes may improve the well-being of a fraction of the population, but it will not solve the group-based harms I have identified. Indeed, the adoption strategy bolsters the stereotype of black family incompetence." The privatization of child care perpetuates social and racial inequality by ignoring the material and social deprivation that confronts many families. Moreover, this model delays state intervention until parents have failed in some way rather than helping to provide adequate care in the first place. Finally, the dominant ideology results in child protective proceedings with a punitive character more concerned to assign blame to parents than to provide care for children: "Child welfare interventions become a way both to punish black parents for their perceived moral depravity and to place black children in the state's superior care."

The fact is that black parents are more likely to have their parental rights terminated and that their children are less likely to be adopted. Roberts effectively argues that these outcomes result from a failure to recognize the validity of informal sharing of child care within extended families and among friends, from the state's refusal to take responsibility for providing assistance to poor children, and from the perpetuation of stereotypes that define black parents as inadequate and their children as undesirable. The child welfare system in these ways fails in its promise to individual children and works to maintain the subordination of African Americans as a group: "The disproportionate removal of individual black children from their homes has a detrimental impact on the status of blacks as a group because it weakens their collective ability to overcome institutional discrimination and because it reinforces stereotypes about black people's need for governmental supervision." The disruption of black families by the state and its agencies perpetuates the cycle of racial inequality. As Goldstein and his collaborators insist, the removal of young children from their families is experienced as abandonment and undermines their capacity to form lasting ties: "[T]hey not only suffer separation, distress and anxiety but also setbacks in the quality of the next attachments, which will be less trustful. . . . [T]he children's emotional attachments become increasingly shallow and indiscriminate."[48] They get caught in a downward spiral through which they become less capable of establishing the relationships they most need, often with devastating effects:

> [W]here children are made to wander from one environment to another, they may cease to identify with any set of substitute/parents. Resentment toward the adults who have disappointed them in the past makes them adopt the attitude of not caring for anybody; or of making the new parent the scapegoat for the shortcomings of the former one. In any case, multiple placement at these ages puts many children beyond the reach of educational influence, and becomes the direct cause of behavior which the schools experience as disrupting and the courts label as dissocial, delinquent, or even criminal.[49]

Here the state's creation of "parentless" children awaiting incorporation into "as if" families that never arrive perpetuates the very suffering it is supposed to cure. For African Americans, the harm of the child welfare system may ultimately result in disparate rates of unemployment and incarceration for young men, early pregnancies for women, and continuing strains on their families.

Aware of the inevitable tendency of child care systems to delay and of the exigent needs of growing children, Goldstein and his colleagues urged that *every* placement decision be treated as an emergency. Greater attention to the range of ages, diversity of familial histories, and intensity of need that characterize children awaiting adoption helps recast the policy issues. The number of children and the urgency of their needs for security underlines the irrationality of arbitrarily excluding any class of adults from consideration. Not only the claims to equal treatment by the adults but the "best interests" of the children require that single people, unmarried couples, lesbians and gay men, and members of any and all races and religions who are capable of providing long-term care should be enabled to adopt as quickly as possible. Even more importantly, every effort should be made to provide families, friendship networks, and local communities the material and social support to raise their children. The alternatives offered by the welfare system contribute far too much to individual suffering and racial harm. Perhaps ultimately, the paradigm of modern adoption itself must be challenged. The deliberate severing of one set of ties and creation of others to form quasi-natural families that mirror norms of heterosexual monogamy may exact too high a cost from the children and adults it excludes. Legal fictions that support collective fantasies that many do not share have failed the test of providing care for children in need.

NOTES

I would like to acknowledge gratefully my debt to those without whom this essay would not have been possible: Stephen Macedo and Iris Marion Young, for inviting me to participate in the proceedings at Atlanta in 1999; Mary Shanley and Dorothy Roberts, for their papers; Carol Sanger, for her commentary; Jamie Mayerfeld, for introducing me to *The Kid*; Jay Katz and the late Joseph Goldstein, for their courses in family law and psychoanalytic theory. It is a great tribute to the teaching of the latter that they raised questions that have remained with me for almost three decades. My thinking about children, families, and the law has been informed by several years' experience as a trial attorney with the Legal Aid

Society of New York. I dedicate this essay to the memory of Charles Schinitsky, founder and attorney-in-charge of its Juvenile Rights Division; of Judge Kathryn McDonald of the New York Family Court, once my supervisor in the Manhattan office; and of Joseph Goldstein, Professor of Law at Yale University.

1. Plato, *The Republic,* trans. Allan Bloom (New York: Basic Books, 1968), 139 et seq. (Stephanus: 460a).

2. John Boswell, *The Kindness of Strangers: The Abandonment of Children in Western Europe from Late Antiquity to the Renaissance* (Chicago: University of Chicago Press, 1998).

3. Michel Foucault, *The History of Sexuality: An Introduction* (New York: Vintage, 1976).

4. Thomas Hobbes, *Leviathan,* ed. C. B. Macpherson (New York: Penguin, 1968), 254, chap. 20.

5. Judith Butler, Ernesto Laclau, and Slavoj Zizek, *Contingency, Autonomy, Universality* (New York: Verso, 2000), 172.

6. Joseph Goldstein, Anna Freud, and Albert J. Solnit, *Beyond the Best Interests of the Child* (New York: Free Press, 1973), 11.

7. Ibid., 5–6.

8. Ibid., 6.

9. Ibid., 12–13.

10. Ibid., 13.

11. Ibid., 20.

12. Ibid., 23.

13. Sigmund Freud,"Moses and Monotheism" (1939), in *The Standard Edition of the Complete Psychological Works of Sigmund Freud,* ed. James Strachey, vol. 23 (New York: Vintage, 2001), 12.

14. Sigmund Freud, "Family Romances" (1909), in *The Standard Edition of the Complete Psychological Works of Sigmund Freud,* ed. James Strachey, vol. 9 (New York: Vintage, 2001), 237–38.

15. Ibid., 238.

16. Ibid., 239.

17. Ibid., 240.

18. Ibid., 238.

19. Ibid., 240–41.

20. Ibid., 241.

21. Drucilla Cornell, *At the Heart of Freedom: Feminism, Sex, and Equality* (Princeton, N.J.: Princeton University Press, 1998), 97.

22. Ibid., 99.

23. Ibid., 105, 107.

24. Ibid., 108–9.

25. Dan Savage, *The Kid (What Happened after My Boyfriend and I Decided to Go Get Pregnant): An Adoption Story* (New York: Dutton, 1999).
26. Kath Weston, *Families We Choose: Lesbians, Gays, Kinship*, rev. ed (New York: Columbia University Press, 1997), xiv–xv, citations omitted.
27. Morris B. Kaplan, *Sexual Justice: Democratic Citizenship and the Politics of Desire* (New York: Routledge, 1997), 227–35.
28. Savage, *The Kid*, 25.
29. Ibid., 34.
30. Ibid., 36.
31. Ibid., 44.
32. Ibid., 46.
33. Ibid., 48.
34. Ibid., 46–47.
35. Ibid., 69–70.
36. Ibid., 47.
37. Ibid., 70.
38. Family Research Council, quoted in Savage, *The Kid, 57.*
39. Savage, *The Kid,* 57.
40. Family Research Council, quoted in Savage, *The Kid, 57.*
41. Butler, *Contingency,* 146.
42. Ibid., 180.
43. Ibid., 146.
44. Don Westervelt, "National Identity and the Defense of Marriage," *Constellations: An International Journal of Critical and Democratic Theory* 8, no. 1 (2001).
45. Savage, *The Kid,* 55.
46. Ibid.
47. It is no accident that much of the most interesting work on the intersections of multiculturalism and liberal theory has emerged from thinkers like Will Kymlicka and Charles Taylor, who have been engaged by the specific challenges posed in Canada by indigenous people and the Francophone population of Quebec.
48. Goldstein et al., *Beyond the Best Interests,* 33.
49. Ibid., 34.

PART II

EDUCATION AND PARENTAL AUTHORITY

7

PARENTS, GOVERNMENT, AND CHILDREN: AUTHORITY OVER EDUCATION IN THE LIBERAL DEMOCRATIC STATE

WILLIAM A. GALSTON

I. Introduction

Some years ago, my wife and I engaged in a series of discussions about where to send our son to school. His experience in a District of Columbia primary school had been perfectly satisfactory, and we could have easily let him continue there. Ultimately, although neither my wife nor I am particularly religious, we decided to send him to a Jewish day school. The determining factors were, first, our desire that our son learn systematically about his heritage and second, that he learn in a recognizably moral community where shared premises—justice, care for others, moral responsibility, and self-discipline, among others—are applied to the concrete issues of school life.

Our decision occurred within a context of assumptions that we took for granted without much thought. The government has the right (and perhaps duty) to require the education of all children up through the mid-teens and to regulate some basic features of their education. Parents bear principal responsibility for seeing to it that their children meet this requirement, but they have the right to choose among a wide range of options for meeting it. While government has the right to tax all its citizens to finance and operate a system of public schools open to all, it cannot create a public school monopoly that prevents parents from sending their children to nonpublic schools.

Each of these assumptions was contested earlier in the history of the United States; all now enjoy near-universal support. In my judgment, this shift represents more than bare historical contingency or practical necessity. These widely accepted assumptions are consistent with a defensible version of liberal democratic theory as well as with the practical requirements of life in liberal democracies under modern circumstances.

The underlying theory goes something like this: In establishing the aims of—and control over—education, three sets of considerations must somehow be coordinated. First, the conditions for the normal development of children must be secured, their ability to become contributing members of the economy and society must be fostered, and the growth over time in their capacity for sound independent judgment must be recognized. Second, the liberal democratic state must act, not only to safeguard the developmental interests of children, but also to promote the effective functioning of its basic institutions. Third, the special relationship between parents and children must be reflected in the allocation of educational authority, and so must what I shall call the "expressive interest" of parents in raising their children in a manner consistent with their understanding of what gives meaning and value to life.

While each of the values must find appropriate expression in practical decisions, there is no guarantee that they will fit together into a harmonious whole. Pressed to the hilt, any one of them will entail costs to the others that may well be judged excessive. Sound education policy cannot be exclusively state centered, parent centered, or child centered. Among other implications, this schema means that civic concerns do not function as trumps in discussions of educational policy. A particular course of action designed to promote important civic objectives may nonetheless be the wrong thing to do for other reasons: for example, the government cannot rightly compel school children to join in a flag salute ceremony contrary to the dictates of their conscience.[1] This remains the case even if the flag salute proves to be an effective means of fostering patriotism. It is equally true that parental concerns do not function as trumps; in some cases the damage to core civic concerns, or to the child's interests, will be too extensive.

While I shall not offer anything like a full exposition (let alone defense) of this thesis, I should underscore three of its features at the outset.

First, liberal democracies are not civic republics. The liberal democratic state does not have plenipotentiary power, and public-spirited aims need not govern the actions of its citizens in all spheres and circumstances. And while feminism has reinterpreted and relocated the boundary between public and private matters, it does not necessarily deny the appropriateness of the distinction as such or the value of privacy, rightly understood, in human life.[2] If the liberal democratic state were to legislate a conception of child or governmental interests that in effect nullified parental educational choice, it would exceed the legitimate bounds of its authority.

Much the same can be said of liberal democratic justice. Whichever conception of liberal democratic justice one prefers, it cannot be so comprehensive and stringent as to expunge a substantial zone of diversity and choice. Justice establishes a framework of claims that individuals and (for some purposes) groups may ask the state to enforce. But potential claimants need not press their justified claims to the hilt. They may choose not to exercise some of their entitlements in return for other goods that seem preferable, all things considered. The proposition "It would be unjust for you to deprive me of A" does not imply the conclusion "It would be wrong for me not to exercise my claim to A against you." The nonexercise of a justified claim becomes questionable when the potential claimant is subject to intimidation or is deprived of the information and self-confidence required for independent judgment. The free exercise of independent and group choice within the framework of liberal democratic judgment generates a zone of diverse ways of life that are permissible and safeguarded from external intervention even when we could not imagine choosing them for ourselves.

At this point, I should confess a theoretical interest. In recent years I have inclined increasingly to the view that Isaiah Berlin's depiction of the moral universe we happen to inhabit is roughly right—a multiplicity of genuine human goods, no one of which is dominant for all persons, groups, or circumstances, and many combinations of which serve to structure ways of life that are worthy of moral respect. Liberal democracy as I understand it is particularly sensitive to this moral diversity and to the importance of social spaces within which it may find expression.[3] If so, I might add, liberal democratic civic education must emphasize the beliefs and virtues that enable citizens to respect the boundaries of free social spaces.

Second, when I invoke parental authority over education, I presuppose a fair division of decision-making power between the parents (assuming that more than one is in the picture). I make no assumptions about who can be a parent, about how one becomes a parent, or about the parent's legal status in relation to another parent or to the child. I do not address the circumstances in which the presumption in favor of the parent may be rebutted by parental misconduct or incapacity. Nor do I intend to enter into, or to prejudge, the knotty questions that arise when marriages dissolve or when a child's relatives other than parents (grandparents, for example) make claims on a share of decision-making authority. My discussion, then, takes place within a simplified model of family life. I leave for another occasion the question of how my arguments and conclusions would change in response to various real-world alterations of the model.

Third, to insist, as I do, that control over education is a function of distinct and sometimes competing normative dimensions is to say almost nothing about how these variables should be weighted or rank-ordered in determining individual decisions. This gap can be filled only by thick descriptions of specific decision contexts and by deliberative arguments about the relative importance of different dimensions of value within these contexts. Even after careful description and deliberation, in many situations it will not prove possible to reach full closure, leaving wide latitude for appropriate processes of political decision making.

While the multivalued pluralist perspective I am urging is not enough to produce unique affirmative results, it does yield an important negative consequence. This approach makes it impossible to argue directly from the premise "Option A yields important gains along dimension X" to the conclusion "We should choose A," for others may reasonably contend that the sacrifices of value along other dimensions are significant enough to outweigh the gains along X. From this perspective, then, it never suffices to claim that a particular course of action serves the interests of children, or parents, or civic life; all must somehow be taken into account.

II. Education in U.S. History

John Stuart Mill regarded the right of the state to compel parents to educate their children as "almost a self-evident axiom." Yet writing in 1859, he observed that in practice few of his fellow citizens were willing to affirm its force. While most acknowledged the moral duty of parents to educate their children, they denied that the state had the right to enforce it.[4] Much the same situation prevailed on the other side of the Atlantic. Despite the spread of the "common school" ideal in the early nineteenth century, as late as the eve of the Civil War, only two states (Massachusetts and New York) had enacted compulsory education statutes.[5] Many citizens who conceded that the policy would promote the general welfare nonetheless denied that the state could properly—and constitutionally—go down this road.

Within decades, matters had changed radically. By 1900, thirty-two states had passed compulsory attendance laws. By 1918, such laws were universal throughout the United States. Despite its readiness to strike down a wide range of social legislation as infringements of individual liberty, not even the *Lochner*-era Supreme Court was willing to raise constitutional questions about the power of the states to enforce such laws. (Given the late development of the policy of universal compulsory education, this agreement is all the more noteworthy.)

It is instructive to review the arguments in favor of public education that gained currency in the century between the onset of the common school debate and the establishment of universal compulsory education. The first may be called "limited perfectionism": a certain measure of education was necessary for normal intellectual and moral development and for full participation in cultural and associational life. The second revolved around basic social obligations: education enabled individuals to maintain their economic independence and to discharge their duties to family members. Third, education was thought to promote a range of public goods: economic growth, appropriate civic beliefs and virtues, national unity and "Americanization," and a strong national defense. The increased credibility of these claims represented a response to key developments—in particular, the industrialization of the economy, the diversification of the population through immigration, and the emergence of the United States in world affairs.

Early in the twentieth century, the U.S. Supreme Court acted to ratify, but also to limit, the evolving power of government in educational affairs. Three decisions handed down in the 1920s helped define the constitutional context within which education policy has operated ever since.

Reflecting in part the nativist passions stirred by World War I, the state of Nebraska passed a law forbidding instruction in any modern language other than English. Under this statute, a Nebraska trial court convicted a teacher in the Lutheran parochial school for teaching a Bible class in German. In *Meyer v. Nebraska*, decided in 1923, the Supreme Court struck down this law as a violation of the Fourteenth Amendment's liberty guarantee.

Writing for seven members of the Court, Justice McReynolds noted that "it is the natural duty of the parent to give his children education suitable to their station in life; and nearly all the States, including Nebraska, enforce this obligation by compulsory laws."[6] This kind of legislation is not in itself constitutionally dubious: "The power of the State to compel attendance at some school and to make reasonable regulations for all schools . . . is not questioned."[7] The question is whether the prohibition of all instruction in modern languages other than English meets this test. Justice McReynolds argued that it did not: "That the State may do much, go very far, indeed, in order to improve the quality of its citizens, physically, mentally and morally, is clear; but the individual has certain fundamental rights which must be respected. A desirable end cannot be promoted by prohibited means."[8] Nebraska's action represented such prohibited means because it violated both Meyer's right to teach German and the right of parents to engage him to instruct their children in that language:[9] "The desire of the legislature to foster a homogeneous people with American ideals prepared readily to understand current discussions of civic matters is easy to appreciate. But the means adopted, we think, exceed the limitations upon the power of the State."[10] In a remarkable if controversial passage, Justice McReynolds expanded the discussion beyond even constitutional bounds. He identified the underlying theory of the Nebraska law with the practices of Sparta and the pedagogical principles of Plato's Republic. But "their ideas touching the relation between individual and State were wholly different from those upon which our institutions rest" and could not be implemented "without doing violence to both letter and spirit of the Constitution."[11] Our constitutional conception of liberty guarantees parents a wide though not unlimited sphere of discretion to educate their children as they see fit.

The Supreme Court handed down a second key ruling just two years later. The background can be summarized briefly: Through a ballot initiative, the people of Oregon adopted a law requiring parents and legal guardians to send all students between the ages of eight and sixteen to public schools. In practice, this amounted to outlawing most if not all nonpublic schools. The Society of Sisters, an Oregon corporation that maintained a system of Catholic schools, sued, claiming that the law was inconsistent with the Fourteenth Amendment. In *Pierce v. Society of Sisters,* decided in 1925, the Court emphatically agreed. Justice McReynolds, this time writing for a unanimous court, declared:

> [W]e think it entirely plain that the Act . . . unreasonably interferes with the liberty of parents and guardians to direct the upbringing and education of children under their control. . . . The fundamental theory of liberty upon which all governments in this Union repose excludes any general power of the State to standardize its children by forcing them to accept instruction from public teachers only. The child is not the mere creature of the State; those who nurture him and direct his destiny have the right, coupled with the high duty, to recognize and prepare him for additional obligations.[12]

Consider, third, *Farrington v. Tokushige,* decided in 1927. Faced with a proliferation of schools teaching the Japanese language to students of Japanese ancestry, the Territory of Hawaii enacted a law strictly regulating all foreign-language schools. Among its other provisions, the law imposed a per capita tax on these schools and gave the territorial government the right to determine hours, course of study, entrance requirements, textbooks, and teacher qualifications.

The Court found that this law and the administrative measures adopted pursuant to it "go far beyond mere regulation of privately supported schools . . . . They give affirmative direction concerning the intimate and essential details of such schools." Enforcement of the act, the Court concluded, would destroy most of the regulated schools and would deprive parents of a fair opportunity to obtain instruction, not obviously harmful, that they desired for their children. "The Japanese parent has the right to direct the education of his own child without unreasonable restrictions," but the law in question represented "a deliberate plan to bring foreign language schools under a strict governmental control for which the record discloses no adequate reason."[13] Because the law was inconsistent with the liberty guarantees of the Fifth Amendment, it could not stand. The Fifth Amendment rather than the Fourteenth applied because Hawaii was at that time a territory rather than a state, and the Fourteenth Amendment constrains only state governments.[14]

Taken together, these cases stand for three propositions. First, in the U.S. Constitution's version of liberal democracy, there is in principle a division of authority between parents and the state. Government has the right to require parents to educate their children and to specify some basic features of that education, wherever it may be conducted. Parents, however, have a wide and protected range of choices as to how to discharge that duty to educate. Second, the state may not deploy its regulatory power to deny in practice what it grants in principle. In particular, government may not require nonpublic educational institutions to conform themselves to public schools as a condition of their continued existence. And third, there are some things the government may not rightly do, even in the name of forming good citizens. The appeal to the requisites of civic education is powerful, but not always dispositive when opposed by claims based on parental authority or individual liberty. In short, the legal framework of education in the United States reflects the fact that the underlying theory of the U.S. Constitution is liberal rather than civic-republican.

These three cases have framed the constitutional discussion of education since they were handed down seven decades ago. And thus it is that today no U.S. governmental authority can prevent my son's Jewish day school from existing or so tightly regulate the content of the education it offers as to preclude its distinctive two-track curriculum. And even if there were substance (which there is not) to the sometimes voiced charge that learning about Israel complicates or weakens students' allegiance to the United States, the government would not ipso facto have the right to intervene.

As Barbara Bennett Woodhouse argues, the context of these cases is more complex than their status as "liberal icons" would suggest. The impulse behind the Oregon law was populist egalitarian as well as nativist; the legal theory underlying these cases (substantive due process) also yielded *Lochner v. N.Y.* and *Hammer v. Dagenhart*; the argument could be read as endorsing an understanding of children as parental property.[15] Still, the holdings of these cases have never been seriously questioned, and they enjoy almost universal support today.

III. From History to Theory

So much by way of brief historical and constitutional background. But of course, appealing to basic features of U.S. educational practices does not suffice to justify them. A resort to theory may not prove conclusive, but it is surely necessary.

As we have seen, John Stuart Mill regards it as virtually self-evident that the state "should require and compel the education, up to a certain standard, of every human being who is born its citizen." In his account, the state's authority derives from parental responsibility. The bare fact of causing the existence of another human being brings into play more responsibilities than does virtually any other human act.[16] In particular, "[I]t is one of the most sacred duties of the parents (or, as law and usage now stand, the father), after summoning a human being into the world, to give to that being an education fitting him to perform his part well in life toward others and toward himself." The failure to do so is a "moral crime, both against the unfortunate offspring and against society; and . . . if the parent does not fulfill this obligation, the State ought to see it fulfilled."[17]

Mill assumes that this educational duty flows directly from the fact of biological generation, coupled with broad features of the individual and social good. Parents do not have the right to neglect the education of their children in ways that impose avoidable burdens on their fellow citizens—for example, by raising children unable to contribute to the economy or unwilling to obey the law. Nor do they have the right to deprive their children of what Mill assumes to be the profound and pervasive benefits of education: the development of human faculties is at the core of what he terms the "permanent interests of man as a progressive being."[18] Mill accepts a version of the thesis I earlier termed limited perfectionism; the necessity of education reflects, not only the contextually specific requisites of advanced economies, but also noncontextual features of the human condition. The state has a legitimate interest in enforcing parental responsibility, both to enhance social utility and to create human beings in the "maturity of their faculties" who are "capable of being improved by free and equal discussion."[19]

Mill suggests that this parental responsibility is material as well as moral: parents must finance their children's education to the extent they can. His insistence on individual responsibility is striking: the "moral crime" lies not only in willfully depriving a child of education but also in bringing a child into the world without a "fair prospect" of being able to afford a basic education. (He even endorses the legitimacy of Continental laws forbidding couples to marry unless they have the means to support a family.[20]) But he also stresses the element of social responsibility: when the state makes education compulsory, it must provide sliding-scale subsidies for lower-income families and pay outright for the education of children whose parents cannot afford to contribute anything. So all members of the society must do their part to sustain a system of compulsory education that benefits society as a whole.

Mill distinguishes between state-enforced compulsory education and direct state provision of education. He opposes all policies that lead to state dominance over or monopoly of education. Diversity of character and opinion is the key to both individual flourishing and social progress. But a state-dominated system of education is a "mere contrivance for molding people to be exactly like one another" that "establishes a despotism over the mind." A state system of education "should only exist, if it exist at all, as one among many competing experiments, carried on for the purpose of example and stimulus to keep the others up to a certain standard of excellence."[21]

This is not to say that the state has no interest in defining a basic common education or no legitimate power to enforce it. A wide range of parental choice makes sense only in the context of publicly defined educational standards that can serve as regular and reliable benchmarks of educational attainment. Mill proposes a universal system of public examinations, beginning with basic literacy at an early age and widening out annually to ensure the acquisition and retention of core general knowledge. He is confident that these examinations can be structured to prevent the state from exercising an improper, homogenizing control over the formation of opinion through a strict focus on "positive science." To the extent that examinations on disputed topics such as religion and politics are administered, for example, they should be confined to facts about the views of specific authors or denominations and the stated grounds of those views.[22]

Clearly, Mill is offering a generalized defense of educational diversity and parental choice. But what kind of theory is it? At first glance, Mill's theory is child centered: a state educational monopoly disserves the best interests of children because it is bound to foster mental despotism and personal unhappiness by repressing individuality. By implication, Mill's account of individuality rejects the thesis of social construction. Rather, each of us is born with a "nature"—a distinctive ensemble of talents, dispositions, and potentialities of character. To the extent that this ensemble is able to flourish, our lives gain value, for ourselves and for those around us. If not, our capacities wither and starve, and we lose touch with ourselves.

One may of course question Mill's point of departure. But there is much to be said in favor of the proposition that children are not uniform blank slates that others may inscribe as they please. Most parents I know have been led by their own experience to acknowledge the existence and importance of each child's natural bent. Good parenting—and by extension good education—finds ways of accomplishing its essential purposes with rather than against the grain.

The crucial issue is whether our upbringing will accommodate and encourage, or rather pinch and repress, the development of our distinctiveness. But there is no guarantee that a system of parental educational choice would promote individuality as Mill understands it. He is critical of patriarchy, but he does not draw the obvious connection that a father's choice may prove just as Procrustean for a child as would the state's. Instead of a single despotic power there might be a multiplicity of smaller ones. (Mill of all people should have been exquisitely sensitive to this possibility.) Mill's proposed system would promote educational diversity, to be sure, but not necessarily individuality.

There is more to be said in defense of Mill's position, however. Educational diversity is at least a necessary condition for the cultivation of individuality. Assuming, as Mill does, the diversity of human types, it is hard to see how any single unitary system of education could accommodate all of them equally well. The existence of a range of educational choices offers the possibility of a better fit between institutional settings and individual needs.

While children can be consulted, moreover, they cannot make these choices for themselves, especially in the early years. Either parents will make these choices, or the state will make them for them. While parents may often fail to choose wisely, there are reasons to believe that the state typically will do even worse. On average, parents understand their children's individual traits better than public authorities do, their concern for their children's well-being is deeper, and they are not subject to the homogenizing imperatives of even the best bureaucracies in the modern state. In practice, the legal system must create a presumption in one direction or the other, and the case for a presumption in favor of parents is strong.

But that presumption is rebuttable. While the range of parental discretion is wide, the state properly enforces numerous limits on parental authority. Laws against abuse and neglect mean that parents are not free to injure their children or to deprive them of the basic goods needed for normal physical, mental, and emotional development. Nor may parents invoke their deepest religious convictions to prevent their children's immunization or deprive them of essential medical care. By the same token, the state may act to prevent what amounts to educational abuse and neglect, through measures such as compulsory education statutes and basic standards of education attainment. But the state cannot legitimately define a concept of the child's best interests so extensive and detailed that its enforcement would in practice eviscerate the power of parents to make decisions concerning their children's education.

Eamonn Callan offers a useful example. Suppose that the parents of a musically talented child can afford either to buy a piano or to take the child on an expensive holiday. Judged from the standpoint of the developmental best interests of the child, the right choice is reasonably clear. But we draw the line at state authority with the power to compel parents to buy the piano instead of going to Disneyland. There must, it appears, be a protected zone of parental discretion, even when the judgments parents make look mistaken to outsiders.[23]

Why should such a zone exist? One standard liberal answer is fear of the overweening state: even if the judgment of bureaucratic experts were systematically superior to that of parents, a government with the power to make us buy the piano would be unlikely to leave any of our liberties intact. But a fuller answer includes as well the expressive interests of parents in raising children in a manner consistent with their own understanding. It is to this theme that I now turn.

IV. Expressive Liberty and Parental Interests

By *expressive liberty* I mean the absence of constraints imposed by some individuals or groups on others that make it impossible or significantly more difficult for the affected individuals or groups to live their lives in ways that express their deepest beliefs about what gives meaning and value to life. An example of such constraints is the Inquisition, which forced Iberian Jews either to endure persecution or to renounce their religious practices.

Expressive liberty offers us the opportunity to enjoy a fit between inner and outer, conviction and deed. Not all sets of practices will themselves rest on, or reflect a preference for, liberty as ordinarily understood. For example, being Jewish is not always (indeed, is not usually) understood as a matter of choice. But once that fact is established through birth and circumstance, it becomes a matter of great importance for Jews to live in a society that permits them to live in accordance with an identity that is given rather than chosen and that is structured by obligations whose binding power does not depend on individual acceptance. For Jews, and for many others as well, the ability to revise one's conception of the good is hardly a good thing. In short, because not all sets of beliefs and practices value (let alone give pride of place to) liberty, expressive liberty protects the ability of individuals and groups to live in ways that others would regard as unfree.

Expressive liberty is an important value because it is a precondition for leading a complete and satisfying life. The reason is straightforward: part of what it means to have deep beliefs about how one should live is the desire to live in accordance with them. Only in rare cases (perhaps certain kinds of Stoicism) do constraints imposed by other individuals and by social structures have negligible effects on the ability of believers to live in accordance with their convictions. Most of us experience impediments to acting on our deepest beliefs as sources of deprivation and unhappiness, resentment and anger. The absence of expressive liberty is a misfortune that few would willingly endure.

Although expressive liberty is a great good, it is not the only good, and it is certainly not without limits. No one would seriously argue that the expressive liberty of parents would legitimate the ritual sacrifice of their children or that expressive liberty could be invoked to blunt the force of responsibility to our fellow citizens and to legitimate public institutions. But because it is a core value, it cannot rightly be infringed without countervailing reasons of considerable weight.

Expressive liberty is possible only within societies whose members do not needlessly impede one another's opportunity to live their lives as they see fit. To be meaningful, the ethic of liberty requires a politics and sociology of liberty. Suitable institutional arrangements can help police a zone of mutual abstention, but these institutions must be bolstered by the pervasive belief among citizens that it is wrong to deprive others of expressive liberty. Citizens must internalize norms, not of substantive indifference, but rather of self-restraint, in the face of practices that reflect understandings of the good life that they reject. Fostering this self-restraint—the principled refusal to use individual or collective coercion to deprive others of expressive liberty—is a legitimate object of liberal civic action.

What I want to argue is that the ability of parents to raise their children in a manner consistent with their deepest commitments is an essential element of expressive liberty. As Eamonn Callan rightly suggests, parenting is typically undertaken as one of the central meaning-giving tasks of our lives. We cannot detach our aspirations for our children from our understanding of what is good and virtuous. As Stephen Gilles insists, loving and nurturing a child cannot in practice be divorced from shaping that child's values. In so doing as parents, we cannot but draw on the comprehensive understanding that gives our values whatever coherence and grounding they may possess.[24] Moreover, we hope for relations of intimacy with our children, as they develop and when they are grown. But estrangement is the enemy of intimacy. It is understandable for parents to fear that their children may become embroiled in ways of life they regard as alien and distasteful and, within limits, act to reduce the risk that this fear will be realized. Callan links these parental expressive interests with core liberal freedoms:

> The rights to freedom of conscience and association are widely accepted as among the necessary requirements of any recognizably liberal regime. But the freedom to rear our children according to the dictates of conscience is for most of us as important as any other expression of conscience, and the freedom to organize and sustain the life of the family in keeping with our own values is as

> significant as our liberty to associate outside the family for any purpose whatever.[25]

Conversely, one of the most disturbing features of illiberal regimes is the wedge their governments typically seek to drive between parents and children and the effort they make to replace a multiplicity of family traditions with a unitary, state-administered culture.

The appropriate parental role is structured in part by the vulnerability, dependency, and developmental needs of children. The model of fiduciary responsibility developed by Locke and endorsed by contemporary thinkers such as Richard Arneson and Ian Shapiro well captures this dimension of the parent-child relationship.[26] But the expressive interests of parents are not reducible to their fiduciary duty to promote their children's interests. A better model is more nearly reciprocal: parents and children serve, and are served by, one another in complex ways. To quote Callan once more:

> [I]f a moral theory interprets the child's role so as to make individual children no more than instruments of their parents' good it would be open to damning moral objections. But parallel objections must be decisive against any theory that interprets the parent's role in ways that make individual parents no more than instruments of their children's good. We should want a conception of parents' rights in education that will not license the oppression of children. But we should also want a conception that will do justice to the hopes that parents have and the sacrifices they make in rearing their children.[27]

This reciprocity model must do justice to the particularity of the relationship between specific parents and specific children. Everyone can agree that children are not the "property" of their parents. Still, when I say that this child is "mine," I am both acknowledging responsibilities and asserting authority beyond those I owe or claim vis-à-vis children in general. As parent, I am more than the child's caretaker or teacher, and I am not simply a representative of the state delegated to prepare the child for citizenship. The hopes and sacrifices to which Callan refers reflect the intimate particularity of the parent-child bond, the fact that the child is in part (though only in part) an extension of ourselves. This fact helps explain the multiplicity of moral claims sons and daughters must balance: to themselves (the duty of integrity), to the state (the responsibilities of citizenship), and to their parents (the obligation of gratitude, if not always obedience).

Like any other value, the expressive interests of parents can be pushed too far. To begin with, as children develop, their own expressive interests must be given increased weight. Consider the well-known case of *Wisconsin v. Yoder.*[28] This case presented a clash between a Wisconsin state law, which required school attendance until age sixteen, and three Old Order Amish parents, who claimed that mandating their children's school attendance after age fourteen would undermine their community-based religious practices. While the Supreme Court decided in favor of the parents, a number of justices declared that the adolescent children had liberty claims independent of their parents. The record offered no evidence of religious disagreement between the Amish children and their parents. If the children had expressed the desire to continue their education, these justices would have voted to uphold the state's enforcement of its attendance laws against the wishes of the parents. At a minimum, the children's freestanding religious claims imply enforceable rights of exit from the boundaries of community defined by their parents. I would add that the exit rights must be more than formal. Communities cannot rightly act in ways that disempower individuals—intellectually, emotionally, or practically—from living successfully outside their bounds.

But should the expressed views of the children be taken as dispositive? Arneson and Shapiro say not: even if the children acquiesce, the parents may still be in violation of their fiduciary responsibility. A parent, they insist, "cannot pretend to speak for the child while really regarding the child as an empty vessel for the parent's own religious convictions. As a fiduciary, the parent is bound to preserve the child's own future religious freedom."[29] Even if we accept this premise (and it may be questioned from several perspectives), it is by no means clear what practical conclusions we are compelled to draw from it. Does respect for a child's religious freedom mean that the parent is required to treat all comprehensive views equally, taking the child on a tour of different faiths and secular philosophical outlooks and then saying in effect, you choose? Few parents, whatever their outlook, would accept this proposition; even fewer would endorse its enforcement by the state; and I do not see considerations weighty enough to warrant such a sharp break with established practices. At the very least, parents are entitled to introduce their children to what they regard as vital sources of meaning and value and to hope that their children will come to share this orientation. One might also argue that instructing children within a particular tradition, far from undermining intellectual or religious freedom, may in fact promote it. Knowing what it means to live within a coherent framework of value and belief may well contribute to an informed adult choice between one's tradition of origin and those encountered later in life.

Now consider a thought experiment at the other extreme. Suppose a group raises its children with the result that as adults, none ever question or reject the group's basic orientation. To achieve this result, the group seals itself off from the outside world and structures its internal education so that children are not even aware of alternatives to the group's way of life. In effect, the group has become a kind of mental and moral prison. Because diversity and disagreement typically arise even in circumstances of considerable repression, their absence in this case is a sign of extreme suppression of individuality that warrants external scrutiny and perhaps intervention. Parents abuse their expressive liberty if they turn their children into automatons, in part because in so doing they deprive their children of the opportunity to exercise their own expressive liberty.

In this respect, I agree with Eamonn Callan's argument that servility is a vice and that parental actions fostering servility in children amount to illegitimate despotism. As a parent, I cannot rightly mold my child's character in a way that effectively preempts "serious thought at any future date about the alternatives to my judgement." Every child has a prospective interest in personal sovereignty (Callan's term) or, in my terms, expressive liberty, that parents cannot rightly undermine.[30]

There are, however, formative forces other than parental despotism that also foster servility. Children immersed in a culture defined by advertising, entertainment media, and peer pressure are often dominated by influences that they neither understand nor resist. In the face of such challenges, to have any realistic possibility of exerting countervailing formative power, parents may be compelled to take a strong countercultural stance that involves a substantial measure of family or communal separation from external influences. Parental actions that may be judged despotic in some circumstances may well be necessary, or at least justified, in others.

While these arguments clarify some moral intuitions, they also suggest that practical issues of educational authority cannot be resolved on the plane of moral abstractions. The acceptability of parental decisions must be evaluated within the full context of influences shaping children's awareness of alternatives and ability to weight them. And it is not enough to judge the intention of parents' educational decisions; we must also look at their concrete results.

These considerations highlight some relevant empirical dimensions of the *Yoder* controversy. The Amish community is not a prison. Young adults must explicitly choose to become full members. Substantial numbers decide not to join at the threshold, and others leave later. While there are transitional difficulties for some, there is no evidence that many former members find themselves unable to cope with the demands of a modern economy and society.

This is hardly surprising. In a contemporary liberal democratic society, it is impossible for small groups to seal themselves off from ways of life very different from their own. At most, even a coherent separationist community such as the Amish can only serve as a counterweight to the dominant culture. It cannot prevent children from learning about alternatives, and while it can offer young adults various incentives to stay, it cannot prevent them from leaving.

Even if *Yoder* does not violate the present or potential expressive liberty of Amish young people, it may be argued that the decision gives inadequate weight to the state's interest in fostering good citizens. According to this line of argument, good citizens participate actively in public affairs, using developed powers of critical reason to deliberate on and decide among competing policies and representatives. But Amish education discourages both active participation and critical reasoning and thus fails to meet legitimate basic state requirements.[31]

There are three sorts of reply to this line of argument. First, as we have seen, the proposition that X is instrumental to (or even necessary for) the creation of good citizens does not, as a matter of constitutional law or liberal democratic theory, warrant the conclusion that X is right or legitimate, all things considered. There may be compelling moral and human considerations that prevent the state from enforcing otherwise acceptable policies on dissenting individuals or groups.

Second, even if we accept the premise that critical reasoning is a sine qua non of liberal democratic citizenship, there is no reason to believe that the Amish are incapable of exercising it in the relevant respect. I recently read a newspaper article (regrettably I cannot locate the reference) written by a Catholic theologian concerning U.S. tactics in the Kosovo conflict. Reasoning from and applying the principles of Catholic "justice in war" doctrine, he concluded that high-altitude bombing safeguarded pilots at a morally unacceptable cost in civilian lives. This is an example of critical reasoning *within* or *from* a tradition rather than *about* that tradition. But it would be unreasonable for a conception—especially an enforceable conception—of liberal democratic citizenship to demand that citizens somehow set aside, or adopt a stance of open-minded neutrality toward, the beliefs around which they organize they lives when reasoning about public affairs. The Amish have demonstrated their capacity for critical reasoning in the ways that it is publicly reasonable to expect.[32]

Finally, the active deliberative/participatory virtues are not the only virtues of citizenship we should care about. Law-abidingness, personal and family responsibility, and tolerance of social diversity are also important for the successful functioning of contemporary liberal democracies.[33] In these respects, among others, the Amish score high. They may not be the best of citizens, but may we not say that they are good enough? At least they fulfill the political version of the Hippocratic oath—to do no harm. I might add that if nonvoting and civic withdrawal are taken as sufficient evidence of parental and pedagogical failure warranting state intervention, then our indictment extends far beyond the minute

numbers of Amish to implicate more than half the families and graduates of public schools in the United States.

V. Parental Authority, Expressive Liberty, and Public Education

Today, after two decades of hand-wringing about the quality of public education, roughly 90 percent of all school-age children still attend public schools. There is no compelling reason to believe that the emphasis I have placed on expressive liberty and the role of parents, if taken as the basis for actual policy, would significantly erode the dominant position the public schools now enjoy. Nor does my thesis undermine the legitimate role of the state in requiring all parents to educate their children and in establishing basic standards for all educational institutions. (In these important respects, all elementary and secondary education in the United States is "public.") Rather, my account merely makes explicit the moral and theoretical underpinnings of the long-standing U.S. constitutional commitment to the principle that parents may choose among a range of options—public and private, secular and religious, heterogeneous and homogeneous—for discharging their obligation to educate their children.

Nonetheless, my stance does reflect an underlying understanding that some may find objectionable. I believe that in a society characterized by a deep diversity of moral and religious views, and accordingly by diverse family and communal ways of life, both empirical consent and normative legitimacy require that, to the maximum extent consistent with the maintenance of civic unity and stability, all permissible ways of life be able to find expression in the key choices families and communities must make. Among these choices, the venue and conduct of education rank high. I would argue that genuine civic unity rests on unforced consent. States that permit their citizens to live in ways that express their values are likely to enjoy widespread support, even gratitude. By contrast, state coercion is likely to produce dissent, resistance, and withdrawal.

Granted, sometimes the state has no choice. If families, schools, or local communities are acting in ways that violate the basic rights of citizens, then the state must step in. And if the result is resistance—even "massive resistance" in the face of compulsory school desegregation—that is the price that must be paid for defending the rightful claims of all citizens. My point is rather that the state must be parsimonious in defining the realm in which uniformity must be secured through coercion. An educational program based on an expansive and contestable definition of good citizenship or civic unity will not ordinarily justify the forcible suppression of expressive liberty.

NOTES

For a fuller statement, see William A. Galston, *Liberal Pluralism: The Implications of Value Pluralism for Political Theory and Practice* (New York: Cambridge University Press, 2002).

1. As the Supreme Court recognized in *West Virginia v. Barnette,* 319 U.S. 624 (1943).
2. See Susan Moller Okin, *Justice, Gender, and the Family* (New York: Basic Books, 1989), 127-28.
3. For initial sketches of this position, along with some consequences for educational policy, see William A. Galston, "Expressive Liberty, Moral Pluralism, Political Pluralism: Three Sources of Liberal Theory," *William and Mary Law Review* 40 (March 1999): 869-907; and "Value Pluralism and Contemporary Liberal Theory," *American Political Science Review* 93 (December 1999): 769–78.
4. John Stuart Mill, *On Liberty,* ed. Currin V. Shields (Indianapolis: Bobbs-Merrill, 1956), 128.
5. R. Freeman Butts and Lawrence A. Cremin, *A History of Education in American Culture* (New York: Holt, Rinehart and Winston, 1953), 415.
6. 262 U.S. 400.
7. 262 U.S. 402.
8. 262 U.S. 401.
9. 262 U.S. 400.
10. 262 U.S. 402.
11. 262 U.S. 401–2.
12. 268 U.S. 4534–35.
13. 273 U.S. 298.
14. 273 U.S. 299.

15. Barbara Bennett Woodhouse, "'Who Owns the Child?': *Meyer* and *Pierce* and the Child as Property," *William and Mary Law Review* 33 (Summer 1992): 995-1122.
16. Mill, *On Liberty*, 132.
17. Ibid., 128.
18. Ibid., 14.
19. Ibid., 13, 14.
20. Ibid., 132.
21. Ibid., 129.
22. Ibid., 130–31.
23. Eamonn Callan, *Creating Citizens: Political Education and Liberal Democracy* (Oxford, England: Clarendon, 1997), 146-47.
24. Stephen G. Gilles, "On Educating Children: A Parentalist Manifesto," *University of Chicago Law Review* 63 (1996): 960-67.
25. Callan, *Creating Citizens*, 143.
26. See Richard Arneson and Ian Shapiro, "Democratic Autonomy and Religious Freedom: A Critique of *Wisconsin v. Yoder*, in *Democracy's Place*, ed. Ian Shapiro (Ithaca, N.Y.: Cornell University Press, 1996), chap. 6.
27. Callan, *Creating Citizens*,145.
28. *Wisconsin v. Yoder*, 406 U.S. 205 (1972).
29. Arneson and Shapiro, "Democratic Autonomy," 154.
30. Callan, *Creating Citizens*, 152-54.
31. This is the core of the Arneson/Shapiro critique of *Yoder* in Arneson and Shapiro, "Democratic Autonomy."
32. See, e.g., the essays assembled in Albert N. Keim, ed., *Compulsory Education and the Amish: The Right Not to Be Modern* (Boston: Beacon, 1975).
33. See William A. Galston, *Liberal Purposes: Goods, Virtues and Diversity in the Liberal State* (New York: Cambridge University Press, 1991), chap. 10.

8

TAKING CHILDREN'S INTERESTS SERIOUSLY

MARTHA L. A. FINEMAN

As Professor William Galston clearly states, educational policy requires a balancing of interests. As with many other decisions affecting children and families, the rights and responsibilities of parents and the state must be components of any consideration of what is appropriate for children. The problem is that bringing parents and the state into the discussion often diverts attention away from children. Perhaps it is evidence of our inability to rise much above binary thinking, but what tends to happen in balancing discussions is a kind of either/or thinking, with the child as a "prize" rhetorically shuttled back and forth between the competing rights holders—the parents and the rival state. The independent interests of the child, if recognized at all, are submerged as we slip into a consideration of the competing claims of authority over children made on behalf of parent and state.[1]

It is not surprising that the child tends to disappear as an independent focus in discussions about rights and authority. The very existence of the child presents a dilemma for the liberal theorist concerned with the individual and preserving autonomy and choice. The child is clearly an individual, but one who is not fully actualized or capable of autonomous decision making. Children are dependent in many ways—economically, emotionally, and, often, physically. We are uncomfortable with the idea of children, even adolescents, exercising unsupervised "choice," and we structure legal and social relationships so that someone is empowered to act for them and in their interest.

In our system, the family (headed by the parent) is the social institution to which children with their dependency are referred. The family is designated as "private" and thus distinguished from the public and political realms, which are appropriately subjected to policy making in the liberal tradition. Secured within the private family, the dependent child becomes the primary responsibility of the parent. This conceptualization renders most considerations of the child independent of the family (parent) inappropriate because they are potentially adversarial. In most cases, the family is presumed to function appropriately, and the child, invisible within the private sphere, can conveniently be ignored in fashioning public policy.[2]

Of course, the child does not always remain subsumed within the family and is occasionally separated out as the state seeks to supplement or displace the parents as decision maker. This occurs when the child is the object of specific public policy, such as education. But the dependency and lack of autonomy inherent in the status of child seem to mandate that the real terms of debate are when the rights of the "natural" custodian (the parent) are trumped by the residual *parens patriate* power of the state. Despite the well-documented possibilities of harm to children, we are still suspicious of the state as protector of children against parents.

The reduction of the balancing to a consideration only of the parents and the state is evident in the area of education. This is an area in which the state has well-established interests and has long been active. In fact, the state mandates that parents educate their children. Three objectives are typically articulated in justification of compulsory education. Each of these objectives ostensibly emphasizes different interests.

The first objective has a public aspect, and the interests of the state are dominant. If we argue that compulsory education is necessary to produce an informed and disciplined citizenry able to create and maintain necessary social institutions, we emphasize the interests of the state. By contrast, the emphasis is on social or parental interests when the objective of education is cast as teaching children responsibility with regard to the family, the community, and civic institutions.

If we concentrate on the "self-actualization" possibilities provided by education, however, the child's interest should be moved to the foreground. Education from this perspective has the potential to position the child in opposition to both parent *and* state. The parents' dilemma is that educational opportunities often produce paths for advancement and mobility out of the family circumstances (providing escape from the family's class, neighborhood, etc.) and thus ways for the child to assert her or his individuality. From the state's viewpoint, education for self-actualization is often geared more toward developing personal critical capacity than toward securing social conformity and obedience. This potential tension may interfere with both parental and state advocacy of the child's self-actualization interest in education.

Professor Galston correctly points out that sometimes the objectives of education are at odds with each other. Choosing from among them can lead us to different conclusions about how we should allocate control or authority over decision making. Professor Galston resolves this in a balance that first concedes the mandatory nature of education, but thereafter strongly favors parental discretion. He also concedes that it is necessary to have some standard requirements concerning substance and content.[3]

Parental discretion can be exercised by choice of the location of the child's education—whether it will be in a private or public institution, in a religious or secular setting, and so forth. Parents also have choices with regard to supplementing their child's education with enrichment courses or specialized instruction beyond the state-mandated core curriculum. The lessons of *Meyer* and *Yoder* are that the state is denied rigorous regulatory power over both arenas of parental discretion—private schools and supplemental education—even when it asserts an interest in protecting the child's interest in self-realization. But this leads to the questions of how much structure the state can impose on parental decisions about supplementation of core education in the interest of protecting the child as an individual.

The next, obvious question is: How does the child's interest manifest itself in this scheme where the state is foreclosed from meaningful regulation? At this point Professor Galston's strong preference for parental decision making in education derails the balancing process and allows the parents' interest to subsume the interest of the child. This is done in a manner that suggests that the allocation of the child's interest to parental authority is the best way to protect that interest. His first claim is that leaving the decision making to parents will provide greater diversity of educational choices. Choices will allow them to find a better fit between the child and his or her educational setting. This, Galston believes, will promote the possibility of the growth of individuality in a child. He views this result as a positive good.

His second claim is that parents have superior knowledge about their child. It is presumed that this knowledge will allow them to make superior, even if not perfect, decisions for that child. The implication certainly is that typically parental decisions will be superior to those made by the state in this regard.

Both of Galston's arguments assume that parents typically act in the best interests of children. Both arguments are offered as "child-centered" justifications for parental control.

But in examining these claims an initial observation leaps to mind. Specifically in regard to the claim that parental choice leads to child individuality, an argument could be made, on the basis of psychological and other observations, that the family is one of the most difficult contexts in which to assert one's individuality, at least as that term is used to connote independence. Further, Galston may be overstating not only the possibility of diversity in a parental choice (private) system but also the uniformity or conformity of the state system.

It is not clear what constitutes "the state" in Galston's analysis. There are few nationally imposed requirements that deal with educational substance. In fact, the idea of national content control (even in the form of national testing) has been vigorously rejected throughout American history. In actuality, "the state" system is many systems that vary by state and locality. One response to Galston is that within the state system there is always a great deal of choice. The curriculum of schools in Kansas is not the same as that in New York. If parents do not want their children taught the theory of evolution, they can simply relocate to a state with a different science curriculum.

Even if the state were to articulate a unitary standard of core requirements, diversity would show up at the implementation stage as differences within districts, schools, and classrooms. Furthermore, an important potential for diversity in public education is presented by public school systems' access to tax revenues. These resources, collected from everyone in the district, are specifically committed to the education of that district's children. While there are "politics" to be played in this regard, the state school systems have the ability to garner public funds to supplement core education with a variety of pluralistic/secular school-affiliated clubs, groups, and associations. Thus the possibility for diversity of experience in some public settings goes well beyond that provided by smaller individual private institutions dependent on tuition.

Just as Galston understates the relative superiority of public schools in providing diversity, he overstates the possibility for diversity inherent in giving parents choice among educational options. There may well be some diversity *among* private institutions, but there is more likely to be homogeneity *within* them. Education, after all, is a group activity, practiced in institutions. Private institutions may become the choice of parents precisely because they are likely to be far more homogeneous, providing fewer opportunities for children to encounter alternatives to parental values or biases.

Perhaps the entire argument about the possibilities for diversity is rather specious. If there is a core curriculum, then diversity is merely conceived of as supplemental to some extent. Of course, as noted above, differences may be introduced in the process of implementation, but that type of diversity is not confined to the private setting. Further, even if there are opportunities for supplements beyond the imposed core curriculum, external pressures such as standardized tests, college entrance requirements, and the influence of culture will probably push private institutions to replicate public choices. Teaching materials are also relatively uniform in content and perspective, and there is not a great deal of variety and choice.

Thus significant constraints limit the viability of theoretical options. Even in cases in which there are unconstrained economic resources, time, and energy, other factors will make uniformity and conformity attractive if not inevitable. I am not arguing that there are no diversity distinctions, only pointing out that the difference in diversity opportunities supplied by private as contrasted with state systems is less stark than Galston suggests.[4]

Galston's second justification for parental control is that parents have special or superior knowledge about their child. I concede that this may be true when the knowledge at issue is highly personalized, such as whether the child's favorite color is red or blue or whether the child prefers carrots to beets. However, I question whether parents have superior knowledge when the issues involve what subjects and methods of preparation are most likely to prepare the child for a future in a complex, technical, and rapidly changing world.

My comfort level with leaving decisions to parents is profoundly affected by the extent to which any decision is likely to have implications for the child in the future. Some parental choices will not have much long-term effect on the developmental well-being of an individual. Children are very resilient and can often recover from parental selfishness, shortsightedness, mistakes, bias, or ineptitude. Thus, to use Galston's example, a child can recover (or never experience real disadvantage) from being deprived of piano lessons for the sake of a trip to Disneyland. Other choices, however, may not inspire confidence about children's assumed resilience. Certain parental decisions can create handicaps and inhibit a child's entry into the secular and complex world in which she or he must live and function as an adult.

Galston begins his essay with his decision to send his son to a religious school. His expressive parental interest is to educate his child according to his values and morals. But what if the parental values and morals to be expressed in making choices for the child are not so conveniently exemplary by secular standards as those of Galston? What is the role for expressive interest of parents who believe in the value and morality of white supremacy or resistance to the "jack-booted" officials of a federal government poised to take over and enslave free people? What weight should be given to the choices for their children of parents who believe that women should be sequestered and confined, that they are actually a form of "property" to be passed from father to husband according to God's will? The point is that parental expressive interest can reflect oppressive, hierarchical belief systems. Such systems are designed to destroy any possibility of the very individuality and independence that Galston argues diversity can foster.

When one considers these types of expressive communities, it is important to realize that parents may not be the "real" or sole interest holders in regard to their children. Parents in these contexts are often part of a larger religious or ideological community, a community with an independent interest in and intent to indoctrinate children. Such communities conspire with member parents to separate their children from diverse secular, and therefore competing and dangerous, alternatives.

The big question is not whether the state must recognize parents' expressive interest in their children's education, but where we draw the line separating that expressive interest from the *child's* interest in the diversity and independence-conferring potential of a secular and public education. When does the state's interest in protecting children come into play? Galston mentions the concept of educational abuse and neglect as the place to draw that line. The examples I mentioned would not fall into that category, however, since the children in question would be educated and could function at or above a minimal level.

One final point in criticism of Galston's position has to do with his expressed notion or idea of "choice." Choice in the individual family situation that he begins with as the basis for his arguments is a positive good, freely available to all parents. Galston was able to explore alternatives, identify a particular school consistent with his values and beliefs, secure entry for his child, navigating entrance tests and requirements, and afford the tuition. He had options for manifesting his expressive interest. What about those parents with fewer options, however—those whose children are excluded by tuition or tests or those who reject the necessity of affiliation with religious groups in order to secure that type of subsidy for a private education?

Choice is not equally available to everyone in our American education system—some are kept out. It is particularly important to remember this crucial point given our history of race relations. Historically in the United States the expressive interest of one set of parents resulted in the segregation of and discrimination against the children of another set of parents. Allowing some to opt out of the public system today is reconstituting a new reality of segregation and neglect in many urban areas.

Perhaps the more appropriate suggestion for our current educational dilemma is that public education should be mandatory and universal. Parental expressive interest could *supplement* but never *supplant* the public institutions where the basic and fundamental lesson would be taught and experienced by all American children: we must struggle together to define ourselves both as a collective and as individuals. Perhaps when parents could not buy their children's way out of a public system, they would begin to buy into the idea that we should all be concerned with every child's opportunities, not just with those of our own.[5]

NOTES

1. I myself have been guilty of this type of lapse and usually find myself on the side of greater parental (caretaker) control over decisions affecting children. In considering education, however, my inclination is the opposite. I want a more active state and well-defined public presence.

2. In contrast to liberal theorists, who have paid scant attention to the issue of the child's independent interests, focusing on the fully framed and independent adult as the object of theory, some feminist theorists have used the position of the child to argue that the concept of autonomy is flawed. Further, concentrating on the child suggests that the boundaries between state and family are blurred. Feminists have also pointed to the paradox that while the substitution of private (family) for public (state) power occurs in the name of protecting the autonomy and interests of some individuals (parents), this can produce the possibility of harm to other individuals within the family (children).

3. In this regard, note attempts on the part of parents to opt their children out of certain classes within public school. Some may feel it is appropriate to excuse a child from sex education classes, but how do we feel about that same child's being excused from the science curriculum because it teaches the theory of evolution and the big bang theory?

4. Paradoxically, allowing parental choice of private as compared with public education may provide diversity across institutions, but it may result in the child's actually experiencing less diversity *within* an institution if it is private.

5. One of my favorite statistics to make this point is that one out of every 270 (or so) people in the United States is a child in the New York City public schools. In what way can we continue to think of education as a "local" concern? Such a viewpoint is even more ludicrous when we add to the more than a million New York City public school students those in Los Angeles, Chicago, Philadelphia, and so on.

9

THE PROPER SCOPE OF PARENTAL AUTHORITY: WHY WE DON'T OWE CHILDREN AN "OPEN FUTURE"

SHELLEY BURTT

Adult rule over children is so widespread that an effort to explain or justify it might seem beside the point: part of what it means to be a child is to be subject to the authority of adults. Yet there is little consensus in either real-world or scholarly debates concerning the nature and extent of such authority. While few question the overall justice of age-based inequality, the precise parameters of a parent's right to make child-rearing decisions independent of state interference or oversight are constantly contested. It is perhaps not surprising that views on this question differ between regimes, cultures, and religious traditions, but disagreement also persists if we narrow our focus to liberal democratic polities. Courts, legislatures, and scholars in both the United States and Europe have all grappled with how far the right of parents to make decisions regarding children's discipline, medical care, and education (to mention only the most prominent areas of dispute) extends. In the American constitutional context, these disagreements are often filtered through the lens of the free exercise of religion clause.[1] But the issues at stake reach beyond questions of religious freedom to the more general right of parents to raise children as they see fit and, in particular, to control and direct the education they receive.

Most, if not all, parents believe that they bear some responsibility for their child's moral, spiritual, cultural, and civic education. And for almost everyone, being a good parent involves ensuring that children acquire the habits and virtues characteristic of a good person and responsible citizen. Many parents, in addition, hope their children will embrace the particular values and ways of life that they, the parents, find worthy of commitment, seeking to educate their children consistently with this end. But how far can parents go in shaping their children's values without running afoul of the values of democratic citizenship and liberal autonomy? When must parental aspirations give way to public values and expectations regarding the next generation of the nation's citizens?

One obvious limiting principle turns on the moral importance of at least some minimum level of autonomy in any plausible conception of the good life. Thus Eamonn Callan has argued forcefully that neither family nor state is justified in creating "ethically servile" individuals, and nothing I say here is meant to conflict with this position.[2] Persons so deeply in thrall to parental power or religious authority figures that they cannot think at all independently about questions of identity and morality are neither good citizens nor morally autonomous individuals. No community should either encourage or tolerate educations that aim in this way at the complete subordination of one person's will to that of another.[3] But while we can safely rule out of bounds parenting directed toward such ends, doing so still leaves the appropriateness of many parents' educational agendas unresolved.

In this essay, I pay particular attention to what I will call "fundamentalist" educational practices. The fundamentalism I reference here is one that takes fundamental truths about the good and right as given and aims to convey these truths intact to the next generation. In fundamentalist educations, children are not encouraged to choose their values or way of life in reflective contrast to their parents'. Rather, they are taught that the best way of life, the way of life they ought to adopt, is one that affirms and reproduces the faith, worldview, and moral understandings of their parents. Typically, such fundamentalist educations are associated with religious upbringings, but we can imagine this sort of education occurring around questions of cultural and national identity as well.

Liberal philosophers have always characterized the purpose of children's education in ways deeply antagonistic to such fundamentalist aims, and contemporary writing on the subject is no exception. In an influential article written a generation ago, at a high point of scholarly interest in the nature and extent of children's rights, Joel Feinberg argued that children have a "right to an open future," one in which they, rather than their parents, choose the orienting principles by which they will guide their lives.[4] While Feinberg's argument is rarely referenced in recent debates on the subject, its central idea of preserving for the child an "open future" directly captures what contemporary liberal theorists take to be the dividing line between a just and unjust exercise of parental educational authority. Good educations keep children's options open as regards their values, roles, and way of life, encouraging them to choose these goods for themselves as they develop the capacity rationally to reflect on ultimate values.[5] Fundamentalist educations, by contrast, go beyond the allowable scope of parental authority by seeking to narrow children's choices regarding the best way of life to those that their parents or their faith community find acceptable.

I agree with Amy Gutmann that the distinctions often drawn between political and comprehensive or perfectionist liberalism are not relevant here.[6] Both political and perfectionist liberals, though for different reasons, argue explicitly for the importance of exposing all children to diverse points of view regarding understandings of the good life—a position that necessarily sets these theorists at odds with the educational aims of fundamentalist parents. Perfectionist liberals insist that only such exposure, undertaken with the aim of eliciting children's "sympathetic and critical engagement" with ways of life other than the one their parents value, can ensure that children develop the capacity for critical self-reflection on which the characteristic liberal virtues of autonomous thought and action depend.[7] Political liberals take a slightly softer line, professing agnosticism regarding the development of the "liberal personality" but insisting on exposure to diversity as a necessary element of developing the tolerance for social diversity required of a good citizen.[8]

It is possible to object that these arguments turn not on what parents may or may not teach their children, but rather on what public schools may or may not legitimately require of children enrolled in them. Most theorists engaged with questions regarding parents' educational authority concede that parents who disagree with the "open future" provided by public school curricula are free, as a matter of constitutional entitlement, to choose private or home schooling for their children. But while the possibility of opting out is acknowledged, the moral thrust of liberal arguments is that children whose parents choose fundamentalist educations for them are being unjustly treated and remain in danger of being deprived of a good—education for autonomy or education for democratic citizenship—that they deserve to receive.[9]

In the following pages, I stake out a position very much at odds with this view, defending fundamentalist educations as not only permissible, but well within the bounds of parents' educational authority. While this authority is not unlimited, neither is its scope delineated by the value of liberal cosmopolitanism, which represents but one view of the good life to which parents may seek to commit their children. Parents who wish to expose their children to a wide variety of possibly worthy lives both in and out of their formal schooling experience may certainly do so, just as they may choose to teach them that decisions about the good life are intensely personal matters that must and should be made by each individual after appropriate critical reflection on the values and chosen lifestyles of their parents. But the creation of liberal cosmopolitans is not the only just exercise of parental authority. Parents may, with equal legitimacy, raise their children to understand themselves as in some important way *lacking* a choice about what they do or who they are. Fundamentalist educations aim to produce such encumbered selves, providing upbringings in which children are not encouraged to choose their ends but are rather urged to grow into roles and life goals already affirmed as worthy by their family and faith community. Not every fundamentalist education will posit goals that a liberal democracy can or will tolerate, but simply to influence or seek to influence a child in this manner is neither to overstep the appropriate bounds of parental authority nor seriously to threaten the autonomy of future citizens.

The extent to which fundamentalist educations compromise the development of individual autonomy is a legitimate concern, but not the focus of my discussion here. My own view is that the sorts of fundamentalist educations on offer in liberal democracies today do not impede the development of individual autonomy properly understood. While children receiving such educations may not understand themselves as able to choose freely from among a range of worthy life plans, the effort to tie children to a particular way of life already judged as worthy by their parents neither automatically nor even frequently creates "ethically servile" individuals. To the extent that this outcome is avoided, and I explore elsewhere why this expectation is legitimate,[10] liberal democracies need not fear for either the autonomy or the civic capacities of individuals receiving fundamentalist educations.

This is not to say that all fundamentalist educations deserve toleration. As already stated, the creation of ethically servile individuals is out of bounds. Politically, a state may at a minimum act to prevent parents from raising individuals with a deep-rooted antipathy to the state's constitutional order and/or a settled indifference to widely held principles of international law and human rights. As I write, the despicable example of Muslim boys and girls being raised to embrace the life of suicidal martyrs comes to mind as particularly abhorrent. But the problem with such parental malfeasance is the unworthiness of the way of life glorified, as well as the deliberate flouting of legal norms that the encouragement of terrorist activity implies, not the fundamentalist impulse itself or any supposed deprivation of a child's autonomy.

While we can safely rule out of bounds parenting directed toward such ends, an additional concern regarding fundamentalist educations remains. Do fundamentalist educations, in their effort to decide for children their ends and values, overstep the appropriate limits of parental authority? It is to this question that I now turn.

How far may parents go in socializing their children to particular values and ways of life? Which choices regarding curriculum, values, peer group interaction, and educational attainment are properly made by parents, and which must be shared with the state or the child? Typically, these questions have been answered by focusing on the outcomes of fundamentalist educations. Those defending a robust view of parental educational authority will often emphasize its benign consequences—Amish children are not as lacking in autonomy as may be feared; girls raised within strict Muslim households still possess the necessary democratic civic virtues, and so on—while those critical of fundamentalist educations will take the opposite tack. This essay takes a somewhat different approach, looking not at the results of fundamentalist educations to determine their acceptability but at the principles that ground parental educational authority in the first place.

Proponents of a liberal education sometimes write as if the immense influence parents exercise over their children's understanding of self and world is a regrettable feature of family life that good parents will do their best to avoid. My own view is that parents who seek to exercise decisive influence over their children's worldviews and values act justly with regard to their children as long as they concomitantly fulfill the primary responsibility of parenting, which is to meet their children's developmental needs. From this perspective, the state properly intervenes in family decision making only when these developmental needs are demonstrably in jeopardy. Once this standard for the proper scope of parental authority is accepted, deciding for or against the legitimacy of fundamentalist educations requires a discussion of what children need to develop well and whether the ends of fundamentalist educations are in any way at odds with these goals. I turn to these questions in part II of this essay. In part I, I discuss liberal theories of paternal authority and why I believe the proper scope of parents' educational authority should be set not by the "open future" standard of liberal theory but by this focus on meeting developmental needs.

I.

Do parents overreach their authority when they raise their children to affirm only those goods and values the parents themselves believe to be true and worthwhile? Does the state act justly in insisting that children be exposed to views, values, and ways of life that their parents believe are inconsistent with living well? Because these are questions about the proper scope of parental authority over children, answering them correctly requires us to reflect on the reasons we give adults authority over children in the first place. Why, in the face of legal and moral antagonism to virtually all forms of inequality, do we continue to affirm the necessity and appropriateness of treating children unequally?

Some might argue that the issues at stake in deciding for or against fundamentalist educations are far removed from such foundational questions. But all arguments for or against particular distributions of authority over children rest on certain assumptions regarding the grounds of children's inequality. *Some* morally relevant difference between children and adults must be asserted to justify the former's near complete social and political domination of the latter. And the difference that we point to in order to justify children's unequal treatment will in turn influence the range over which we are willing to let parental authority extend.

In the following pages, I argue that liberals take too narrow a view of the sort of authority parents may exercise over their children in part because they lack a sufficiently expansive picture of what children lack as compared to the adults who care for them. Because liberal theorists miss crucial features of what children need from adult authority figures in their journey to adulthood, their conclusions regarding the appropriate scope of parental authority are compromised. Against the liberal focus on rational capacity as the primary feature distinguishing children from adults, I offer a conception of children's deficits that focuses on their developmental needs. In this view, children are best understood as comprehensively needy adult "works in progress," who require a tremendous amount of caring attention from adults in general and parent figures in particular to grow into mature individuals able to flourish in the communities of which they are a part. Once children are understood in this way, the notion that parents' primary educational responsibility to a child is to preserve for him or her an open future becomes less compelling. Parents act justly toward children when they play their part in providing the goods and resources required to guide them toward a productive, responsible, rewarding maturity. With these propositions in mind, I return in part III to the question of the moral permissibility of fundamentalist educations. I conclude that fundamentalist educations are not the only way for parents to meet their children's developmental needs, but neither do they represent a prima facie abuse of parental power.

What features of childhood render children sufficiently unlike adults that their comprehensive subordination is not (in theory at least) a form of oppression? Locke's answer to this question provides the template for most later liberal thought on the subject, although its primary motivation is very much to counter what Hobbes and other absolutists had to say about the grounds of parental authority. For Hobbes, parental authority is political authority and is justified (by consent) and exercised (absolutely) in the same way as a monarch's assertion of authority over his subjects. In fact, Hobbes's model is unique in maintaining a formal equality of infant and adult as civic persons, even though its thrust is to legitimate parental dominion. The child chooses a relation of inequality, and it is the evident rationality of this choice, given the child's utter dependence on its potential caregiver, that legitimates its subordination. Beginning with Locke, liberal theory deliberately dissociates parental authority from political power. Consent becomes the only legitimate ground of political subordination (rule of one adult over another) but is explicitly rejected as the basis of parental authority. Children are described as properly subject to adult authority because they lack the qualities or capacities necessary for rational self-government.

Just as Hobbes shaped his account of parental dominion to serve his argument for the rationality of absolutist regimes, so Locke re-visions parental power to support his critique of political patriarchy. Debunking Robert Filmer's popular defense of absolutism (which, like Hobbes's, linked the absolute power of the father to the absolute power of the monarch) required challenging the patriarchal conception of familial authority in which a child's subjection to his parents lasted a lifetime—without opening the door to the absurd proposition that parents had no authority over their children at all. Locke argued that lifelong subordination could not be legitimate given men's natural equality with each other. Rather, the child's subjection to his parents was temporary and made necessary by certain deficiencies. Children are not "born in [a] full state of Equality"; they are lacking certain goods or capacities common to all unimpaired adults. It is thus possible to exercise authority over them without their consent and without injustice. But because these deficiencies are remedied over time, the grounds for authority will weaken until, like swaddling clothes, "they drop quite off, and leave a Man at his own free Disposal."[11]

Locke gives as the most important reason for children's temporary subjection their incapacity to live by the "Law of Reason." (Issues of physical dependence and self-sufficiency, including a child's "inability to provide for his own support and Preservation," figure as well but receive less emphasis.) God intends for all human beings to live by and under the law of reason, yet the capacity to "keep his actions within the Bounds" of the law is not yet present in the "imperfect state of Childhood." This imperfection (or deficit) explains and justifies the subordination of children to their parents. "Whilst he is in an Estate, wherein he has not Understanding of his own to direct his Will, he is not to have any Will of his own to follow: He that understands for him, must will for him too."[12]

It is important to note, especially in contrast to the liberal paternalists to whom I turn next, that Locke's account of what children are missing in terms of rational capacity is neither particularly robust nor defined in terms of a capacity for critical self-reflection. One commentator, for example, glosses it as "the capacity to manage your own private affairs while keeping out of trouble with the law."[13] Locke's view seems to be that the rational capacity he requires as the precursor to equal treatment emerges some time in midadolescence as part of the normal process of human maturation. Until then, the parents' job is to supply the reason their children lack, literally substituting their will for their children's imperfectly guided one.

How successful is Locke's effort to explain and justify the root causes of children's persistent inequality? The central question of the *Two Treatises* is obviously not the appropriate scope of or limits to parental power. The ground of children's subordination is discussed primarily to drive home the point that the sort of rule appropriate to children who have not yet developed their full powers of reason must be very different from the authority to which fully rational individuals are legitimately subject. But since the picture of childish deficits that Locke provides is shared by most liberal theorists writing on the subject of parental authority, it is still worth examining the implications of Locke's account in more detail.

Considered solely as a justification of children's inequality, Locke's account has a number of limitations. In particular, his focus on rational deficit, while superbly conceived as a response to the problem of political patriarchy, produces a distorted understanding of what children are lacking vis-à-vis adults and, in consequence, an incomplete picture of what authority over them exists to supply. I have two problems particularly in mind here. First, as every parent knows, the only or primary thing children lack as compared to adults is not the ability to use reason to regulate their behavior. Children require a broad range of goods and resources if they are to grow into adults capable of flourishing in the community of which they are a part.[14] Locke the philosopher may well share this more complex view of what children lack as compared to adults, but this multidimensional picture is still absent from the one text in which he explicitly discusses the rationale for children's subordination to their parents. Here, children's inequality is both measured and justified solely in terms of their lack of rational capacity and thus fails to capture the full extent of what it is about children that leads adults to treat them unequally. As such, we cannot confidently turn to it to guide our discussion of the proper *limits* of that power.

A second difficulty is that even if lack of rational capacity were the primary deficit that justified children's unequal treatment, Locke has not necessarily characterized correctly the manner in which such deficit is remedied. And, as I have already argued, we must characterize what children lack correctly in order to specify properly the scope of parental power. For Locke, the rational capacity that children lack emerges as surely and spontaneously as the more physical manifestations of adulthood. The job of the caring adult is not so much to develop that capacity as simply to supply the deficiency until such time as the child is sufficiently mature to make decisions for him- or herself. I call this approach one of substituted judgment. Since the child cannot reason his way to obedience to human and divine law, it is legitimate to place him under the control of others who will enforce this obedience. A different picture of children's needs will produce a different picture of what adult authority over them exists to supply—with a corresponding change in how we judge the scope and limits of that authority. For example, it is not at all clear that what children need to flourish as adults is supplied in the normal process of human maturation (as Locke believes of humans' rational capacity). While all children able to survive through their adolescence will become adults physically and cognitively, the sort of adults we wish to live with and to whom we must entrust our world's and nation's future will not emerge from the children we are responsible for without considerably more attention. The ability to act morally, to respond to personal and public challenges with emotional maturity and due attention to the competing claims of self, family, and community, is a learned capacity, not an inevitable milestone in the maturation of the human being. Any fully adequate account of the distribution of authority over children must incorporate this fact, acknowledging that adult rule over children exists not simply to supply a deficit until such time as the child matures but rather actively to shape the child's morals, goals, dispositions, habits, and virtues.

Of course, acknowledging this necessity does not in itself establish an exclusive parental right to shape the child's understanding of the world or to decide what the totality of the child's developmental needs are and how to meet them. While I defend fundamentalist educations as legitimate, I do not believe parental power is absolute or unlimited. In part III I discuss the proper dividing line between state and family input into decisions affecting children's well-being. Here I want simply to make the point that what separates children from adults and justifies their quite comprehensive subordination is not simply an underdeveloped reasoning faculty. Locke's focus on rational deficit is completely understandable given the purposes of his political theory, but it produces a distorted picture of developmental needs and thus of the sort of authority that should be exercised over children.

More recent liberal theorists follow closely enough in Locke's footsteps that their work is subject to similar criticism. Like Locke, they explain and justify children's unequal treatment by reference to rational deficiencies. However, there is a shift in emphasis derived from their taking into account new questions raised by Mill's distinctive view of liberal principles. For Locke, the obvious legitimacy of parental rule over children and the equally obvious fact that the child has not consented to it present a challenge to his claim that any power exercised without the individual's consent is unjust. Children's inequality poses a different sort of explanatory problem for contemporary liberals, who must grapple not only with the idea of persons' natural moral equality but also with Mill's insistence that no one may justly impose his or her own view of the good life on others. Children appear to represent an important exception to this rule. Even Mill agrees that children's liberty should be curtailed by adults' views of what is good for them and not by the harm principle alone. But such exceptional treatment requires an explanation. What differences between adults and children justify such unequal treatment?

As with Locke, the most plausible answer appears to be some form of rational incapacity on children's part. "Children . . . are not be accorded exactly the rights adults enjoy because they lack 'experience,' 'rationality,' 'the capacity for choice,' or some other 'adult' faculty or attribute."[15] "Lacking some of the emotional and cognitive capacities required in order to make fully rational decisions," in particular "an adequate conception of their own present and future interests," children are properly subordinated to those without such deficits.[16] I have already identified a number of problems with Locke's effort to justify children's inequality simply in terms of their rational incapacities. I want here to suggest difficulties with adopting the paternalist version of this argument as well.

A paternalist account of the nature of adult authority over children would appear at first glance to hold much promise. The idea of responsible parenting (or at least fathering) seems to be built into the very word itself. But "paternalism," understood as the principle that guides exceptions to Mill's harm principle, is first of all a guide to the question of how best to treat *adults* who are judged incapable of self-determination. And while the idea of paternalistic authority is perhaps meant to evoke the sort of caring governance a father exercises over his offspring, there is little reason to suppose that what children are lacking as compared to adults has much similarity to what mentally ill or disabled adults are lacking as compared to their typically able counterparts.

The first problem, then, with paternalist theories of authority over children is their oxymoronic character. Paternalist principles within contemporary liberalism were developed to account for those exceptional cases of mature human beings who, due to either disease, decadence, or disability, lacked the mental competence to make informed, autonomous decisions about their life plans. In these cases, and these cases alone, it was permissible to set aside Mill's harm principle and restrain or direct other putatively equal adults "for their own good." Paternalist theories of parental authority derive their initial plausibility from the observation that children, too, lack the mental competence to make informed, autonomous decisions about their life plans. The ground and limits of the authority that it is appropriate to exercise over them are thus assumed to be of the same sort as those developed to account for the unequal treatment of mentally incompetent adults. As with Locke, the primary idea is that those in authority are to substitute their judgment for the immature or disabled judgment of the person ruled.

However, children differ from mentally incompetent adults in ways substantial enough to make the analogy implicit in paternalist theories of parental authority inappropriate. True, young children lack the mental competence to care for themselves or to choose wisely regarding their future. But unlike mature adults with mental retardation, mental illness, or profound physical disabilities, they have not yet reached their physical and mental maturity and should be partially defined by the fact that their development toward adulthood is still in progress. From this perspective, an authority that simply substitutes its judgment of what a child needs until the child is old enough to make such judgments is not enough. Those in positions of authority over children have the obvious responsibility of teaching them to exercise their maturing judgment responsibly, developing within them not only a capacity for critical reflection but a range of moral virtues, dispositions, and self-understandings that will enable them to live happily and productively in the world they inherit from the previous generation.

While few persons would object to this more comprehensive characterization of children's needs, the fact remains that in discussing the ground and nature of adult authority over children, liberal theorists focus almost exclusively on children's rational deficits, intentionally or unintentionally obscuring the differences between children and other categories of mental incompetents, all of whom are said to be properly subject to some sort of paternalistic rule. The problem with this approach, as already indicated, is not just that it elides the distinctive nature and challenges of childhood but that in doing so it distorts the premises from which the proper scope of parental power is deduced. If children's needs are narrowly conceived, the extent of the power properly exercised over them will be correspondingly curtailed. Fundamentalist educations, in which parents aim to supply children not just with the power of reason so obviously lacking in the immature human but also with concrete ideas regarding the right, the good, and the best way of life that they are expected to embrace as adults, will appear an overreading of parental power if children are subject to adult authority for the sole reason that they temporarily lack the ability to reason through these issues for themselves. Such educations appear in a different light when we understand what children lack in a more comprehensive way.

A second problem with paternalist justifications of children's inequality concerns how the "open future" ideal that it incorporates is to be realized in practice. Liberal paternalists share Locke's view that the primary deficiency of children as compared to parents is that of rational capacity and that the proper role for parental power is that of substituted judgment. But where Locke charges parents to enforce children's obedience to an objective law, human or divine, parents in the paternalist vision are supposed to decide as children themselves would, if fully rational. The idea here is that exercising authority in a paternalistic fashion involves as far as possible making "the kind of enlightened decisions [the person subject to authority] would make for himself, were he capable of doing so."[17] Of course, this standard cannot be completely realized when dealing with children, as the whole point of treating them unequally is that they lack the "settled preferences and interests" that Rawls says ought to guide those who find themselves ruling paternalistically over others.[18]

The solution, in David Archard's lucid account, is that "the paternalist caretaker must choose what the child would choose if competent to make choices, and choose with regard to the interests of the adult the child will become."[19] This recommendation taps into the dominant, freedom-maximizing strain of modern theories of paternalism in which authority is most justly exercised over children, as it is over mentally incompetent adults, when it "preserves and enhances for the individual his ability to rationally consider and carry out his own decisions."[20] In this view, a good parent is one who does the least to form or settle his or her child's views, deliberately abstaining from such indoctrination so as to leave important life decisions up to the rational adult who will emerge in the future. In other words, the just exercise of adult authority is one guided by principles of liberal neutrality.[21] The standards that should "best guide parents . . . are [those] more neutral between competing conceptions of the good life."[22]

Obviously, such a perspective on parental authority renders fundamentalist educations inherently suspect: while children are developing the ability to reason critically and deliberately (ideally as part of an autonomy-facilitating school curriculum), parents are not to skew the outcome of any adult exercise of this rationality by imposing their own views of the best way of life on their children. Rather, the parents' responsibility is to substitute for children's currently immature judgments the judgments parents believe children would make as fully mature adults themselves were they not unfortunately (temporarily) incapacitated from doing so. But while the insistence on neutrality successfully resolves a theoretical dilemma arising within paternalist theories of parental authority, what sense does this directive make if taken seriously as a guide to parental action? The parent must choose "what the child would choose if competent to make choices." But what are the grounds of the grown-up child's choice to be if not the understanding of the world, self, and other made available by the parents during its infancy and childhood? The decision to preserve for a child an "open future" by infusing its upbringing with the values of liberal cosmopolitanism is as significant a judgment about the choices a rational adult would independently make as the decision to urge upon the child the traditionalist practices of a conservative faith community. While there is a genuine difference between these upbringings, the relevant difference is not that one is "neutral" as regards the child's good and the other is engaged. Rather, the difference concerns what parents believe is the best way to prepare their children for reaping the pleasures and discharging the responsibilities of adulthood.

If we accept the premise that the only morally relevant difference between children and adults is the former's lack of rational capacity, then the limits on parental authority proposed by paternalists make sense. As I have already argued, authority over other human beings should extend only so far as making up the deficits that legitimate their subordination. If rational capacity is all that children lack in comparison to adults, the job of parents should be to make good children's rational deficit without predisposing children to choose or value goods that, in exercising their own mature reason, they might assess differently. Yet this reasoning, while internally consistent, produces a strangely truncated picture both of children's needs and of parental responsibilities. The logic of neutrality applies most reasonably to persons, whatever the level of their mental ability, who are thought to have matured to the extent they can; it is at this point that their already developed preferences and interests deserve respect as part of their "settled understanding of the good." Children by contrast are adult "works in progress." The reason we exclude them from the community of social and political equals is that they lack a range of social, emotional, and cognitive capacities that cannot be developed apart from their subordination to caring adults who take responsibility for their education and that, when developed, ground the possibility of their successful integration into a larger political and cultural community. If we return to the principle that authority over others should extend only so far as making up the deficits that legitimate their subordination, we can see that this more expansive picture of children's needs brings with it a different understanding of the nature and extent of parental power.

II.

In the previous section, as part of my critique of the dominant liberal perspective on parental authority, I allude to an alternative account of children's incapacities that focuses not on rational deficit but on developmental need. I want now to further refine this alternative way of conceiving and justifying children's inequality. The main idea driving this argument is the proposition that the way we think of children and their needs determines the sort of authority we think it is appropriate to exercise over them. If we think of children as lacking only or primarily critical rationality, ceding to parents the authority to encumber children with unchosen obligations, to point them toward particular views of the good life as right for them because of who they are, may not seem justified or appropriate. To think of children as comprehensively needy shifts our expectations regarding the scope and purpose of parental authority. In this view, children are properly treated unequally because they have not yet had a chance to cultivate the skills, capacities, and emotional resources necessary to thrive as full members of their community. (I say more below about this way of describing the fully developed adult; like the account of developmental needs itself, what it means to thrive as a full member of one's community is a concept open to both philosophical reflection and political debate.)

In this developmental model, authority over children flows not from the child's consent or will, or from adult identification of children as (merely) lacking in rational capacity, but from a recognition that children are adult works in progress, the vulnerable, plastic, raw material from which we must build the next generation of our polity and the world. Considered from this perspective, the question is not how little impact a parent can make on a child's view of the world (how neutral parenting can be) but how fully parents can discharge their obligation to guide children to a productive, satisfying adulthood. Children require a great deal of care if they are to become adults capable of flourishing in the social and political communities of which they are a part. Not all of it can be provided by parents, who must work toward this end in partnership with the community at large. But nothing about fundamentalist educations obviously or necessarily thwarts such an achievement. Particular parents may choose poorly as regards the ends with which they wish to encumber their child. If such choices compromise children's developmental needs or the stability or constitutional integrity of the polity, the state may justly intervene to prevent such a dysfunctional education. But the problem here lies with the particular values a parent seeks to impose, not with the commitment to raising children to embrace particular values per se.

This developmental model of children's inequality distinguishes children from adults not by their rational incapacity alone but by a broader conception of developmental needs. The precise parameters of these needs will differ between cultures and across time and are open not only to scholarly debate but to democratic deliberation. To orient an account of the appropriate scope of parental authority by reference to children's developmental needs is thus to begin a discussion of considerable length. However, a few preliminary remarks can indicate the direction in which a more thorough analysis of children's developmental needs might go.

One starting point would be a provisional description of the sorts of goods children must receive to grow, at a minimum, into socially competent, civically responsible, financially resourceful adults.[23] In their recent book *The Irreducible Needs of Children*, a prominent pediatrician and a child psychiatrist identify six needs of the growing child without which his or her development would be seriously compromised. These are the need for ongoing nurturing relationships; the need for physical protection, safety, and regulation; the need for experiences tailored to individual differences; the need for developmentally appropriate experiences; the need for limit setting, structure, and expectations; and the need for stable, supportive communities and cultural continuity.[24] The distinguished child psychologist Urie Bronfenbrenner offers a similarly demanding account of what children need to develop well. His list begins with "good health care and adequate nutrition," while emphasizing the "developmentally sensitive interaction" necessary for the child "to grow socially, psychologically, and cognitively." Most important for Bronfenbrenner is the presence of at least one adult completely in love with a child and available to care for him or her on a continuous basis.[25] There must be effective communication and mutual accommodation between the home and the other "principal settings in which children and their parents live their lives," and there must be wide-ranging public support, both cultural and institutional, for the practices that best meet children's needs.[26] These lists offer only a beginning for a more extensive discussion of the goods and capacities children require in order to flourish as members of their community.

Another way to approach this question would be to begin by asking what we want our children to be capable of at the time that they begin to live independently from our (legal) authority over them. Most parents wish their children to be, at a minimum, socially competent, law abiding, morally and civically responsible, capable of supporting themselves financially, and able to nurture long-term loving relationships. This list is not exclusive and could obviously be extended in a number of directions. The next step is to ask what goods and resources we must supply to encourage these capacities to develop. In answering this question we would begin to get a picture of our children's developmental needs as well as a sense of the shared nature of adults' responsibility for meeting them. One would probably want to give first priority to meeting children's emotional, physical, and cognitive needs, while recognizing that children have spiritual, moral, and cultural needs as well. Yet no parent could ever meet the range of his or her child's developmental needs alone. As Bronfenbrenner emphasizes in his account, the local and national community, and civic and political organizations, must be committed to this end as well.

Assuming some agreement on a general set of developmental needs, how do we translate such a list into a guide to the parameters of legitimate parental authority? From the point of view of the comprehensively needy newborn, its parents' choices regarding discipline, education, religion, cultural community, place of residence, and so forth are inescapably arbitrary. The helpless, wordless, desiring infant is shaped from the moment of its birth (if not before) by the choices of the adults who have power over it. By what standard is it appropriate to judge these choices? I have already given my reasons for rejecting preservation of an open future as an appropriate measure of legitimate parenting. My suggestion here is that as long as parental choices fulfill children's developmental needs in some reasonable, if not optimal, way, they remain legitimate, if not ideal, exercises of parental authority. We may wish for as few parents as possible to choose fundamentalist educations for their children; we may believe that both children and the polity they live in are better off when the dominant values to which they are exposed are those of liberal individualism. But not all socially competent, civically responsible, independent adults adhere to such values, and as long as the educational choices of parents advance these ends, they do not overstep the bounds of legitimate parental authority.

I do not go so far as to argue that closing children's futures in the way aimed at by fundamentalist educations is itself a developmental need. Parents may choose, as part of their way of preparing children for a fulfilling, flourishing adult life, to teach the values of liberal cosmopolitanism to their children and emphasize the virtues of bringing them to adulthood with an "open future." But my reconception of the role of the good parent makes the paternalist emphasis on preserving an open future as the litmus test of good parenting seem somewhat beside the point. Children require the active, loving guidance of at least one trusted adult committed to their well-being in order to develop the complex set of cognitive, emotional, social, and intellectual resources that will enable them, as adults, to make a reasonably happy, successful, responsible life for themselves within the community in which they were born. Certainly, any persuasive account of what equipping children to flourish in today's world involves must include the development of a critical rationality that gives individuals an ability to examine thoughtfully competing understandings of the good life and to deliberate nondogmatically on their ultimate aims and goals. But it is possible to preserve an open future for a child without giving him or her the skills associated with critical rationality, and it is possible to value critical rationality without rejecting the encumbered self.[27]

This developmental model of children's deficits emphasizes the degree to which children need adult care and control if the qualities prized as markers of adulthood are to be manifested in them. Adults who govern children must in consequence provide much more than the minimum authority and direction necessary to remedy deficits of a child's intellect. Their responsibility (and prerogative) is affirmatively to socialize the next generation of adults, to elicit from the bundle of capacities to be found in the infant and maturing child the sort of adult they understand to be good for the community as well as morally exemplary.

If the characteristic feature of paternalistic parenting is its disinterestedness, the developmental model of parental authority emphasizes an interested approach to parenting. At least in part because they perceive the morally relevant difference between children and adults so narrowly in terms of rational deficit, liberal theorists favor a model of parenting that seeks to minimize the formative influence of adult caregivers on children's beliefs, values, and habits. Parents stand to children as the state does to its citizens. And just as the state owes the citizens over which it exercises authority a neutral stance on questions of the good life, so too do parents owe such neutrality to their children. The developmental model endorses a more engaged, even prejudicial, role for adult caregivers in which imparting the family's and community's understanding of the good life is an acceptable, and even intrinsic, part of caring well for children.

It should now be sufficiently clear that quite a bit is at stake when it comes to specifying what deficiencies in children make their subordination to adult authority legitimate. In particular, the idea that parents owe children an "open future" and must condition their exercise of educational authority accordingly loses its plausibility when a developmental model of children's deficits is accepted. But any argument for an expanded scope for parental power must address the concerns of overreaching. As I have made clear from the beginning of this essay, parental power is not absolute and cannot be exercised in such a way that children are treated unjustly. My concern so far has been to show that subjecting children to fundamentalist educations is not an example of this problem, and I want now to conclude with the argument that a theory of parental authority grounded in developmental needs sets appropriate and effective limits on the abuse of parental power, limits that compare favorably to the division of authority over children generally countenanced in liberal theories.

III.

I take it that any account of parental power satisfactory to liberal democracies will structure the division of authority over children such that (1) children are adequately protected from justiciable maltreatment and (2) adults are given meaningful freedom in the educational, disciplinary, and lifestyle choices they make as parents. By *justiciable maltreatment,* I have in mind at a minimum the currently accepted legal definitions of child abuse and neglect. I have argued elsewhere for the expansion of this term to include all corporal punishment of children by adults,[28] but anyone who reads the metropolitan pages of any major daily newspaper knows well enough that children are inadequately protected from even gross forms of abuse under current family law. *Meaningful freedom* is a deliberately subjective term meant to reference the expectation citizens have in liberal polities that, within minimal limits, they will be free to pursue their own distinctive understandings of the good life. The vehemence with which many religious parents react to public school efforts to expose their children to a diversity of roles and values suggests to me that requiring such exposure would represent for these parents a meaningful incursion on their freedom to be a good parent (which is itself one instantiation of the good life). Such incursions are of course appropriate to protect both the state's constitutional order and children's basic autonomy. But neither of these goods is threatened by fundamentalist educations per se.

To return, then, to the standard I have just proposed: in delineating the appropriate scope of parental power, we are looking for an account that gives children protection against justiciable maltreatment while affirming adults' meaningful freedom in the choices they make as parents. My aim in this formulation has been to translate the twin liberal principles of harm prevention and expansion of the realm of individual freedom into guidelines appropriate to the parent-child relationship, and my worry has been that structuring parental authority by reference to children's rational deficits can lead to policies that advance neither of these ends. However, a theory of parental authority organized around meeting children's developmental needs satisfies both criteria in a way that Lockean and paternalist alternatives do not.

The idea that authority over children is linked to developing capacities for rational self-government is often used by liberal theorists to justify state supervention of parents' educational choices.[29] Parental concerns about children's spiritual development and moral uprightness, as well as more general parental assessments of children's educational interests, are subordinated to the supposedly overriding goal of giving children the capacity to choose freely among competing conceptions of the good life. Such constraints limit parents' freedom to seek their children's good, not in order to prevent actual maltreatment of a child, but in order to promote alternative state-approved understandings both of the good life and of the best way to develop the capacity for meaningful choice. In so doing, these principles run afoul of the liberal ideal that adults be given adequate scope to advance their own understanding of the good life independently and in their chosen role as parents. Of course, such an ideal does not give unlimited scope to parental preferences. But setting the limits to the realization of parental preferences in terms of not compromising children's developmental needs gives wider scope to adult freedom without shortchanging children's interest in a just upbringing.

The developmental model I argue for teaches that when developmental needs (or fundamental civic interests) are not at stake, parents may choose among a broad range of educations for their child without running afoul of the limits of parental authority. What parents may not do is compromise their children's ability to participate responsibly and meaningfully in the broader social and political community, regardless of the ultimate ends such education may be said to serve. Of course, there is room for disagreement over what preparation for responsible and meaningful participation in the broader community involves, and my intention with such a standard is to rule out of bounds educations chosen by groups such as the Christian Identity movement, survivalists, and hermetic cults such as the Branch Davidians. The fundamentalist educations that hundreds of thousands of American citizens hope to offer their children as part of an evangelical Christian or other private religious or home schooling remain legitimate exercises of parental authority unless and until such educations are shown radically to compromise children's ability to contribute constructively to their community at large.

The liberal preference for dividing educational authority over the child so as to "balance" parental input with the values of the public school curriculum is just that—a preference. Some parents find such an option desirable and welcome the range of perspectives on offer in the public schools. But other parents believe such "balancing" is better described as a competition for the minds and hearts of their children. As long as these parents meet their children's developmental needs, broadly defined, acting on this belief and keeping children out of the public school system so as to give a fundamentalist education the best chance possible of succeeding is a legitimate exercise of parental authority.

Is exposure to a diversity of roles, values, and understandings of the good life a developmental need of children growing up in the United States in the twenty-first century? Simply living in the United States provides a great deal of exposure to diverse persons and ways of life, more than is available in many other societies. Parents who systematically wall their children off from any and all interaction with the outside world are harming their children's emotional, moral, and civic development, and such educational preferences (e.g., hermetic cults such as the Branch Davidians) need not be tolerated. But the decision to teach one's children that there is a right way of life for them and that their flourishing as individuals depends on assuming certain roles or affirming certain beliefs or living by certain traditions does not in itself impede the development of the various capacities that contribute to being a socially competent, civically responsible, morally upright human being and may at times enhance this process. Exposure to diversity is a central tenet of liberal cosmopolitanism, but the refusal to countenance cosmopolitan experiences for one's children does not in itself make one a bad parent.

My final point concerns an aspect of children's welfare that looms large in policy debates but receives little attention in political theory: the prevention of child abuse. One of the most pervasive and disturbing abuses of parental authority is harsh and abusive physical violence. But understanding children as subordinated to their parents primarily because they lack the rationality to govern their own behavior generates no internally supported constraints to the use of force to control children. In fact, beating, spanking, or paddling children is often justified by the claim that children aren't rational enough to be guided by other means.[30] Locke's educational theory discourages the use of corporal punishment, and no paternalist theory of parental authority that I am aware of recommends it at any point. However, it is an irony of the recent debate that so much effort is devoted to protecting children from the supposedly stultifying effects of fundamentalist educations, while the very concrete power of the parental fist is left unchallenged. Perhaps this is because parental choices regarding discipline are seen having less impact on children's autonomy than educational choices. But this position is difficult to maintain if one thinks about physical punishment in terms of its impact on children's developmental needs. Recall the lists cited above. None of the goods mentioned there as crucial to children's optimal development are advanced in any way by the regime of harsh physical punishment to which many American children are subjected, both in and outside school. An argument that parental power must be exercised in the service of children's developmental needs or be curtailed could provide the means for ruling corporal punishment out of bounds in the United States (as it is now in Europe) as an abuse of the power over children with which the state entrusts parents.

As this example suggests, a theory of parental authority that takes as its basis children's developmental needs has sufficient bite to impose substantial limits on what parents may do to and for their children. But it sets these limits in a way quite different from the approaches to parental power currently in favor. I began this essay by citing the prevalent liberal concern with fundamentalist educations. The effort by parents to choose for their children a good way of life and to back this choice up with substantial constraints on the children's education strikes many theorists as an undesirable and inappropriate exercise of parental authority. Certain fundamentalist educations may well be undesirable, as are those parental abdications of responsibility that leave a child with an open future and no tools with which to make sense of it. But the idea that fundamentalist educations are illegitimate exercises of parental authority over children does not make sense apart from an unduly truncated account of what distinguishes children from adults and thus legitimates their subordination. Once we understand children correctly as subject to adult authority because of their comprehensive neediness, concerns about the legitimacy of fundamentalist educations vanish. Most educations to particular understandings of the good life can be shown to meet a wide range of children's developmental needs, including the development of critical rationality and individual autonomy, properly understood. But parents' power over children still extends only as far as their willingness and ability to meet their children's developmental needs. As I have tried to show with the example of corporal punishment, this standard is robust enough to rule out certain fundamentalist educations as well as parenting practices still widely accepted as legitimate expressions of parental preference.

NOTES

For comments on earlier versions of this chapter, I am grateful to Rupert Gordon, John Gould, and the editors of this volume.

1. See, e.g., *Wisconsin v. Yoder,* 406 U.S. 25, and *Mozert v. Hawkins County Board of Education,* 827 F.2d 1058 (6th Cir. 1987), as well as the extensive commentary elicited by both cases.

2. Eamon Callan, *Creating Citizens: Political Education and Liberal Democracy* (New York: Oxford University Press, 1997), 152–57.

3. For a further discussion of this point, see Shelley Burtt, "Comprehensive Educations and the Liberal Understanding of Autonomy," in Kevin McDonough and Walter Feinberg, eds., *Collective Identities and Cosmopolitan Values: Group Rights and Public Education in Liberal Democratic Societies* (New York: Oxford University Press, 2002).

4. Joel Feinberg, "The Child's Right to an Open Future," in William Aiken and Hugh LaFollette, eds., *Whose Child? Children's Rights, Parental Authority, and State Power* (Totowa, N.J.: Littlefield, Adams, 1980).

5. See, e.g., Bruce Ackerman, *Social Justice in the Liberal State* (New Haven, Conn.: Yale University Press, 1980); Harry Brighouse, *School Choice and Social Justice* (New York: Oxford University Press, 2000); Eamon Callan, *Creating Citizens: Political Education and Liberal Democracy* (Oxford, England: Clarendon, 1997); James Dwyer, *Religious Schools v. Children's Rights* (Ithaca, N.Y.: Cornell University Press, 1998); Meira Levinson, *The Demands of Liberal Education* (New York: Oxford University Press, 1999); and Robert Reich, *Bridging Liberalism and Multiculturalism in Education* (Chicago: University of Chicago Press, 2002).

6. Amy Gutmann, "Civic Education and Social Diversity," *Ethics* 105 (1995): 557–79.

7. Callan, *Creating Citizens,* 133.

8. See, e.g., Stephen Macedo, "Liberal Civic Education and Religious Fundamentalism: The Case of God v. John Rawls?" *Ethics* 105 (1995): 468–96. William Galston, *Liberal Purposes: Goods, Virtues, and Diversity in the Liberal State* (New York: Cambridge University Press, 1991), is an important exception among liberal philosophers of education, specifically affirming the legitimacy of fundamentalist educational aspirations within the liberal state. For Galston, parents' right to pursue illiberal educations follows from the principles of political liberalism; I take a different tack in this essay, reasoning from the arguments we use to justify setting children under the authority of adults in the first place.

9. Dwyer, *Religious Schools,* and Reich, *Bridging Liberalism,* argue for much more stringent regulation of religious schools and home schooling respectively as both constitutional and morally imperative.

10. Burtt, "Comprehensive Educations."

11. John Locke, *Two Treatises of Government* (New York: Cambridge University Press, 1960), 304 (II, § 55).

12. Ibid., 305, 307, 306 (II, § 57, 59, 58).

13. David Archard, *Children: Rights and Childhood* (New York: Routledge, 1993).

14. This discussion leaves undetermined the scope of the community with which the child identifies. My formulation is meant to accommodate local, national, cultural, religious, and even global understandings of community.

15. Lyla H. O'Driscoll, "Toward a New Theory of the Family," in Joseph R. Peden and Fred R. Glahe, eds., *The American Family and the State* (San Francisco: Pacific Research Institute for Public Policy, 1986), 81.

16. Gerald Dworkin, "Paternalism," in Richard Wasserstrom, ed., *Morality and the Law* (Belmont, Calif.: Wadsworth, 1971), 119.

17. Richard T. DeGeorge, *The Nature and Limits of Authority* (Lawrence: University Press of Kansas, 1985).

18. John Rawls, *A Theory of Justice* (Cambridge, Mass.: Harvard University Press, 1971), 248.

19. Archard, *Children,* 53.

20. Dworkin, "Paternalism," 125.

21. Dworkin, "Paternalism," offers the less successful formulation that parental authority is justified only if children "eventually come to see the correctness of [their] parents' interventions" (much as Rousseau's Emile comes to see the wisdom of his tutor's education). In

this view, children's inequality is just only so far as children give "subsequent recognition of the wisdom of these restrictions" (119). One obvious problem with this approach is that we must await a child's maturity to pass judgment on the justice of the regime to which he or she was subjected. A second problem is that any consent secured to treatment received within a fundamentally unequal power relationship is necessarily suspect. It seems to be a feature of human psychology that vulnerable individuals will seek to make sense of ill treatment by legitimating it as deserved or for their own good. Violent parents often justify even abusive physical punishment of their children as appropriate because their parents treated them in the same way (Richard Gelles and Murray Straus, *Intimate Violence: The Causes and Consequences of Abuse in the American Family* [New York: Simon and Schuster, 1988]). Thus the measure of just parenting cannot be the ability to create an adult willing to "sign off" on the character he or she has acquired. While we hope our children will come to be satisfied with what we did to and for them, the legitimacy of the authority exercised will rest on grounds other than retrospective consent.

22. Amy Gutmann, *Liberal Equality* (New York: Cambridge University Press, 1980).

23. The following section draws on material presented in somewhat different contexts in Shelley Burtt, "Reproductive Responsibilities: Rethinking the Fetal Rights Debate," *Policy Sciences* 27 (1994): 179–96; and Burtt, "Comprehensive Educations."

24. T. Berry Brazelton and Stanley I. Greenspan, *The Irreducible Needs of Children: What Every Child Must Have to Grow, Learn, and Flourish* (Cambridge, Mass.: Perseus, 2000).

25. Urie Bronfenbrenner, "Discovering What Families Do," in David Blankenhorn, Jean Bethke Elshtain, and Steven Bayne, eds., *Rebuilding the Nest: A New Commitment to the American Family* (Milwaukee, Wis.: Family Service America, 1990), 29.

26. Ibid., 36–37.

27. Eamonn Callan, "Autonomy, Child-rearing, and Good Lives," in David Arehard and Colin Macleod, eds., *The Moral and Political Status of Children: New Essays* (Oxford University Press, 2002).

28. Shelley Burtt, "Discipline, Assault, and Justice: Violent Parents and the Law," *Law and Policy* 19 (1997): 343–61.

29. E.g., see Reich, *Bridging Liberalism.*

30. Irwin Hyman, *Reading, Writing, and the Hickory Stick: The Appalling Story of Physical and Psychological Abuse in America's Schools* (Lexington, Mass.: Lexington Books, 1990).

PART III

SAME-SEX FAMILIES

10

CHILDREN'S RIGHTS IN GAY AND LESBIAN FAMILIES: A CHILD-CENTERED PERSPECTIVE

BARBARA BENNETT WOODHOUSE

I. Reconceptualizing Rights for Children

When I entered law school over twenty years ago, most family law casebooks devoted very little attention to gays and lesbians. Since they were forbidden to engage in "homosexual" sex, their rights to marry, raise children, and share a home were overshadowed by the fear of persecution merely for cohabiting with another man or woman. Rights of gays and lesbians are now a major topic in all areas of law, from constitutional law, to health care and employment law, to family law. Gays and lesbians claim the right to be treated equally with other adults, regardless of their sexual orientation.

As gay and lesbian rights have emerged from the closet, another new group of rights claimants has begun to command the attention of legal scholars and policy makers. Children, while not closeted, have been treated as inherently unequal and lacking in capacity—consigned to being "seen but not heard." During the past twenty years, children and youth have gained an increasing voice in disputes with the state and in intrafamily disputes. They have moved from the status of property to the status of person, from objects to subjects. Custody, adoption, marriage, and assisted conception all involve rights of children as well as of adults. In some settings, claims of gay and lesbian adults and claims of children may conflict, and in other settings, their claims of rights may be mutually reinforcing.

In this essay, I will explore the intersection of gay and lesbian rights with the children's rights movement, applying a purposefully child-centered perspective to the analysis.[1] This exercise is important in its own right to the many children growing up in gay and lesbian families. It also provides a lens through which to examine relations among children, the adults who care for them and claim family relationships with them, and the state. In reforming family law to recognize gay and lesbian families, we are presented with a fresh opportunity to think about the larger subject of justice within the family. The same impetus toward perfecting our understanding of justice unites those who advocate for children and those who advocate for other excluded and marginalized groups.

Finally, this exercise is important because of novel proposals from defenders of the traditional family that intentionally penalize children of gay and lesbian parents in their access to government-funded programs. These proposals include giving priority to children of married heterosexual families over children in gay and lesbian families in distributing financial aid and in allocating slots in programs like Head Start.[2] A children's rights analysis quickly exposes the unconstitutionality of policies that single out children for less favorable treatment on the basis of the sexual orientation of their parents.

A. Traditional Understandings of Rights within the Family

Traditionally, the law has described family rights in strongly hierarchical terms. The biological father (the patriarch) had a right to custody and control of the child and to autonomy in child rearing and education.[3] As women gained greater equality, parental rights in the intact family were shared by mothers and fathers. These rights go beyond the positive law (enactments by legislatures and decisions by judges). They have been characterized since the 1920s as fundamental rights of liberty and privacy protected by constitutional guarantees.[4] Whatever individual rights children might possess were subsumed in those of t[illegible]ents. The parent, not the child, had authority to assert the child's rights in conflicts with the state, and the state was enjoined from intervening in the parent's management of conflicts within the family. The parent also had a duty to nurture and educate the child, creating a right on the part of the child to be nurtured and educated by the parent. While protection of parental autonomy has been the rule, gross failure to perform parental duties—that is, abuse or neglect of the child—might provoke state intervention and result in loss or curtailment of parental rights. In such cases, custody of the child would be transferred to the state or to a new parent or guardian selected by the state.

Divorce has been the other major exception to the rule of nonintervention. Once women began to assert equal rights, a mechanism was needed to resolve custody disputes between mothers and fathers, and the family courts provided the forum for these disputes. The era of fathers' rights was followed by an era of mothers' rights, in which mothers were presumed to be best suited to caring for children.[5] Gradually, whether parents were married became less important than their biological relationship to the child. For the past fifty years, since neither adult has a superior right conferred by gender, the basic principle applied to disputes over custody between parents has been "the best interest of the child." In disputes with so-called "third parties" (persons who claim an interest in the child but who are not biological or legal parents), many jurisdictions require a showing of detriment to the child or of parental unfitness before they will consider the best interest of the child.[6] Likewise, only in rare circumstances may children seek protection of the state or seek to enforce their own rights against their parents or against the state without parental permission.[7]

Modern scholars have challenged the traditional account on many fronts. Some feminists have argued that it allocates parental rights too broadly by giving equal rights to fathers who may have contributed minimally to the work of childbearing and child rearing.[8] Fathers' rights groups have contended that the best-interest standard has resulted in mothers' winning the custody wars at the expense of children who need relationships with both parents. Scholars concerned with nontraditional families have argued that it defines family too narrowly, excluding extended and de facto families and imposing a nuclear family model of two married heterosexual parents and their biological children where there ought to be greater respect for diversity.[9] The state has traditionally held the power to define who is inside and who is outside the family circle. At one time unmarried parents and interracial parents were excluded, and currently gays and lesbians are denied family status. On the other side, conservatives are alarmed at the "breakdown" of family values and see exclusion of deviant family forms as essential to defense of marriage and the traditional family.[10]

As an advocate for children, I have challenged the traditional description of parental rights on different grounds. In my view, it overlooks children's personhood and fails to treat them as people with rights of their own. In a world in which "rights talk" dominates all other forms of discourse, I have argued that the least powerful members of society are most in need of a theory of rights.[11] I would start from a child-centered perspective, reshaping our analysis to reflect the fact that children are persons with rights of their own. If children, like adults, have fundamental rights of liberty and equality, the sweeping authority that law gives to adults can be justified only by a theory of adult stewardship or trusteeship. Adult authority is predicated on and justified by children's lack of capacity and must respect their emerging capacity as they mature. Adult power is conferred as an adjunct to the adult's obligation (analogous to a fiduciary duty) to protect the rights and meet the needs of dependent children.[12]

My account is difficult to square with the prevailing American approach to rights, which tends to conceptualize the rights bearer as an autonomous individual with the capacity to choose when and whether to invoke his or her rights. How can children have rights if they lack the capacity to understand, let alone exercise, their rights? Who will protect them from themselves if they make unwise choices? Or shall we simply "abandon" children to their rights?[13] Clearly, if children are to be treated as having equal "rights," we must rethink the meaning of the term as it applies not only to children but to adults. In the next section, let me describe a child-centered approach to rights.

B. Children's Needs-Based Rights and Dignity Rights

A child-centered framework for thinking about the rights of children and youths is useful not only in providing a normative language but also in critiquing the way courts and legislatures currently approach cases involving children.[14] Currently, while courts have moved past the property-based notion of rights "in" children, they frequently stop short of explicitly recognizing the rights "of" children. Instead, they tend to use a dual concept of "interests"—focusing on the "state's interest" in protection of the child and on the "best interest" of the child as the benchmark for decision making. This rhetoric of "interests" masks the claims of children to "rights" under the law.

A "right" implies the existence of a corresponding "duty"—recall the description of how the parent's duty to nurture the child created reciprocal rights on the part of the child to be fed and clothed by the parent. An "interest," by contrast, is the sound of one hand clapping. The state may have a legitimate, even a compelling "interest" in educating children, and children certainly have an "interest" in receiving training to equip them for adult roles. It may be "in the best interest" of children in foster care to be consulted before the state terminates their legal relationship with their birth family. But unless children have a "right" to be heard or to be educated, creating a "duty" on the part of the state, the state has no obligation to protect or promote the interests of children. It comes as a profound shock to most first-year law students when they learn that American children have no constitutional "right" to education. And few Americans realize that every day hundreds of the six hundred thousand American children in foster care are subjected to wrenching changes in their lives without any notice or opportunity to be heard. Clearly, the difference between rights and interests is more than mere semantics to an incarcerated fifteen-year-old denied access to education or to a ten-year-old who faces losing all legal ties to his parents and siblings.[15]

Children, being people and not property, are entitled to basic human rights. The "best interest of the child" standard is a step in the direction of a child-centered perspective on rights, but only one component of a larger universe of rights for children. Rights must mean something more than a paternalistic protection of the best interest of the child as perceived by the adult decision maker. However, rights for children inevitably involve some measure of paternalism (or maternalism) in the best sense of the word. They cannot be understood as purely rights of choice or privacy, contingent on the rights bearer's capacity for autonomy. Instead, children's rights should be defined by children's "capacity for growth to autonomy." Reconceptualizing rights for children as including "needs-based rights" allows us to acknowledge children's essential dependency at birth but also each child's inherent capacity for growth to maturity. Children's "needs-based rights" include rights to form intimate attachments and to receive nurture, education, food, medical care, shelter, and other positive goods without which children cannot grow into autonomous adults and productive citizens. Children's "needs-based rights" would also encompass the child's need to test the wings of increasing autonomy.

The category of children's "dignity rights" acts as a necessary complement to the notion of "needs-based rights" because it acknowledges that children are individual persons with the same claims to dignity as autonomous adults. Dignity rights are not dependent on autonomy. As infants, children rely on others to articulate and protect their rights, but the framework of decision making evolves as the child's capacity for autonomy evolves. The capacity for autonomous action need not be a necessary attribute for asserting or vindicating dignity rights. For example, a patient in a hospital has what we usually think of as a "negative right" to refuse a medical procedure. Should that patient fall into a coma and be unable to object or consent to medical procedures, she does not lose her right to protection from state intrusion. She still retains the right to be treated as an individual with claims to dignity, but her rights are exercised on her behalf by a family member or a court-appointed guardian. The fact that these are still her rights is clear in the legal standards requiring her guardian to be faithful to her wishes, to the extent they can be known or discovered, and to place her interests before his own if her wishes are not known.

Recognizing children's dignity rights and assigning the protection of these rights to parents is one route to acknowledging that childhood is a journey to autonomy. While a child's ability to reason and understand evolves over time, his or her dignity rights are fully present at birth. Dignity rights call on the legal system to respect that the child, though lacking autonomy, does have rights based on his or her present humanity as well as his or her potential for autonomy. In making these rights operational, the law must reflect the child's dependency but also his or her emerging capacity for participation and, ultimately, control. This analysis requires that we work harder to integrate children's needs with their capacities, acknowledging that dependency and autonomy are two sides of the same coin. A scheme of rights that focuses exclusively on one or the other will be incomplete, whether applied to adults or to children.

The questions remain: Who is responsible for meeting the needs of children? Who is responsible for speaking for the preverbal or very young child and vindicating his or her rights? Who is responsible for guiding the older child to an informed decision? I have argued that parents, society, and children themselves all play important roles in this endeavor and must all share responsibility.[16] When the courts take on a protective role, as in deciding disputes about child custody and visitation, I have argued that a children's rights analysis would require that best interest be the test in all cases—but a best-interest test that is informed by a child-centered perspective.[17]

Conflicts will arise not only in balancing children's "needs" for external support and direction against their "capacity" for autonomy but also in balancing the competing claims of children against those of parents and government. No right is absolute, and children's rights must be weighed in the balance with other competing claims of rights and authority. However, the power adults exercise over children—as parents, as legislators, and as judges—should not be taken for granted but must be justified as furthering children's interests and meeting their special needs.

This scheme for analyzing family relationships and for thinking about children's relationships with adult authority shifts the focus from adults' rights to adults' responsibilities. In this scheme, parents exercise the fiduciary powers of a guardian or a trustee, with special authority to make decisions about the needs and interests of the beneficiary, their child. Parenthood is seen not as a form of ownership of children but as a form of trusteeship. Parents are given the broad authority and freedom from state interference that they must have to nurture and protect their children in their journey to autonomous adulthood.[18] Government must act responsibly toward children and use its awesome authority in ways that further children's needs and interests and respect their dignity as human beings.

C. Tailoring Basic Human Rights Principles to Children

Five principles should guide us in thinking about rights generally: (1) the equality principle; (2) the individual dignity principle; (3) the privacy principle; (4) the protection principle; and (5) the empowerment principle.[19] Each of these principles represents a basic value that ordinary people as well as judges would agree should be reflected in the scheme of human rights. They are reflected, if not fully realized, in the U.S. Constitution and subsequent interpretations of it by the Supreme Court.[20] These principles provide a lens for examining past developments in children's rights and exploring how to shape an agenda for the future. They have developed in an adult-centric world. Each of these principles must be reexamined through a child-centered lens that resolves the paradox of children's rights by seeing clearly both children's dependency and their capacities and that honors both their needs-based rights and their dignity rights.

For example, the equality principle does not require that children be treated identically with adults but rather that their capacities, as well as their differences from adults, be respected. It does require that similarly situated children be treated equally and protected from discrimination. Because children are in the process of becoming, the focus must be on equality of opportunity rather than formal equality.

The individual dignity principle requires that children be treated as individual human beings with rights and interests of their own and not as pawns or chattels to be manipulated, traded, and fought over. Children caught in family struggles often become the focal point for adults' battles, in gay and lesbian families as well as in straight families. Sadly, children have often been the pawns in political struggles as well.

The privacy principle may differ from the principle as applied to adults. The right to be let alone is meaningless to infants and dependent children, who would die in isolation from others. Instead, children's privacy is defined by the circle of care. Rather than privacy in the adult sense, children need privacy in the sense of protection from unwarranted state intrusion in relationships with those who nurture them.

The protection principle, the right of the weak to be protected from the strong, is the most basic of all social compacts. If I know anything as a member of a civil society, it is this: I cannot use physical violence to force you to comply with my demands. Children have been excluded from this most basic protection by laws that ignore or condone the use of violence against them.[21] In protecting children from violence, however, we need to place the violence in context. Many loving parents use corporal punishment. A child should not be separated from a loving parent unless the risk of harm truly outweighs the child's privacy right to the parent-child relationship.

Finally, the empowerment principle establishes that children, like adults, have a right to notice and the opportunity to be heard. Empowerment may not give children a completely autonomous choice, but it must give them a voice. Even very young children have views and experiences that can be understood with the aid of expert testimony and studies of child development.[22] Children's perspectives must be an important element in decision making within families and in public institutions.

With this basic frame for analyzing children's rights, let me examine various contexts in which it applies to children in gay and lesbian families. In some areas, we will see that courts have interpreted the U.S. Constitution or state constitutions in ways that open the door to children's rights arguments. In other areas, the courts have remained closed to the kind of arguments I am making here. Rather than an analysis of what exists now, this will be an analysis of what will be and a blueprint for advocates seeking to challenge an adult-centric vision of family rights.

II. Children's Rights in the Context of Gay and Lesbian Families

In cases involving gay and lesbian families, children's rights are implicated in a variety of contexts, including (1) disputes over custody and visitation, (2) state-created barriers to same-sex marriage and adoption by gays and lesbians, and (3) laws regarding children's access to court process, to people, and to information. Clearly, these cases implicate the rights of children as I have outlined them.

A. Children's Rights in the Context of Custody and Visitation Disputes

This category covers many different scenarios and alignments of parties. Viewed through a traditional lens, such cases are classified according to the status and alignment of the adults involved. Here are four common scenarios, all of which can be found in case law:

1. A biological parent, who is gay or lesbian, asserts his or her parental rights to custody of a child born in a prior heterosexual union in the face of claims by the other biological parent.
2. A nonbiological co-parent, who is gay or lesbian and has formed a relationship with a child born to or adopted by a partner, seeks rights to custody or access, based on equitable doctrines or in loco parentis status, after the breakup of the same-sex relationship.
3. A third party (e.g., a grandparent) seeks to overcome the parental rights of a gay or lesbian parent by attacking the parent's fitness on the basis of his or her sexual orientation.
4. A biological parent outside the gay or lesbian family (a sperm donor or surrogate mother) seeks to assert parental rights in order to gain custody or visitation.

Viewed from a child-centered perspective, these cases take on a different meaning. Whenever the state cuts off access to people the child knows as family, or allows the biological parent to do so, the privacy principle, as I have conceptualized it above, is clearly implicated. The equality principle is violated when children are treated differently from children in heterosexual families simply because of the status of their parent as gay or lesbian. And children's individual dignity and rights to a voice are infringed when they are treated like chattel lacking individual interests of their own, denied a voice, and excluded from the decision process. I will recast the scenarios listed above from a child-centered perspective, identifying what is at stake for the child and the principles that should guide adults in their resolution of these disputes.

The first scenario, involving a battle between two biological parents, one gay and one straight, when viewed from a child-centered perspective, concerns the rights of a child born in a heterosexual union to continue his or her relationships with both parents after they separate.

> GUIDING PRINCIPLE: Every child has a right to continued contact with both parents absent a showing of harm to the child and to be in the custodial arrangement that is in the best interest of the child. Children in gay and lesbian families are entitled to be treated equally with all other children.
>
> *Discussion*: By far, the most commonly reported cases are cases that follow this scenario.[23] Applying moral judgments to custody disputes is nothing new. At one time, a parent (especially a female) who engaged in adultery would have been seen as inherently unfit to care for a child. From an adult-centric perspective, how could it be in a child's best interest to be raised by an immoral parent? The modern rule properly rejects examination of the heterosexual parent's "moral character," including sexual conduct, unless there is a clear connection between the parent's conduct and detriment to the child.[24] The equality principle dictates that children of homosexual parents be treated the same as those of heterosexual parents. Only if a parent's sexual conduct actually harms the child should it become an element in the best-interest calculus.
>
> Here, I may part company with some in the gay and lesbian community who oppose any examination of the gay or

lesbian parent's sexual conduct, fearing it will give too much discretion to homophobic judges. I would retain the modern standard, but I would work to purge it of homophobia. Children suffer when parents who suddenly become single place their sexuality ahead of the child's sense of stability and emotional health. Overt sexual activity in front of or including a child can be confusing and damaging to a child. I am not talking about holding hands, hugging, or discreetly sharing a bedroom. One individual who consulted me reported that the other parent, during in-home visitation, would seek to arouse jealousy by engaging in deep and prolonged french kissing with a new lover, with both in a state of sexual arousal. This conduct occurred in front of the children, who were obviously highly disturbed by the conduct. I do not need to know the sex of any of the adults to know that this conduct is relevant to the parent's ability to meet the needs of the children. As it happens, the mother's new lover was a woman.

I recognize that women historically have suffered from a double standard. Male extramarital sexual activity has been excused while female extramarital sexual activity has been condemned. Heterosexuality is all-pervasive and lionized, while homosexuality is to be hidden and demonized. As far as children are concerned, bad sex knows no sexual orientation. We need to listen to the mother who is alarmed when she arrives to pick up her kids after a visit and is greeted at the door by her ex-husband and his nude girlfriend . . . or his nude boyfriend. Families differ in their attitudes toward nudity, but when parents part, they should avoid exposing their children to sexually explicit conduct that violates the privacy norms established in the child's intact family.

Another common syndrome is the succession of lovers appearing and then disappearing from the child's home. This lack of stability and continuity can be painful and damaging to a child who is grieving over the dissolution of a family, regardless of whether the new lovers are of the same or opposite sex.[25] Children have varying needs for privacy, just as adults do. A friend of my son described her childhood as a succession of moves from one place to another as her mother fell in and out of love and insisted that her daughter join her in loving each new man totally and completely. If a shy and sensitive child seems to be suffering detrimental effects from a parent's casual attitude toward bringing sexual partners into the child's home and in and out of the child's life, this harm should figure in the custody decision. As an advocate for children, I oppose adjusting the legal scales to correct judicial bias against other groups (such as racial, religious, or sexual minorities) if the adjustment results in making justice blind to the reality of children's lives. But the showing of harm to the child must be supported by competent evidence and testimony, and not by mere speculation. The custodial arrangements of a child who is doing well in school, attached to his or her parent, and generally happy should not be modified because he or she expresses some embarrassment about the parent's sexuality—a normal reaction regardless of the sexual orientation of the parent.

The second custody scenario, involving a battle between gay or lesbian co-parents, when viewed from a child-centered perspective, concerns the rights of a child whose relationship with a bonded caregiver is being threatened because that person is not the biological or legal parent.

GUIDING PRINCIPLE: A child who has formed a parent-child relationship with a nonbiological co-parent or de facto parent has a right to legal recognition and protection of this relationship regardless of the marital status and sex of the adults involved.

Discussion: Let's begin with the "equitable arguments," which have deep roots in common law. The thrust of equitable arguments is that courts should not be used to create an unjust result, regardless of the legal rights of the parties. Cases in many jurisdictions hold that a man who is encouraged to form a relationship with a child he believes is his biological child, investing financially and emotionally in the child-parent relationship, should be treated as a parent. The biological parent should be barred on basic fairness grounds from challenging the relationship.[26] However, under traditional legal theories, courts will often rule against the husband or lover if he knew or should have known that he was not the biological father. Gay and lesbian couples rarely surmount this defense because the adults involved generally know that the child is neither legally nor biologically their own.

How would these cases play out from a child-centered perspective? In deciding whether a biological parent who has encouraged formation of a parent-child relationship between his or her child and a gay or lesbian co-parent/partner should be barred from challenging it once the parties separate, I would look at how heavily and trustingly the child has invested in the child-parent relationship.[27] We know that children have a natural need to bond with a caring adult and that breaking these attachments can be harmful to the child. Moreover, the child has invested an irreplaceable resource (the small child's ability to attract the irrational adoration of a bonded adult).[28] If anything, the child's claim to protection of the relationship will be stronger than the adult's, since no one can attribute to the infant who is forming these precious attachments the knowledge of any legal impediments to the relationship or argue that the child comprehends that he or she is unlikely to be biologically related to two mothers or two fathers. In fairness to the child, the biological parent's change of heart cannot be dispositive, and the case must be decided on the basis of whether custody or contact with the nonbiological parent is or is not in the best interest of the child.

The third custody scenario, involving the grandparent or other caretaker who challenges the gay or lesbian parent for custody, when viewed from a child-centered perspective, concerns the rights of a child who is caught in a dispute between a biological parent and some other person who claims a relationship with the child.

GUIDING PRINCIPLE: A child has a right to a custody decision that is based, not on the sexual orientation of the adults or on the mere fact of biological connection, but on the best interest of the child and, if the child is sufficiently mature, on the child's preference. To base a custody decision on the sexual orientation of a parent is a violation of the child's right to equal protection of the law.

Discussion: In *Bottoms v. Bottoms,* a straight grandmother sought custody of her lesbian daughter's young child.[29] When such cases hit the media, they tend to polarize the "talking heads" along predictable lines. Conservatives, who would normally trumpet the rights of the parent and the sanctity of the traditional family, tend to side with the third party, while liberals, who would normally be supportive of a broader functional definition of family, rise to the defense of the gay or lesbian parent, invoking the constitutional rights of parents as a trump card.

In such cases, we ought to step back and look carefully at the facts from a child-centered perspective. Who does the child perceive as his or her primary attachment, and is that person meeting the child's basic needs? Barring extraordinary circumstances, the gay or lesbian parent who has raised the child will fill this description. Unless the nonparent can show some severe risk to the child, the parent should maintain custody. However, when the parent has left the child in the care of a nonparent (i.e., grandmother or fictive kin) for an extended period of time, the balance of interests may be different. Such cases are not really about the sexual orientation of the parent but about the child's needs for continuity and stability of attachment relationships. The same principles described in the second scenario, involving a parent who encourages a parent-child relationship with a nonbiological parent, should prevail in this scenario.

The fourth custody/visitation scenario, involving a dispute between a semen or egg donor and the gay or lesbian parent raising the child, when viewed from a child-centered perspective, concerns the rights of a child born through assisted reproduction who becomes the object of a dispute over his or her custody or visitation.

GUIDING PRINCIPLE: Children have the right to form families and to protection of their family privacy, just as adults do. No child should be deprived of relationships with those who function as his or her parents, and with whom the child has bonded as a family, because of claims based solely on biology that are brought by people who are strangers to him or her.

Discussion: The case of *Thomas S. v. Robin Y.*[30] is an example of this scenario. Robin had used sperm donated by Thomas S., a gay male friend, to conceive a child to be raised by herself and her female partner. The biological father had contact with the child from the time she was four until she was nine. When he sought to expand his visitation in a manner the mothers perceived as undermining the family's solidarity, the biological mother invoked her parental rights to exclude him from the family circle.

It is fundamentally unfair to the child to allow a party who willingly consented to the creation of a bond between the child and a nonbiological parent to invoke biological rights as a means to destroy or imperil that bond. Biology is only one way of defining family—family is also created when people commit, to themselves and to the world, to a lifelong relationship. Children's family ties are formed through daily experiences of caregiving and nurture. Children do not stand up before a judge or minister to publicly "plight their troth," but they definitely do give their hearts, as anyone observing a bonded parent and child can see. They also remain attached with far more constancy and commitment than adult lovers, who form and dissolve grown-up relationships with relative ease. While courts and scholars looking for a better measure than biology alone have tended to approach these cases according to the "intent" of the adults,[31] a child-centered perspective would focus on the experiences of the child. This approach would emphasize the welfare of the child, in concert with the dominant themes of modern family law.[32] Has the donor or surrogate played an important part in the child's life, and is he or she recognized by the child as a family member? If not, it is appropriate for the law to keep the stranger from invading the family circle.[33]

In the case of *Thomas S. v. Robin Y.*, the court carefully evaluated the child's perspective. While she knew and liked her biological father, he was a relative stranger, and she did not consider him a family member. His dispute with her mothers caused her grave concern and threatened her sense of safety within her family. Wisely, the family court followed the child's lead in this controversial case and refused the sperm donor's petition for visitation. But one can imagine a very different outcome if the sperm donor had indeed become a central figure in the child's pantheon of parenting resources, tipping the balance in favor of continued access.

B. Barriers to Marriage and Adoption Also Occur in Many Variations

The barriers to marriage and adoption, generally viewed from the adults' perspective, entail a different set of scenarios than those in the custody context.

1. Two adults of the same sex claim a violation of their rights because they are prohibited by law from marrying.
2. Gay or lesbian adults claim discrimination due to laws that fail to provide for adoption of a gay or lesbian coparent's biological child by his or her partner.
3. Gay or lesbian adults claim that they are harmed by laws that disqualify homosexuals from becoming adoptive or foster parents of children who are available for adoption by heterosexuals.

When viewed from a child-centered perspective, these cases all share a similar feature: they deprive children of legal recognition of their relationships with existing or prospective parents purely because of the parent's sexual orientation and not because of the best interest of the child.

The marriage scenario, involving adults who cannot marry because of their sex, when viewed from a child-centered perspective, involves the rights of a child who is deprived of a two-parent family because of barriers to the parents' marriage.

GUIDING PRINCIPLE: The child's right to legal recognition of the child's family and equal access to the benefits of legitimation is infringed when the child's parents are forbidden to marry.

Discussion: Arguments against laws that treat gay and lesbian families differently gain added force when made by children and their advocates. The scientific jury may be out on whether sexual orientation is a lifestyle choice, like cohabitation, or an inherent and immutable status, like sex, or something far more complicated. But no one can argue that a child being raised in a gay or lesbian family has made the choice to forfeit the equal protection of the laws by not choosing to be raised in a heterosexual family. Laws treating children in gay and lesbian families less favorably than those in heterosexual families should be constitutionally suspect and require an empirical showing that they are based on protection of children from harm or other equally weighty public policies.

A mere twenty-five years ago, it was commonplace for laws to punish the innocent child for the "sins" of the parent. Children born to unmarried parents were stigmatized as bastards, denied the right to support and inheritance from their fathers, and denied equal access to government benefits and causes of action available to children of married parents. In a series of cases during the 1970s, the Supreme Court recognized the injustice to children of such laws. It applied heightened scrutiny to them and struck many of them down as unconstitutional.[34]

Critics might argue, however, that the nonbiological parent (often the partner of the biological parent) is not "really" a parent and that the child therefore has no protected relationship with this biological stranger. It all depends, however, on how one defines "the family." In the past quarter-century, we have seen a shift from defining family solely by biology toward defining family in terms of function. Increasingly, children's relationships with de facto parents, stepparents, and extended family have been recognized as valuable relationships meriting protection. These changes pave the way for advocates to argue that children's rights are violated when they are denied benefits because the law prohibits the people who are their functional parents from marrying or in some other way assuming the legal obligations of parenthood.

The second scenario involves access to a special form of adoption (called stepparent or second-parent adoption) to turn a single-parent family into a nuclear family. When viewed from a child-centered perspective, this scenario concerns the rights of a child who is prevented from having two parents by laws that give this option to heterosexual couples (who are or may become married) but not homosexual couples (who are barred from marrying).

GUIDING PRINCIPLE: Children in gay and lesbian families have a right to be treated equally with children in heterosexual families, and that right is infringed when the state denies them access to the benefits of stepparent or second-parent adoption.

Discussion: Typically, adoption laws have facilitated the creation of two-parent families. Divorced and never-married mothers have been encouraged to form two-parent families through marriage and stepparent adoption. In a traditional adoption, the rights of all biological family members are terminated and the new family completely displaces the old. In a stepparent or second-parent adoption, the child can gain a "second parent" through a streamlined adoption process that creates a new legal tie without dissolving the custodial parent's legal tie to the child. Only the child's relationship to the absent or unknown biological parent is dissolved.[35] In *Quilloin v. Walcott*, the Supreme Court upheld termination of the rights of a biological father who had never legitimated or supported his child, remarking that stepparent adoption would give legal protection to the already functioning family unit.[36]

As Theresa Glennon has argued, bringing a child advocacy perspective to second-parent adoption, the refusal to extend these processes to cover children whose parent is gay or lesbian precludes these children from the obvious benefits of a two-parent family.[37] These benefits include access to health insurance coverage, rights to child support, custodial continuity and stability in the event of death of the biological parent, rights to inheritance and to wrongful death or tort recovery for injuries to the second parent, and protections of the child's relationship with both parents should the parents separate. To pass constitutional muster, the unequal treatment of these children must be justified by competent empirical evidence that the gay or lesbian two-parent family is somehow detrimental to the welfare of the child or fails to provide the benefits of a heterosexual two-parent family. Much ink has been spilled on the subject of whether same-sex couples are as good as heterosexual couples at child rearing. Critics of same-sex families have used data about single mothers and their children to argue that being raised in family forms other than the married heterosexual couple is harmful to children. But the analysis fails to take into account the complex socioeconomic factors related to single-parent households, as well as ignoring the very fact at issue in our debates on same-sex marriage—that two parents can provide more resources than one.[38] While there is always room for debate on so complex an issue, the accumulating data have prompted more and more nationally respected authorities to conclude that children can and do thrive in same-sex families. On February 4, 2002, the American Academy of Pediatrics (AAP) issued a policy statement favoring legalization of gay and lesbian adoption. According to the AAP, the weight of the evidence persuasively establishes that there is no systematic difference between gay and nongay parents in child rearing and no risk to children growing up in a family with one or more gay parents.[39] The AAP recommended tearing down the legal barriers that unfairly discriminate against children in gay and lesbian families.

New reproductive technologies have made even more salient the harm suffered by children who are denied access to second-parent adoption. Where the child is conceived through artificial insemination by an anonymous donor (AID), he or she is born with only one legal parent—her biological mother. In a heterosexual union, the husband of the woman who gives birth is automatically the legal father, under most states' statutes on parentage. But because lesbians cannot marry, this route to the two-parent family is closed to the child of a lesbian mother conceived through AID. The same is true of a child who is born to a gay father who engages a surrogate mother to gestate an anonymous donor egg fertilized in vitro (IVF) with the father's sperm. In a heterosexual family, the intended co-parent could use second-parent adoption to legalize her relationship to the child. Where the family unit is composed of a gay father and his partner, the child is limited to one legal parent.

Some states have attempted to prevent such high-tech scenarios entirely by barring single or homosexual parents from using the laws on AID or surrogacy.[40] Proposals have been made in the federal arena as well.[41] But the Supreme Court has quite clearly held that policies aimed at discouraging single parenthood are unconstitutional when they visit the consequences of adults' actions on innocent children, condemning them to be half-orphans forever. Like the laws that penalized children born out of wedlock, which deprived them of equal protection, the law on adoption should not punish children produced through these technologies.

The third scenario, which involves adoption of a child who has no legal parents, when viewed from a child-centered perspective, involves the rights of a child who is available for adoption but is foreclosed from being adopted by a prospective gay or lesbian adoptive parent because of the adoptive parent's sexual orientation.

Guiding Principle: All children have a fundamental right to grow up in families of their own. Children in state care are entitled to reasonable efforts on the part of the state to place them in a permanent home. A state that burdens the child's access to adoption must show that its rules are narrowly tailored to serve a compelling government interest or are at the very least rationally related to a legitimate state interest.

Discussion: I would argue that all children have a positive right to grow up safe and secure in their own homes and that government is charged with ensuring that they have the opportunity to do so. This position is consistent with the United Nations Convention on the Rights of the Child, which recognizes positive as well as negative rights. But one need not go beyond the traditional American realm of negative rights to argue that a law that prohibits adoptions of children by eager, fit, and willing families burdens children who are in need of homes. By analogy to the rights of adults to marry and form a family, children's equal access to adoption as a means to form a family must be considered a fundamental right.

This is no abstract argument. Currently, more than half a million children are in foster care, and in 1998 an estimated 110,000 had been freed for adoption.[42] Many of these children have special needs that create barriers to their adoption. Critics of racial matching have urged that barriers to adoption by different-race families be torn down in fairness to these children. Less attention has been given, however, to the effects on children of barriers to adoption by same-sex families. A federal district court recently upheld a statute in the state of Florida that barred homosexuals from adopting.[43] The case involved a petition by Lofton, a gay foster parent, to adopt "John Doe," a ten-year-old boy whom Lofton had taken in as an HIV-positive infant and nurtured into health. Lofton had fostered no less than ten HIV-positive babies and had received the Outstanding Foster Parent Award from the Children's Home Society. He wanted to adopt the one who had survived and now tested HIV negative, but his petition was denied solely because of his sexual orientation. The court used circular reasoning, dismissing the fundamental rights claim because adoption is a creature of statute and rejecting the equal protection claim on the basis that, while no evidence had been presented, it was at least "arguable" that homosexual couples were not as good at parenting as heterosexual couples. The court failed to grapple in any meaningful way with the child's "rights" in this case. The harm to John Doe, and to other children awaiting adoption, is real and tangible.

One counterargument is that the prospective adoptive parent is a stranger to the child. How can the child lay claim to a family relationship before it is formed? But the arguments I make for the rights of the child to a family, in this scenario, do not depend on an already established relationship.[44] The Court has consistently rejected state laws on marriage that significantly interfere with the right to marry unless supported by an important governmental interest and closely tailored to support that interest.[45] The Court in *Lofton* distinguished adoption from marriage as a "creation of statute" and therefore not deeply rooted in American history and tradition. But entry into marriage in modern America is also a creation of statute, and legal adoption as a means of providing new families for displaced children dates back to the 1850s.[46]

Of course, the child does not normally initiate the relationship or "petition" to be adopted, making it more difficult to see how the child's fundamental liberty is burdened. The exceptional case that illustrates this rule is the case of Gregory K., the child who tried to "divorce" his parents.[47] In that case, eleven-year-old Gregory Kingsley petitioned to be adopted by his foster family. The appellate court denied him standing to file a petition on his own, but it granted the adoption. This case illustrates how the state child welfare agency, in whom guardianship of the child has been vested by the court that placed the child in foster care, is normally the entity that has standing to act on the child's behalf. In some jurisdictions, an attorney is appointed to represent the child and has authority to bring a petition seeking the child's adoptive placement. Clearly, however, the state functions in a fiduciary relation to the children in its care. As a fiduciary, it is charged with protecting the child's rights and interests. To pass constitutional muster, laws and policies preventing a child from finding an adoptive home must be supported by evidence that adoptions by gay and lesbian parents are not in the best interest of the child.

Some, including Lynn Wardle, have argued that a two-parent heterosexual family is better than a gay and lesbian family.[48] As noted above, I am not alone in harboring significant doubts about the empirical evidence he employs to support his arguments.[49] Critics of gay and lesbian adoption draw heavily on data about single-parent families and presume that the deficits of single-parent families flow from the absence of an opposite-sex parent rather than from other factors such as parental immaturity, lack of stability, or socioeconomic status.[50]

But in this scenario, where the choice is between a gay or lesbian family and no family at all, the prohibition surely fails the most basic tests of reasonableness and fairness. It punishes the child who might otherwise be adopted for the sexuality of the prospective parent without regard to the child's individual needs.

C. Children's Access to People, Courts, and Information

This is a category far less examined because it surfaces only when and if we shift to a child-centered perspective. Because children traditionally have lacked standing to assert rights of their own and have been perceived at best as dependents and at worst as property of the parent, these issues have been considered matters of parental right. We take for granted laws that allow parents to bar contact with others, to preclude separate representation for children in court cases affecting them, and to preclude children from access to information, especially information regarding their biological heritage. I have left these issues for last because they are most likely to arouse dissent from those who might otherwise support my arguments for the rights of children in gay and lesbian families. They potentially pit the rights of parents, abetted by the state, to control their children's access to information against the children's independent and conflicting rights. I will lump them into a single scenario that seems to capture the nature of the conflict.

These cases involving adult control over children's access to people and information, when viewed from a child-centered perspective, involve the rights of a child who is prevented from access to people and information because of the objection of the child's legal parent, by state laws denying the child standing to appear in court, or by laws sealing the adoption records.

GUIDING PRINCIPLE: Children have a right to access to useful and nonharmful information necessary to the formation of their individual identities.

Discussion: Traditionally, parental rights have included the right to exclude others from access to the child, the exclusive authority to speak for the child and determine when and how the child's rights would be asserted, and the right to bar access to information about subjects as diverse as the child's adoptive status, the practices of other religions, and ways of life other than those of the parent.[51] In some cases, such as rules on standing and procedures for sealing adoption records, the state weighs in with laws that further limit children's rights of access. I believe that neither parents nor the state should bar children from access to the courts, when the child's critical interests are at stake, or from access to useful and nonharmful information essential to the formation of the individual's identity. In children's growth to autonomy, the right to access people and information may be integral to vindication of children's dignity, privacy, and equality rights.[52]

It is not surprising that marginalized and excluded groups seeking recognition as parents would want to claim the full panoply of parental rights. This eagerness to have full-blown rights over children was a part of the activism of women and people of color in past centuries[53] and will surely play a role as gays and lesbians gain greater recognition. I have argued that rights are not a zero-sum game and that a victory for children's rights strengthens rather than weakens the rights of all. I would urge that gay and lesbian families, sensitized by their own struggle for justice, think expansively about the rights of their children.

As this discussion illustrates, there are cases involving custody and adoption in which children's rights may seem to come into conflict with those of their parents. When parents' and children's interests are in direct conflict in matters of great significance, the child must be entitled to appointment of a guardian ad litem and/or representation of counsel. Discussion of the precise role of the child's representative is beyond the scope of this essay.[54] But for purposes of this discussion, it is sufficient to note that the importance of the child's right to a representative dwarfs any debates about the precise role the child's representative should play. Of course, courts should appoint a guardian ad litem or counsel only when they find that to do so is in the child's best interest and does not unduly infringe on parental autonomy.

To make plain where I would draw the line, a child's objections to taking out the garbage are simply not sufficient to create a cause of action, meaning they would never get through the courthouse door. Nor are decisions about such ordinary authority issues as curfews, homework, and social companions. But when the issue directly implicates the child's basic rights to maintain relations with a family member, to knowledge of the child's own identity, or such other fundamental issues (e.g., education rights, reproductive rights, religious rights), the parent's opposition cannot be given dispositive weight.

Finally, children have rights, recognized in international law, to know their identities. The practice that dates to the mid-twentieth century of sealing birth records and refusing to disclose even to adult adoptees the identity of their biological parents is a gross violation of the rights of the individual. Gays and lesbians may be tempted to support these laws to ensure that the child will never know the identity of the opposite-sex individual who contributed the genetic material necessary to conception of a child. Gays and lesbians are understandably wary of the risk that a biological parent may intrude on the family unit's autonomy. However, adoptive parents have learned the hard way that many children have a burning need to know. Although I would place the functional family higher in the hierarchy of family rights than a simple biological connection unaccompanied by a developed relationship, it does not follow that biology is meaningless. I realize, as an adoptive parent, that biological connections also have very deep meaning to us and to our children. Parenthetically, I was just reunited with a seventy-two-year-old half-brother whom I had never met. This experience has taught me in a most direct and basic way what it meant to my adopted son to meet his biological parents, uncles, and half-brothers who looked like him and shared his genetic heritage.

III. Balancing Children's Rights with Values of Family Autonomy and Privacy

In the scheme I have sketched above, I take it as axiomatic that children, being persons, are entitled to claim legal protection not only against an abusive state (the normal sphere of negative rights) but also against an abusive or exploitive parent. This position is not without its risks. It challenges, to some degree, the dominant norms according a veil of privacy to conduct within the home and to parenting choices. Traditionally, law was loath to intervene in an "intact" family. Law has conceptualized the family as an entity with its own internal governing structures and balances of power. The patriarch, as head of the family, spoke and acted on behalf of all. In cases like *McGuire v. McGuire*,[55] judges argued that husbands and wives must resolve their own internal disputes without state intervention. Having joined in voluntary unions, men and women must work out their problems in the privacy of the family. To allow state intervention would be to encourage micromanagement of intimate relationships and would drive a wedge between family members, or so the theory goes.

But this account has substantial flaws even as it applies to consenting adults. Laws that prevented husbands and wives from suing each other in tort or contract have been repealed as women and men gained equal standing under the law. Moreover, even if a noninterventionist stance were proper in the case of consenting adults who enter into a marital unit, children and adults are not similarly situated. First, adults, unlike children, choose their mates and choose (purposefully or negligently, as the case may be) to have children. Children do not choose their parents, nor do they choose to be born. Second, adults have an exit option from an oppressive family situation through legal separation or divorce. Except in extraordinary cases, children do not. Even for adults, termination of the relationship is not always a fair price to charge for access to justice. Only recently have women been able to persuade judges and legislatures that some protection short of the exit option was needed in cases of domestic violence, threats to property rights, and torts against the person. Children are even more deserving of protection within the family than women, since they are smaller than adults, do not have the exit option, and are not in the relationship by free choice.[56]

I am not suggesting that family autonomy is outmoded or has no value. Even from a purely child-centered perspective, family autonomy is a valuable commodity indeed. Children thrive in families where the adults who care for and protect them enjoy a large measure of autonomy and authority. The family serves as a crucial buffer between the child and the large, cold, impersonal state. To avoid meddlesome and destructive interventions, we should generally presume that parents are motivated to act in the best interest of their child, know the child's needs better than anyone else, and, therefore, function as the most effective advocates of children's rights. But when this presumption fails, the duty shifts to the state to protect the child's rights. Whether the child's "family" is constituted by a traditional heterosexual married couple, gay or lesbian partners, or a single parent, family autonomy should not become a cover for ignoring the needs and rights of children.

IV. Conclusion

In this essay, I have applied a child-centered perspective to rights within the family to examine the status and rights of children in gay and lesbian families. Here, as in most family settings, the rights of children complement and reinforce the claims of adults to protection of intimate relationships. Barriers to marriage and adoption and child custody and visitation laws that discriminate against gays and lesbians infringe the rights of children to just and equal treatment as much as they infringe the rights of adults.

Government bears a heavy burden of justification when it adopts laws and policies about adults that cause collateral damage to children. What, then, of laws and policies that on their face explicitly single out children in nontraditional families for less favorable treatment? Clearly, there is no place in a constitutional system grounded on equal justice under the law for policies, such as those proposed by conservative welfare reformers, that discriminate directly against the children themselves by conditioning children's access to programs like Head Start on having two married heterosexual parents

While children's and parents' rights, in same-sex as in heterosexual families, are normally mutually reinforcing, there are rare situations when vindicating the adult's claim to autonomy and privacy may come at too great a cost to the child. Complete freedom and autonomy for adults must give way to children's rights to protection, to preservation of family relationships, and to knowledge of their genetic identities.

NOTES

1. This article was inspired by Nancy Polikoff, author of the groundbreaking article "This Child Does Have Two Mothers: Redefining Motherhood to Meet the Needs of Children in Lesbian-Mother and Other Nontraditional Families," 78 *Georgetown Law Journal* 459 (1990). While a few scholars who write about same-sex families have discussed the rights of children—see, e.g., Lewis A. Silverman, "Suffer the Little Children: Justifying Same Sex Marriage from the Perspective of a Child of the Union," 102 *West Virginia Law Review* 411 (1999)—scholars of children's rights have not devoted sufficient attention to this topic. Polikoff recently challenged me, as an advocate for children, to analyze the treatment of children in gay and lesbian families using my theory of children's rights.

2. See Sean Cahill and Kenneth T. Jones, *Leaving Our Children Behind: Welfare Reform and the Gay, Lesbian, Bisexual, and Transgender Community,* National Gay and Lesbian Task Force Report (New York: Policy Institute of the National Gay and Lesbian Task Force, 2001).

3. See Mary Ann Mason, *From Father's Property to Children's Rights: The History of Child Custody in the United States* (New York: Columbia University Press, 1994); Michael Grossberg, *Governing the Hearth: Law*

and Family in Nineteenth Century America (Chapel Hill: University of North Carolina Press, 1986).

4. See *Meyer v. Nebraska,* 262 U.S. 390 (1923), and *Pierce v. Society of Sisters,* 268 U.S. 510 (1925), two seminal Supreme Court cases whose impacts are discussed in Barbara Bennett Woodhouse, "Who Owns the Child? Meyer and Pierce and the Child as Property," 33 *William and Mary Law Review* 995 (1992).

5. Mason, *From Father's Property*; Michael Grossberg, *A Judgment for Solomon: The d'Hauteville Case and Legal Experience in Antebellum America* (New York: Cambridge University Press, 1996); Barbara Bennett Woodhouse, "The Status of Children: A Story of Emerging Rights," in *Cross Currents: Family Law and Policy in the U.S. and England,* ed. Sanford Katz et al. (New York: Oxford University Press, 2000).

6. Barbara Bennett Woodhouse, "Hatching the Egg: A Child-Centered Perspective on Parents' Rights," 14 *Cardozo Law Review* 1747 (1993).

7. Catherine J. Ross, "From Vulnerability to Voice: Appointing Counsel for Children in Civil Litigation," 64 *Fordham Law Review* 1571, 1579 (1996).

8. Karen Czapanskiy, "Volunteers and Draftees: The Struggle for Parental Equality," 38 *University of California at Los Angeles Law Review* 1415 (1991).

9. Nancy Dowd, *Redefining Fatherhood* (New York: NYU Press, 2000); Barbara Bennett Woodhouse, "It All Depends on What You Mean by Home: Towards a Communitarian Theory of the Nontraditional Family," 1996 *Utah Law Review* 569 (1996).

10. David Blankenhorn, *Fatherless America* (New York: Basic Books, 1995).

11. Barbara Bennett Woodhouse, "Children's Rights," in *Handbook of Youth and Justice,* ed. Susan O. White (New York: Kluwer Academic/Plenum, 2001).

12. Woodhouse, "Hatching the Egg"; Barbara Bennett Woodhouse, "Child Custody in the Age of Children's Rights: The Search for a Just and Workable Standard," 33 *Family Law Quarterly* 815 (1999).

13. Bruce C. Hafen, "Children's Liberation and the New Egalitarianism: Some Reservations about Abandoning Youth to Their 'Rights,'" 1976 *Brigham Young University Law Review* 605 (1976).

14. See Woodhouse, "Hatching the Egg"; Barbara Bennett Woodhouse, "Out of Children's Needs, Children's Rights: The Child's Voice in Defining the Family," 2 *Brigham Young University Journal of Public Law* 321 (1994); Woodhouse, "Children's Rights."

15. See www.law.ufl.edu/centers/childlaw for amicus briefs by this author in cases like *Brian B. v. Pennsylvania Department of Education,* 320 F.3d 582 (2000), and *DeBoer v. Schmidt,* 509 U.S. 1301 (1993), urging courts to recognize children's rights to education and to a voice in foster care and adoption cases, respectively.

16. Woodhouse, "Who Owns the Child."

17. Woodhouse, "Child Custody."

18. Woodhouse, "Hatching the Egg."

19. Woodhouse, "Children's Rights."

20. Woodhouse, "The Status of Children"; Barbara Bennett Woodhouse, "The Constitutionalization of Children's Rights: Incorporating Emerging Rights into Constitutional Doctrine," 2 *University of Pennsylvania Journal of Constitutional Law* 1 (1999).

21. Susan H. Bitensky, "Spare the Rod, Embrace Our Humanity: Toward a New Legal Regime Prohibiting Corporal Punishment of Children," 31 *Michigan University Journal of Law Reform* 353, 359 (1998).

22. James Garbarino and Frances M. Stott, *What Children Can Tell Us: Eliciting, Interpreting, and Evaluating Critical Information from Children* (San Francisco: Jossey-Bass, 1992).

23. See, e.g., *Boswell v. Boswell,* 352 Md. 204, 721 A.2d 662 (Md. Ct. App. 1998); *Jacoby v. Jacoby,* 736 So. 2d 410 (Fla. App. 2d Dist. 2000).

24. See § 401, Uniform Marriage and Divorce Act, 9 U.L.A. 147 (1987).

25. Judith Wallerstein, Julia Lewis, and Sandy Blakeslee, *The Unexpected Legacy of Divorce: A 25 Year Landmark Study* (New York: Hyperion, 2000).

26. See Woodhouse, "Hatching the Egg," discussing *Boyles v. Boyles,* 466 N.Y.S.2d (App. Div. 1983).

27. Woodhouse, "Hatching the Egg," 1844–51.

28. Barbara Bennett Woodhouse, "Of Babies, Bonding and Burning Buildings: Discerning Parenthood in Irrational Action," 81 *Virginia Law Review* 2493 (1995).

29. 444 S.E.2d 276 (Va. App. 1994).

30. 599 N.Y.S.2d 377 (N.Y. Fam. Ct. 1993).

31. John A. Robertson, "Assisted Reproductive Technology and the Family," 47 *Hastings Law Journal* 911 (1996).

32. See Marsha Garrison, "Law Making for Baby Making: An Interpretive Approach to the Determination of Legal Parentage," 113 *Harvard Law Review* 835 (2000), for a fascinating discussion of how family law principles can be brought to bear to resolve issues of parentage in reproductive technology cases.

33. See Mary Lyndon Shanley, *Making Babies, Making Families: What Matters Most in an Age of Reproductive Technologies* 136 (Boston: Beacon, 2001), 136.

34. See Woodhouse, "The Status of Children," discussing illegitimacy cases such as *Clark v. Jeter*, 486 U.S. 456 (1988).

35. For discussions of the second-parent adoption controversy, see Mark Strasser, "Courts, Legislatures, and Second-Parent Adoptions: On Judicial Deference, Specious Reasoning, and the Best Interest of the Child," 66 *Tennessee Law Review* 1019 (1999).

36. 434 U.S. 246 (1978).

37. Theresa Glennon, "Binding Family Ties: A Child Advocacy Perspective on Second Parent Adoptions," 7 *Temple Political and Civil Rights Law Review* 255 (1998).

38. See Lynn Wardle, "The Potential Impact of Homosexual Parenting on Children," 1997 *University of Illinois Law Review* (1997): 833–920 (arguing that gay parents are injurious to children), and Woodhouse, "Hatching the Egg" (arguing that two parents are better than one).

39. American Academy of Pediatrics, Committee on Psychosocial Aspects of Child and Family Health, *Pediatrics* 109 (Feb. 2002): 339–40, citing Ellen C. Perrin et al., "Technical Report: Coparent or Second-Parent Adoption by Same Sex Parents," *Pediatrics* 109 (Feb. 2002): 341–44. A full analysis of the literature on children raised in homosexual families is beyond the scope of this essay. However, there is a broad consensus among existing studies, which generally conclude that gay and lesbian parents are not detrimental to their children and may well provide superior parenting to a matched sample of heterosexual couples. In this highly charged area, there will always be some experts who disagree. Currently, the battle of the experts continues in a series of affidavits by experts submitted in the Ontario case of *Halpern v. Canada* (A.G.) et al. (on file with author).

40. See Garrison, "Law Making for Baby Making," 847–48.

41. See Cahill and Jones, *Leaving Our Children Behind.*

42. Elizabeth Bartholet, *Nobody's Children: Abuse and Neglect, Foster Care Drift, and the Adoption Alternative* (Boston: Beacon, 1999), 25.

43. *Lofton v. Kearney*, 99-10058-CIV-KING (USDC SDFL Aug. 30, 2001).

44. My arguments build on those sustained in cases like *Turner v. Safely* and *Zablocki v. Redhail*, where the Supreme Court applied heightened scrutiny to laws barring a class of persons from entry into a family relationship through marriage. 482 U.S. 78 (1987) (rights of prisoners to marry); 434 U.S. 374 (1978) (rights of poor parents to marry).

45. See *Zablocki v. Redhail*, 434 U.S. 374 (1978).

46. Grossberg, *Governing the Hearth.*
47. *Kingsley v. Kingsley*, 623 So. 2d 780 (Fla. Dist. Ct. App. 1993).
48. Wardle, "Potential Impact," 833.
49. Glennon, "Binding Family Ties," 13.
50. See ibid. and Marc E. Elovitz, "Adoption by Lesbian and Gay People: The Use and Mis-Use of Social Science Research," 2 *Duke Journal of Gender Law and Policy* 207 (1995), for a critique of interpretations of social science research.
51. Woodhouse, "Who Owns the Child."
52. Catherine J. Ross, "An Emergent Right for Mature Minors to Receive Information," 2 *University of Pennsylvania Journal of Constitutional Law* 223 (1999); Naomi Cahn and Jana Singer, "Adoption, Identity, and the Constitution: The Case for Opening Closed Records," 2 *University of Pennsylvania Journal of Constitutional Law* 150 (1999).
53. See Peggy Cooper Davis, *Neglected Stories: The Constitution and Family Values* (New York: Hill and Wang, 1997); and Grossberg, *A Judgment for Solomon.*
54. See *Special Issue: Ethical Issues in the Legal Representation of Children*, 64 *Fordham Law Review* (March 1996).
55. 59 N.W.2d 336 (Neb. 1953).
56. For a fuller discussion of this issue, see Woodhouse, "The Dark Side of Family Privacy," 67 *George Washington Law Review* 1247 (1999).

11

RELATIONSHIP RIGHTS FOR A QUEER SOCIETY: WHY GAY ACTIVISM NEEDS TO MOVE AWAY FROM THE RIGHT TO MARRY

VALERIE LEHR

The debate over whether gay and lesbian couples should have marriage rights in Vermont has continued even after passage in 2000 of legislation that grants these couples the right to register their relationships as civil unions and receive, in essence, the benefits of marriage. Proponents supported the civil union law as a way to extend protection to gay relationships without actually allowing gays/lesbians to marry. The passage of this legislation left proponents of gay marriage not altogether satisfied, and it left conservative opponents, encouraged by the fact that polls show a majority of Vermonters opposed to civil unions, organizing to defeat legislators who had supported the bill's passage.[1] In addition to introducing a bill to repeal passage, conservative Representative Peg Flory tried another tactic. She challenged the gains of gay men and lesbians by proposing that the coverage of the legislation be expanded in a manner that would change it from a "civil unions" law to a "reciprocal partnership" law. Under the proposal, which was passed by the Republican-controlled House, any two people age eighteen or older who are legally prohibited from marrying would be allowed to form a contractual partnership. "Gay couples would be eligible, but so would other couples who cannot legally marry—primarily blood relatives, such as an elderly woman and her adult child."[2] This proposal gained the support of those promoting traditional marriage, while it was opposed by gays who fought for marriage rights. "One of the House's two openly gay members said there was no comparison between the relationship between himself and his partner of 18 years and the one he enjoyed with his parents. 'You can't equate the two,' Rep. Robert Dostis said. 'Don't demean, don't demoralize my relationship with Chuck.'"[3] It is, I believe, worth reflecting on why Dostis, Flory, and others think that it demeans gays and lesbians to extend benefits to relatives as members of reciprocal partnerships.

To understand this claim, we need to understand the role that marriage plays in society and in citizenship. As will become clear, I believe that understanding marriage can help us to better appreciate *both* why marriage rights have become so central to lesbian and gay organizing and why focusing energy on gaining these rights reinforces an understanding of citizenship and labor that troubles many feminists, as well as some gay and lesbian scholars. Applying feminist theoretical arguments to the question of gay marriage leads me to conclude that by making gay marriage the primary goal of a gay politics of family, we fail to engage other issues in American society that need to be defined as political problems. Despite the promise that marriage will bring economic security, many families do not have the resources they need, even when they are organized around heterosexual marriages, and poor families not organized around heterosexual marriage are furthermore seen as responsible for their own poverty because of their difference. As well as arguing that marriage rights should not be a primary goal, I want to suggest that achieving gay marriage rights is likely to fail until our social understandings of marriage, citizenship, and rights are changed. Unfortunately, queer theory and politics, which in the 1980s and 1990s was the primary alternative within gay and lesbian communities to a politics that prioritized rights gains such as gay marriage, fails to provide a basis for an adequate alternative politics. Queer theory promotes a politics that does not adequately account for the material importance of social change.

This is particularly relevant in relation to the family because although family certainly has a symbolic force, it is also central to the material survival of many Americans. When marriage and the ideal family created by it are understood as both material and symbolic forces, promoting policies such as domestic partnership, civil unions, or even reciprocal partnership becomes a more compelling and more strategic alternative. Even these policies, however, should be seen as a mechanism by which to build coalitions with the power to challenge the centrality of marriage for full citizenship rather than as an ideal end.

I. Marriage and Citizenship

The public rhetoric of gay and lesbian marriage rights advocates indicates clearly that they see attaining marriage rights as central both to enhancing the status of gays as citizens and, for at least some, to further "civilizing" American society. In framing its arguments about gay marriage rights, the Human Rights Campaign, for example, urges gay marriage proponents to assert that marriage is a basic human right. The organization's "marriage organizing booklet" indicates that antimarriage arguments can be countered if marriage proponents frame their points using the following key terms: "basic human right," "personal decision," and "individuals, not government should decide."[4] One way of putting these terms together is to argue that without the ability to exercise freedom in deciding whom to marry, the individual is not a full rights-bearing individual, since the government has interfered with the right to exercise personal autonomy in choosing to enter into the institution of marriage. Two of the most prominent voices in developing such ideas into fleshed-out arguments in favor of progay marriage are writer and former *New Republic* editor Andrew Sullivan and Yale law professor William Eskridge. Sullivan sees marriage rights not just as a necessary reform but as one of the only reforms necessary to achieve gay equality: "If nothing else were done at all, and gay marriage were legalized," he writes, "ninety percent of the political work necessary to achieve gay and lesbian equality would have been achieved. It is ultimately the only reform that matters."[5] It matters so much because it is a mechanism by which equal treatment can be granted by government action—that is, in a way that does not require "private tolerance" and that respects the boundaries between public and private life so central to liberalism.

In explicating why marriage rights can be perceived as this important, it is worth noting the role that marriage has played in American life since the country's founding. Nancy Cott suggests that marriage was a critically important institution because it provided a metaphor for what it meant to be a citizen. "The method of the new nation was union and the essence of the national union was to be the voluntary adherence of its citizens. Allegiance was to be contractual, not coerced—to be motivated by love, not fear. . . . Marriage, being a voluntary and long sustained bond, provided a ready emblem."[6] The mechanisms by which marriage was built into the law, whether in relation to coverture, slavery, or immigration, have been important for regulating citizenship, defining appropriate gender roles, defining appropriate sexuality, and developing "racial formations."[7] To be excluded from the institution is to be seen as inferior or as unable to consent to a "long and sustained bond"; to be brought into marriage is to be civilized. Native people could be brought into American (Christian) culture through marriage: "Both political and religious officials assumed that native Americans' assimilation had to be founded on monogamous marriage, from which would follow conventional sexual division of labor, property, and inheritance. Both envisioned Indians could be educated to embrace Christian values. Indians were not seen as so different from white Americans that they could not *become* civilized."[8] As Peggy Cooper Davis discusses so forcefully, African Americans understood having control over their family lives, which required being able to marry, as a critical component of becoming equal. Thus, the Fourteenth Amendment rights that have been used to carve out private space were necessary for ending slavery. "These men and women [who framed the Fourteenth Amendment] regarded the denial of family liberty as a vice of slavery that inverted concepts of human dignity, citizenship, and natural law. And they regarded the Fourteenth Amendment as the instrument with which to reenshrine family liberty as an inalienable aspect of national citizenship and natural law."[9] Similarly, gay marriage advocates suggest that the continued denial of relationship rights maintains unacceptable inequality, that it helps to reinforce stereotypes of gays as unable to sustain commitment. They argue that gays are close enough to heterosexuals to be able to become more civilized and fully equal with the right to form families through marriage. Although this obviously would not mean accepting traditional gender roles, it would mean accepting other aspects of traditional norms, including monogamy. Putting this fairly simply, Eskridge notes that "[i]n short, long-term commitment to another person is good."[10] Sullivan explicitly contrasts a gay world with marriage as a central institution to the current "ethic more of anonymous and promiscuous sex than of committed relationships."[11] Yet why commitment needs to be sexually monogamous, or even why it needs to be sexual, is not at all clear.

In fact, there is a double-edged sword here that I believe needs to be acknowledged and discussed. Although the right to make decisions about one's private life is critical to meaningful citizenship in a liberal democracy, extending marriage rights has always occurred within the terms set by the dominant culture because monogamous heterosexual marriage was defined as a natural advance over the "primitive" relationships of others.[12] This is clear in Cott's discussion of Native Americans and marriage.[13] Although Peggy Davis tends to focus on the positive aspects of the Fourteenth Amendment, in other words, those aspects that allowed African Americans to counter the horrendous control of their bodies and families by slave owners, she notes that the terms of inclusion also meant the loss of the cultures that many Africans brought to the United States.[14] Finally, it is clear that the over one-hundred-year process of gaining control of Mormons through antipolygamy law is an assertion of cultural superiority. "Mormons," Phelan writes, "were characterized as 'absolutely treacherous,' suffering from moral decay that produced children who were 'a menace to the future of our country' because of the 'licentiousness' to which they were exposed."[15] In part, this resulted from the identification of polygamy with Asian and African cultures.[16] It also resulted from identifying polygamy as fostering, not civilized gender interdependence, but patriarchal domination. Although marriage rights are a central mechanism used by the state to form citizens, simply having access to marriage, and rights within marriage, does not guarantee equality.

The expansion of the right to marriage to African Americans and the provision to women of choices about and within marriage have had limited success in transforming the social status of both groups. Thus marriage, and the norms of heterosexual monogamy and two-parent families that are embedded within marriage, remain potent forces for reinforcing racism and sexism. The continued poverty of African Americans is often attributed, not to the continued power of racism, but to the failure to control sexuality within a particular family structure. There is no reason to believe that nonmarital homosexual sex would not continue to be defined as deviant even if gays and lesbians were granted marriage rights. Sodomy laws could continue to exist even if gay marriage were to become legal. As Phelan observes, "It is not certain, however, that such a change [marriage rights] would lead to the abolition of anti-sodomy laws. Courts might very well allow that married couples could not be restricted, while leaving sodomy between unmarried persons (either same-sex, heterosex, or other) unaffected."[17] Thus it is not necessarily the case that all gay men and lesbians would become more respected citizens or gain greater rights than they have currently if gay marriage were to become legal.

This history can help us to analyze the rhetoric that Sullivan and Eskridge employ in making their case for gay marriage. In addition to arguments about equal rights and equal treatment, they justify the inclusion of gays in the institution of marriage by asserting that gays need the civilizing influence of marriage, both because the "sexual citizens" that gay men have become are not ideal citizens and because the social and legal norms of (monogamous) marriage can change the behavior of these men and make them better citizens. Marriage will regulate gay men in a way that Sullivan and Eskridge find salutary. This is true to such an extent that other mechanisms, such as domestic partnerships, that might extend rights are rejected by Eskridge as inferior and as lacking transformative potential because such relationships can be ended more easily and do not have the force of tradition.[18] The discourse that Eskridge and Sullivan employ in making this argument draws upon traditional understandings of marriage in asserting that self-control and civil virtue are connected to sexual monogamy and that these are particularly difficult for men to achieve because they are so sexually driven:

> Surely even conservatives who think women are essential to the successful socialization of men would not deny that the discipline of domesticity, of shared duties and lives, of the give-and-take of cohabitation and love with anyone, even of the same sex, tends to benefit men more than the option of free-wheeling, etiolating bachelorhood. But this would mean creating a public moral and social climate which preferred stable gay relationships to gay or straight bachelorhood.[19]

Or, in Eskridge's words:

> In order to achieve committed relationships, gay men need the discipline of marriage more than lesbians do. Gay men are like Ulysses, who directed that he be bound to the ship's mast as it passed the Sirens, sea creatures whose seductive voices enticed men to their deaths. Likewise, gay men realize that they tend to lose their balance and succumb to private sirens if they are not socially or even legally constrained.[20]

It is not clear, however, why a liberal democratic society needs to rest on this foundation, other than perhaps that this has been the guiding dominant understanding. In the past, the basis of the argument has been gendered: that is, it has been asserted that strengths and weaknesses of men and women provide controls on each when one man and one woman form a single marital unit and that, through marriage, men and women can form a unit that is superior to either alone. Given that neither Eskridge nor Sullivan wants to reinforce the gendered basis of this argument (and in fact Eskridge states explicitly that he wants to undermine the sexist nature of marriage), it is hard to maintain a link between monogamy and virtue. Additionally, even if we granted that society would benefit from its citizens' engaging in sustained, committed relationships, the assumption that a committed relationship and promiscuity are mutually exclusive does not fit with gay male experience. In their study of American couples, Blumstein and Schwartz found that of the 339 gay male couples that had been together for over ten years, 71 percent had had nonmonogamous sex and another 23 percent had had a meaningful affair.[21] One can, it would seem, have both a committed relationship and a nonmonogamous one, and if part of gay acceptance by mainstream America requires following the monogamous norm of marriage, it is not at all clear that marriage alone will challenge the nonmonogamous cultural norms of gay male communities. Finally, one could argue, as Mark Blasius has done, that the ethical self is enhanced if individuals are actively engaged in making decisions about whether and how to act sexually and in relationship, rather than acting because they are socially or legally constrained.[22] Valuing gay male and lesbian relationships and families as they exist could help us to better understand how differences in the norms of private life might be positive for citizenship.

Interestingly, the radical potential of gay and lesbian relationships and families is recognized in the promarriage arguments of Sullivan and Eskridge, yet each either denies the radical potential or simply skips over the radical implications. In *Virtually Normal,* Sullivan notes that many gay men have been able to form positive nonmonogamous relationships, yet in the afterword he backs away from the implications of this statement, stating that marriage should be the preferred form of relationship and that it should be monogamous.[23] In discussing family more broadly as a structure that often nurtures children, Eskridge is quite aware of the challenge that gay and lesbian families can pose because of the possibility of multiple parenting: "Because procreation will necessarily involve a third party, children will introduce differences. For instance, third-party sperm donors and surrogate mothers (and perhaps their partners) are more likely to be part of the gay or lesbian family than heterosexual families."[24] This seems a clear example of where marriage (assuming that spouses continue to be defined as a child's legal parents, regardless of biology) would retard the development of the extended family that might serve gays and lesbians (and others) well. Instead of exploring this potential challenge in more detail, at other points Eskridge restates the conservative argument that children are best raised in two-parent families, whether lesbian/gay or heterosexual, even though it is unclear whether the inferiority of single-parent families is a result of family structure or of confounding variables, such as poverty or education, which could be equalized through social policy.[25] Eskridge's position leaves single parents continuing to be condemned, while the dominant ideology that reinforces the superiority of two-parent families does not recognize more parents as better, or even desirable. Thus, norms are reinforced that go against the interests of many, including many gay people, and against one of the innovations that gay families can make that Eskridge himself believes to be positive. Among those who are harmed by these norms are single mothers, some of whom are lesbians, struggling to survive in a society that provides little economic assistance and much condemnation.

Eskridge does not believe that gay couples will gain only equal protection and stable monogamy with the right to marry. He also argues that marriage is a central mechanism by which one can receive "social insurance." Yet he does not discuss the substantial burden that such "social insurance" has placed on women by relegating much care work to the private realm and defining it as naturally more appropriate for women. It is this argument that I want to explore in greater detail, because if Sullivan and Eskridge achieve what they desire and, by extending marriage rights to gays, reinforce marital norms among both gays and lesbians and heterosexuals, they will have helped to reinforce norms that continue to deny status and resources to many in society: those who provide the labor of care, whether within their family or as paid workers, those who choose not to marry, single parents, and those who do not have adequate social insurance despite being married and monogamous.

The greatest opposition to making marriage rights a primary goal of gay/lesbian/queer politics has come from those whose work is based in feminist theory and ideas, such as Paula Ettelbrick, Shane Phelan, Michael Warner, and Ruthann Robson.[26] One of the first and clearest statements of the difference between seeing a gay family politics centered on marriage rights and a gay family politics that is necessarily tied to a more extensive agenda is in the 1989 exchange between activists Thomas Stoddard and Paula Ettelbrick. At that time, in response to Stoddard's promarriage essay, Ettelbrick stated, "Only when we de-institutionalize marriage and bridge the economic privilege gap between married and unmarried will each of us have a true choice. Otherwise, our choice not to marry will lack legal protection."[27] In making this argument, she drew upon a body of feminist literature that has since been developed further. This work argues that changes within society that provide expanded rights, but not the cultural change or the material resources necessary to make real choices about how to exercise those rights, do not enhance freedom. Central to this argument is a challenge to the division between public and private life that has been so central to liberalism and that Sullivan believes gay rights advocates must respect and preserve.[28] In conceptualizing what this means for activism, Patricia Boling argues that genuinely political responses to inequity require that we look beyond our allies to address larger collectivities in hopes of transforming institutions, not simply gaining inclusion in them. In this sense, identity politics (or political action intended to extend rights to groups defined by some characteristic of their identity) needs to be understood not as political action but as a precursor to political action.[29] Similarly, Iris Young notes that the failure to engage in political debate about the family leaves intact institutional structures, such as marriage and motherhood, that, as a variety of feminist theorists have argued, reinforce injustice.[30] They even reinforce gender divisions, class divisions, and race divisions within gay and lesbian communities and politics. Although there have been moments when this realization was present in gay political analysis and life, it is not currently present in a way that is likely to lead to the coalition building necessary to reconceptualize the family and institutional structures that support it. To begin to do this work, we need a fuller understanding of the role that marriage and family play in supporting inequality in the United States and how the division between public and private life embedded in American society reinforces race and gender formations in the United States.

II. Inequality and Marriage

Eskridge sees gay marriage as important in part because of the social insurance functions that it plays, but these functions, as I noted briefly, have rested mostly on women, and feminists have analyzed them as a critical force in maintaining gender inequality. As Linda Gordon and Nancy Fraser's discussion of rights and citizenship indicates, we cannot fully understand how marriage fits into a system of rights until we understand social rights. "Social rights" is a concept that has significantly greater currency in many western European and Canadian democracies than in the United States. It is not coincidental that in many of these same countries, gays and lesbians enjoy significantly greater relationship rights, since the existence of greater social rights serves to decrease the benefits of marriage and therefore makes the institution less important.[31]

The distinction between social citizenship and civil citizenship follows the work of T. H. Marshall, who saw society as passing through stages of development that increasingly expanded the rights to which citizens were entitled.[32] The final stage in this progression, social citizenship, marked the advance of society to a point where citizenship entitled individuals not simply to civil and political rights but also to economic security and access to benefits, such as health care and education, that enabled them to develop their capacities. As Fraser and Gordon observe, this is a view of citizenship that has never been achieved in the United States.[33] Further, as they also discuss, coverture and slavery were each important in the United States for expanding civil rights to white men: "The legal consumption of wives in coverture, and the legal classification of slaves as property, therefore, were not simple matters of exclusion. They actually helped instead to define civil citizenship, for it was by protecting, subsuming, and even owning others that white male property owners and heads of household became citizens."[34] The result of this definition of civil citizenship is that dependencies, such as those of wives and children on husbands or slaves on masters, were located in the private sphere, with full citizenship contingent on the ability of these private units to remain self-supporting and independent. One legacy of this understanding is that those who depend on the state for benefits, rather than on themselves or their spouse, do not have the same civil rights as those who are "independent." It is critically important, however, to recognize that the myriad benefits that marriage provides even to the wealthy are not seen as challenging "independence." Equally important, the carving out of this ostensibly private, independent realm allowed family and private life to become the preferred site of the labor that would become public if social rights were expanded.[35]

Gender, class, and race asymmetries are particularly important to consider because the minimalist state that is most thoroughly justified by liberal political theory requires that human dependency not be located in the public sphere. Instead, as legal theorist Martha Fineman notes, such dependency is located in the "sexual family":

> The idea of the family as natural coincides with the idea that it is the repository of "inevitable dependencies." The idea of the natural family—the unit to which responsibility for inevitable dependency is referred—establishes a relationship between the "public" state and the "private" family. Dependency is allocated away from the state to the private grouping. These ideas of natural and privatized dependency reinforce one another on an ideological level. They perversely interact so that the societal tasks assigned to the natural family inevitably assume the role differentiation that exists within the sexually affiliated family.[36]

Thus, we have to understand the sexual family as an institution through which the fact of dependence can be denied and the labor of dependence can be provided at minimal social cost.

If coverture initially guaranteed that the ideal of women's labor would be unpaid care work for the benefit of the family, later policies and programs have enabled this understanding to continue. The ability of families to be "independent" within industrial society resulted from a combination of state policies and union policies that supported the family wage; enacted social security legislation, including provisions that provided for widows and their children; banned women from employment in a number of fields and regulated the hours they could work; mandated school attendance (thus removing children from the workforce); and stigmatized single mothers by setting benefits for them at significantly lower levels than benefits for widows and allowing the state to monitor and regulate their private lives. All of these policies contained gendered assumptions that allowed for the location of dependence within the family. For example, Eileen Boris and Peter Bardaglio observe, "The family wage had a dual function: it bolstered men's power over women and children, and it facilitated the efforts of capital to segment the labor force along gender lines."[37] Cott extends this analysis by observing, "New

Deal policy innovations revivified the fading connection between citizenship and marital role through economic avenues. These choices diluted the formal political equality of women and deeply imprinted marriage on citizenship and entitlements, while refiguring what those entitlements were."[38] This occurred with the creation of a dual-track welfare system in which benefits targeted to white male breadwinners and their dependents were defined as entitlements and those targeted to nonbreadwinning males and women who were not dependent on men were defined as either charity or "welfare" programs that marked the recipient as inferior.[39]

The sexual division of labor is not, of course, the only mechanism by which the "labor of care," as Joan Tronto refers to it, is denied as a necessary social function. This work has also been defined as somehow more "natural" for people of color, regardless of gender. As she notes, "the disdain of 'others' who do caring (women, slaves, servants) has been virulent in our culture. This dismissal is inextricably bound up with an attempt to deny the importance of care. The mechanisms of this dismissal are subtle. One form of dismissal is to equate people of color and women with caring roles."[40] The same policies that reinforce women's inequality are not simply gendered; in a variety of ways, they have also been part of the process of racial formation[41] in the United States. Professions with high percentages of black workers were often explicitly excluded from public policy and unionization. For example, Social Security rules restricted those who were eligible to participate. Importantly, excluded work often took place not in the industrial sphere but in the private sphere of the home or farm.[42] The result was that many white working-class and middle-class families gained stability because social policy encouraged and rewarded a particular kind of family formation and rewarded those who followed its guidance. At the same time, state policies guaranteed that the labor required to make these families "independent" without imposing too great a burden on some white women would be inexpensive for the upper middle class and wealthy. Obviously, this had serious implications for the ability of care workers to meet the needs of their own dependents and construct their own families. In this way, among others, even after slavery was outlawed, the demands of labor continued to exert a negative pressure on black private life. The exclusion of black men from well-paid, unionized jobs through much of the twentieth century continues to have a significant impact on the economics of race.[43] Judith Stacey comments: "If marriage was a form of racial privilege under slavery, it is rapidly becoming so again. Sociologist William Wilson has contracted a chauvinistic, but still stunning 'marriageable black male index' that graphs the increasing scarcity of Black men who are neither unemployed nor incarcerated. Wilson's index demonstrates that male breadwinning and marriage are becoming interactive badges of race and class status."[44]

It is, of course, tempting to see changes made since the 1960s as providing all that is necessary to address these inequalities. Certainly this is what Sullivan seems to be suggesting when he argues that gays face greater discrimination than women or racial minorities because these groups possess the civil rights necessary to compete successfully, with the right to marry prominent among them.[45] Wilson's index is one form of counterevidence. Additionally, it is clear that gender inequalities continue to be reproduced within marriage. Ursula Vogel notes that although women do have significantly more civil rights now than in even the recent past, this does not mean that they have full citizenship:

> Her citizenship rights are no longer mediated through the status of a wife; they belong to her as an individual. Yet, the pathetically low level of representation in virtually all forums of public decision-making leaves no doubt that women are still second-class citizens. Marriage and family, as we know them, still trap women in a vicious "cycle" of socially caused and distinctly asymmetrical vulnerability.[46]

As Susan Okin has argued, this also means that children continue to be socialized in an institution that is not a school of justice, but a school of injustice that socializes children into gender role differentiation.[47] Families are so successful that most Americans continue to believe that gender role differentiation is either neutral or beneficial.[48] And given the lack of social resources to provide for those who are dependent, it *is* in many senses beneficial.

Although those who see gay marriage as a central focus of activism may want to define gay rights narrowly and fight only for changes that would extend rights to gay men and lesbians, the fate of legal recognition of gay relationships ought to be, and practically may well be, tied to fostering a greater acceptance of social rights within the United States. In an important sense, Sullivan may be correct in asserting that once marriage rights are obtained by gay men and lesbians, much of the work of achieving gay equality, and I would add, gay citizenship, will have been accomplished. But I want to suggest that he is correct not because marriage rights in themselves have this power, but because gays are not likely to achieve marriage rights until marriage becomes an "extinct ritual"[49] or until heterosexuals are sufficiently "homosexualized"[50] that they no longer care whether queers can marry. That is, marriage rights are unlikely until we confront other, equally institutionalized forms of oppression that have been constructed and sustained in part because of the "civilizing" role that marriage has played since our country's founding. Two kinds of evidence support this position: comparing social policy in the United States to that of other countries and examining the rhetoric that has enabled the right to develop an anti–gay rights coalition.

In writing about the tendency to a politics of assimilation by gay activists in Denmark, Karen Lutzen acknowledges that what appears to be assimilation in Denmark is often an ideal for those in other countries, especially America. She attributes this difference to the strength of the welfare state in Denmark, as well as a tradition of "enlightened tolerance" combined with "a social commitment to establish the conditions for individuals to think and live as they prefer."[51] This culture and the welfare state that supports it have combined to create conditions in which "marriage is no longer an entrance fee to cohabitation, to being part of a couple, or to founding a family with children."[52] Similarly David Rayside notes that although the attempt to win marriage rights in Ontario failed, it had a much greater chance of passage than it would in the United States. One factor in this was that common-law heterosexual relationships already receive greater recognition in Canada; thus marriage does not have the same symbolic power. "The case for same-sex benefits was also made easier by the Canadian medicare system: the universal availability of basic health services made the extension of benefit programs to same-sex couples much less expensive than in the United States."[53] That is, when the state takes greater responsibility for helping people to receive the care that they need, gay people have greater success in having relationship rights recognized.

Rayside's discussion also makes clear the extent to which limited benefits and security for all citizens can make building a progay coalition difficult: "One Conservative MP from a rural constituency commented that most workers in areas like his do not have benefits at all, and would say, 'We're talking about people who have full-time, good-paying jobs who want ice cream afterwards, and I'm really having trouble getting the meal on the table.'"[54] One strategy that has been employed by gay groups to persuade politicians and corporations that gays are worthy of positive attention has been to premise acceptance on studies demonstrating that gays have high disposable incomes. Even though better social scientific studies indicate that gay households are similar to heterosexual households and lesbian households are poorer than heterosexual ones,[55] this legacy makes countering such arguments difficult. It also makes it easy for those opposed to gay rights to suggest that these issues are much less important than making the lives of married heterosexuals and their families more secure, particularly at a time when women's necessary paid labor can make it difficult for anyone to provide the labor of care within families. Progay marriage arguments that appeal to reason, such as those of the Human Rights Campaign, Sullivan, and Eskridge, are not likely to be successful in a debate that is, for many people, not at all about reason. For many, any question about family is really about survival in a world where class divisions are growing, and along with them the insecurity of many people who feel the family is not only a sphere for exercising freedom outside the purview of the public realm but also a place of material support. Until their families feel more secure, expanding rights to others is a low priority. The right seems to understand this much better than gay marriage proponents; thus they have been able to develop a divisive discourse of "special rights," one that is able to take advantage of stereotypes of gays as wealthy and secure to impede the development of more extensive gay citizenship or of questioning the social circumstances that keep so many citizens insecure.

To the extent that the family system that is dominant in the United States is intimately connected with a social devaluation of care, a gendered division of labor that helps to reproduce this division, and an undeveloped welfare state that leaves the provision of the vast majority of care work located in the private realm, changes in social policy or law that are perceived as challenging these systems are likely to be perceived as threats to multiple systems of power and privilege. Gay marriage fits into this category by creating the expectation that people should be able to build private lives without the gender interdependency that has been built into American society. If monogamous heterosexual marriage (or the sexual family) is not simply a natural and progressive way to live, then it becomes possible to ask a number of questions that can otherwise be avoided: Are two-parent heterosexual families inherently superior to single-parent families, or do we live in a society that does not adequately value and support children? Can we have gender equality or racial equality without providing greater social resources for the labor of care? Can people build stable, supportive, committed relationships without marriage and without monogamy? What social guarantees would individuals need to enable them to build such relationships without economic and/or social power? Why is heterosexuality seen as necessary for society? To the extent that these questions are connected, achieving gay marriage rights will not end antigay discrimination because the threat of homosexuality is connected to a system that relies, in part, not just on marriage but on heterosexual marriage with gender differentiation. The right to gay marriage would not in itself change the fact that a society constituted around the (hetero)sexual family will continue to discourage or suppress homosexuality. Thus, it would not change the reality that gay people are legally discriminated against in multiple ways, that schools are often legally prohibited from challenging heterosexual supremacy, or that it remains socially acceptable to create antigay prejudice, whether through jokes, positions on public policy, religious pronouncements, or other forms of speech. In other words, rights for gays are limited by culture and material resources just as they are limited for women and people of color.

One of the defining features of the 1980s and 1990s has been a reaction to the "permissiveness" that developed during the 1960s, permissiveness often tied pejoratively to feminism, welfare rights, gay rights, and other progressive social movements. Challenges to the dominant understanding of family were prominent in each of these movements. The rhetoric of "ending welfare as we know it" has been embedded in the assertion that those who fail to create a particular form of family, one with proper masculine and feminine roles that allow for economic independence, need to be transformed into more psychologically and morally mature people who understand that marriage and the sexual family, along with paid labor, will make them better citizens and, particularly, parents. Fraser and Gordon suggest that the new image of dependence is "the black, unmarried, teenaged, welfare-dependent mother. This image has usurped the symbolic space previously occupied by the housewife, the pauper, the native, and the slave, while absorbing and condensing their connotations."[56] The rhetoric of "appropriate family" is used not only to continue to oppress African Americans. "Arguments on the floor of the Senate for the Defense of Marriage Act, which defined matrimony as a status that could be conferred only on a heterosexual couple," Alisa Solomon argues, "sounded the same fear and loathing as the welfare reform debates: both sought to draw strict lines around what constitutes an American family unit."[57] Margaret Cerullo and Marla Erlien's observations from fifteen years ago seem prescient today: "If the cultural assumptions about female sexuality, 'normal' families, proper relations between men and women, and 'good' mothering are not challenged, any defense of welfare rights will be inadequate."[58] To the extent that gay marriage proponents either reinforce or fail to challenge this rhetoric, the conditions of insecurity and the symbolism of family that lead many to support antiwelfare policies, to be threatened by homosexuality, and to reject gay marriage are reinforced. In fact, Cerullo and Erlien's statement could just as accurately be rewritten: "If the cultural assumptions about female sexuality, 'normal' families, proper relations between men and women, and 'good' mothering are not challenged, any attempt to gain equality for gay/lesbian/queer relationships will fail."

III. Queer Politics and the Politics of Family

If, as I have argued, gay marriage rights are not adequate for addressing family issues, it is important to consider whether other strains of gay activism might provide a more solid base from which to build a politics of family. The 1980s and 1990s saw the rise of an alternative perspective—queer politics. Although this perspective has much to contribute to rethinking family, it has not done so. To understand this failure, I want to explore the roots of this alternative, the theory that has fostered political activism, and the limits of this theory and activism in relation to family. As a result, I hope to demonstrate that queer theory and politics can contribute to a new politics of family but that this potential will be realized only if the focus on challenging cultural norms that is at the center of this perspective is combined with political goals that expand the material security of both queer and nonqueer citizens.

The search for an alternative to gaining gay/lesbian equality through state recognition stems from two problems that civil rights–oriented political activism has encountered, each of which I already discussed in my analysis of the limits of fighting for marriage rights. First, as sociologist Steven Seidman suggests, this is not an approach that has demonstrated an ability to counter the power of the right backlash.[59] The Christian right's argument that gay rights are really not equal rights but special rights has received a depressingly positive reaction. Momin Rahman argues that one of the problems with equal rights, even if one can enshrine them in the law, is that they do not bring with them moral approval; in fact, quite the opposite may be the case. "I would argue," he writes, "that there is no guarantee that the importance of legal liberties will take precedence over essentialist morality. In the realm both of sexuality and sex and gender, the traditional liberal formula is revered."[60] The right seems to fully understand this and is willing to exploit it by constructing legal changes as affronts to traditional morality. Manuel Castells captures the fear that many in the United States have experienced over the past twenty years, fear that aids the right:

> Unable to live under secular patriarchalism, but terrified of solitude and uncertainty in a wildly competitive, individualistic society, where family, as a myth and a reality, represented the only safe haven, many men, women, and children, pray God to return them to the state of innocence where they could be content with benevolent patriarchalism under God's rules. This is why American fundamentalism is deeply marked by the characteristics of American culture, by its familistic individualism, by its pragmatism, and by the personalized relationship to God, and to God's design, as a methodology for solving personal problems in an increasingly unpredictable and uncontrollable life.[61]

In the process, those on the right have used their opposition to gay civil rights, whether antidiscrimination measures, the possibility of marriage rights, or discussions of gay issues in schools, in a way that allows them to consolidate their white base of support, while they try to use these issues to build alliances with African Americans. To the extent that they succeed, as the analyses of Suzanne Pharr and Barbara Smith each suggest, they are successful because they can exploit the lack of multiethnic and multiracial organizing in gay and lesbian organizations.[62] To counter this, gays and lesbians need to engage in discussion internally and with others about the meaning of sexuality and moral regulation, particularly as these interact with racialized discourses in the United States. As the discussion above indicates, the fact that this morality reflects the needs and values of a particular segment of the population means that serious reflection on these values could yield something different. As yet, prominent, well-funded gay groups have rarely understood "gay issues" as all those that have to do with the social regulation of private life, preferring to focus on those issues that are specifically "gay." Queer activists, on the other hand, understand that the dominant moral discourses must be challenged. "Queer theorists shift their focus from an exclusive preoccupation with the oppression and liberation of the homosexual subject to an analysis of the institutional practices and discourses producing sexual knowledge and the ways they organize social life, attending in particular to the ways these knowledges and social practices repress differences."[63]

At the same time that some gay and lesbian activists have seen the need to create an alternative approach to politics for pragmatic, as well as epistemological, reasons, others have seen this need as arising from problems that have developed as identity politics created a plethora of identity groups. The need to define new identities has consistently arisen as exclusions and contradictions within gay/lesbian life became apparent: What, if anything, do gay men and lesbians have in common? Does gay politics, as defined by white gays, include an understanding of the needs of gays of color? How do bisexuality and bisexual people fit into gay politics? How do transgendered people fit into a politics defined by gay identity? Should any and all gay sexual practices be supported in the name of sexual freedom? As a result of the reality that gay groups have often not had very good answers to such questions, the movement has faced a proliferation of identities, organizations, and communities as people try to account for the totality of their experiences and senses of self, rather than simply their same-sex desire and (perhaps) their gender. One impetus behind the development of queer theory and queer activism, both of which have roots in Foucauldian analysis of power and subjectivity, is to provide an alternative to the development and consolidation of such identities. Queer activism, queer theorists argue, should not create a politics premised on the existence of gay or lesbian identity, which can itself become a new discourse of power; it should focus on making identities more open. Queer critics of marriage rights might point out, for example, that marriage rights would be a quite effective mechanism of power to control and limit gay sexuality, rather than fostering freedom.[64] As a result, they argue, one needs to challenge the discourses that create subjugated sexualities. Such deconstruction, at least in theory, opens up the possibility that people affected by these discourses in diverse ways may work together in challenging power. Steven Seidman explains his understanding of queer politics and theory:

> Queer theory has accrued multiple meanings, from a merely useful shorthand way to speak of all gay, lesbian, bisexual, transgendered experiences to a theoretical sensibility that pivots on transgression or permanent rebellion. I take as central to Queer theory

> its challenge to what has become the dominant foundational assumption of both the homophobic and affirmative homosexual theory: the assumption of unified homosexual identity. I interpret Queer theory as contesting this foundation and therefore the very telos of Western homosexual politics.[65]

Arlene Stein and Ken Plummer basically agree with this formulation but also point out that one result of this new theorization is "a rejection of civil-rights strategies in favor of a politics of carnival, transgression, and parody which leads to deconstruction, decentering, revisionist readings, and an anti-assimilationist politics."[66] This is a new kind of politics, still located in the streets, but the goal of which, unlike its liberationist forerunners, seem less clearly motivated by direct engagement with the state.

Queer politics and queer theory have been critiqued for not developing strategies that will allow them to meet their goals. The primary goal of queer activists is to challenge dominant understandings of normality. In so doing, the intent is not to set forth an alternative standard; it is to deconstruct the discourses that produce "normality." The combination of the focus on discourse and textual analysis and the lack of desire to make demands of the state for structural change results in activism that is focused on transgression. It is not always clear, however, what the point is of transgressing social norms. Perhaps the most forceful critique of transgression as a political end is stated by activist and scholar Elizabeth Wilson. "The concepts of transgression, dissidence, subversion, and resistance—which have become familiar in radical discourses since the mid-1980s—are oppositional, negative," she writes. "They are the politics of being *against*, they are the politics of rebellion. Yet since they are cast in the terms set by that which is being rebelled against, they are the politics, ultimately, of weakness."[67] That is, since they can only react to what already exists, they lack the power to redefine social institutions in ways that enhance the possibility of freedom or democracy.

Exploring a Queer Nation action intended to challenge norms of family and sexuality exemplifies the problem of transgression as a primary tool of political action. By interrupting daily life, queer activists suggest, it is possible to help people to see the ways by which hegemonic norms are constructed (invisibly) in everyday life. We can see such an attempt at revelation in some of the strategies of Queer Nation, strategies designed to challenge understandings of normalcy by "performing" roles that the dominant culture defines as abnormal and, through this, revealing the hidden content of everyday life. In analyzing the actions of the Queer Shopping Network of New York and Suburban Homosexual Outreach Program (SHOP) of San Francisco, Lauren Berlant and Elizabeth Freeman write:

> Whereas patrons of the straight bar at least understand its function in terms of pleasure and desire, mall-goers invest in the shopping mall's credentials as a "family" environment, an environment that "creates a nostalgic image of [the] town center as a clean, safe, and legible place." In dressing up and stepping out queer, the network uses the bodies of its members as billboards to create what Mary Ann Doane calls "the desire to desire." As queer shoppers stare back, kiss, and pose, they disrupt the antiseptic asexual surface of the malls, exposing them as sites of any number of explicitly sexualized exchanges—cruising, people watching, window-shopping, trying on outfits, purchasing of commodities, and having anonymous sex.[68]

By interrupting the normal and using parody to bring to the surface the hidden values and desires of American citizens, Queer Nation attempted to create more space for alternative understandings by displaying the extent to which homosexual desire is everywhere, including perhaps in the bodies of (heterosexual) shoppers, even though most heterosexual people do not recognize the presence of homosexuality and may deny their own desires.

Yet it is impossible to determine how people will actually interpret such actions. For some, they may be parodic actions that provoke laughter and self-reflection, but for others, they will be felt not as challenges to an unnatural binary but as a threat that provokes negative reactions or even violence. Even if they do not provoke an overt reaction, they may simply reinforce existing stereotypes. As Rahman asks, "Don't those who regard gays and lesbians as deviant expect us to be revolting, in both senses of the word?"[69] Further, because there is no challenge to the structural forces that maintain insecurity in order to profit, the action provides no real mechanism by which to even begin to foster discussion about the role of sexuality or family in society. The simple reality is that many people go to spaces such as malls because they seek consumer goods and nostalgic images to counter the turmoil of everyday life; they seek commodities, we might say using the language of Richard Flacks, because they do not wish to "make history."[70] Since neither social structures nor those who might be recognized as having power and privilege are visible in the shopping mall, the enemy must be many of the "normal" people out shopping for the day. Transgression, then, may well increase insecurity, thus reinforcing the cycle that Castells described. In responding to queer theorists who believe that it is simply necessary to take the risk that transgression will not be interpreted as activists wish, Angelia Wilson writes:

> Transgression for its own sake may be personally enjoyable, but as a political tactic its message is too important to leave to interpretation by the "heterosexual other." If we wish to establish "the very terms through which identity is articulated" then surely we must be clear about the message. And in so doing, we must be sensitive to the collage of identities—racial, economic, religious—that individuals struggle to balance in understanding themselves.[71]

In ending as she does, Wilson challenges queer activists to recognize the complex history of the construction of sexual and, I would add, family norms. She asks that queer activists link their work to the broader agendas, something similar to what Urvashi Vaid sees as necessary to move gay and lesbian politics forward and counter the power of the right. As yet, it is not apparent that queer activists have been able to combine these visions or link their attempts at challenging norms to other communities.[72]

In fact, a number of theorists comment that queer activism has failed to build such alliances and in many ways has become little more than a new form of gay identity politics. Rahman, for example, suggests that since many queer actions re-create the opposition between heterosexuality and homosexuality, they may do little more than recreate an essentialist gay and/or lesbian identity.[73] In fact, Rahman challenges queer theorists to confront the reality that even the possibility of being subversive is not the same for people who are situated differently. "Adopting or 'performing' a strategic, marginal position must be recognized as a luxury for most if Queer politics is not to be seen as simply the latest radical chic for those in the know in both academia and broader intellectual circles."[74] The likelihood of recognizing these limitations is lessened by the lack of antiracist analysis within queer politics.[75] In this context, Vaid's observation that Queer Nation is in significant ways nationalistic and dependent on the presence of an external enemy is important. Nationalism is unlikely to be the base on which alliances are built.

Nevertheless, as I noted in the beginning of this section, it is important to recognize that the problems with liberal individualist gay politics that gave rise to queer politics are still significant and that the force of "normality" looms large in the lives of many within our society, particularly at a moment when the right is attempting to use fear to buttress old norms, albeit ones that are shifting, even for heterosexuals. Angelia Wilson concludes her essay on where queer theory "is getting us" with the following observation: "Translating the potentiality of queer theory, of multisubjectivities, cannot be left up to the interpretation of the 'other.' Instead, if that potentiality is to be realised, the articulation process must be more intentional, more connected to the varied structures of oppression, and more committed to the communication of specific issues resulting from those oppressions."[76] For reasons that I will explicate further, I believe that how people receive support for private life and dependence needs must be one of the issues around which queer politics organizes. One needs to ask not only about the norms that queers can transgress but also about the ethical and social norms that queers—and all those whose familial practices create something other than the sexual family—create in our lives that might provide a positive model for others if institutional structures were changed so that these alternatives received the same kind of support as the sexual family. Working with others to achieve this change requires a perspective that is about "making history" by building a left alternative that takes seriously both cultural and material realities.[77]

IV. Building Alliances: Necessity and Possibility

Shane Phelan, discussing lesbian identities, makes a point that is critical for queer activists to remember:

> As lesbians, we (both white lesbians and lesbians of color) are often denied by our families or our communities, cut off from major social institutions, but the fact of our birth and life within those communities and cultures is not so easily erased within us. We may be defined as other, but in fact we are always here, always present before those who would deny us.[78]

This is important in two ways, each of which is suggestive of building a queer politics that takes seriously the issue of family: it reminds us of the complexity of our subjectivity, and it reminds us that gay/lesbian/bisexual/transgendered/queer people are not born to a queer community or, for the most part, to queer parents. One of the fundamental flaws in the social understanding of gay people is believing that a community that largely does not socialize its young people can best build an accepting world by pursuing individualist goals that allow people to live comfortable private lives. The "family" is a particularly important concept for gay/lesbian/queer activists to take on because the construction of children and young people as properly under the purview of parents is particularly deleterious for young queers. As Linnea Due's discussion of gay/lesbian/bisexual youth makes clear, the visible presence of queer adults has, in some ways, made life more, rather than less, difficult for queer youth.[79] In part, policies within schools contribute to these difficulties. The *Florida Times-Union* reports that "nearly 40 percent of teenagers polled last year by *Who's Who among American High School Students* said that they are biased against homosexuals."[80] Despite this, young people in northern Florida find it extremely hard to get schools to allow them to start gay-straight alliances. These groups are also fought by the Christian right, which helps parents to present arguments to school officials that make any progay/proyouth messages difficult.[81] As education theorist and activist Michael Apple asserts:

> The increasing dominance of conservative positions on the entire range of issues involving education, the economy, sexuality,

> welfare, "intelligence," and so on—in the media and in public discussion—means that people in cities such as Citrus Valley[82] and elsewhere live in a world where rightist discourses constantly circulate. It is now increasingly hard *not* to hear such interpretations and even harder to hear positions opposed to them.[83]

One implication of this, Apple suggests, is that a state such as Texas, with its disproportionately large impact on textbooks and therefore the curricula of other states, can pass laws that mandate that "textbooks stress patriotism, authority, and the discouragement of deviance."[84] Children, including many who will at one time question or explore alternative sexualities or gender identities, directly confront values, embedded in subtle and obvious ways in educational materials, that suggest to them that they are deviant, even while they learn many other, even conflicting cultural messages.

Those with queer family members or friends may have the opportunity to question what they learn in school; many, however, do not have this luxury. Instead, some of these young people will learn that there are few options for appropriate gender or sexual identities, and they will have clear (and to a large extent acceptable) targets for their own anger and frustrated dreams—those who fail to conform to sex and gender norms. Given the extent to which parents fear that they will have little to contribute to their children in a world of constant change, the one thing that they have to hold onto—control of education and moral values—is also the primary target of the right. In other words, not just queers but anyone who wishes to see a challenge to the power of corporate America needs to take seriously the ways in which family values, education reform, and welfare reform respond not to the real problems and issues that people face but to the need to organize various groups around identities. As Rosalind Petchesky has argued, such identities are ultimately quite effective for allowing the state to use its resources to create a new kind of privatism, "corporate privatism," rather than to help citizens exercise greater freedom.[85] The recognition by queer theorists and activists of the need to challenge dominant constructions of sexuality and family is crucial in this regard.

This leaves us with the question of how queer approaches might be rethought in ways that retain the power of queer theory to recognize that challenging "normalcy" needs to be a target of politics, even while a transformative politics is proposed.[86] Feminist theorists such as Drucilla Cornell, Zillah Eisenstein, and Wendy Brown set out visions of politics that are helpful.[87] Writing about the social requirements necessary for women to control their bodies, Eisenstein and Cornell each recognize that simply extending the rights that white men have had historically does not provide adequate protection. Cornell suggests that "equivalent rights" need to replace equal rights. To make judgments about what equivalent rights might be, a discussion of needs is necessary. Writing about her understanding of the process of politics, Wendy Brown notes, "Such judgments require learning how to have public conversations with each other, arguing from a vision of the common ('what I want for us') rather than from identity ('who I am'), and from explicitly postulated norms and common values rather than false essentialism and unreconstructed private interest."[88] Similarly, Shane Phelan recommends that we "get specific," by which she means that we engage in conversation about specific issues in ways that draw on and recognize the ways the communities from which we speak have been constructed.[89] To talk about sexuality and family issues, we need an understanding of the role that marriage and the sexual family have played for many in the United States, including how the institution has aided and harmed many. In relation to marriage, family, and sexuality, the process suggested by these theorists would not, I believe, lead either to gay men and lesbians' seeking the right to marry or to the desire to challenge the power of marriage simply by transgressing its norms. Rather, it would ask that queer people engage with others in reflecting on what marriage offers to people and whether there are alternative mechanisms (equivalent rights) by which the state could help individuals and those with whom they wish to build their private lives. I want to very briefly return to the question of how Vermont is approaching the issue of gay marriage in order to suggest how "getting specific" would be a helpful strategy for building new visions of private life.

The desire to find alternatives to traditional marriage seems to inform the perspectives of many of the lesbians and gay men interviewed by Suzanne Sherman for her book *Lesbian and Gay Marriage: Private Commitments, Public Ceremonies.*[90] As Michael Warner notes, it is not at all clear that marriage would be what many queer people would choose if the choice in the kinds of polls that marriage proponents cite were not so limited.[91] The desire to be able to form a plethora of relationships informs the evaluation of domestic partnership by one of Sherman's interviewees, Kathie Cinnater: "What I like about domestic-partnership legislation is that it includes people who live in households and do not necessarily have a traditional, sexual relationship. I like to think that there are a great variety of ways to live with people and relationships you can call families or partnerships."[92] Domestic partnerships provide an interesting example of how rights may be redefined and extended in ways that open up new possibilities, which in turn can help to build alliances and perhaps result in the development of new, more extensive demands. The fight for domestic partner benefits in the United States, Desma Holcomb notes, arose to extend health insurance benefits to partners. Because of the lack of state-provided health benefits, especially as employers have sought increasingly to limit them, unions have been particularly concerned with extending health benefits. The movements for domestic partner benefits arose in major metropolitan areas in which several necessary preconditions existed: "[F]irst, the lesbian and gay rights movement had achieved basic non-discrimination municipal laws or ordinances; second, city workers were already organized in unions; and third, these unions were already bargaining creatively on 'work and family' issues such as new parent, family, and medical leave, child care, and elder care."[93] In other words, gay activism had created some space for maneuvering, but equally importantly, family needs of gays and lesbians could be connected to wider union agendas that sought to deal with the conflict between worker needs and a society that relegates care and dependence needs to the private sphere. In fact, Holcomb's argument is that domestic partnership demands have been most successful when such coalitions have been possible.

The policies that have been passed as a result of union activism gained support from union members because those who wrote the policies recognized that gays and lesbians are not the only ones harmed by public policy that assumes people will marry. For example, as Holcomb describes:

> AFSCME DC 37's Disability Rights Committee and Retirees Committee joined forces with the Lesbian and Gay Issues Committee in this campaign for partner benefits. The coalition was based on a related set of circumstances: Workers receiving government medical disability income and widows and widowers receiving surviving spouse government Social Security income risked losing these benefits (and their financial independence within the relationship) if they married their domestic partners. As unmarried partners, however, they could not share health insurance benefits, unless domestic partner health benefits were available.[94]

The inclusion of straight couples in the domestic partnership negotiations prevented the then recently elected New York Governor George Pataki from rescinding the promise of his Democratic predecessor, Mario Cuomo. "The fact that partner benefits had been implemented for straight couples had saved partner benefits from a vigorous Republican and homophobic attack."[95] These, then, are policies that allow many to have greater power to define their relationships, while also allowing them to meet essential material needs and garner political support.

I would not, however, want to go as far as Kathie Cinnatar and see these policies as providing the degree of freedom she suggests. In general, domestic partnership policies only cover two cohabiting, nonrelated partners who share support for another. In other words, they try to recreate the sexual family to as large an extent as possible. Even in doing this, they do not adequately confront issues connected to having and raising children. Thus, they do not mandate that domestic partners can adopt or that they have access to artificial insemination, issues that a gay/lesbian politics of family should consider. And, obviously, they expand support only for those who are employed in jobs that provide benefits, something that is decreasingly likely for many Americans. What is important about this example is that domestic partnerships provided a mechanism by which different groups could engage in the process of discussing an issue, defining equivalent needs, and making these needs political. The challenge now is to continue to broaden the coalition and broaden the definition of needs and the definition of relationships that would qualify for benefits.

If one sees the politics of family in this way, it is easier to understand how a proposal such as Peg Flory's "reciprocal partnership" law might be seen, not as a devaluation of gay and lesbian relationships, but as a further expansion of relationship justice.[96] That is, if one understands the process of politics as being not just about gaining recognition within systems that already exist but about changing definitions of rights and needs in ways that allow people greater freedom to define the households in which they wish to live, without having to take into consideration whether they can afford to live in these households, then the opposition between "comprehensive benefits for blood relatives" and valuing gay relationships becomes meaningless. Again, reciprocal partnerships are not the ideal that one might envision coming out of this process because they implicitly promote the superiority of marriage by allowing only individuals who cannot legally marry to enter into them[97] and they do not allow for more than two adults to enter into them.[98] Supporting changes such as that proposed by Flory (and ideally supporting legislation that is this broad to begin with so that it cannot become an antigay weapon), and the more progressive alternatives discussed by Young, Phelan, Lehr, and Warner, could be a central strategy of gay organizations wishing to expand political support for nonmarital relationships.[99] Instead, most choose to reinforce the supremacy of marriage by defining it as *the* acceptable legal change. In the process, they allow the right to continue to build coalitions with the power to define queer relationships as abnormal and in need of control or, as Flory is attempting, to seduce gays into fighting *against* expanded rights for others in a way that can seem to reinforce the idea that gay people really do want "special rights." As this focus on marriage fails, gay/lesbian/queer people remain not full citizens but bearers of a legacy of domination and inequality that promises only to enhance the appearance of freedom for some while reinforcing second-class status for too many queers and those who must be allies.

NOTES

1. "Vermonters Divided on Civil Unions," Associated Press, May 4, 2001 (cited October 17, 2001). Available from web.lexis-lexis.com /univers...5=a8915743ce305c8f1f99016a48b81596.

2. "Vermont House Tries Shift in Gay-Union Law," *Newsday*, May 24, 2001, A44.

3. Ibid.

4. Human Rights Campaign, "A Basic Human Right: Talking about Gay Marriage: A Guide for Organizers, Candidates and Public Speakers" (cited October 19, 2001). Available from www.hrc.org/issues/marriage/background/guide/key.asp.

5. Andrew Sullivan, *Virtually Normal: An Argument About Homosexuality* (New York: Vintage, 1996), 185.

6. Nancy F. Cott, *Public Vows: A History of Marriage and the Nation* (Cambridge, Mass.: Harvard University Press, 2000), 16.

7. Michael Omi and Howard Winant, *Racial Formation in the United States: From the 1960s to the 1980s* (New York: Routledge and Kegan Paul, 1986).

8. Cott, *Public Vows*, 26.

9. Peggy Cooper Davis, "Neglected Stories and the Lawfulness of Roe V. Wade," *Harvard Civil Rights–Civil Liberties Law Review* 28 (1993): 309.

10. William N. Eskridge, Jr., *The Case for Same-Sex Marriage* (New York: Free Press, 1996), 72.

11. Sullivan, *Virtually Normal*, 13.

12. Julian Carter, "Normality, Whiteness, and Authorship: Evolutionary Sexology and the Primitive Pervert," in *Sciences and Homosexualities*, ed. Vernon A. Rosario (New York: Routledge, 1997), 155.

13. Cott, *Public Vows*.

14. Peggy Cooper Davis, *Neglected Stories: The Constitution and Family Values* (New York: Hill and Wang, 1997), 63.

15. Shane Phelan, *Sexual Strangers: Gays, Lesbians, and the Dilemmas of Citizenship* (Philadelphia: Temple University Press, 2001), 63.

16. Davis, *Neglected Stories*, 52.

17. Phelan, *Sexual Strangers*, 73.

18. Although Eskridge notes that domestic partnerships and marriage are not mutually exclusive, he clearly believes that marriage is a superior alternative and should therefore be the priority of the gay rights movement. See Eskridge, *The Case for Same-Sex Marriage*, 78–79.

19. Sullivan, *Virtually Normal*, 109.

20. Eskridge, *The Case for Same-Sex Marriage*, 83.

21. Philip Blumstein and Pepper Schwartz, *American Couples: Money, Work, Sex* (New York: William Morrow, 1983), 280.

22. Mark Blasius, *Gay and Lesbian Politics: Sexuality and the Emergence of a New Ethic* (Philadelphia: Temple University Press, 1994), chap. 3.

23. Sullivan, *Virtually Normal.*

24. Eskridge, *The Case for Same-Sex Marriage*, 117.

25. Judith Stacey, *In the Name of the Family: Rethinking Family Values in the Postmodern Age* (Boston: Beacon, 1996).

26. Paula L. Ettelbrick, "Since When Is Marriage a Path to Liberation?" *Outlook* 2 (Fall 1989): 14–16; Phelan, *Sexual Strangers*; Michael Warner, *The Trouble with Normal: Sex, Politics and the Ethics of Queer Life* (New York: Free Press, 1999); Ruthann Robson, "Mother: The Legal Domestification of Lesbian Existence," in *Adventures in Lesbian Philosophy*, ed. Claudia Card (Bloomington: Indiana University Press, 1994); Ruthann Robson, "Our Children: Kids of Queer Parents and Kids Who Are Queer: Looking at Sexual Minority Rights from a Different Perspective," *Albany Law Review* 64 (2001): 915–48.

27. Ettelbrick, "Since When?"

28. See, e.g., Wendy Brown, *States of Injury: Power and Freedom in Late Modernity* (Princeton, N.J.: Princeton University Press, 1995); Susan Okin, *Justice, Gender, and the Family* (New York: Basic Books, 1989); and Carol Pateman, *The Sexual Contract* (Stanford, Calif.: Stanford University Press, 1988).

29. Patricia Boling, *Privacy and The Politics of Intimate Life* (Ithaca, N.Y.: Cornell University Press, 1996).

30. Iris Young, "Reflections on Families in the Age of Murphy Brown: On Gender, Justice, and Sexuality," in *Revisioning the Political*, ed. Nancy J. Hirschmann and Christine De Stefano (Boulder, Colo.: Westview, 1996), 252.

31. Although I will not develop this point in this essay, I think it is important to note that even in these countries social rights exist within a framework that generally assumes interdependent sex/gender roles. As a result, although individuals are able to enjoy greater relationship rights, gay marriage has most frequently been defined in a way that makes parenting difficult, either by restricting adoption for gay male and lesbian spouses or by denying access to artificial insemination for lesbian couples. This is the case, I believe, because it is possible and common to provide significant social rights with the assumption that these benefits generally flow to families headed by male breadwinners. Thus extending the rights of gay men and lesbians requires challenging this assumption of social policy.

32. T. H. Marshall, *Citizenship and Social Class* (New York: Cambridge University Press, 1950).

33. Nancy and Linda Gordon Fraser, *Civil Citizenship against Social Citizenship? On the Ideology of Contract-Versus-Charity* (Thousand Oaks, Calif.: Sage, 1994), 90–91.

34. Ibid., 98.

35. Ibid., 97–98.

36. Martha Albertson Fineman, *The Neutered Mother, the Sexual Family, and Other Twentieth Century Travesties* (New York: Routledge, 1995), 161.

37. Eileen Boris and Peter Bardaglio,"The Transformation of Patriarchy," in *Families, Politics, and Public Policy,* ed. Irene Diamond (New York: Longman, 1983), 81.

38. Cott, *Public Vows,* 174.

39. This is a much discussed and analyzed issue within feminists writing on the welfare state. See, e.g., Gwendolyn Mink, *The Wages of Motherhood: Inequality in the Welfare State* (Ithaca, N.Y.: Cornell University Press, 1995), or Virginia Sapiro, "The Gender Basis of American Social Policy," in *Women, the State, and Welfare,* ed. Linda Gordon (Madison: University of Wisconsin Press, 1990).

40. Joan Tronto, *Moral Boundaries* (New York: Routledge, 1993), 174.

41. Omi and Winant, *Racial Formation.*

42. See Jill Quadagno, *The Color of Welfare: How Racism Undermined the War on Poverty* (New York: Oxford University Press, 1994), and Mink, *The Wages of Motherhood.*

43. See William J. Wilson, *The Declining Significance of Race: Blacks and Changing American Institutions* (Chicago: University of Chicago Press, 1980).

44. Judith Stacey, *In the Name of the Family,* 73.

45. Andrew Sullivan, quoted in Barbara Smith, "Blacks and Gays: Healing the Great Divide," in *Dangerous Liaisons: Blacks, Gays, and the Struggle for Equality,* ed. Eric Brandt (New York: New Press, 1999), 17–18.

46. Ursula Vogel, "Marriage and the Boundaries of Citizenship," in *The Condition of Citizenship,* ed. Bart van Steenbergen (Thousand Oaks, Calif.: Sage, 1994), 85.

47. Okin, *Justice, Gender, and the Family.*

48. Jyl Josephson and Cynthia Burack, "The Political ideology of the Neo-Traditional Family," *Journal of Political Ideologies* 32 (1998): 213–31, esp. 223.

49. Karin Lutzen, "Gay and Lesbian Politics: Assimilation or Subversion: A Danish Perspective," *Journal of Homosexuality* 35, no. 3/4 (1998): 239.

50. Ibid., 241.

51. Ibid., 235.
52. Ibid., 238.
53. David Morton Rayside, *On the Fringe: Gays and Lesbians in Politics* (Ithaca, N.Y.: Cornell University Press, 1998), 150.
54. Ibid., 155.
55. M. V. Lee Bladgett, "Income Inflation: The Myth of Affluence among Gay, Lesbian, and Bisexual Americans," Policy Institute of the National Gay and Lesbian Task Force and the Institute for Gay and Lesbian Strategic Studies, 1998 (cited October 1, 2001). Available from www.ngltf.org/library/index.cfm#2.
56. Nancy Fraser and Linda Gordon, "Genealogy of Dependency: Tracing a Keyword of the US Welfare State," *Signs* 19 (1994): 327.
57. Alisa Solomon, "Nothing Special: The Specious Attack on Civil Rights," in Brandt, *Dangerous Liaisons,* 65.
58. Margaret Cerullo and Marla Erlien, "Beyond the 'Normal' Family: A Cultural Critique of Women's Poverty," in *For Crying out Loud: Women and Poverty in the United States,* ed. Rochelle Lefkowitz and Ann Withorn (New York: Pilgrim, 1986), 251.
59. Steven Seidman, "Introduction," in *Queer Theory/Sociology,* ed. Steven Seidman (Cambridge, Mass: Blackwell, 1996), 10.
60. Momin Rahman, *Sexuality and Democracy: Identities and Strategies in Gay and Lesbian Politics* (Edinburgh: Edinburgh University Press, 2000), 46.
61. Manuel Castells, *The Power of Identity* (Malden, Mass.: Blackwell, 1997), 27.
62. Lisa Cagan, "Community Organizing and the Religious Right: Lessons from Oregon's Measure Nine Campaign: Interview with Suzanne Pharr," *Radical America* 24 (1990): 72; Barbara Smith, "Blacks and Gays."
63. Seidman, "Introduction," 13.
64. See Warner, *The Trouble with Normal.*
65. Seidman, "Introduction," 10.
66. Arlene Stein and Ken Plummer, "'I Can't Even Think Straight': 'Queer' Theory and the Missing Sexual Revolution in Sociology," in Seidman, *Queer Theory/Sociology,* 134.
67. Elizabeth E. Wilson, "Is Transgression Transgressive?" in *Activating Theory: Lesbian, Gay, Bisexual Politics,* ed. Joseph Bristow and Angelia R. Wilson (London: Lawrence and Wishart, 1993), 109.
68. Lauren Berlant and Elizabeth Freeman, "Queer Nationality," in *Fear of a Queer Planet: Queer Politics and Social Theory,* ed. Michael Warner (Minneapolis: University of Minnesota Press, 1993), 210–11.
69. Rahman, *Sexuality and Democracy,* 128.

70. Richard Flacks, *Making History: The American Left and the American Mind* (New York: Columbia University Press, 1988).

71. Angelia R. Wilson, "Somewhere over the Rainbow: Queer Translating," in *Playing with Fire: Queer Politics, Queer Theories,* ed. Shane Phelan (New York: Routledge, 1997), 105.

72. Urvashi Vaid, *Virtual Equality: The Mainstreaming of Gay and Lesbian Liberation* (New York: Anchor, 1995), 186–87. Cathy Cohen and Tamara Jones's discussion of homophobia/heterosexism among black leftists makes a similar point about race-based political organizing. See Cathy J. Cohen and Tamara Jones, "Fighting Homophobia versus Challenging Heterosexism: 'The Failure to Transform' Revisited," in Brandt, *Dangerous Liaisons.*

73. Rahman, *Sexuality and Democracy,* 126–27.

74. Ibid., 128.

75. See Smith, "Blacks and Gays," and Vaid, *Virtual Equality.*

76. Wilson, "Somewhere over the Rainbow," 110.

77. Flacks, *Making History.*

78. Shane Phelan, "Lesbians and Mestizas: Appropriation and Equivalence," in Phelan, *Playing with Fire,* 84.

79. Linnea A. Due, *Joining the Tribe: Growing up Gay and Lesbian in the '90s* (New York: Anchor, 1995).

80. Alliniece T. Andino, "Gay Students Say Schools Should Help Fight Prejudice Educators, Peers Seem Closed to Forming Clubs," *Florida Times-Union,* January 11, 2001, A1.

81. Family Research Council, "How to Protect Your Children from Pro-Homosexuality Propaganda in Schools," 1999 (cited March 1, 2000). Available from www.frc.org/infocus/i99jlhs.html.

82. Citrus Valley is the fictional name of a city that is central to the case study Apple examines.

83. Michael W. Apple, *Cultural Politics and Education* (New York: Teachers College Press, 1996), 65.

84. Ibid., 48.

85. Rosalind Petchesky, *Abortion and Women's Choice: The State, Sexuality, and Women's Freedom* (Boston: Northeastern University Press, 1990), 248.

86. See Wilson, "Is Transgression Transgressive?"

87. Drucilla Cornell, "Gender, Sex, and Equivalent Rights," in *Feminists Theorize the Political,* ed. Judith P. Butler and Joan Wallach Scott (New York: Routledge, 1992), 292–93; Zillah R. Eisenstein, *The Color of Gender: Reimaging Democracy* (Berkeley: University of California Press, 1994); and Wendy Brown, *States of Injury.*

88. Ibid., 51.

89. Shane Phelan, *Getting Specific: Postmodern Lesbian Politics* (Minneapolis: University of Minnesota, 1994).

90. Suzanne Sherman, *Lesbian and Gay Marriage: Private Commitments, Public Ceremonies* (Philadelphia: Temple University Press, 1992).

91. Warner, *The Trouble with Normal,* 143–45.

92. Sherman, *Lesbian and Gay Marriage,* 34.

93. Desma Holcomb, "Domestic Partner Health Benefits: The Corporate Model vs. the Union Model," in *Laboring for Rights: Unions and Sexual Diversity across Nations,* ed. Gerald Hunt (Philadelphia: Temple University Press, 1999), 107.

94. Ibid., 111–12.

95. Ibid., 115.

96. See Young, "Reflections on Families," and Warner, *The Trouble with Normal,* for discussions of how private relationships might be arranged to better accord with justice.

97. Warner makes this argument in relation to Hawaii's domestic partnership law. He argues that, as a result of this provision, the law is not progressive. Warner, *The Trouble with Normal,* 26.

98. In her discussion of the justice of allowing multiple adults to register their partnership, Iris Young notes: "[I]t might be reasonable to declare a limit to the number of persons who can register as domestic partners to one another." Young, "Reflections on Families," 265. Although this is certainly a pragmatic position, I disagree for two reasons: (1) there are currently no limits on the number of children that one might parent and have covered under various employer benefits, and (2) if one's goal is to enhance social rights and social justice, putting pressure on private employers may be an important step in putting pressure on government to create a more equitable system that provides benefits to people regardless of their relationship status.

99. Ibid.; Phelan, *Sexual Strangers,* chap. 3; Warner, *The Trouble with Normal,* chap. 3; Lehr, *Queer Family Values: Debunking the Myth of the Nuclear Family* (Philadelphia: Temple University Press, 1999).

PART IV

BIRTHRIGHT CITIZENSHIP

12

CHILDREN OF A LESSER STATE: SUSTAINING GLOBAL INEQUALITY THROUGH CITIZENSHIP LAWS

AYELET SHACHAR

I. Introduction

Imagine a world where there are only five continents. Each represents a separate political entity. Also assume that in this alternative world, there is zero human mobility across continent-states. There are also no class, ethnic, national, cultural, or social conflicts in this world, and there is nothing to be gained by tampering with the existing continent-state structures. In short, there is no motivation for change or migration in this fully stable world system. Each continent-state operates as an autonomous unit where people live, love, work, and eventually pass away. Assuming that there are no natural disasters, children and grandchildren are likely to pursue the same path as their progenitors. In such a world, it does not matter to which continent-unit a child belongs because he or she enjoys equal opportunities regardless of the specific entity into which he or she happened to be born.

When we relax these assumptions to fit them more closely to the reality of our own world, with its omnipresent social, economic, and national struggles—a world where political instability, human mobility, and inequality among individuals and nations continue to persist—things begin to look quite different. In our world, membership in a *particular* state (with its specific level of wealth, degree of stability, and record on human rights) has a significant impact on the well-being of children, as do government decisions that shape marriage and divorce law, welfare entitlement, public education, health care, environmental protection, investment in infrastructure, national security, and the like. But perhaps the most dramatic consequences for children's lifelong prospects follow from the basic determination that any political community must make: defining *which* children that polity views and protects as its "own."

According to the current governing norms of international law, countries are free to define the outer limit of the circle of their citizens.[1] The right to define who is "inside" and who is "outside" the political community is rooted in the concept of sovereignty: the exclusive power held by a legitimate government to exercise its authority over a bounded territory and the permanent population that resides on that bounded territory.[2] Indeed, distribution of what Michael Walzer calls "the most important good" can be seen as the key expression of the power of sovereignty: how we distribute membership in our human communities.[3] At present, different states have different rules governing the entry and stay of those defined as "aliens." However, most countries make determinations concerning who is automatically included as a citizen by creating a formal, legal connection between *entitlement to membership* and *circumstances of birth*, thus inviting some children into a world of immense opportunity and condemning others to a life with little hope.

Specifically, two legal principles govern the automatic attribution of citizenship to children: birth to certain parents (*jus sanguinis*) or birth in a certain territory (*jus soli*).[4] Both the *jus soli* and the *jus sanguinis* principles rely on (and sustain) a prior conception of closure and exclusivity; if everyone had access to the benefits of full membership in any polity of his or her choice, then there would be no need to formally distinguish insiders from outsiders, since both would be able to enjoy the benefits of citizenship.[5]

While a growing body of scholarship describes the different principles involved whenever immigrant populations apply for political membership, less attention has been paid to principles of *jus soli* and *jus sanguinis,* which attribute citizenship at birth. There have also been scholarly efforts to correlate different citizenship regimes with different understandings of national identities (the "civic-ethnic" divide), yet there is almost no literature dealing with the understanding of birthright identities. This has been ignored even though it is the principle that underpins the decision, for the vast majority of the world's population, as to who is entitled to rights, opportunities, and wealth. What is missing from the current literature is a critical evaluation of how existing birthright rules contribute to defining and solidifying political membership boundaries between peoples and to translating them into seemingly invisible (and thus uncontroversial) mechanisms for securing the propertylike entitlement of citizenship and its accompanying benefits to "natural-born" members—at the expense of excluding all non–right holders from claiming access to equivalent entitlements and benefits. National affiliations, guaranteed or denied on the basis of considerations such as ancestral pedigree or the brute and random luck of birthplace, should no longer be taken for granted, however.[6]

In this essay, I will risk opening a Pandora's box by scrutinizing the connection between birth and political membership in a given state. We reject heredity as a determining factor in almost any other admissions criteria (such as those concerning competitive job offers or selective university programs). However, family ties and birthright entitlements still dominate our imagination and our laws when it comes to articulating principles for allotting membership in a state. It is particularly important to reexamine current citizenship laws in light of the indications that in spite of economic predictions suggesting that the reduction of national barriers (e.g., to trade and commerce) would guarantee a larger slice of the pie to all (including members of the least well-off countries), the distribution of such global gains is still extraordinarily unequal.[7] If greater disparities in the "wealth of nations" are indeed the trend of the foreseeable future, then access to the rights, goods, opportunities, and resources offered to individuals on the basis of their national political membership may become more, not less, significant in our increasingly "global" world.[8]

My motivation in pursuing this discussion is not to call into question the rights and benefits that children (including those born to undocumented migrants) currently enjoy in many democratic countries. If anything, I would urge an expansion of these entitlements. But the desire to ensure equality among all children who reside *within* the same polity still does not relieve us of the moral responsibility to address the basic question of why *these* children deserve such entitlements, whereas others are deprived of them. In posing these questions, I am also not challenging the important role that families perform in creating a web of relationships and a context of meaning for their members. This context is often more important than any formal, legal connection between the child and the state. Instead, my purpose is to show how membership status (or lack thereof) can exert an impact on a child's life chances, particularly in terms of citizenship as an inherited entitlement.

The time is ripe for us to reconsider the justifications for allotting citizenship (the basic "right to have rights"[9]) according to birthright, because such attribution has served too long as a veil that separates questions about the distribution of power and wealth from the realm of *demos* definition. I hope to invoke such a discussion by recognizing the propertylike qualities of citizenship status, which secures the ability of its holders to enjoy a share in specific rights, protections, and wealth-creating assets held in common by those who count as members, while excluding all others (i.e., those deemed as "noncitizens" by the state's membership rules) from such control powers and use privileges.

My aim throughout this essay, then, is to destabilize and "denaturalize" the entrenched normative concept and legal practice of allotting full membership in democratic polities on the basis of birthright ascription, as manifested in existing citizenship laws. The discussion of these sensitive and topical issues proceeds in three main steps. First, I introduce the basic principles of birthright citizenship attribution: *jus soli* and *jus sanguinis.* I elucidate their basic governing rules, as well as the problems of overinclusiveness and underinclusiveness that each principle engenders, drawing on a set of examples taken from recent American, Canadian, German, and Israeli case law and legislation. This is followed by a brief exploration of the rules governing naturalization. Second, I explore the prevailing assumption that "civic" and "ethnic" nations follow fundamentally distinct rules and principles in allocating membership to their citizens. If this were the case, we could reasonably expect to find that civic nations allot membership in their polities on the basis of criteria substantively different from those of ethnic nations. However, in practice the supposed distinction between the principles of *jus soli* (generally associated with civic nationalism) and *jus sanguinis* (often described as a manifestation of ethnic nationalism) is not borne out. Like their ethnic counterparts, civic polities tend to reserve a privileged place for the criteria of blood and soil—not consent and choice—in attributing membership to the vast majority of their permanent members.

Third, I examine critically prevalent defenses of the *jus soli* and *jus sanguinis* principles, including arguments premised on democratic self-governance, administrative convenience, and respect for constitutive relationships and distinct cultural identities. While we might want to retain some of the insights drawn from these arguments, they fail to address the detrimental effects that current membership rules impose on the life chances of individuals (across national borderlines) "because of birthright"—involuntary circumstances that none of us control. Ultimately, extant theories of law and morality fail to provide justifiable grounds for upholding apportionment criteria of membership that currently limit the opportunities open to the vast majority of the world's population simply on the basis of considerations as arbitrary as ancestry or birthplace.

In light of my critique of prevalent *jus soli* and *jus sanguinis* citizenship rules, the concluding section of this essay offers a more radical, alternative understanding of the persistence of birthright citizenship principles. It reconceptualizes membership status in affluent political communities as a complex form of property right that perpetuates not only privilege but also access to a disproportionate accumulation of wealth and opportunity, while at the time insulating these important distributive decisions (through reliance on birthright) from considerations of justice and equality.

II. How Does a Child Become a Member of a Political Community?

As stated above, two dominant legal principles govern citizenship attribution rules in the world today: *jus soli* and *jus sanguinis.*

A. *Jus Soli*

This principle, which originates in the common-law tradition, implies a territorial understanding of birthright citizenship. It recognizes the right of each person born within the physical jurisdiction of a given state to acquire full and equal membership of that polity. The present-day *jus soli* principle finds its basis in the feudal system of medieval England, where "ligeance" or "true and faithful obedience" to the sovereign was owed by a subject from birth.[10] In the landmark *Calvin's* case, decided in 1608, Lord Coke employed the concept of ligeance to explain the mutual relationship that is created for life between the monarch and all subjects born in the monarch's dominion.[11] In its modern variant, *jus soli* no longer refers to a connection between a monarch and his or her subjects. Instead, it refers to the political relationship between governments and their citizens. Nevertheless, this principle continues to emphasize *place of birth* as the definitive criterion for allocating or withholding birthright membership. In its purest form, *jus soli* is blind to any considerations *but* birthplace. Accordingly, any child born under the jurisdiction of a given polity must automatically acquire citizenship—regardless of the circumstances of the parents' entry into the country, their legal (or illegal) residence, the child's length of stay in the state, effective ties to the polity, and so on. The only relevant factor is the question whether the child was born within the territory over which the state maintains (or in certain cases has maintained or wishes to extend) its sovereignty.[12]

Assuming that the rationale for attributing citizenship on the basis of territoriality is to serve as a proxy for those who actually live in a given country, *jus soli* may prove to be overinclusive. We repeatedly find in American literature that argues against the pure application of *jus soli* the example of a Mexican woman who crosses the border illegally just as she is about to give birth, in order to ensure that her child is born on American soil. In this way, she secures for her child the advantages of being a U.S. citizen.[13] The mother might later return to Mexico with her newborn child, but that does not change the fact that the child is already entitled to full membership in the U.S. polity.[14] Criteria such as residency, need, consent, or effective ties to the polity are not part of the American *jus soli* principle. Instead, the arbitrary fact of birthplace is elevated to an absolute norm: if the accident of birth occurs within the territory, then that child is one of us; if not, he or she is a total stranger, an outsider, a noncitizen. Under these conditions, "[w]ho could blame the Mexican mothers for what they do? . . . [T]hey seek to improve the life chances of their children," often at considerable cost and risk to themselves.[15]

From a global welfare perspective, one that weights equally the capacities and well-being of every person on the globe (whatever country they reside in), it could even be suggested that this "abuse" of the American *jus soli* principle by the Mexican mother is in fact no abuse at all.[16] Such actions improve the odds that at least some Mexican children might be able to enjoy greater access to resources and opportunities (in employment, education, and the like) that would otherwise be withheld from them simply because they were born on the "wrong" side of the border.[17]

At present, however, domestic citizenship laws are clearly not designed to correspond with a global welfare matrix. Rather, a main function of these laws is to create a wall that clearly marks off those who are members from those who are not. These distinctions are usually articulated as a means to protect and enhance the interests of insiders, irrespective of the effects of the state's citizenship attribution rules on those deemed "outsiders." Canadian immigration law, for example, explicitly states that determinations concerning who belongs are "designed and administered in such a manner as to promote the domestic and international interests of Canada"[18]—not in a manner to promote the well-being of the world's population. Canada is by no means alone in holding this perspective, which is the sine qua non of the existing global system of state-based citizenship laws.

Jus soli may lead not only to overinclusiveness, as demonstrated by the example of the Mexican mother and child, but also to underinclusiveness. For example, citizenship is withheld from "alien" children raised in the United States by American families if they happen to have been born outside the territory. The most glaring illustration of this problem occurs in the case of foreign-born adoptees who are brought into this country by their adoptive American parents only days or weeks after their birth. Because of the U.S. territorial-based rule of citizenship attribution, foreign-born adopted children are not automatically entitled to citizenship, even if they arrive in their earliest days of infancy and subsequently spend the rest of their lives in the United States. Even for children who gain lawful residency status ("green card" holders), the lack of full membership status has potentially detrimental effects, ranging from exclusion from certain educational loans or federal employment opportunities to the threat of expulsion from the country.[19]

Reliance on a pure *jus soli* rule therefore carries its own exclusionary and punitive elements. To overcome some of the more troubling effects of the territoriality principle, the U.S. Congress recently enacted the Child Citizenship Act.[20] The new act confers U.S. citizenship automatically and retroactively on certain foreign-born children adopted by citizens of the United States. In other words, the United States now attributes "birthright" citizenship to foreign-born adopted children *as if* they were born to American parents. This creates a legal fiction that erases the distinction between biological and adopted children by introducing a parentage component (of *jus sanguinis*) into the otherwise *jus soli*–dominated regime of citizenship attribution professed by the United States.

B. *Jus Sanguinis*

Complex demarcation patterns also inform the second principle of birthright attribution of citizenship, *jus sanguinis*. Unlike *jus soli*, however, *jus sanguinis* does not elevate the first fact of birthplace into a guiding constitutional principle. Instead, it confers political membership on the basis of parentage and family links: it automatically defines children of current members of the polity as the future citizens of that community. Whereas *jus soli* is traditionally followed in most common-law countries, *jus sangui-*

nis is the main principle associated with the citizenship laws of continental European countries.

The modern inception of *jus sanguinis* came with the post–French Revolution Civil Code of 1804, which broke away from the territoriality principle. The French Civil Code held that *as citizens,* parents (specifically, fathers) had the right to transfer their status of political membership to their offspring at birth, regardless of whether the child was born in France or abroad.[21] During the Napoleonic period, the concept of attributing membership on the basis of descent was considered fresh and radically egalitarian. As Patrick Weil explains, the *jus sanguinis* principle broke away from the feudal tradition of *jus soli,* which linked subjects to a particular land (and to the lord who held the land).[22] In contrast, *jus sanguinis* linked citizens to each other (and to their joined political enterprise) through membership in the state. Together, they constituted "a class of persons enjoying common rights, bounded by common obligations, formally equal before the law."[23] Through codification and imitation, the nineteenth century saw the adoption of the *jus sanguinis* principle by many other European countries, including Austria, Belgium, Spain, Prussia, Italy, Russia, the Netherlands, Norway, and Sweden.[24] European colonial expansion further spread the *jus sanguinis* principle to countries outside Europe.[25]

Today, however, *jus sanguinis* has exclusionary overtones often associated with ethnic and national favoritism. It has been argued that *jus sanguinis* serves as a camouflage for discrimination against certain sections of the population by denying them full access to the rights and benefits of citizenship due to a criterion they cannot choose or change—their ancestry.[26] Under such conditions, *jus sanguinis* constitutes an unjustifiable system of legalized ascriptive hierarchy. The underinclusiveness feature of *jus sanguinis,* namely the situation where not all persons residing within a territory are eligible to become members because they do not share the "right" heritage, has led several scholars to associate this membership attribution rule with an ethnocultural perception of citizenship.[27]

Perhaps the most famous example of perpetual intergenerational exclusion (through *jus sanguinis*) of long-term permanent residents from full membership in the polity can be seen in

German citizenship law (before its reform in 2000).[28] Historically, German citizenship law attributed membership exclusively on the basis of descent. Noncitizens (and their children) were thus precluded from becoming citizens. Naturalization was considered exceptional: it was granted only when the applicant was considered to be culturally integrated into German society, and even then only where there was a public interest in approving such naturalization.[29] Thus even long-term permanent residents born and bred on German soil had no legal right to become full members of the body politic because of their "bloodline" or lack thereof. Their noncitizenship was perpetuated over generations as the result of an unchangeable, inherited status: once the parents were excluded from membership, neither they nor their children could alter this designation through residency, consent, or voluntary action. This policy created a class of second- and third-generation children of immigrants who were deprived of German citizenship because of their ancestry.

When the long-awaited change in German citizenship law took effect in 2000, the approximately one hundred thousand children born annually in Germany of long-term permanent residents at last gained the right to acquire German citizenship based on their birth in the territory. These children automatically acquire provisional membership in the polity (whether or not their parents might be entitled to gain full access to German citizenship). By the age of twenty-three, these children must decide whether they wish to keep their German birthright citizenship, on condition that if they are dual citizens, they may retain their German citizenship only if they give up their second nationality.[30] As with the introduction of the Child Citizenship Act in the United States, which added a component of *jus sanguinis* to the American *jus soli* regime, the new German citizenship law represents a retreat from a pure model. In this case, the model of *jus sanguinis* is modified by a *jus soli* component.

The citizenship laws of Germany prior to its modification, exemplified some of the more problematic and blatantly exclusionary impacts of the principle of citizenship attribution through parentage. However, *jus sanguinis* need not necessarily correlate with an ethnocultural conception of political membership. For instance, if a newly established state has a diverse population, and each member of that population is recognized as a full citizen upon independence, then their children will count equally as members through *jus sanguinis* birthright attribution, regardless of their parents' specific ethnic, cultural, linguistic, racial, or religious backgrounds.[31] Even where the "original" political community is largely homogeneous, a *jus sanguinis* citizenship regime combined with a relatively open immigration and naturalization policy can lead to the creation of a heterogeneous society, which in turn may "reproduce" its multiethnicity through a parentage-based birthright regime.[32] Maintaining cultural diversity through *jus sanguinis* is therefore not necessarily a contradiction in terms, although it is not a common use of this membership attribution system either.

However, like *jus soli, jus sanguinis* can also lead to overinclusiveness. According to a system where citizenship is transmitted by descent, the offspring of an emigrant parent gains automatic citizenship at birth to his or her parent's country of origin, regardless of the family's effective ties to the society they left behind. Such a child would then count as a full member of the parents' country, even though the child may never have set foot in that country and may have no substantive knowledge of its language, culture, history, or political structure. Depending on each country's specific citizenship laws, such membership may be attributed for only a limited number of generations or in perpetuity.[33] *Jus sanguinis* can therefore lead to a situation where individuals enjoy the good of membership in a polity (and are thus entitled to all the rights and benefits accorded to this status) without sharing any of its obligations.

A recent illustration of this problem can be found in the case of *Sheinbein,* an American adolescent who was accused of a brutal 1998 murder in a Washington, D.C., suburb, who also held Israeli citizenship though *jus sanguinis* (his father was an Israeli citizen).[34] Sheinbein had lived his whole life in the United States and had no viable ties to Israel. However, after being named a suspect in the murder case, he fled to Israel.[35] The United States requested his extradition, but according to Israeli law (which here follows the Continental tradition), a citizen may not be extradited, not even to stand trial for crimes he is alleged to have committed in another country. This legal battle soon reached the

Israeli Supreme Court. Sheinbein's lawyers argued that the immunity from extradition provided by Israeli law was absolute because it was status based: it required no proof of real or effective ties to the state once a child gained citizenship by birthright.[36]

In a narrow three-to-two decision, the Court accepted Sheinbein's position. However, Chief Justice Aharon Barak (in a minority opinion) ruled that the rights and protections associated with citizenship "can be claimed only by a citizen for whom 'Israel is the center of his or her life and who participates in its life and joins his or her destiny to that of the country.'"[37] In other words, the Chief Justice infused an element of *genuine*, meaningful membership in the polity into the legal understanding of status-based entitlement to the right of citizenship. The *Sheinbein* saga thus represents the flip side of the inclusiveness principle of *jus sanguinis*. Here, a person who had the most tenuous connection with a society was attributed membership solely because of the accident of his descent; he then abused this connection to avoid standing trial in the home country to which he formally and substantively belonged.

C. Naturalization

The only legal method for acquiring citizenship other than through birthright is naturalization.[38] When we speak of naturalization, we refer to the final step in the process of acquiring citizenship *after* birth. Whereas birthright attribution of citizenship is, as we have seen, involuntary and ascriptive, naturalization is a voluntary process. It requires agency, action, and expressed consent by the individual, as well as acceptance by the political community into which he or she emigrates.

To become eligible for naturalization, a person must first be legally admitted as a long-term resident into another polity. In a world of regulated borders, this may prove harder than is commonly thought: each polity is obliged to allow entrance only to its own citizens. An "outsider" has no similar right.[39] Global inequality patterns also make their mark here: citizens of countries perceived to be poorer or less stable are often subjected to more stringent requirements when they seek admission to more affluent countries.[40] These inequalities are felt even when the outsiders are seeking temporary entrance rights only, let alone permanent residence status.[41]

A person seeking to establish lawful permanent residency in another country must apply for immigration status with the relevant state authority (e.g., the Immigration and Naturalization Service [INS] in the United States). Such an application generally requires the provision of detailed information to the host country about one's finances, education, family, and other personal matters. It also involves a medical examination by a state-approved doctor and often requires that applicants undergo an intrusive interview before obtaining an immigration visa. Even then, the final decision concerning acceptance or rejection of one's permanent residency status occurs at the point of entry, namely the border itself, where an immigration official still has the discretion to deny such status.

Each country imposes a further set of requirements on persons who wish to take up membership in its political community but who are not natural-born members. In the United States, for example, the most basic requirement for naturalization is that the applicant must have been admitted as a legal permanent resident—that is, the applicant must first pass thorough the initial "gate" of screening by the country's immigration officials.[42] However, gaining permanent residency status is not enough. The applicant must also have resided continuously in his or her polity of choice for several consecutive years (the United States currently follows a five-year rule, whereas Canada requires only three years of permanent residency before it will consider applications for adjustments of status).[43] If the foreign-born person seeking naturalization is a spouse of a citizen (i.e., the "outsider" is already involved in a legally recognized relationship with an "insider"), then the continuous residency requirement is usually reduced in length. This once more shows the significance of family ties in gaining access to membership in the body politic, this time in relation to a chosen partner, rather than a biological (or adopted) child.

Persons who seek to naturalize without resting their case on family ties must qualify independently for naturalization. As such, they must be at least eighteen years of age. They must also establish their legal residency and physical presence in the country and demonstrate a basic knowledge of their new home country's language, political system, and forms of government. In Canada, would-be citizens must also prove that they have no criminal convictions for indictable offenses. In the United States, the more vaguely defined requirement of "good moral character" must be demonstrated by the applicant. While these requirements are not always simple or straightforward, naturalization operates as an "as-of-right" system in both countries.[44] That is, once the applicant has met these requirements, state officials have little discretion to decline a request for naturalization.

But not all countries follow the as-of-right model. Most European countries follow much stricter policies concerning full access to the commonly held resource of citizenship. This more restrictive approach may translate into longer residency requirements before gaining eligibility for naturalization (such as eight or ten years versus three or five years; a higher degree of language competency; proof of economic self-sufficiency; and, in most cases, a "deeper" integration of the newcomer into the host society). More importantly, even when these requirements are met, the immigrant still has no guaranteed right to citizenship. Instead, the state maintains full discretion over whether to confer or decline access to membership whenever a non-native-born person seeks to acquire (through naturalization) what she failed to gain at birth: entitlement to share in the political community. The naturalization process usually culminates in a symbolic public ceremony where applicants pledge allegiance to their new home country and salute its flag.[45] In certain polities, they must also renounce their previous citizenship. Taken together, these acts are designed to mark the immigrant's "rebirth" into a new political community.

Naturalization, then, serves as a procedure for the acquisition of membership in the state for those who were not born into it. Unlike a natural-born citizen, however, the immigrant is carefully monitored before he or she actually acquires the valued prize of citizenship. In theory, naturalization might be viewed as an ideal route for allowing human mobility and choice, overcoming many of the problems ingrained in the concept of birthright citizenship. Yet we have just seen how selective this process is in practice and how value laden it inevitably becomes. Moreover, the statistics concerning the number of people who actually acquire membership in the state through the consensual process of naturalization rather than birthright are themselves enlightening. The latest figures published by the United Nations Population Division show that only a minuscule percentage of the world's population has managed to acquire citizenship through naturalization: less than 2 percent.[46] While the figures do not reveal the causes for this low rate of voluntary membership acquisition, they clearly establish that in the world today the vast majority of people still acquire citizenship as a function of passive birthright and not as a result of active adult consent.

III. Civic and Ethnic Nationalism: The Power of False Dichotomies

As we have seen, both *jus soli* and *jus sanguinis* base legal and political decisions with far-reaching implications on details of the same event—birth. The territorial principle asks where the child was born and, on the basis of this criterion, determines eligibility for citizenship status. The parentage principle investigates the child's family lineage as the basis for full membership. In light of the brief legal survey offered in the previous section, and assuming that we accept the proposition that citizenship is an important good that may dramatically affect a child's life prospects, we must still ask: What, if anything, justifies the intimate alliance between birthright and political membership?

One way to approach this question is to reevaluate the well-established distinction between "civic" and "ethnic" nationalism.[47] Civic nationalism, it is argued, refers to a political community of equals that is created by the free consent of the governed.[48] Accordingly, inclusion in the state must rest on individual choice to become a member of the polity. Those who are governed must have equal access to political participation and an equal right to determine how sovereign power is exercised.[49]

Ethnic nationalism, on the other hand, reflects an understanding of the political community as a natural order, where a citizen's attachment to a specific political community is inherited, not chosen. This attachment provides the ties that connect the past to the future, permitting the community to preserve its distinct cultural or national character. Citizenship, by this account, establishes a legal mechanism for a society to achieve regeneration—passing down a legacy from one generation to another, while asserting a link back into time immemorial and forward into an indefinite future.[50]

With this typology in mind, we might expect to find two very different legal procedures for establishing membership in these two different types of political communities. In a civic nation, we might expect choice and consent to play a key role in the acquisition of membership. In an ethnic nation, on the other hand, we might expect intergenerational continuity to play a more central role in the reproduction of the collective. Here, ascriptive membership attribution rules that express the idea of citizenship as an inherited status are predictable. These rules reflect a logically consistent manifestation of a "diachronic" dimension of nationhood that privileges the children of current members (at the expense of all others) by automatically entitling them to participate in their forebears' political enterprise.

However, the idea of allocating resources and opportunities, including citizenship itself, on the basis of a natural lottery is at odds with the central notion of civic nationalism, which stresses the value of choice by the governed. But counter to what liberal theory might lead us to predict, even countries that are viewed as archetypes of the civic model (such as the United States and Canada) fail to establish choice and consent as the guiding principles for their citizenship laws. Recall that the U.S. Constitution's Fourteenth Amendment proclaims that "[a]ll persons born or naturalized in the United States, and subject to the jurisdiction thereof, are citizens of the United States and of the State wherein they reside." Similarly, section 3 of the Canadian Citizenship Act ascends any person "born in Canada" to full membership status.[51] In contrast, both Canada and the United States do not open their borders to all persons who voluntarily consent to the authority of their democratic governments, nor do they admit as members all those who deeply identify with their political ideals of freedom and liberty. Instead, just like ethnic nations, they too acquire the vast bulk of their population through inherited membership entitlement rather than individual merit or adult consent.

While one might argue that these civic nations follow birthright citizenship rules on the pragmatic grounds of public choice considerations, such as the reduction of transaction costs (in terms of relocation and resettlement, democratic education, and so on), rather than on normative grounds, it would be difficult to defend the argument that a basic manifestation of sovereignty (determining "who belongs") is indeed determined in this fashion. Moreover, it is hard to sustain the public-choice line of argument when we take into consideration the global welfare matrix. For example, it is estimated that the removal of limitations on the free movement of persons across national borders would result in a net doubling of the annual GNP worldwide and that an optimal migration policy (according to neoclassical economic theory) would be not to have one at all.[52]

Still, it might be argued that birth is a relevant criterion (even in a world fraught with deep inequality) as long as it serves as a tool to predict who might *potentially* be entitled to full membership in the polity. But if that were the rationale for extant *jus soli* rules, we would expect to find supplementary measures (e.g., residency and consent requirements) being used to define who belongs to the political community—over and above the arbitrary event of birth in the territory. In practice, however, civic nations that follow the territorial principle (supposedly associated with consensual rather than inherited membership) do not require continued residence or any other measure of implied consent on the part of those who are automatically ascribed membership at birth. In fact, the reverse is true.[53] Even if a natural-born citizen has left the country voluntarily and no longer bears effective ties to the polity, this would not imply a corresponding loss of membership. This is surprising: it yet again illustrates how civic nations fail to express in their citizenship laws the idea that *jus soli* citizens must accept or reject (rather than merely inherit) their status as stakeholders and beneficiaries in the polity into which they have been born.

The absence of an "affirmation" requirement is all the more glaring when we compare natural-born citizens and naturalized immigrants. The latter acquire admission to full political membership in the state only after proving, through the volitional actions of migration and resettlement, that they have rightly earned the prize of citizenship. As described above, naturalization in most civic nations demands not only the screening of the applicant's background and qualifications by the relevant governmental agencies but also explicit and active participation (e.g., swearing allegiance) on the part of the immigrant.[54]

Furthermore, the fact that we find explicit consent requirements in the immigration laws of *jus soli* states, while there are none with regard to citizenship, further weakens the claim that the consent of the governed can be tacitly attributed. According to the "tacit consent" theory, choice is de facto reduced to a matter of passive consent: a manifestation of free will is (presumably) implied by nonaction—that is, by remaining subject to the jurisdiction of the government under which one is born. But if this is true for the natural-born citizen, why doesn't the same theory apply to others: for example, those who have already taken volitional action in entering the country, such as legal immigrants? Clearly, the latter have made a serious commitment to the new home country by submitting themselves to the authority of its laws while at the same time risking the loss of their former "inherited" membership. If anything, their implied consent seems to be stronger than that of natural-born citizens who have never faced the decision of whether to stay or to go. Yet it is the immigrant, not the citizen, who must undergo a ceremonial "rite of passage" in order to acquire full membership. On the other hand, neither volitional action nor a symbolic manifestation of choice of membership is required of the natural-born citizen.

A defender of birthright citizenship in civic nations might, however, assert that choice is indeed present in a *jus soli* system: a natural-born citizen may renounce his or her citizenship. (This process usually requires that the individual submit a formal expatriation request to an authorized government agency.)[55] But on this account, unlike the standard defense of consent theory, choice is not conceptualized as a *condition for admission*. Rather, it is construed more narrowly as protecting the legal *right to exit* the community (with the important caveat that a citizen cannot, at least in principle, renounce political membership for the sake of evading taxes or avoiding the reach of the law).

Defining consent as tacit (through "nonexit") might serve as a convincing argument in a world with minimal differences in life chances across political units (such as the hypothetical scenario described at the opening of this essay), but this is not the world in which we live. With disparities between countries so great that about half of the population of the world, according to the World Bank, lives "without freedom of action and choice that the better-off take for granted," it seems disingenuous to suggest that "nonexit" implies consent.[56] Even where members of less well-off countries manage to leave their home communities in search of a better future elsewhere, no other country has an obligation in international law to provide them right of entry (unless they are refugees seeking asylum from persecution) because, according to the extant world system of birthright citizenship laws, right of entry is reserved exclusively for insiders: those born on the territory or to parents who are themselves members.[57]

Thus—rhetoric to the contrary notwithstanding—in both *jus soli* and *jus sanguinis* countries, birthright, not choice, plays a determining factor in establishing personal entitlement to the specific political membership that the individual possesses from the cradle to the grave. Parentage and territorial principles share a common reliance on the arbitrary condition of birth as their main criterion for distinguishing insiders from outsiders. In other words, they are both ascriptive.[58] The "right to have rights" in civic nations therefore resembles the inherited pattern of entitlement (usually attributed to ethnic nationalism) more closely than current theory suggests.[59]

But *jus soli* and *jus sanguinis* part company on at least one critical issue: resolving the status of children born of noncitizens who have made the host country their permanent home (the "second generation" problem). Traditionally, *jus soli* countries have addressed this problem more adequately. In the United States and Canada, for example, children born to illegal immigrants within the nation's borders are automatically entitled to unconditional membership. Differently put, the parents' lack of membership status does not pass on to the next generation. Other civic nations, such as Australia and Britain, which also follow the *jus soli* tradition, have in recent years adopted a more qualified approach. They do not automatically attribute membership at birth to children of illegal immigrants. Instead, a child born within their borders to undocumented parents is granted citizenship status only after he or she resides in the country for at least the first ten years of his or her life.

This modification of the territorial birthright principle, which takes into account the status of the parents in attributing citizenship to a child, is part of a growing trend of convergence between the *jus soli* and *jus sanguinis* traditions.[60] Another indication of this convergence is reflected in the infusion of a territorial component into the *jus sanguinis* tradition, as we have seen in our discussion of the recent reform in German citizenship law, which now allows the inclusion of children born in the territory to nonmembers under a cumulative set of requirements that include long-term residency, cultural immersion, and the surrender of any other nationality at the age of majority (for dual citizens). In other words, these children must actively choose to become members and must explicitly consent to the citizenship status conferred upon them at birth. Related provisions concerning a combination of birth, residency, and consent requirements are also found in other *jus sanguinis* countries, such as Belgium, Denmark, Sweden, Finland, Italy, and the Netherlands.[61]

In the maze of citizenship laws, we clearly need to keep track of each country's distinct rules and procedures. But equally, we need to recognize that it is misguided to simply assume that consent and choice are automatically associated with the *jus soli* model. If anything, it appears that the choice to commit oneself to citizenship is more commonly developed in *jus sanguinis* countries, at least as far as the determination of membership status for children born on native soil to foreign parents is concerned. Although we may still find differences in the membership attribution laws of *jus soli* and *jus sanguinis* countries (and also among countries that share the "civic" or "ethnic" traditions), the basic claim that such distinctions can be explained by the dichotomy of "consent versus ascription" is largely refuted by the legal realities we find in practice.

IV. Why Birthright? Extant Defenses and Their Limitations

Can we salvage the *jus soli* and *jus sanguinis* principles of ascriptive membership by thinking of them as an intergenerational mechanism for providing selective access to a bounded system of common meaning and shared history—in *both* civic and ethnic nations? Several arguments may be furnished to provide justifications for the right of each country to define and police its membership boundaries according to birthright rules. These arguments generally fall into three major categories: democratic self-government; administrative convenience; and respect for constitutive relationships and distinct cultural identities. The following section concisely evaluates these arguments. It also points to possible amendments or innovations in current citizenship practices designed to better reflect the principles in question, although, as I will argue, even these innovations have their limitations.

A. Democratic Self-Governance

Democratic self-governance as a justification of birthright membership speaks to the idea that the laws of a polity ought to serve and reflect the interests of all those who habitually reside within its territory and are subject to its authority.[62] An important manifestation of democratic self-governance is the power vested in the people to define the membership boundaries of their communal political enterprise. Such definitions are usually codified in domestic legislation soon after the community has achieved independence and established its own state. International law traditionally refrains from any intervention in the sovereign prerogative of the state in defining citizenship laws. However, this is no longer necessarily the case, as new countries tend to find themselves under international pressure to include long-term residents within their membership boundaries.

The more contemporary understanding of the democratic self-government argument goes beyond a procedural emphasis on open elections and tends to include equal participation as a substantive element of democracy.[63] This creates a strong presumption in favor of including *all* long-term residents in the innermost circle of membership–citizenship. A "democratic legitimacy gap"—that is, a situation where a country prevents some of its permanent residents from participating fully in the political process—is not a problem seen only in seceded states, however. It may also present itself in well-established democracies—for instance, in their treatment of permanent "guest workers."[64] This democratic legitimacy gap stems partly from problems associated with the over- and underinclusiveness of both *jus soli* and *jus sanguinis* principles. As we have seen, hereditary citizenship may lead to a situation where persons with only minimal effective ties with the state are guaranteed all the rights and benefits of membership (overinclusiveness), whereas others who participate in its daily economic and social life are excluded from similar entitlement (underinclusiveness).

Yet if commitment to the democratic ideal of self-governance (conceived as equal participation) is to guide the attribution of political membership in the state, then we need to reconsider our current reliance on birthright entitlement. A principled answer to the question of "who belongs" would require a shift away from the present ascriptive principles of *jus soli* and *jus sanguinis* to a new "genuine connection" principle of citizenship acquisition, which we might label *jus connexio.* I introduce this term because, like *jus soli* and *jus sanguinis,* it conveys the core meaning of the method through which political membership is conveyed: here, *connexio* (Latin), meaning "connection, union, linkage."

This new principle considers membership on the basis of a tangible connection between the individual and the state (e.g., as established by proof of residency). *Jus connexio* allows greater democratic accountability and representation because it ensures that all long-term residents of a state are full members of its political community, irrespective of birthright. In theory, *jus connexio* might require some redrawing of membership boundaries from time to time.[65] The determination of who is and who is not a citizen would then be based on the social fact of membership, which requires a genuine, effective connection between the individual and the state that is stronger than the mere accident of birth.

The idea of using a "genuine link" test is not new.[66] It is recognized in international law as a means for distinguishing between "active" and "passive" citizenship (e.g., in cases where one person holds dual or multiple citizenship). Various domestic laws also use a genuine link test: for instance, in determining a noncitizen's duty to pay taxes. In the United States, for example, this is known as the "substantial presence test."[67] Thus if the *jus connexio* principle were to be introduced in lieu of *jus soli* or *jus sanguinis*, a nonmember could become a citizen on the basis of habitual residency, just as a natural-born citizen could lose his or her citizenship if he or she effectively left the country for an extended period of time and thus no longer complied with the "substantial presence test."

Like *jus soli* and *jus sanguinis*, however, *jus connexio* has several serious drawbacks. Most notably, it lacks an intergenerational component for transferring citizenship to the descendants of members of the current political community. This feature of *jus connexio* can be judged as a liability, just as it may be viewed as an asset. In comparison to existing birthright principles, however, a *jus connexio* residency-based attribution system would unequivocally lack the threads of continuity between past and future that are crucial to most current understandings of citizenship laws. Given the significance of the diachronic dimension of citizenship, it is unlikely that a *jus connexio* will be adopted any time soon by viable political communities that need to establish who belongs within their boundaries not just for today but for tomorrow as well.

Another difficulty presented by a residence-based membership rule is that it still leaves unresolved the representation-of-interests problem, which arises from the fact that those inside the polity can impose potential harms (intentionally or not) upon those outside their *demos*. For example, a wealthy country like the United States may regularly undertake actions with negative environmental externalities that impose severe pollution and health risks upon those residing outside its geographical boundaries.[68] Imagine a sick child who, through no fault of her own, is excluded (by birth) from having a voice in the affluent neighbor country's decision-making processes but who may nonetheless suffer the harsh consequences of environmental contamination caused by those on the other side of the border. The problem here is that the territorial boundaries that shape inclusion in and exclusion from the polity (and its democratic decision-making processes) fail to correlate with the spillover effects of that polity's actions upon the citizens of another state. Existing birthright citizenship rules do nothing to ease such tensions, but a more democratic *jus connexio* membership principle would also assist little in resolving them.

B. Administrative Convenience

Efficiency offers a second possible line of defense for ascriptive citizenship (in either its territorial or its parentage variant). This argument takes two different forms. First, it may be claimed that determining membership according to birthplace or family lineage offers a clear and relatively reliable international "filing system" in which people are automatically sorted into specific political units.[69] Since birth is usually a publicly recorded event, it provides an apparently noncontroversial method of assigning individuals to states. Moreover, this international filing system (if properly managed) can ensure that every child acquires membership within some polity at the moment of joining the larger family of humanity. In theory, an ideal global birthright-attribution system should leave no one in the vulnerable position of statelessness; in practice, however, the combined operation of *jus soli* and *jus sanguinis* has never guaranteed this outcome in a world fraught with political instability and human mobility.

In addition, given that freedom of movement is still regulated across national borderlines, each country is compelled to define its membership boundaries in ways that clearly define who belongs and who does not—who may enter and who may not. Citizenship attribution at birth and the manifestation of this status through documents such as passports and identity cards render these distinctions both "legible" and enforceable in the eyes of immigration officials, customs agents, police officers, and so on.[70] Administrative convenience may therefore explain the prevalence of birthright citizenship rules, but it does not bear the weight of justifying them.

The second variant of this defense moves beyond pure administrative convenience and provides a stronger normative claim in support of ascriptive membership rules. Instead of criticizing the arbitrariness of birthright, this position suggests that we should value the contingency of existing citizenship laws. By making the determination of political membership entirely independent of substantive considerations, we avoid the trap of moral judgment about who deserves to be a citizen. According to this view, it is better to exclude persons on the basis of territoriality and pedigree than on the basis of criteria such as political opinion, national loyalty, or suspected disagreement with the community's basic governing norms. Bernard Yack, for example, claims that "[b]irthright citizenship can promote toleration precisely by removing the question of communal membership from the realm of choice and contention about political principles."[71]

The idea that birthright "blindness" is a blessing seems plausible only if we think of the problem in terms of ensuring internal equality among persons already residing within the same territory. On this account, the need to avoid hard decisions concerning who belongs (and why) is so important that it justifies any presumably neutral rule for conferring the valuable status of citizenship in a blind way, such as according to the accident of birthplace. We need not know the gender, race, creed, or need of a child in order to determine eligibility for birthright membership if such membership is granted automatically. The only thing that matters is whether the child was born in the territory (under a *jus soli* rule) or whether one (or both) of his or her parents is already a member of the polity (under a *jus sanguinis* rule).

While this argument may seem compelling at first glance, *jus soli* and *jus sanguinis* can only artificially be conceptualized as removing the question of communal membership from the political realm. It would be more accurate to suggest that they represent a precommitment to following specific rules and criteria in determining who may become a citizen and who may not. And this precommitment is inevitably born out of specific political, contextual, and historical events that have led to the creation of particular communities that follow particular membership attribution rules. In modern states, such regulation usually falls under the jurisdiction of national governments, and the laws and policies that they issue are always the outcome of human imagination, coordination, and agency—certainly not a preordained "natural order" of things. It thus requires a great leap of faith to assume that exclusion according to predetermined criteria (such as territoriality or parentage) necessarily translates into political toleration through the adoption of (allegedly "blind") birthright membership rules.

Finally, the argument in support of the arbitrariness of birthright (as a means of avoiding substantive debates about belonging) loses much of its force when we think about the external impact of such membership rules. As Joseph Carens points out, existing citizenship attribution principles uphold a sharp distinction between the children of members and the children of nonmembers. But unless we presuppose that people have an entitlement to membership in the community of their parents (or in the territorial community into which they happened to be born), we have only pushed the question of political membership back another level.[72] We have not yet provided satisfactory justification for the assertion that only some children may enjoy entitlement to the full rights and protections of membership in a stable, affluent, democratic polity while other children do not deserve the same.

C. Communities of Character and Constitutive Relationships

A relational approach to citizenship emphasizes the constitutive relationships that shape human communities and the right of each polity to define and assert its own distinct cultural and historical character.[73] According to this defense of birthright entitlement, "Children are not born into the world as isolated individuals, but as members of established social networks."[74] These social networks serve as the bedrock for establishing moral claims concerning political membership. Instead of focusing primarily on the vertical relationships between the individual and the state, this approach looks at the horizontal networks and webs of relationships that are created between persons in various public and private settings, including families. The communitarian variant of the relational approach holds that members of a political community have the right to both construct and reflect a shared culture in their joint enterprise as members of a particular state. Decisions about admission and exclusion are therefore viewed as powerful expressions of a community's identity and autonomy, as well as a means of preserving those particular characteristics. Without control over such decisions, "there could not be *communities of character*, historically stable, ongoing associations of men and women with some special commitment to one another and some special sense of their communal life."[75] Respecting familial, social, and historical ties by attributing membership at birth appears to play an important role in preserving such communities of character. Yet these communities may also turn out to be highly exclusionary, withholding membership from long-term residents, among others, because these "outsiders" fail to share a distinguishing "character" that is possessed only by those who belong to the community. The character argument thus runs the risk of becoming hopelessly circular: a person is deemed not to possess the special character that makes one a citizen because he or she does not belong to the state; but then again, he or she cannot belong to the state because he or she lacks the special character of membership.

Equally troubling, a relational-communitarian approach may come to serve as a justification for overtly discriminating between potential immigrants and citizens on the basis of their ethnicity, religious beliefs, and so on because of the community's desire to maintain a distinct cultural heritage or national identity by carefully selecting its members. While this may be a fair argument for a minority community to raise against the state when that minority is struggling to preserve its identity in the face of severe assimilation pressures, it is far harder to justify the right of a state to exclude persons on the same basis. Taken to its ultimate logic, the communitarian variant of a relational approach suggests that the power of the polity to define its own human boundaries must trump considerations of fairness and equality. Michael Walzer explicitly makes this claim by suggesting that "[t]he distribution of membership is not pervasively subject to the constraints of justice" because "the shape of the community that acts in the world, exercises sovereignty, and so on" is at stake.[76] Other political philosophers and legal scholars, however, have strongly contested this view.[77]

A feminist variant of the relational approach, on the other hand, hopes to infuse specific values, including gender equality and respect for the labor of caregiving, into existing membership attribution rules.[78] According to this line of argument, membership rules ought to reflect the central place of families in constituting citizens and must do so in ways that ensure that women's rights are upheld and respected.[79] Here the emphasis is not necessarily on a shared history or distinct culture on the national level. Rather, attention is given to specific relationships with particular others, such as parents, spouses, lovers, or extended families, who mediate one's inclusion in a larger political community. Citizenship laws must protect and foster the important contribution of such intimate and family-based relationships. A *jus soli* membership rule reflects these contributions in a circumstantial way, but a *jus sanguinis* membership rule does so explicitly. A relational approach that takes family ties and intergenerational continuity seriously therefore provides strong support for inherited citizenship entitlements.

Accordingly, it is argued that if a child is born in a marriage between spouses from different countries, where each parent holds a different nationality, then the child deserves to belong to both membership communities on grounds of safeguarding family relationships and respecting the principle of gender equality.[80] The notion that fathers and mothers should be equally able to transmit membership entitlement to their offspring may seem self-evident today. But the troubling record of gender-based discrimination in citizenship laws worldwide should teach us differently.

Historically, under Roman law, a child acquired citizenship on the basis of his father's status, or according to family links transmitted exclusively through the *pater familias*. In keeping with this tradition, a mother had no right or legal power to pass her citizenship on to her children. Similarly, with the development of the common-law doctrine of coverture, the father became the sole bequeather of citizenship to his children (born of a valid marriage).[81] A married mother had no similar authority or standing. In fact, she risked losing her own (birthright) citizenship upon marriage to a noncitizen husband.[82] Discrimination against women in citizenship attribution rules was first targeted by international law in the early half of the twentieth century. This was not so much because of concern for gender equality as because of concern that such rules might result in statelessness for a child born out of wedlock or to an unknown father.[83]

In most countries, gender-discriminatory citizenship laws have been repealed in many countries since the end of World War II.[84] However, several countries still continue to uphold legal regulations that distinguish between the capacity of male and female parents to transmit citizenship status to their offspring born abroad.[85] An illustration of how patterns of discrimination on the basis of gender and marital status permeated into modern citizenship laws, even in countries that consider themselves enlightened on the matter of gender equality rights, is found in three constitutional battles fought recently over these issues in Canada and the United States: *Benner*, *Miller*, and *Nguyen*.

i. Benner

In the 1997 *Benner* case, the Canadian Supreme Court was asked to determine whether Section 5 of the Canadian Citizenship Act, which restricted access to Canadian citizenship based on the gender of the parent, violated the equality principle enshrined in the Canadian Charter of Rights and Freedoms.[86] According to the act, a child born abroad to a Canadian father was automatically entitled to Canadian citizenship upon registration of his or her birth. However, a child born under similar circumstances to a Canadian mother was denied similar entitlement to membership. Instead, that child's eligibility depended on the absence of a criminal record and his or her willingness to swear an oath of allegiance (neither of these requirements was imposed on a child born abroad to a Canadian father).[87] The Canadian Supreme Court ruled that this statutory provision violated the equality principle because it restricted access to citizenship "on the basis of something so intimately connected to and so completely beyond the control of the [child] as the gender of his or her Canadian parent."[88] This legislation, in the words of the Court, "continues to suggest that, at least in some cases, men and women are not equally capable of passing on whatever it takes to be a good Canadian citizen."[89] Such gender discrimination was ruled unjustifiable in a free and democratic society, and the relevant provision of the Citizenship Act was struck down.

ii. Miller

By contrast, in the 1998 *Miller* case, the U.S. Supreme Court upheld Section 309 of the Immigration and Nationality Act (INA), which distinguished between American men and women in their ability to transmit U.S. citizenship to their offspring born abroad.[90] Unlike the Canadian act, the American act imposed strict requirements for conferring citizenship upon a child born abroad to an unmarried American father, while attributing automatic birthright membership to a child born abroad to an unmarried American mother.[91] According to the act, the citizenship of a child born to an American father could not be established unless and until either the father or the child had taken affirmative steps to confirm their relationship. The act held that unlike the connection between a mother and her child, which was immediately recognized at birth, thereby in turn establishing the child's connection to the political community, the relationship between father and child had to be legally established (e.g., through a court order declaring paternity)[92] if the status of American citizenship was to be conferred upon the child.[93] *Miller*, in short, suggests that mothers are naturally bonded to their children whereas fathers are not. The state is therefore not obliged to recognize children born abroad to unwed American fathers as its citizens. The Supreme Court affirmed this position, leaving unchanged the act's gender discriminatory two-tiered citizenship attribution system.[94]

iii. Nguyen

In 2001, only three years after delivering its controversial *Miller* decision, the U.S. Supreme Court again reviewed Section 309 in the *Nguyen* case, this time focusing on the section's constitutionality.[95] Nguyen was born out of wedlock in Vietnam to a Vietnamese mother and an American father. Unlike the child in *Miller*, who had lived outside the United States prior to seeking American citizenship, Nguyen had been in the care of his American father ever since the relationship between his parents had ended. At the age of six, when his father returned to the United States, Nguyen became a lawful permanent resident of the United States and was raised in Texas by his father. For all practical purposes, he was a full member of the polity. However, at the age of twenty-two, Nguyen pleaded guilty to criminal offenses committed in the United States and, as a noncitizen, was ordered to be deported by the INS. Nguyen's father challenged the order, claiming that his son's blood relationship to him and lifelong association with the American polity should render Nguyen eligible for full membership and thus protect him from deportation.[96]

However, the U.S. Supreme Court rejected the father's argument. It ruled that although a meaningful and lasting parent-child relationship had been established between the American father and his foreign-born son, the failure to follow one of the three affirmative legal steps defined by law for the transmitting of citizenship (legitimization, declaration of paternity under oath, or court order of paternity), meant that Nguyen had no entitlement to full membership status in the American polity. In other words, the state need not treat him as *its* own child.[97]

The Court also held in *Nguyen* that the decision to impose different requirements on unmarried fathers and unmarried mothers was justified by two important governmental interests: first, ensuring that a biological parent-child relationship existed; and second, ensuring that the child and the parent had demonstrated a relationship consisting of "real, everyday ties" that provided a meaningful connection between child and citizen-parent and, in turn, the state. Ignoring the fact that precisely such a connection had been established between the child-parent-state in this particular case, the Court preferred to twist the language of relationship by collapsing it into biological essentialism. According to the Court, the opportunity for developing a meaningful parent-child relationship inheres in the event of birth in the case of a citizen mother and her child but does not result "as a matter of biological inevitability, in the case of an unwed father."[98] The Court further declared that in the context of citizenship attribution rules, American men are legally relieved of personal responsibility for the results of their sexual actions. As the Court put it, "One concern in this context has always been with young people, men for the most part, who are on duty with the Armed Forces in foreign countries."[99] When turning to current conditions, the Court continued, it found "even more substantial grounds to justify the statutory distinction [between men and women]. The ease of travel and the willingness of Americans to visit foreign countries have resulted in numbers of trips abroad that must be a real concern when contemplating the prospect [of mandating] . . . citizenship by male parentage."[100]

Thus, the Court concluded, the legislature was well within its authority to refuse to embrace a child conceived abroad of an American father and a noncitizen mother as a U.S. citizen.[101] A child born abroad of an unwed American mother, on the other hand, automatically acquires such membership (without any requirement of proof of the establishment of a parent-child relationship) because, again to cite the Court's own words, "There is nothing irrational or improper in recognizing that at the moment of birth—a critical event in the statutory scheme and tradition of citizenship law—the mother's knowledge of the child and the fact of parenthood have been established."[102]

Instead of looking at the establishment of a viable relationship between Nguyen and his father, the Court preferred to stick to a gender-based stereotype of female caregiving and bonding as the paradigmatic case of "real, everyday ties" between a parent and a child that merit state recognition. The Court in *Nguyen* upheld, as the minority put it, "a historic regime that left women with responsibility, and freed men from responsibility, for nonmarital children. . . . [R]ather than confronting the stereotypical notion that mothers must care for these children and fathers may ignore them, [the majority] quietly condones the very stereotype the law condemns."[103] Nguyen and his father lost their case, and we received a fresh reminder of the dangers and biases that may be inherent in a relational-based theory of membership attribution.

While it is theoretically possible to develop a relational conception of citizenship that respects the crucially important role that families and other social networks play in children's lives without repeating the mistakes of the past, the risks are nevertheless daunting. For one, the relational approach is likely to embroil citizens, their dependents, and the state in a problematic situation where intimate relationships are regularly scrutinized by state officials because these relationships gain an important public dimension—potentially entitling foreign-born members of the family to citizenship. Such concerns are not hypothetical, as the *Benner*, *Miller*, and *Nguyen* cases demonstrate.[104] Moreover, related concerns are regularly encountered in immigration law practice, where some of the most sensitive and topical legal cases pivot around the definitions of *marriage, child, immediate relative,* or *family* for the purposes of acquiring permanent residency and naturalization status.[105]

Even if a generous definition of who counts as "spouse," "child," or "family member" is adopted, this still fails to resolve the basic difficulty: how to determine *which* human relationships deserve to be recognized as the basis for citizenship, the most foundational attachment to the state. This complexity arises because any definition of political membership that depends on such relations must inevitably contain a normative judgment about what counts as "family." The risk here is that unmarried cohabitants, gay and lesbian couples, and members of families that do not comply with a "standard" household stereotype might not only become vulnerable to societal pressure (as they often do today) but also face the detrimental possibility of noninclusion in the polity. Like current *jus soli* and *jus sanguinis* rules, a relational conception of membership is likely to end up falling into the trap of both underinclusiveness (e.g., excluding same-sex partners) and overinclusiveness (e.g., including remote family members who have no substantial ties to the polity).

These dilemmas have not escaped advocates of the relational approach. Their response has generally been to try to expand the definition of family and to fight vigorously against any gender-biased constructions of political membership. While this effort is laudable, it may prove more relevant for removing residual inequalities that still persist in membership attribution rules (as in *Miller* or *Nguyen*) than for offering a comprehensive alternative to *jus soli* and *jus sanguinis.* Specifically, it is hard to conceptualize what a general schema of relational citizenship would require in practice. For example, if citizenship is to be defined relationally, based on a web of attachments to meaningful others, should one be deprived of citizenship because of the lack (or breakdown) of relationships? Would residency be required, or would it be sufficient to have family members in the host country? Should all persons belonging to a "transnational" family carry multiple affiliations, and if yes, for how long (one generation, two generations, or in perpetuity)? And if constitutive relationships are at the heart of this approach, could citizenship be attributed in a counterdiachronic direction: that is, would children be entitled to pass on political membership to their parents (e.g., where the parents entered the country illegally)? Unlike birthright membership, which at least rests on a factual and usually clearly recorded event (birth), reliance on "relations" for granting access to the good of citizenship almost inevitably invites political, cultural, and legal debate about the values upon which acceptable forms of marriage and family are based. A relational approach to citizenship is likely to deepen these problems further, especially if one's definition of a "spouse" or "child" becomes the prime sorting mechanism for including individuals in the political community, in lieu of reliance on *jus soli* or *jus sanguinis.* According to the latter scenario, all citizens would have to establish their status in the political community on the basis of their affective ties to the state or its citizens.

Add to these definitional problems the troubling realization that a relational approach may unwittingly place children and spouses in a dependency trap because their status as members of the polity rests on their ongoing connection to another individual who happens to be a citizen. As such, they lack the security and agency that are gained when a person establishes an *un*mediated relationship with the rest of the political community. In the history of citizenship, the struggle (ongoing in many parts of the globe) to ensure that all adult women and men, rich and poor, literate and illiterate, property owners and free slaves, whites and blacks, gain equal membership in the state and an equal standing before the law has been no small feat. This achievement was seen as a great victory over the previously mediated relationships in which individuals were entangled, where entities such as the guild, the family, or the church defined the set of rights and duties that were attached to the person. It would be unwise to turn back the clock and risk the independence that women and other historically vulnerable groups have won through the acquisition of full citizenship by reintroducing interdependency (here, through family and marriage, instead of church and guild) as a condition for entitlement to equal political standing in the polity.[106]

Furthermore, gender equality itself may not be served by emphasizing a relational approach to citizenship. Again, the realm of immigration provides a useful context for considering such problems. There is troubling evidence to show that regulations originally intended to address concerns about possibly fraudulent marriages may end up burdening the weaker party in the relationship. For example, a two-year "conditional status" provision was recently introduced in the United States, requiring the foreign spouse to stay married for that length of time before being able to qualify for lawful permanent residence.[107] These regulations have been criticized by feminist activists and scholars who explain that foreign spouses are often so desperate to escape the poverty and hardship of their home countries that they remain in abusive relationships out of fear that leaving the marriage will jeopardize their chances of adjusting their status in their spouse's home country. Unfortunately, their fears are not unsubstantiated.[108] This regulatory framework leaves foreign spouses vulnerable to abuse by their partners who hold the key to membership in the desired polity.[109] Such a system projects existing power inequalities between nations onto intimate family relationships, usually to the detriment of women from poorer and less developed regions of the world.[110]

V. Sustaining Global Inequality through the Property of Birthright Citizenship

To conclude this investigation of the connection between birthright and political membership, I now turn to a relatively unexplored possibility: thinking about citizenship status as a complex type of property right that plays an important role in maintaining an unequal distribution of wealth and opportunity according to national affiliation. By considering this, we move from a search for justifications of such membership attribution rules (as described in the approaches above) to a more critical analysis of the functionality of birthright-citizenship attribution in a world fraught with deep inequality. The discussion that follows is intended only to provide the bare bones of this argument, which I call "reconceptualizing citizenship status as property." It is not intended as a full exploration of the multilayered implications of such a reconceptualization, an investigation that I undertake at greater length elsewhere.

When we speak about property as a legal concept, we are talking about relations between people and things.[111] Modern theories of property extend the concept beyond concrete and tangible objects (my car, your house) to refer to a host of more abstract entitlements (shares in a company, intellectual property in the form of patents and copyrights, professional licenses and university degrees, genetic information, even folklore practices).[112] Changes in human relations and social values, along with new developments and discoveries in the physical world, constantly modify our understanding of what counts as protected property.[113]

Once we categorize certain relationships as falling under the rubric of property, important questions of allocation are raised: Who gets what, and why? When applying contemporary understandings of property to the realm of citizenship, we soon recognize that what each citizen holds is not a private entitlement to a tangible thing but a relationship to other members and to a particular (usually a national) government that creates enforceable rights and duties. From the perspective of each member of the polity, reconceptualizing one's entitlement to citizenship as a form of property fits well within the definition of "new property," a phrase famously coined by Charles Reich that refers to the power to control a particular portion of the well-being and wealth of valuables accumulated by governments.[114]

Another important feature of property is the ability of its holder to exclude others from access to the entitlement. Citizenship not only serves important internal functions (such as those of democratic self-governance or respect for constitutive relationships) but also has a vital external dimension: it serves to structurally restrict access to commonly held resources by excluding non–rights holders from enjoyment of the goods of membership.[115] Unlike traditional forms of wealth, which are held as private property, valuables associated with citizenship derive specifically from holding a *status* that is dispensed by the state, one that bestows exclusive goods and benefits to a select group of status holders.[116] The value of an entitlement such as citizenship depends at least in part upon governmental power. For example, by limiting the number of persons who can qualify as full members, the government can make the status of citizenship extremely remunerative for those who hold it. In a similar way, if citizens are the only ones guaranteed access to resources administered by the state, they gain a tremendous competitive advantage. Even in the current age of globalization, governments still control significant amounts of land, mineral wealth, routes of travel and commerce, various communications facilities and avenues of broadcasting, public facilities, and other infrastructural assets. Use of these resources generates wealth, and national governments often privilege domestic owners and entrepreneurs over foreign investors hoping to gain access to these same goods.

Reich's analysis intended to establish that governments owe an obligation to distribute public goods in ways that are predicated on an assessment of collective interests and that guarantee each member certain minimal rights to "intangible" entitlements (such as welfare payments in the event of need).[117] My intention, however, is to begin to explore what might be gained by thinking about citizenship as property in a different context: in terms of the global distributive effects of the extant system of inherited citizenship, which is currently facilitated through *jus soli* and *jus sanguinis* membership attribution rules.

Clearly, citizenship status per se is no guarantee against the persistence of inequalities between members of the same polity. But it does anchor certain basic interests as irrevocable once a person is inducted into the innermost circle of members.[118] The advantages of citizenship can be seen most clearly when we expand our horizons from the domestic scenario to the global one. Citizenship status creates an apparently "invisible" shield of entitlement and protection that applies only to those who "naturally" belong to the state. This collective power to limit access to the goods of membership in a stable, rich, political community creates a border between those who deserve to enjoy the disproportionate spoils in these countries (by virtue of birth) and those who are classified as nonmembers (and thus presumably "nondeserving"). But once we understand citizenship to be a form of property, we can no longer hide the important distributive implications behind the "naturalizing" veil of birthright. At the very least, we need to pay closer attention to the principles and procedures governing admission to and allocation of the property of citizenship.

Once we begin to think of citizenship as property, we are in a better position to appreciate how birthright subtly but surely perpetuates privilege. It does this by creating a mechanism of closure that excludes the concerns (and pains) of nonmembers—not on substantive grounds related to specific disputes at issue but by defining them as falling outside our jurisdiction. Outsiders are those who (by definition) are not counted as stakeholders and rights holders in our communal enterprise, so they have no say in determining how we should define "internal" issues (such as membership boundaries). But it is precisely the nature of the property we call citizenship that builds this boundary between "us" and "them," while at the same time making this distinction appear natural, apolitical, and noncontroversial.

"The will to (boundary) power" inherent in both *jus soli* and *jus sanguinis* citizenship laws can thus be seen in a new light.[119] By privileging the event of birth first and foremost, the principles of *jus soli* and *jus sanguinis* actually camouflage the property-related, exclusionary aspects of citizenship because attributing automatic membership to a newly born child seems so benign and easily justifiable. Yet once conceived as a valuable resource, citizenship itself becomes subject to the arguments of distributive justice, just like any other form of property entitlement. Differently put, if we view citizenship as a specific kind of property that secures access to certain valuable rights and benefits associated with political membership in particular communities, we can infuse this concept with questions of justice, specifically those dealing with power, selection, and allocation.

By exploring the different ways in which *jus soli* and *jus sanguinis* are less different in reality than they are often thought to be in theory, I hope to have shown how both these birthright attribution principles collude in the pretense that human-made distinctions between nations, countries, and peoples are "natural" and "inherited" boundaries. These boundaries, in turn, preserve selective access to scarce resources and goods according to an entitlement-allocation scheme that is neither just nor fair in its distributive implications for those children who, through no fault or merit of their own, end up enjoying far more limited life prospects than their counterparts in wealthier and more stable countries. Even the most sophisticated defenders of property rights and inherited entitlements recognize the need to provide justifications for severe and persistent inequalities of accumulation. It is therefore vital that we sever the Gordian knot that has long obscured the connection between birthright, political membership, and differential access to the wealth of nations. In so doing, we tear off the mask of naturalness surrounding inherited entitlements and open the door for new ideas about how to better allocate political membership in a world of scarce resources.

NOTES

This essay was written during my fellowship year at the Institute for Advanced Study, Princeton, 2000–2001. I wish to thank Alex Aleinikoff, Steve Macedo, and Michael Walzer for their helpful comments on earlier versions. I also thank Dan Friedman, Catherine Frost, John Holzwarth, Maya Johnson, and Helen Moffett for their assistance in preparing this manuscript for publication. I am indebted to Ran Hirschl for his incisive criticism and many hours of insightful discussion. Generous funding for this research was provided by the University of Toronto Faculty of Law and the Institute for Advanced Study, Princeton.

1. Art. I of the 1930 Hague Convention on Certain Questions Relating to Conflict of Nationality Laws, Apr. 12, 1930, 178–179 L.N.T.S. 90, 99, provides that "[i]t is for each State to determine under its own law who are its nationals." For further discussion, see William Rogers Brubaker, "Citizenship and Naturalization: Policies and Politics," in *Immigration and the Politics of Citizenship in Europe and North America*, ed. William Rogers Brubaker (Lanham, Md.: University Press of America, 1989), 99–127.

2. This definition is an adaptation of the provisions encoded in the 1933 Montevideo Convention on the Rights and Duties of States, Dec. 26, 1933, art. I, 49 Stat. 3097, T.S. No. 881.

3. See Michael Walzer, *Spheres of Justice: A Defense of Pluralism and Equality* (New York: Basic Books, 1983), 29.

4. Most countries use a combination of these two principles in assigning political membership by virtue of birthright.

5. While international law and regional covenants may force governments to respect a baseline of fundamental negative rights toward all persons within their jurisdiction (e.g., prohibition of torture), as a formal status, citizenship creates a host of positive rights and obligations that are enforceable first and foremost between the state and its members. For

example, only citizens have an unqualified right to enter, and remain in, their home country—and this is the case even in polities that extend various civil, economic, and political rights to their noncitizen residents.

6. The paucity of scholarship addressing this question may partly be explained by the fact that debates over the question of "who belongs" usually arise in the context of disagreements about immigration, not about citizenship.

7. The data on this issue are too vast to cite. But some figures are pertinent. According to the World Bank's "World Development Report 2000/2001," the aggregate average income in the wealthiest twenty countries is more than thirty-seven times greater than the average income in the world's twenty poorest countries—a gap that has doubled in the past forty years. Of the world's 6 billion people, almost half (2.8 billion) live on less than $2 a day, and a fifth (1.2 billion) live on less than $1 a day. In rich countries, fewer than one in a hundred children die before the age of five, while in the poorest countries, as many as a fifth of children do not live to that age. Varying infant mortality rates across the world also correlate to income disparities (the ratio of infant mortality rate per thousand live births is approximately 1:15 between the richest and the poorest countries). In rich countries, less than 5 percent of all children under five are malnourished. In poor countries, on the other hand, as many as 50 percent are malnourished. The report is available at http://www.worldbank.org/poverty/wdrpoverty/report/overview.pdf.

8. Clearly, even optimal citizenship and immigration policies would not serve as a panacea for these much broader problems of economic inequality. Economists tend to stress the need to develop appropriate forms of international cooperation, stronger and more effective forms of foreign and developmental aid, and policies promoting high levels of economic growth as important potential substitutes for immigration by redistributing resources and opportunities to individuals across national lines. For a lucid analysis of the relationship between national and global welfare perspectives on immigration policy, see Michael J. Trebilcock, "The Case for a Liberal Immigration Policy," in *Justice in Immigration*, ed. Warren F. Schwartz (New York: Cambridge University Press, 1995), 219–46. While the salience of economic analysis in the immigration debate is well established, it still does not resolve the basic legal and moral questions surrounding birthright citizenship: Why do some people "naturally" belong to the developed countries of the world, while others who may equally wish to hold such privileged status are not entitled to it by reason of birthplace or genetic inheritance?

9. *Perez v. Brownell*, 356 U.S. 44, 64 (1958) (Warren J., dissenting).

10. See Michael Robert W. Houston, "Birthright Citizenship in the United Kingdom and the United States: A Comparative Analysis of the Common Law Basis for Granting Citizenship to Children Born of Illegal Immigrants," *Vanderbilt Journal of Transnational Law* 33 (2000): 698–701.

11. *Calvin's Case,* 77 Eng. Rep. 377 (K.B. 1608). A detailed analysis of this case is offered by Polly J. Price, "Natural Law and Birthright Citizenship in *Calvin's Case,*" *Yale Journal of Law and the Humanities* 9 (1997): 73–145.

12. See Patrick Weil, "Access to Citizenship: A Comparison of Twenty-Five Nationality Laws," in *Citizenship Today: Global Perspectives and Practices,* ed. T. Alexander Aleinikoff and Douglas Klusmeyer (Washington, D.C.: Brookings Institution Press, 2001), 17–35.

13. As Carens points out, this example is often given by those who wish to restrict the application of the territorial birthright principle in the United States to children of citizens and legal residents aliens (thus excluding children born to undocumented migrants from automatic entitlement to American citizenship). See Joseph H. Carens, "Who Belongs? Theoretical and Legal Questions about Birthright Citizenship in the United States," *University of Toronto Law Journal* 37 (1987): 413. Similar pressures emerged in Canada and were actually enforced in the United Kingdom when the British Nationality Act, 1981 (Eng.) changed the previous common-law rule (where the place of birth was the sole determination in citizenship) to a birthright principle that now takes into consideration the parents' residency status. For further discussion of British nationality law, see Ann Dummett and Andrew Nicol, *Subjects, Citizens, Aliens and Others: Nationality and Immigration Law* (London: Weidenfeld & Nicolson, 1990).

14. The U.S. Constitution's citizenship clause provides that "[a]ll persons born or naturalized in the United States, and subject to the jurisdiction thereof, are citizens of the United States and of the State wherein they reside." U.S. Const. Amend. XIV, § 1.

15. See Carens, "Who Belongs?" p. 413. Carens concludes that the ascriptive principle is morally defensible as long as it is accompanied by adequate legal measures to naturalize long-term residents (whether or not they entered the country legally in the first place). Carens seems to be more concerned with the question of equalizing the status of nonmembers who are already resident within the host society than with scrutinizing the ethical and legal assumptions sustaining a global regime of birthright ascriptions of citizenship, as I hope to do in this essay.

16. For defense of the argument that we need to move toward a global perspective on the social welfare function in evaluating immigration policy, see Gillian K. Hadfield, "Just Borders: Normative Economics

and Immigration Law," in Schwartz, *Justice in Immigration*, 201–11. Hadfield, like Carens, focuses on immigration policy, not on citizenship law per se.

17. While NAFTA could have expanded the scope of citizenship rights by providing a common citizenship to the residents of Canada, the United States, and Mexico, it still remains primarily a trade agreement and not a common citizenship project. See Christopher J. Cassise, "The European Union v. the United States under the NAFTA: A Comparative Analysis of the Free Movement of Persons within the Regions," *Syracuse Law Review* 46 (1996): 1343.

18. See Immigration Act, 1976–77, R.S.C., ch. I-2, § 3 (1985) (Can.).

19. Until 1996, § 244(a)(1) of the Immigration and Nationality Act (INA) allowed aliens who lived in the United States continuously for at least seven years, with or without documents, to obtain permanent residency through a form of relief called "Suspension of Deportation." The standard for granting suspension was high but not impossible to meet, particularly for young adults who came to the United States as children and had no other way to legalize their status. Immigration judges, and even INS attorneys, were often sympathetic to the plight of individuals who came to the United States at a young age, were raised essentially as Americans, and then were subjected to being deported to countries of which they had no memory or experience. See Jonathan Montag, "Involuntary Migrants Face Harsh Consequences of Immigration Law Reforms," http://www.ilw.com/cgi-shl/pr/pl. The 1996 immigration reform laws changed this legal situation, however, by diminishing these exemptions. Specifically, the "Suspension of Deportation" was replaced with a new form of relief, entitled "Cancellation of Removal and Adjustment of Status for Certain Nonpermanent Residents," found in INA § 240A(b), 8 U.S.C. § 1229b (1997), which set stricter provisions that came into force in 1996.

20. See Child Citizenship Act of 2000, H.R. 2883, Public Law 106-395, amending § 320 of the INA, signed into law on October 30, 2000 (effective date February 27, 2001).

21. See Weil, "Access to Citizenship," 19.

22. Ibid.

23. See Rogers Brubaker, *Citizenship and Nationhood in France and Germany* (Cambridge, Mass.: Harvard University Press, 1992), 39.

24. See Weil, "Access to Citizenship," 21.

25. Various countries outside Europe sought expert legislative advice from leading Continental countries. For example, this process of legal imitation is considered one of the main sources for Japan's current reliance on the principle of *jus sanguinis*. See Chickako Kashiwazaki, "Citi-

zenship in Japan: Legal Practice and Contemporary Development," in *From Migrants to Citizens: Membership in a Changing World*, ed. T. Alexander Aleinikoff and Douglas Klusmeyer (Washington, D.C.: Brookings Institution Press, 2000), 437–39.

26. See Diane F. Orentlicher, "Citizenship and National Identity," in *International Law and Ethnic Conflict*, ed. David Wippman (Ithaca, N.Y.: Cornell University Press, 1998), 296–325.

27. This problematic aspect of *jus sanguinis* has manifested itself, for instance, in the citizenship laws adopted by the postcommunist states of Estonia and Latvia in 1991 and 1992 respectively. These citizenship laws failed to recognize all persons who resided within the territory as citizens of the newly established states upon secession from the former Soviet Union. Instead, they privileged the descendants of the pre-Soviet Estonian and Latvian states, while imposing obstacles on long-term Russian residents, who were barred from simple registration for citizenship. To become citizens, they were required to naturalize, and even then under restrictive terms—the most significant of these being the requirement that they demonstrate a command of the Estonian or Latvian language as a precondition for entitlement to full membership. This exclusion from automatic citizenship resulted in large numbers of people becoming stateless. Children of these individuals were deprived of membership in the state as well, even if they were born after independence. International pressure eventually led to the adoption of less exclusionary provisions in the citizenship laws of Latvia and Estonia. For a detailed discussion of these citizenship laws, see Lowell W. Barrington, "Understanding Citizenship Policy in the Baltic States," in Aleinikoff and Klusmeyer, *From Migrants to Citizens*, 253–301.

28. See Germany Information Center, "Citizenship Reform and Germany's Foreign Residents" (June 1999), available at http://www.germany-info.org/content/np_3c.html. Japan's treatment of persons of Korean origin is another such example.

29. See Kay Hailbronner, "Citizenship and Nationhood in Germany," in Brubaker, *Immigration*, 67–79.

30. The memory of the involuntary denationalization of certain classes of German citizens before and during World War II still looms large. This may make the decision to surrender their formal affiliation to another country harder for descendants of some immigrants (e.g., those of Turkish origin).

31. Weil, for instance, explains that the revived *jus sanguinis* principle in the post–French Revolution era had few ethnic or other exclusionary overtones. See Weil, "Access to Citizenship," 18.

32. Sweden represents a classic example of this type of model. See Brubaker, "Citizenship and Naturalization," 110.

33. Many countries now limit the automatic attribution of citizenship *jure sanguinis* to one generation only or impose minimal residency requirements on the child and the parent if the child was born abroad.

34. C.A. 6182/98, *Sheinbein v. Attorney General* (decision given on Feb. 25, 1999—not yet published) [Hebrew]; F.H. 1210/99, *State of Israel v. Sheinbein* (decision given on Mar. 18, 1999—not yet published) [Hebrew].

35. In this way, he escaped the threat of a heavier punishment, which would most likely have been imposed upon him in the United States. For example, Israeli law does not permit the death penalty for a convicted criminal offender, whereas various American states both allow and implement such punishment.

36. In all likelihood, Sheinbein would not have been entitled to receive Israeli citizenship by virtue of the Law of Return because § 2(B) of that law was interpreted to bar admissibility on grounds of criminality that might endanger the public welfare. See the Israel Supreme Court decision in H.C. 442/71, *Lansky v. Minister of the Interior,* 26(2) P.D. 337 [Hebrew]. For further discussion, see Ayelet Shachar, "Whose Republic? Citizenship and Membership in the Israeli Polity," *Georgetown Immigration Law Journal* 13 (1999): 240–41.

37. In light of the Israel Supreme Court decision, and to the dismay of the U.S. Justice Department, Sheinbein was not extradited to the United States. Instead, his trial for murder took place in Israel. He pleaded guilty and was sentenced to twenty-four years in prison. He is now serving his term in an Israeli prison.

38. See *United States v. Wong Kim Ark,* 169 U.S. 569, 702 (1898) (holding that there are "two sources of citizenship, and two only: birth and naturalization").

39. The exception here is the obligation that nations that signed the 1951 Hague Convention have taken upon themselves to provide a safe haven to persons who qualify as refugees. Even then, the receiving country is obliged to provide temporary shelter only, not necessarily long-term residency. See the 1951 Convention Relating to the Status of Refugees, Apr. 22, 1954, 189 U.N.T.S. 137, as amended by the Protocol Relation to the Status of Refugees, Oct. 4, 1967, 606 U.N.T.S. 267.

40. Although racial, ethnic, national origin, and similar distinctions may not be taken into account in immigration decisions, since they were expunged from the law books in the late 1960s, the anxieties surrounding "old" distinctions still linger. For further exploration of this "phantom distinction" theme in the American context, see, e.g., Ian F. Haney

López, *White by Law: The Legal Construction of Race* (New York: NYU Press, 1996); for a comparative perspective, see Stephen Castles and Alastair Davidson, *Citizenship and Migration: Globalization and the Politics of Belonging* (New York: Routledge, 2000), 54–83.

41. For comprehensive research examining these trends, see National Intelligence Council, *Growing Global Migration and Its Implications for the United States* (Washington, D.C.: NIE 2001-02D Publication, March 2001). This report can be found at http://www.odci.gov.nic/nic_homepage/nic/publications/index.htm.

42. Naturalization is generally open only to those who have already passed the initial (and more difficult) stage of entry by gaining lawful admission and establishing permanent residency status. Tomas Hammar identifies three "entrance gates" through which an immigrant must pass in order to become a citizen: (1) lawful admission to the territory; (2) permanent residency; and (3) naturalization. (Exceptions to this threefold process are found in amnesty programs that allow illegal immigrants to adjust their status.) See Tomas Hammar, *Democracy and the Nation-State: Aliens, Denizens and Citizens in a World of International Migration* (Aldershot, England: Avebury, 1990), 16–18.

43. The specific requirements for naturalization in Canada are specified in the Citizenship Act, R.S.C., ch. C-29, § 5(1) (1985) (Can.), which stipulates that an applicant must be eighteen years of age or older, have been lawfully admitted into Canada for permanent residency, have accumulated at least three years of residence in Canada, have adequate knowledge of one of the official languages (English or French), have adequate knowledge of Canada and the responsibilities and privileges of citizenship, and not be under a deportation order. Australia also imposes related admission criteria (i.e., the requirement that an applicant must be eighteen years of age or older; have basic knowledge of the English language; be of good character; have an understanding of the obligations of Australian citizenship; and have lived in Australia as a permanent resident for at least two years). An applicant for Australian citizenship must also renounce "all other allegiances." See Citizenship Act, 1948 (Cth), § 13(1) (Austl.). For further discussion of the Australian Oath of Allegiance, see *Sykes v. Cleary* (1992) 176 C.L.R. 77. In the United States, an applicant for citizenship must be eighteen years or older, have been lawfully admitted as a permanent resident, have resided in the United States for the five years immediately before filing a petition for naturalization, be able to speak and understand simple English, as well as read and write it, show good moral character, and prove that he or she is "attached to the principles of the Constitution of the United States, and well disposed to the good order and happiness of the United

States." The applicant must also take an oath of renunciation and allegiance in open court. See INA, §§ 334(b)(1), 316(a), 312(1), 316(a), 337(a), 8 U.S.C. §§ 1445, 1427, 1423, 1448 (1952).

44. I borrow this term from Rogers Brubaker. See Brubaker, "Citizenship and Naturalization," 108.

45. The symbolic meaning of such acts is discussed by Sanford Levinson in "Constituting Communities through Words that Bind: Reflections on Loyalty Oaths," *Michigan Law Review* 84 (1986): 1440.

46. See the United Nations Population Fund, *The State of the World Population 1999*, chap. 2, fig. 5, http://www.unfpa.org/swp/1999/chapter2d.htm.

47. The civic-ethnic dichotomy is used by many well-known experts on nationalism. See, e.g., Anthony Smith, *National Identity* (New York: Penguin, 1991). See also Liah Greenfeld, *Nationalism: Five Roads to Modernity* (Cambridge, Mass: Harvard University Press, 1992). For a more journalistic account, see Michael Ignatieff, *Blood and Belonging: Journeys into the New Nationalism* (New York: Farrar, Straus and Giroux, 1993).

48. For a detailed discussion, see Peter H. Schuck and Rogers M. Smith, *Citizenship without Consent: Illegal Aliens in the American Polity* (New Haven, Conn.: Yale University Press, 1985), 9–22.

49. They must also acquire basic protections against abuse of power by the state, including the security that their membership will not be unilaterally revoked by the government, no matter how critical they are of their government's actions.

50. The diachronic dimension of citizenship law is elegantly captured by Donald Galloway, "The Dilemmas of Canadian Citizenship Law," *Georgetown Immigration Law Journal* 13 (1999): 201–31.

51. See Citizenship Act, R.S.C., ch. C-29 § 3(1)(a) (1985) (Can.). Australia and the United Kingdom are also quintessential examples of the civic national model.

52. For a detailed discussion, see Michael Trebilcock, "The Fourth Freedom: Towards a Liberalized Immigration Policy," *American Law and Economics Journal* (forthcoming).

53. This is an absolute rule in Canada and the United States. Interestingly, Australia and the United Kingdom have modified their versions of the birthright principle to apply only to children of citizens and permanent residents.

54. Some may object to such expressions of loyalty for reasons of religion or conscience, in which case specific clauses need to be established (as in the case of military exemptions). Any exemptions represent the exception, however, rather than the rule.

55. In the rare instances where citizens specifically declare an intent to give up citizenship, such formal renunciation usually requires approval by the political community before it takes effect. The approval process is handled by the relevant government agencies within the country or its representatives abroad.

56. See World Bank, "The World Development Report 2000/2001," 1.

57. Unless they are subject to persecution in their home country and thus fit the Geneva Convention definition of refugee status. This demands that a host country provide them with a temporary shelter and provides that they may not be returned home if such a step would place them in real danger—the right of non-refoulement.

58. As just mentioned, the only place where consent theory can apply coherently is in explaining the rules that govern immigration policy in *jus soli* and *jus sanguinis* countries, where the individual must come forward and express his or her willingness to accept the host country's political norms, often under oath. The ceremony of naturalization culminates the process of mutual consent between the individual and the political community: the state must approve the individual's candidacy, and he or she must pledge allegiance to his or her new home country, its constitution, and its governing political principles. No similar act of explicit consent and "rebirth" is ever demanded of individuals who happened to be born into the political community.

59. I explore this deep and inherent reliance on birthright ascription, rather than adult choice, as well as other complexities associated with the implied consent theory, in Martha Minow, "The Thin Line between Imposition and Consent: A Critique of Birthright Entitlements and Their Implications," in *Cycles of Hatred: Memory, Law, and Repair,* ed. Nancy L. Rosenblum (Princeton, N.J.: Princeton University Press, forthcoming).

60. See Weil, "Access to Citizenship,"p. 20.

61. Ibid.

62. For a detailed account of the importance of self-governance (or the "responsive" principle) in justifying the U.S. *jus soli* rule, see Christopher L. Eisgruber, "Birthright Citizenship and the Constitution," *New York University Law Review* 72 (1997): 54–96.

63. For further discussion, see Orentlicher, "Citizenship and National Identity."

64. Several scholars have pointed out the need to amend this "democratic legitimacy gap" in western Europe and North America. Some have suggested extending the rights currently enjoyed only by citizens to permanent residents as well. Others have suggested adopting more

generous naturalization policies that would facilitate adjustments of status to full membership. A more radical proposal is discussed by Ruth Rubio-Marin, who defends the granting of automatic citizenship to legal and illegal long-term permanent residents after a period of ten years of continuous residence in their new political community. See Ruth Rubio-Marin, *Immigration as a Democratic Challenge: Citizenship and Inclusion in Germany and the United States* (New York: Cambridge University Press, 2000).

65. A suitable opportunity for such a redrawing of boundaries based on *jus connexio* might be at every decimal census.

66. See the Nottebohm case (*Liechtenstein v. Guatemala*), 1955 I.C.J. 4 (concerning whether the nationality conferred on Nottebohm by Liechtenstein could be validly invoked as against Guatemala in order to afford Nottebohm diplomatic protection).

67. For a discussion and critique of the "substantial presence test" in the context of American taxation, see David Williams II, "Back to the Future: A Time for Rethinking the Test for Resident Alien Status under the Income Tax Laws," *Vanderbilt Journal of Transnational Law* 21 (1988): 965; J. Scott Kircher, "The Substantial Presence Test Exemptions: Taxing Problems for the Alien," *San Diego Law Review* 24 (1987): 531; Robert J. Misey, Jr., "Simplifying International Jurisdiction for United States Transfer Taxes: Retain Citizenship and Replace Domicile with the Green Card Test," *Marquette Law Review* 76 (1992): 73.

68. See Nick Johnstone, "International Trade, Transfrontier Pollution and Environmental Cooperation: A Case Study of the Mexican-American Border Region," *Natural Resources Journal* 35 (1995): 33; and Matthew Tuchband, "The Systemic Environmental Externalities of Free Trade: A Call for Wiser Decisionmaking," *Georgetown Law Journal* 83 (1995): 2099.

69. I borrow the "filing system" metaphor from Rogers Brubaker, "Citizenship and Naturalization," 101.

70. For a detailed discussion of the systems of identification developed by modern states to regulate and control who may and may not enter and leave their territory, see John Torpey, *The Invention of the Passport: Surveillance, Citizenship and the State* (New York: Cambridge University Press, 2000).

71. See Bernard Yack, "The Myth of the Civic Nation," *Critical Review* 10 (1996): 208.

72. See Carens, "Who Belongs?" 423. Joseph Carens, "Aliens and Citizens: The Case for Open Borders," *Review of Politics* 49 (1987): 251–73, makes a strong argument about the need to take specific contingencies into account. These include considerations of whether one is a citizen of

a rich or poor country as well as whether one is already a citizen of a particular country (among other divisive issues that could set people at odds behind a Rawlsian veil of ignorance). Carens claims that a fair procedure for choosing principles of justice requires exclusion of knowledge of these circumstances, together with exclusion of knowledge of an applicant's sex, race, or social class. Carens goes on to suggest that this would be likely to lead us to conclude that few restrictions on migration are morally justifiable. Note, however, that Carens assumes that we need to adopt the perspective of the alien who may want to immigrate (as the person most disadvantaged by these restrictions) but he does not challenge the basic distinction between citizen and alien.

73. This approach is clearly articulated, for example, by Karen Knop, "Relational Nationality: On Gender and Nationality in International Law," in Aleinikoff and Klusmeyer, *Citizenship Today*, 89–124.

74. See Carens, "Who Belongs?" p. 424.

75. See Walzer, *Spheres of Justice*, 62.

76. Ibid., pp. 61–62.

77. The writings of Carens eloquently represent this line of critique. See, e.g., Carens, "Citizens and Aliens." See also Jules L. Coleman and Sarah K. Harding, "Citizenship, the Demands of Justice, and the Moral Significance of Political Borders," in Schwartz, *Justice in Immigration*, 19–62.

78. For further elaboration of a feminist theory of relational rights, see, e.g., Martha Minow and Mary Lyndon Shanley, "Revisioning the Family: Relational Rights and Responsibilities," in *Reconstructing Political Theory: Feminist Perspectives*, ed. Mary Lyndon Shanley and Uma Narayan (Pittsburgh: Pennsylvania State University Press, 1997), 84–108. More generally, see Joan Tronto, *Moral Boundaries: A Political Argument for an Ethic of Care* (New York: Routledge, 1993).

79. See, e.g., Jennifer Nedelsky, "Citizenship and Relational Feminism," in *Canadian Political Philosophy*, ed. Ronald Beiner and Wayne Norman (New York: Oxford University Press, 2001), 131–46.

80. See Knop, "Relational Nationality.".

81. For a detailed discussion, see Candice Lewis Bredbenner, *A Nationality of Her Own: Women, Marriage, and the Law of Citizenship* (Berkeley: University of California Press, 1998).

82. For illuminating critiques of this gender-biased rule, see Virginia Sapiro, "Women, Citizenship, and Nationality: Immigration and Naturalization Policies in the United States," *Politics and Society* 13 (1984): 1–26; Nancy F. Cott, "Marriage and Women's Citizenship in the United States, 1830–1934," *American Historical Review* 103 (1998): 1440–74. Such discrimination continued until late in the twentieth century, when married

women in most countries finally acquired the right to transmit their nationality to their children independently.

83. For further discussion, see the Committee on Feminism and International Law, *Final Report on Women's Equality and Nationality in International Law* (International Law Association, 2000).

84. See Lisa C. Stratton, "The Right to Have Rights: Gender Discrimination in Nationality Law," *Minnesota Law Review* 77 (1992): 195.

85. Ibid.

86. See *Benner v. Canada (Secretary of State)* [1997] 1 S.C.R. 358.

87. See Citizenship Act, R.S.C., ch. C-29, § 5(2)(b) (1985) (Can.).

88. *Benner v. Canada,* 401.

89. Ibid., 403.

90. INA, § 309, 8 U.S.C. § 1409 (1952).

91. See *Miller v. Albright,* 523 U.S. 420 (1998).

92. INA, § 309(a) (codified as amended at 8 U.S.C. § 1409(a) (1986)). The section imposes four requirements that must be met to confer citizenship "as of the date of birth" of a child of an unwed American father and a non-American mother outside the United States:

(1) a blood relationship between the person and the father is established by clear and convincing evidence;
(2) the father had the nationality of the United States at the time of the person's birth;
(3) the father (unless deceased) has agreed in writing to provide financial support for the person until the person reaches the age of eighteen years; and,
(4) while a person is under the age of eighteen years,
  (a) the person is legitimated under the law of the person's residence or domicile,
  (b) the father acknowledges paternity of the person in writing under oath, or
  (c) the paternity of the person is established by adjudication of a competent court.

93. *Miller v. Albright,* 434.

94. International law, on the other hand, clearly provides that men and women deserve equal rights to acquire, change, or retain their nationality and to confer citizenship on their children. See, e.g., Article 9, Convention on the Elimination of All Forms of Discrimination against Women, Dec. 18, 1979, 1249 U.N.T.S. 13.

95. See *Tuan Anh Nguyen v. I.N.S.,* 121 S. Ct. 2053 (2001) (decision given on June 11, 2001).

96. Nguyen's father obtained an order of parentage from a state court, based on DNA testing, proving their blood relationship as father and son. Ibid., 2057.

97. Ibid., 2060.

98. Ibid., 2061.

99. Ibid., 2061–62.

100. Ibid., 2062.

101. Ibid.

102. Ibid., 2063.

103. Ibid., 2066 (O'Connor J., dissenting) (internal quotation marks omitted).

104. Immigration agencies (such as the INS in the United States) were criticized for their "invasions of privacy [in marriage-based immigration] which even the boldest of government agencies have heretofore been hesitant to enter." See *Chan v. Bell*, 464 F. Supp. 125, 130, n. 13 (D.D.C. 1978); *Stokes v. INS*, No. 74 Civ. 1022 (S.D.N.Y. Dec. 1, 1976) (consent judgment), reprinted in 54 *Interpreter Releases* 77 (1977) (ordering particular procedural guidelines for New York INS marital fraud investigation processes); *Doe v. Miller*, 573 F. Supp. 461 (N.D. Ill. 1983) (granting an injunction against implementation of state policies that forced undocumented alien parents to withdraw food stamp applications or disclose information about their alien status).

105. Unlike the automatic nature of citizenship attribution at birth, the naturalization process requires a noncitizen seeking admission on the basis of marriage to prove his or her eligibility for such inclusion. The burden is on the applicant to show that the relationship is genuine—that is, not merely a pretext for gaining access to the rights and benefits of full membership.

106. Of the now established body of feminist literature on this problem, see, e.g., Iris Marion Young, "Mothers, Citizenship, and Independence: A Critique of Pure Family Values," *Ethics* 105 (1995): 535–56.

107. INA § 216, as part of the Immigration Marriage Fraud Amendments of 1986 (IMFA).

108. If a petition for adjustment of status is not filed or the marriage relationship dissolves at any time during the conditional residency, the foreign spouse becomes a deportable illegal alien. The Immigration Act of 1990 was designed to alleviate some of the problems that this system created, specifically the vulnerability of foreign spouses to domestic violence and abuse. See INA, § 216 (c)(4)(C); (codified as amended at 8 U.S.C. § 1186a (c)(4)(C) (1990)). However, the current statutory and regulatory framework still allows husbands to control the petitioning

process for most women and establishes evidentiary requirements that make it almost impossible for a foreign spouse to independently establish her permanent residence status even if she or her children have suffered abuse or extreme hardship. For detailed discussion, see Michelle J. Anderson, "A License to Abuse: The Impact of Conditional Status on Female Migrants," *Yale Law Journal* 102 (1993): 1401–30. See also Linda Kelly, "Domestic Violence Survivors: Surviving the Beatings of 1996," *Georgetown Immigration Law Journal* 11 (1997): 303–27. On the history of spouse-based immigration to the United States and its detrimental impact on women, see Janet M. Calvo, "Spouse-Based Immigration Laws: The Legacies of Coverture," *San Diego Law Review* 28 (1991): 593.

109. Conditional permanent residents receive documents that clearly mark that their status expires at the end of the two years. Within the last ninety days of the two-year period, both spouses must petition the INS to have the conditional status removed. This creates a power imbalance between the anchor spouse (the American citizen) and the foreign spouse. Moreover, staying in the marriage relationship (however abusive) becomes the foreign spouse's only route to lawful status in the United States upon expiration of the two-year conditional period, which further adds to her vulnerability.

110. See Anderson, "A License to Abuse."

111. "[Property] is not a term of art and in itself no more than a convenient expression to denote a legal relationship between a person and a thing, from which it can be inferred that a person is the owner of a particular thing." D. G. Kleyn et al., *Silberg and Schoeman's The Law of Property*, 3d ed. (Durban, South Africa: Butterworths, 1992), 1.

112. For further discussion, see Jennifer Hill, "Visions and Revisions of the Shareholder," *American Journal of Comparative Law* 48 (2000): 39; Brian F. Ladenburg, "Unilateral Refusals to Deal in Intellectual Property after *Image Technical Services, Inc. v. Eastman Kodak Co.*," *Washington Law Review* 73 (1998): 1079, 1086–87; Timothy S. Harris, "Do Professional Degrees and Licenses Earned during Marriage Constitute Marital Property? An Irrelevant Issue," *Ohio State Law Journal* 48 (1987): 1171; Catherine M. Valerio Barrad, "Genetic Information and Property Theory," *Northwestern University Law Review* 87 (1993): 1037; Paul Kuruk, "Protecting Folklore under Modern Intellectual Property Regimes: A Reappraisal of the Tensions between Individual and Communal Rights in Africa and the United States," *American University Law Review* 48 (1999): 769.

113. Scientific research on the use of stem cells in the treatment of disease, for instance, has precipitated a new debate about what constitutes private property. For a description of the novel relationship be-

tween stem cells and conceptions of property, see Jodi K. Fredrickson, "Umbilical Cord Blood Stem Cells: My Body Makes Them, but Do I Get to Keep Them? Analysis of the FDA Proposed Regulations and the Impact on Individual Constitutional Property Rights," *Journal of Contemporary Health and Policy* 14 (1998): 477.

114. See Charles A. Reich, "The New Property," *Yale Law Journal* 73 (1964): 732.

115. Only those who are defined as insiders have a formal share in various state-created rights and benefits, as well as goods and services attached to the special relationship between the rights holder (the citizen) and the government.

116. Thus, as with other types of "new property" (such as a professional license to practice law or medicine), a rights holder cannot lawfully trade or sell his or her entitlement to citizenship. In other words, each citizen enjoys the benefits of full membership in a state-held asset but not the power to transfer it through market activity. The only way in which an individual can automatically transmit this valuable entitlement to another person is through intergenerational inheritance: that is, by virtue of birthright.

117. See the landmark case of *Goldberg v. Kelly*, 397 U.S. 254 (1970), which is considered to have been influenced by Reich's concept of "new property" (affirming that the due process clause of the U.S. Constitution requires that a recipient of state financial aid be afforded an evidentiary hearing before the termination of benefits).

118. Each insider differs from outsiders by virtue of enjoying a share in the protection conferred only on those counted as full citizens and holding a right not to be deprived of the valuable good of membership. Other scholars have termed this particular type of entitlement "communitarian property." For further discussion, see, e.g., J. W. Harris, "Private and Non-Private Property: What Is the Difference?" *Law Quarterly Review* 111 (1995): 421–44.

119. See Friedrich Nietzsche, *The Will to Power*, ed. Walter Kaufmann and R. J. Hollingdale (New York: Random House, 1968).

13

MORAL EQUALITY AND BIRTHRIGHT CITIZENSHIP

MICHAEL BLAKE

It is harder to be a liberal today than it used to be. When liberalism understood itself as a theory about the relation between citizen and state, the liberal project had nicely defined boundaries. The inequalities about which liberals had reason to be concerned were well defined, and liberal theorists agreed—at least in broad outline—about what a liberal political order would look like. The difficulty with this vision of liberalism, of course, is that it ignores many forms of inequality just as troubling as those liberalism traditionally addressed. Consistency demands an extension of liberal concern. Inequalities within the family, and inequalities across international borders, have therefore become the subject of much recent egalitarian concern. This extension makes liberal theorizing more difficult, and liberal conclusions potentially more radical, than was previously the case. Liberal theorists, however, seem to have no option but to pursue liberal thinking wherever it may lead.

In this project, thinkers such as Ayelet Shachar deserve much credit for their willingness to examine afresh what the egalitarian premise of liberalism really demands. Shachar's excellent essay argues that, in the present political world, citizenship in a wealthy democratic society represents a valuable form of property—a form of property whose distribution is now made in accordance with arbitrary and ascriptive rules. In our world, citizenship in such a society represents a form of birthright privilege—an inherited advantage not morally distinct from inherited advantages of class, race, or gender. If liberals are to live up to their egalitarianism, they must consistently reject such inherited structures. Liberals have reason to treat the assignment of citizenship—including the traditional legal standards of *jus soli* and *jus sanguinis*—with considerably more skepticism than they currently do.

I think Shachar is largely right in the concerns that motivate these arguments. Right now, fortuitous birth determines life chances in a deeply objectionable way. In what follows, I want to outline a distinct vision of how these conclusions might be established. I will introduce my approach by asking two questions. First, what, exactly, can we conclude from the fact that our rules of citizenship are arbitrary and ascriptive? And second, are all inequalities that follow from ascriptive attributes genuinely objectionable from a liberal point of view? In both questions, I think my answers will be considerably more deflationary and modest than those given by Shachar. Shachar and I will agree that the currently global allocation of resources is problematic. We will disagree, however, about the degree to which those institutions must promote equality of well-being before they could be justifiable. Neither of us, then, would accept the world as it stands; my vision of an acceptable world order, however, will likely prove much less demanding than hers.

I. Birthright Citizenship: Arbitrariness and Liberal Concern

Liberal theory has long had a hostility to arbitrary and ascriptive forms of group membership. Hierarchies of class, race, and gender form the traditional focus of liberal concern—part of that concern being motivated by the fact that these hierarchies are not "natural" in the sense generally assumed by those who benefit from their imposition. To this list, Shachar adds citizenship. There is, she argues, nothing "natural" in the allocation of citizenship—there is no single method of allocating citizenship, forced upon us by aspects of the world beyond our control. Citizenship is a human creation, subject to human analysis. Since citizenship seems morally akin to the traditional hierarchies liberals reject—since it is an ascriptive form of membership associated with inequalities in life chances, falsely portraying itself as a natural and inevitable part of the world's order—liberals have good reason to challenge the allocation of citizenship itself.

There are, however, two ways of understanding how we ought to respond to arbitrary forms of membership such as citizenship. The first is to say that this form of membership is itself a good and to argue that the good ought to be redistributed in some less arbitrary fashion. An alternative, however, would be to take the arbitrary nature of the distribution as itself unproblematic and to argue that the moral harm arises in what membership currently implies for other areas of life. The first strategy, in this context, would be to respond to the arbitrary nature of *jus soli* and *jus sanguinis* by redistributing citizenship. The second would be to accept these arbitrary ways of allocating state membership, but to argue that they ought not have the drastic consequences they currently do for life chances. Shachar's strategy here is the former; I want to examine what might be said in favor of the latter.

We might examine this distinction with reference to the family. As many of the articles in this volume explore, there is nothing particularly "natural" about the attribution of family membership. Membership in the family has all the hallmarks of arbitrariness we see in the case of citizenship. Family membership is *ascriptive* in that it is assigned to children without knowledge or consent; while we can choose what relationship we will have to our parents as we get older, the selection of parents is not itself a matter of individual choice. Family membership is also *exclusive*—your concern with your own children displaces, to some degree, concern with children more generally; and I cannot become the subject of your parental concern simply by voluntarily affiliating myself with your family. (Children do not have, for example, the right to "emigrate" from their own families to other families simply because they believe the other families have more to offer.) Family membership, finally, is to some degree *arbitrary*, in at least two senses: no one can take credit for his or her own familial status, and there is no single set of rules in the world that determines who counts as a family member. The latter form of arbitrariness is often disguised by the illusory "naturalness" of genetic parentage; however, as Jonathan Kaplan reminds us, there is nothing "natural" about the use of genetics as a surrogate for familial respect and concern.[1] In all relevant respects, it seems, familial membership is as non-"natural" as citizenship.

The liberal response to familial membership, however, is generally not to abolish family status or to replace our arbitrary rules of family membership with some alternative system of just distribution. The strategy liberals have adopted is to seek to make family membership less relevant to the distribution of other goods—such as education, wealth, and political power—rather than to advocate the redistribution of family membership *as* a good. We may seek to alter the specific parts of our arbitrary system of family membership that violate liberal precepts, such as the legal bias against gay parenting. But we accept that, whatever we do, we will be left with some arbitrary, ascriptive, and non-"natural" means by which family status will be allocated to children. We accept that this pattern is arbitrary, but this sort of arbitrariness is not in itself problematic. The only problem arises when this pattern serves as a basis for inequalities in some other area of liberal political concern.

We are willing, then, to accept some arbitrary pattern of allocations in family membership. The reason for this, I think, is that we are aware that familial authority can be justified, even if the pattern by which it is allocated is arbitrary. The authority of the family is justified, in rough outline, by the usefulness of family relationships in protecting those who are vulnerable. What a given child requires—what gives the family its license to operate—is the protection and guidance the family will provide. The child needs a protector, and even if there is nothing inevitable in the way such protectors are allocated, we have no reason to abandon the distributive mechanism if no child is left behind.

This last assumption, of course, is often false—families can lose their claims on their children if they do not serve their function as protector and guardian of the children's interests. In this, however, we do not seek to overcome the arbitrariness of family relationships themselves; we seek only to make sure that each family, however its composition is determined, does its job well. Liberals seek to ensure two things: that each family serves its protective function and that family membership is not associated with unjustified inequalities in other areas of life. In a world in which both of these results were attained, I think liberals would have very little reason to worry about the arbitrary ways in which family membership is distributed.

Membership in a territorial state, I think, can be understood in a like manner. Citizenship is even less "natural" than parentage, but from this fact I do not think all that much can be inferred. States, like families, obtain their authority at least in part because of their protection of certain vital human interests.[2] States can lose their title to authority when they fail to protect those within their sphere of authority—as they often do. State membership can also become associated with objectionable inequalities in life chances, just as family membership does. But neither of these facts should force us to reexamine the principles by which state membership is allocated to individuals. These facts should, rather, make us look for principles by which objectionable inequalities and objectionable state actions toward individuals could be identified. This would be a project, however, of asking what citizenship ought to *mean* as regards other entitlements—not a project involving the reallocation of citizenship itself.

I think we might therefore regard the allocation of citizenship—like the allocation of family membership—as a coordination problem for which there is no single solution dictated as a matter of "natural" compulsion. What individuals require is that they have agents to protect their vital interests—as parents must protect their children, and as states must protect their citizens, if their respective claims to authority are to be valid. But in neither case does the process of allocation itself require more than some arbitrary convention by which membership should be allocated. States and families are justified by what they do for those individuals over whom they claim authority; they need not also show that the pattern by which that authority was granted was anything other than arbitrary.

We might, therefore, take even arbitrary principles such as *jus soli* and *jus sanguinis* as legitimate solutions to the problem of allocating individuals to states. Indeed, I think there are three good reasons to regard such birthright principles as decent solutions to this particular problem of allocation. Children are, first, more likely to live within the authority of the state of their birth than any other state. Despite the problematic cases Shachar notes, birthright citizenship based upon descent or residence still reflects a plausible prediction: the child is more likely to live his or her life within this society than within any other, and a principle reflecting this makes some sense. American children may emigrate to Canada, but giving American citizenship to children born in America still reflects the fact that most of these children will live their lives within the political authority of the United States. The state, second, does have a distinct relationship to the parents of the children in question. These parents generally live within the sphere of authority of the state in question—not always, as Shachar points out, but in the vast majority of cases. The state can ask things of these parents that it cannot ask of nonmembers—it can take their money, their freedom, and even their lives. It cannot ask the same of foreign nationals. This, it seems to me, gives rise to unique duties of justification to those citizens. Part of this justification might involve giving parents the right to pass on their membership to their children; the human desire that one's children have at least the *option* to follow on one's life within the community is not in itself objectionable, and birthright citizenship makes it possible for this desire to be fulfilled. This might be understood, not as an objectionable form of feudal privilege, but as part of the package of rights and duties by which the state establishes the legitimacy of its authority over its citizens. Birthright citizenship, finally, represents at least one means by which the problem of stateless persons is to be avoided. Ascription of citizenship status at birth serves to ensure that every child has at least one political community that is obligated to protect that child in certain ways. This is surely something we have reason to pursue—just as we have reason to pursue a world in which every child has some sort of family, some specific set of adults who regard themselves as uniquely obligated to protect and guide that child to maturity. The arbitrariness of the allocation ought not blind us to the good this sort of system can provide. This good is provided by our current legal structures in a deeply imperfect manner. But fixing the system so that all children are protected is a very different thing from seeking to reallocate citizenship status as a good in itself.

What all this means, I think, is that the arbitrary patterns of distribution that we have in the case of citizenship might not be all that problematic in themselves. So long as all states protect the interests of their citizens, and so long as state membership is not associated with any objectionable inequalities in other spheres of life, then it seems not to matter whether the pattern of allocation is itself arbitrary. These last two conditions, however, deserve our attention. In our world, they rarely hold. Many states are predatory as regards their own members, and state membership determines life chances in a deep and thoroughgoing way. These facts may indicate a need for radical alteration in global institutions. Shachar and I would arrive at such conclusions in different ways, but we would both accept that international legal and political structures ought to reduce the effects of citizenship upon life chances. States that do not protect the interests of their citizens lose their claim to authority; and international structures that associate citizenship with objectionable inequality are unjustified.

We have now to face, however, the second question identified above. What, in this context, constitutes an "objectionable inequality"? What, in other words, would the international world have to look like before it could be justified to all those within it? This is an enormous topic, and I cannot hope to give an adequate answer to this question here. What I do want to do, however, is to articulate an alternative to the approach used by Shachar to answer this question.

II. Moral Equality and Equal Treatment

Equality is a famously slippery term; there is a sense of the word in which virtually all political philosophers count as egalitarians.[3] It is therefore tricky to determine the specific variant of equality with which liberals ought to be concerned. I want here to examine two forms of equality and see how each is implicated in the international context. The first is the basic notion of *moral equality*—what Ronald Dworkin calls treatment *as* an equal.[4] This form of equality is expressed in the attitudes implied by institutional action and policy, or by the forms of justification offered for political agency; it expresses an attitude toward persons in which all individuals are of equal moral concern from the standpoint of the political community. This notion of equality is, we might say, equality of respect. The second notion of equality involves equalization in terms of some form of desirable goods or outcomes. This broad notion—which Dworkin calls *equal treatment*—is meant to capture equality in a variety of specific forms, including equality of income, wealth, welfare, capabilities, rights, and so on. What is common to all these latter forms of equality is that they involve not simply an equality of moral concern but the equalization of some aspect of individual experience as a consequence of that moral concern.

I believe, with Dworkin, that the former notion is morally primary. What matters about a given inequality in treatment is that it demonstrates, constitutes, or otherwise implicates some inequality in respect. This leaves open, however, the question of what might be inferred from a given case of unequal treatment, when that inequality tracks some ascriptive or unchosen aspect of the person. There are, I think, two possibilities here. The first is to argue that any such inequality constitutes an inequality of moral respect. The existence of an inequality in some valuable outcome—be it well-being, rights, or something else—is enough to establish an objectionable inequality of moral concern if that inequality of treatment mirrors some arbitrary aspect of the person. The alternative view, I think, would be to say that there is still some argument required when unequal treatment is premised upon an ascriptive characteristic. While many such cases will reflect unequal moral concern, many will not. On this view, we do not always have to assume that unequal treatment—even unequal treatment based upon unchosen characteristics—is itself an affront to liberal values.

Shachar's argument, I think, involves a commitment to the first strategy. Her moral test for political institutions is welfarist; the fact that ascriptive birthright citizenship can ground a difference in well-being is sufficient, on this analysis, to implicate this form of citizenship as unjustified. The fact that well-being tracks citizenship—together with the fact that such citizenship is distributed in a morally arbitrary way—is enough for us to conclude that the contemporary institutions of citizenship fail the liberal principle of moral equality. We can read back, in this case, from the unequal treatment to an inequality of concern and respect.

My own preference is for the second strategy outlined above. On this analysis, the fact that a given inequality of treatment is premised upon an ascriptive aspect of the person is not sufficient to ground the conclusion that an inequality of respect has occurred. We have some more work to do, on this analysis, before we can assert that something objectionable is taking place. Identifying a disadvantage based upon some ascriptive characteristic begins the liberal argument; it does not conclude it.

This latter strategy, I think, can be defended on the basis of the simple fact that it is not always easy to determine what sort of treatment moral equality actually demands.[5] Equality of respect demands that we treat relevantly similar cases alike—which demands an analysis of what counts, in the present context, as the relevant sort of similarities. We can take voting rights as a good example here. The denial of the franchise to a French citizen resident in France would seem to stand as at least a prima facie violation of liberal principles. Denying the same right to vote in French elections to an American citizen—one who is neither subject to French legal authority nor understands him- or herself to be obligated to the French state—seems utterly unobjectionable. To my way of thinking, this conclusion persists even if we accept Shachar's point that the distribution of citizenship is itself rather arbitrary. However much arbitrariness is to be found in the principles of distribution, the French citizen and the American citizen are situated in different contexts and bear different relationships to the French state. This is sufficient to argue that a difference in treatment here reflects, rather than offends, the liberal principle of moral equality.[6] The fact of differential treatment following on ascriptive status is not always enough to make a liberal concerned.

What this means in the present context, I think, is that figuring out when a given difference in treatment is truly objectionable might be more difficult than we tend to assume. This conclusion holds true even in the context of well-being itself. I do not think we are able to assume that inequalities in well-being necessarily offend liberal principles, even when those inequalities track ascriptive aspects of persons. Shachar and I agree that the sorts of poverty and deprivation found in the developing world today are morally repugnant; to the extent that institutions such as citizenship now help maintain privilege in the face of such poverty, we have a duty to reorganize such institutions. My view, however, is that we can establish this conclusion with reference to poverty and deprivation—which are absolute, rather than relative, concepts—and not, as Shachar would have it, with reference to inequalities in well-being. These latter sorts of inequalities, I suggest, represent inequalities of respect only under certain highly specific circumstances; we cannot always assume that political institutions are unjustified unless they leave everyone as equals in well-being.

To establish this, we can shift from equalities of well-being to the more empirically tractable idea of equality of income. Imagine, in this context, two states, each of which is well beyond whatever threshold we imagine as the baseline of decent functioning. One state is quite wealthy, so that its citizens enjoy a rather nice form of life. The other state, however, is absurdly wealthy, so that its citizens enjoy an utterly sybaritic existence. Is there, in this case, a liberal impulse toward international redistribution? I do not think so; even though an inequality of life chances persists, and this inequality is associated with birthright privilege, I think few liberals would argue that birthright citizenship here reflects or perpetuates any inequality of respect. I cannot see any reason for insisting that the merely very wealthy citizens of the first state are being treated in an objectionable manner if the second state refuses to give them transfer payments. What this means, however, is that unequal treatment is not always something we have reason to condemn. Inequalities in wealth and income, it seems, do not always constitute the sort of moral inequalities liberals have reason to resist.

We should note that this conclusion is compatible with the idea that there are some reasons why income inequality might be relevant *within* each of these states. It might be the case that the legitimate authority of political institutions could be established only when citizens do not face certain sorts of inequalities in income. We might think, for instance, that certain forms of income inequalities would make political self-government impossible, by removing the possibility of each citizen having an equal stake in governance. I cannot argue here that only concerns such as this give rise to a liberal concern with distributive equality—although

I think this conclusion is likely true. All I want to establish here is the possibility that equality in the distribution of income might not matter everywhere. Political institutions might be justifiable even when they do not produce such equalities of treatment at all times and between all persons. We therefore have to find an argument before we can conclude that any given inequality of treatment is objectionable.

In the present context, this means that an inequality of welfare cannot, in itself, establish the conclusion that anything objectionable can be found in our current methods of allocating citizenship. We still require an argument about why this particular form of inequality would represent an inequality of respect, and no such argument, I think, is likely to be persuasive. It simply does not seem plausible to assert that global institutions must equalize well-being before they are morally acceptable.

All of this, of course, is to disagree with Shachar's methodology, not with her practical conclusions. I have tried, in this essay, to establish an alternative framework by which the legitimacy of birthright citizenship might be evaluated. I have not, however, tried to disagree with Shachar's condemnation of current global poverty and immiseration; she is right, I believe, to point out that citizenship in a wealthy state now represents an illegitimate form of privilege. Shachar and I thus agree about the injustice of the current distribution of the world's resources. We disagree about whether this is to be understood with reference to the institution of birthright citizenship itself, rather than with the implications of such citizenship in the world today. We also disagree, I think, about how much the global institutions producing this world would have to change in order to be justified to liberals. These points of disagreement, however, represent distant concerns, given how far away the world is from any remotely acceptable distribution of resources. Neither Shachar's view nor my own could countenance the current world situation as morally permissible. Liberalism, to live up to its own ideals, must continue to develop its ideas in a more global context. As I said at the beginning of this essay, this makes liberalism a more difficult doctrine to understand—and a more difficult doctrine to uphold. This is, however, the only path open to a consistent liberal; and theorists such as Shachar deserve our gratitude for having furthered our progress along this road.

NOTES

1. Jonathan Kaplan, *The Limits and Lies of Human Genetic Research* (New York: Routledge, 2000), 151–65.

2. See Robert Goodin, "What Is So Special about Our Fellow Countrymen?" *Ethics* 98 (July 1998): 663–86; see also Robert Goodin, *Protecting the Vulnerable* (Chicago: University of Chicago Press, 1985).

3. See Amartya Sen, *Inequality Re-Examined* (New York: Russell Sage, 1992).

4. See Ronald Dworkin, *Taking Rights Seriously* (Cambridge, Mass.: Harvard University Press, 1977), 227.

5. It can also be defended, I think, by the idea that not all forms of inequality of treatment are legitimate subjects for political concern. Hierarchies of sexual attractiveness no doubt contribute to individual well-being; very few of us, however, think that sexual attractiveness itself—as opposed to the ways in which sexual attractiveness interacts with the other institutions such as the market—is a proper subject of political attention. It seems perfectly plausible to me that such forms of inequality, however regrettable, are simply not the sorts of things with which a liberal state ought to be concerned; the problems involved in a political state seeking to compensate the unattractive go beyond the merely administrative. On this, see Elizabeth Anderson, "What Is the Point of Equality?" *Ethics* 109 (1999): 287–337.

6. This example is borrowed from my "Distributive Justice, State Coercion, and Autonomy," in *Philosophy and Public Affairs* (forthcoming).

INDEX

Abortion, 28, 75–78, 81
Adoption, 3–6, 8, 15–97, 106–7, 120–22, 170–205; and abandonment, 5, 18, 38–40, 45, 47–49, 62; and adoptees' rights movement, 27–28; and "as if" biological families, 4, 5; and Native Americans, 30–33, 43–45, 54n, 59, 72–73, 199; and religion, 67, 69–71, 73; "clean break" model, 25, 38–39, 59, 176–77; of foreign-born children, 352; gay and lesbian, 3, 8, 25, 74–75, 83, 177, 189–97, 205, 282, 289, 291–96, 300, 335; "open" and "closed" records, 3–5, 15–17, 19, 21, 23–30, 37, 39–40, 45–47, 58–59, 61–62, 75, 78–87, 93n, 170, 176–77, 180, 189–90, 192–93, 198, 203, 296–99; role of birth parents in, 5–6, 17–19, 25–29, 39–44, 47–48, 61–65, 72–85, 87–88, 179, 186–89, 193–94, 199; single parent, 25, 205; stepparent, 291; "stranger," 20, 38, 174; transracial, 4, 5, 15–17, 19, 21–22, 25–27, 30–38, 41–47, 58–63, 68–73, 75, 120–22, 166, 170, 176–77, 179–80, 197–201, 294. *See also* Children; Family; Parents
Adoption and Safe Families Act (1997), 106
Adoption of Kay C., 96n
Aid to Families with Dependent Children, 154–55
Allegiance oaths, 373
American Academy of Pediatrics, 292
Amish, 227, 229–231, 248
Apple, Michael, 331–32
Archard, David, 257
Aristotle, 172
Arneson, Richard, 226–27
Association, freedom of, 225–26
Australian aborigines, 121
Australian Citizenship Act, 389n

Banks, Richard, 35–36, 44, 63–64
Barak, Aharon, 356
Bardaglio, Peter, 317
Bartholet, Elizabeth, 33–35, 41, 63–64
Benner v. Canada (Secretary of State), 373, 376
Berlant, Lauren, 328
Berlin, Isaiah, 214
Black pride, 31
Blake, Michael, 11–12, **398–409**
Blanchard, Evelyn, 41
Blasius, Mark, 313
Blumstein, Philip, 312–13
Boling, Patricia, 315
Boris, Eileen, 317
Bottoms v. Bottoms, 287
Bowen, James, 32, 41, 54n
British Nationality Act, 385n

Bronfenbrenner, Urie, 260–61
Brown, Wendy, 333
Burtt, Shelley, 10, **243–70**
Butler, Judith, 179–80, 195–96

Callan, Eamonn, 223, 225–26, 228, 244
Calvin's Case, 350
Canadian Charter of Rights and Freedoms, 373
Canadian Citizenship Act, 373, 389n
Care and caregiving, 8, 153, 155–59, 163–67, 314, 318, 322. *See also* Dependency
Carens, Joseph, 370, 385n, 392–93n
Castells, Manuel, 324, 328
Catholic Charities, 77–78
Cerullo, Margaret, 323
Child abuse and neglect, 102, 105, 149–50, 160, 167n, 223, 240, 264, 266, 299
Child care, 149–50
Child-centered perspective, 10–11, 17, 60, 221, 237, 273–74, 276–77, 279, 282–300
Child Citizenship Act (2000), 352, 354
Children: access to courts, 282, 298; as autonomous individuals, 5, 15–19, 26, 30, 36–37, 45, 48, 58–61, 170, 175, 178, 234; and autonomy, 10, 235, 244–47, 267, 278–79; capacity for critical judgment, 212, 236, 245–46, 257, 262; and citizenship, 346–48, 377, 402–3; dependency of, 150, 152–53, 234–35, 278–79, 401; developmental needs, 249, 260–62, 265–66, 268; as "encumbered" or "embedded," 5–6, 15–19, 26, 30, 36–37, 44–45, 48, 58–62, 64–72, 75, 85, 170, 175, 178, 262, 370; and family fantasies, 184–85; gay and lesbian, 331–32; and identity, 15, 17, 21, 29, 36, 59, 178–79, 297–98; and individuality, 9–10; interests of, 4, 60, 177–78, 180–81, 199, 205, 234, 236–37, 240, 265, 275, 277–79, 283, 286, 295, 298, 300; moral development of, 253, 255, 258, 263; and "open futures," 245–46, 248–49, 256–57, 261–63, 267; rights of, 2, 17, 25–26, 175, 273–83, 285, 287, 289–91, 293–98, 300–301; under slavery, 20, 22. *See also* Adoption; Education; Family
Child Welfare League of America, 31, 71
Child welfare system, 4, 148, 151–52, 160, 165, 295; racial disparities in, 6–8, 98–107, 114–15, 118–24, 134–42, 145, 150, 154, 159, 162, 201–4
Citizenship, 5, 11–12, 157–58, 227, 229–30, 232, 316, 320, 345–83, 387n, 394n, 399–408; active versus passive, 366; as form of property, 1, 347–48, 379–82, 398; *jus connexio*, 366–68; *jus sanguinis*, 11, 346–50, 352–56, 359, 363–64, 366–69, 372, 377–78, 381–82, 386n, 387n, 388n, 391n, 399–400, 402; *jus soli*, 11, 346–52, 361–64, 366–69, 372, 377–78, 381–82, 391n, 399–400, 402; and "substantial presence" test, 367; and United States law, 389–90n
Civil rights, 30–31, 144, 198, 200–201, 319
Civil unions, 306, 308
Common schools, 215
Communitarianism, 37, 59, 62, 65, 68, 75, 157, 370–71. *See also* Children, as "encumbered" or "embedded"; Culture; Identity
Conley, Dalton, 103–4
Conscience, freedom of, 212–13, 225–26
Constitution, United States, 22, 27, 217–19, 280–81; citizenship clause, 385n; equal protection clause, 44, 201; Fourteenth Amendment, 118, 151–52, 216–18, 309, 360
Constitutions, state, 281
Cornell, C. P., 102
Cornell, Drucilla, 185–89, 333

Corporal punishment, 264, 266–67, 281
Cott, Nancy, 309–10, 317–18
Coverture, 309, 316–17, 372
Culture, 42, 238, 370, 372; and gender, 195–96; black, 109, 115–16, 121
Cuomo, Mario, 335
Custody, 168n, 282–83, 286–87, 300

Davis, Angela, 119
Davis, Peggy Cooper, 117–18, 151, 166, 309–10
Dawson, Michael C., 116
Defense of Marriage Act (1996), 196, 323
Democratic self-governance and legitimacy, 365–68, 380, 391–92n
Dependency, 151–53, 156–59, 164–66, 378. *See also* Care and caregiving
Dignity, 278–81, 283, 297
Distributive justice, 11, 381–82, 401, 407–8
Domestic partnerships, 308, 334, 342n
Dostis, Robert, 307
Doulia, 158, 163–66
Drummond v. Fulton County Department of Family and Childrenís Services, 52n
Due, Linnea, 331
Due process, 159–60
Duncan, Greg, 101
Dworkin, Gerald, 269–70n
Dworkin, Ronald, 404–5

Education, 2, 8–10, 211–68; civic, 212, 214, 218–19, 229–30, 235, 244, 246; diversity and school choice, 9, 10, 212–13, 221–22, 231–32, 237–41; "fundamentalist," 244–50, 253, 256–57, 259, 262–68; and individuality, 222; moral, 117, 216, 220, 239, 244, 255; parental authority over, 1, 9, 214, 218, 223, 234, 236–39, 243; public and private, 9–10, 212, 215, 221, 231–32, 236, 238, 240–41, 246, 266; and race, 240–41; and religion, 211, 223, 240, 244, 265; state authority over, 8–9, 211–23, 227, 229–32, 234–41, 264. *See also* Children
Eisenstein, Zillah, 333
Eliot, George, 73, 92–93n
Empowerment, 280–81
Environmental externalities, 367
Equality, 157–58, 280, 283, 290, 297, 348–49, 369, 371, 381, 383, 398, 402, 404–8; economic, 48, 104, 356, 379, 384n, 407; equal opportunity, 116, 137, 140, 345; equal participation, 365; equal protection, 35–36, 44, 187, 201, 287, 293, 314; equal treatment, 17, 134–35, 205, 249, 253–54, 259, 273, 300–301, 311, 405–6, 408; gay and lesbian, 320, 324; gender, 372–73, 378; moral, 404–8; racial, 38; social, 185
Erlien, Marla, 323
Eskridge, William, 308, 310–15, 321
Estonia, 387n
Ethical life (*sittlichkeit*), 178–79
Ettelbrick, Paula, 314
Exit rights, 227, 362
Expressive liberty, 223–32

Family, 1, 87–88, 324, 331; "as if," 18–21, 24–25, 29–30, 35, 37, 45–46, 48–49, 60, 170, 173–78, 181, 187–89, 195, 197–98, 203–4; black, 98–102, 106–11, 134–35; and citizenship, 370–72, 377; "deviant," 162, 276; gay and lesbian, 10–11, 18, 177, 187–90, 194–95, 274, 276, 281–301, 313–14, 377; membership in, 400–401; multiracial, 35, 276; single-parent, 3, 18, 105, 161, 177, 313–14, 322; as socially constructed, 8, 48, 170, 172–74; traditional ideal of, 2–3, 16, 21, 26, 31, 37, 87, 164, 173–76, 194, 276, 287. *See also* Children; Parents
Family Research Council, 194–95
Farrington v. Tokushige, 218
Feinberg, Joel, 245

Feminism, 186, 213, 241, 307, 315, 323, 333, 371–72, 379
Fifth Amendment, 218
Filmer, Robert, 250
Fineman, Martha L. A., 9–10, **234–42**, 317
Flacks, Richard, 329
Flag salute, 212–13
Flemming Rule, 159–60
Flory, Peg, 306–7, 336
Fogg-Davis, Hawley, 35–36
Foster care system, 6–7, 99–100, 105–6, 123, 277, 294
Foucault, 172, 178–79, 326
Fraser, Nancy, 315–16, 323
Freeman, Elizabeth, 328
French Civil Code (1804), 353
Freud, Anna, 180–83, 202, 204–5
Freud, Sigmund, 183–84

Galston, William A., 8–9, 113, **211–33**, 234, 236–40, 269n
Gasco, Elyse, 74, 84, 86
Gay and lesbian activism, 315, 320, 324, 326, 331, 334
Gay and lesbian rights, 319–24. *See also* Adoption, gay and lesbian; Family, gay and lesbian; Marriage, gay and lesbian; Queer activism; Queer politics; Queer theory
Gay politics, 330
Gelles, R. J., 102
Geneva Convention, 391n
German citizenship law, 354
Gilles, Stephen, 225
Glennon, Theresa, 291
Goldsmith, Donna, 41
Goldstein, Joseph, 180–83, 202, 204–5
Gordon, Linda, 69, 315–16, 323
Gordon, Robert, 49
Gutmann, Amy, 245

Habermas, Jurgen, 115
Hague Convention (1930), 383n
Hague Convention (1951), 388n
Hammar, Tomas, 389n
Hammer v. Dagenhart, 219
Hartman, Ann, 105
Head Start, 274, 301
Hegel, 178
Heretier, 195–96
Hobbes, Thomas, 20, 173, 250
Holcomb, Desma, 334–35
Howe, Ruth-Arlene, 47
Human Rights Campaign, 308, 321

Identity, 115, 153, 245, 315, 326; birthright, 347; black, 116, 120, 162–63; community, 370; cultural, 365, 371; national, 347, 371. *See also* Children, and identity; Communitarianism; Culture
Illegitimacy and unwed motherhood, 4, 22–24, 45, 48, 61, 109–10, 176, 290
Immigration, 200, 309, 346, 351, 354–55, 357, 361–62, 371, 376, 378, 384n, 391n, 393n
Immigration and Nationality Act (1986), 373–75, 386n, 394n
Indian Child Welfare Act (1978), 32–33, 35, 41, 43, 45, 54n, 55n, 59, 67, 72, 120–21, 199–200
In re Marriage of B and R, 121
Integrity, 227
Interethnic Placement Act (1996), 33, 200–201
International law, 346, 365, 394n

Jacobs, Harriet, 151
James, P. D., 85
Judicial system, 145–46
Justice, 349, 371, 381–82, 393n
Juvenile crime and race, 110–11

Kaplan, Jonathan, 401
Kaplan, Morris, 8, **170–207**
Kennedy, Randall, 35–36, 103
Kittay, Eva Feder, 7–8, **148–69**

Latvia, 387n
Lehr, Valerie, 11, **306–42**

Liberal cosmopolitanism, 246, 257, 262, 266
Liberal democracy, 212–14, 218, 230
Liberal individualism, 262
Liberalism, 245, 264–65, 315, 398–402, 406–8
Liberal neutrality, 257–58, 263
Lindsey, Duncan, 100
Lochner v. New York, 219
Locke, John, 226, 250–56, 264, 267
Lofton v. Kearney, 294–95
Lord Coke, 350
Loving v. Virginia, 26, 75
Lutzen, Karen, 320

Macedo, Stephen, **1–12**
Mahoney, Maureen, 40
Malcolm X, 117
Mansbridge, Jane, 118
Marriage, and citizenship, 372–73, 376, 379, 395–96n; gay and lesbian, 11, 187–88, 190, 194, 196, 273, 282, 289–91, 293, 300, 306–11, 313–16, 319–24, 333–36; interracial, 22, 26
Marshall, T. H., 316
May, Larry, 123, 160
McGuire v. McGuire, 299
McReynolds, Justice James, 216–17
Mead, Lawrence, 7, 130n, **134–47**, 155–58
Merritt, William, 31
Meyer v. Nebraska, 113, 216, 236
Mill, John Stuart, 215, 219–22, 254–55
Miller, Jacques-Alain, 196
Miller v. Albright, 373–74, 376
Mississippi Band of Choctaw Indians v. Holyfield, 72–73
Mnookin, Robert, 76
Monogamy, 310–13
Moral remainders, 18, 49, 64, 86
Mormons, 310
Moynihan Report (1965), 43, 109
Multiculturalism, 17
Multiethnic Placement Act (1994), 33, 35–36, 41, 45, 60, 200
Murray, Charles, 110–12, 162

National Association of Black Social Workers, 31, 63, 120, 122, 166, 199
National Committee for Adoption, 78
Nationalism, civic, 349, 359–62, 364–65
Nationalism, ethnic, 349, 359–60, 364–65
Naturalization, 348–49, 354–59, 361–62, 389n, 391n
New York Sisters of Charity, 68–69
Nguyen v. I.N.S., 374–77
North American Free Trade Agreement (NAFTA), 386n

Okin, Susan, 319

Parenting, 1, 222
Parents: authority over children, 1–3, 6, 10, 48, 243–68, 275–76, 279–80, 298; de facto, 285–86, 290; due process rights of, 113; "expressive interest" in parenting, 9–10, 113, 212, 223–32, 239–41; gay and lesbian, 3–4, 10–11, 190, 192, 273, 282–87, 291, 293, 304n; responsibilities to children, 2, 63, 211, 220, 226–27, 235, 237, 244, 251–52, 255, 257–58, 275–76, 280; and sexual activity, 284–85; sperm and egg donors, 287–89, 313; stepparents, 290. *See also* Adoption; Children; Education, parental authority over; Family
Parham v. J.R., 63
Pataki, George, 335
Paternalism, 254–56, 269–70n, 278
Patriotism, 213
Perfectionism, limited, 215–16, 220
Perry, Twila, 37, 41, 47, 122
Personal Responsibility and Work Opportunity Act (1996), 106, 169n. *See also* Welfare system
Petchesky, Rosalind, 332
Pharr, Suzanne, 325
Phelan, Shane, 310–11, 314, 331, 333, 336
Pierce, William, 76

Pierce v. Society of Sisters, 217–18
Plato, 171–72, 179, 217
Plummer, Ken, 327
Pluralism, 214
Polygamy, 188, 310
Poverty, 6, 12, 45, 89–90n, 100–101, 103–4, 106, 111–12, 114, 118, 134, 136–38, 142–43, 151, 154, 163, 165, 176, 307, 311, 379, 406–8. *See also* Welfare system
Privacy, 17–18, 27–28, 179, 213, 280–81, 283–84, 287, 297, 299
Property, 380, 397n
Protection, 280–81

Queer activism, 324–29, 331–32. *See also* Adoption, gay and lesbian; Gay and lesbian activism; Gay and lesbian rights; Family, gay and lesbian; Marriage, gay and lesbian
Queer Nation, 327–28, 330
Queer politics, 11, 314, 326–27, 330
Queer theory, 307, 324–27, 330, 332–33
Quilloin v. Walcott, 291

Racism and racial stereotypes, 4, 6–7, 22–23, 31, 35, 37, 41, 43–44, 98, 100–104, 107–12, 114–16, 119–20, 122, 134–42, 151, 153–55, 159–62, 176, 198, 201–3, 311. *See also* Adoption, transracial
Rahman, Momin, 324, 328
Ramo, Roberta Cooper, 168–69n
Rationality, 10
Rawls, John, 157, 256, 393n
Rayside, David, 320–21
Reciprocal partenerships, 306–8, 336
Reciprocity, 157–58, 226
Refugees, 391n
Reich, Charles, 380
Religion, freedom of, 227–28, 243
Roberts, Dorothy, 4, 6–8, 43, 47, **98–133**, 134–46, 148, 150–52, 154, 156–57, 159–60, 162–63, 166, 176, 197, 201–3
Robson, Ruthann, 314
Roe v. Wade, 76
Rubio-Marin, Ruth, 392n

Sanger, Carol, 6, 27, 39, **58–97**, 177
Santosky v. Kramer, 113
Savage, Dan, 74, 189–97
Schwartz, Pepper, 312–13
Sears, Richard, 28
Seidman, Steven, 324, 326
Sexism, 7–8
Schneider, David, 20, 26
Shachar, Ayelet, 11–12, **345–97**, 398–400, 403–8
Shanley, Mary, 5–6, 8, **15–57**, 58–67, 84–85, 170–80, 185–87, 199, 201
Shapiro, Ian, 226–27
Sheinbein v. Attorney General, 355–56
Sherman, Suzanne, 334
Slavery, 108, 115, 117–19, 150–51, 160, 173, 309, 316
Smith, Barbara, 325
Smith, James Farrell, 18
Sodomy laws, 311
Solnit, Albert, 180–83, 202, 204–5
Solomon, Alisa, 323
Stacey, Judith, 319
Stack, Carol, 102
State: authority over children, 1–2, 4–5, 277, 279–80, 295; interventions into families, 2, 65–66, 98–102, 105–7, 112–14, 117–19, 123–24, 134, 141, 150, 152, 159, 162–63, 197, 201, 243, 247–49, 260, 275, 281, 299; right to exclude, 371. *See also* Child welfare system; Citizenship; Education
State of Israel v. Sheinbein, 355–56
Stein, Arlene, 327
Stoddard, Thomas, 314
Sullivan, Andrew, 308, 310–15, 319–21
Supreme Court, Canadian, 373
Supreme Court, Israeli, 356
Supreme Court, United States, 9, 22, 26–27, 63, 72–73, 81, 113, 215–19, 227, 280, 290–91, 293, 373–76
Sweeney, Maureen, 40

Tacit consent, 362
Temporary Assistance for Needy Families, 155
Thomas S. v. Robin Y., 288–89
Toleration, 230, 244–47, 266, 309, 320, 369
Tronto, Joan, 318

Union activism, 334
United Nations Convention on the Rights of the Child, 294
United Nations Population Division, 359

Vaid, Urvashi, 329–30
Vogel, Ursula, 319

Walker, Alice, 119
Walzer, Michael, 346, 371
Wardle, Lynn, 296
Warner, Michael, 314, 334, 336
Weil, Patrick, 353
Welfare system, 2, 111–12, 153–57, 160, 165, 318, 323; global, 351; reform, 106–7, 136, 143, 159, 163, 202, 301. *See also* Poverty
Westervelt, Don, 196
Weston, Kath, 190
Williams, Bernard, 178–79
Wilson, Angelia, 329–30
Wilson, Elizabeth, 327
Wilson, William, 319
Wisconsin v. Yoder, 227, 229–31, 236
Wood, Cheri, 168–69n
Woodhouse, Barbara Bennett, 10–11, 219, **273–305**
World Bank, 363, 384n

Yack, Bernard, 369
Yngvesson, Barbara, 25, 29, 40, 47
Young, Iris Marion, **1–12**, 315, 336, 342n